CATHOLIC BIOETHICS
AND THE
GIFT OF
HUMAN LIFE

CATHOLIC BIOETHICS
AND THE
GIFT OF
HUMAN LIFE

WILLIAM E. MAY

Our Sunday Visitor Publishing Division
Our Sunday Visitor, Inc.
Huntington, Indiana 46750

Nihil Obstat
Reverend Paul F. deLadurantaye, S.T.D.
Censor Deputatus

Imprimatur
✠ Most Reverend William E. Lori, S.T.D.
Vicar General for the Archdiocese of Washington
June 29, 2000

The Nihil Obstat and Imprimatur are official declarations that a book or pamphlet is free of doctrinal or moral error. No implication is contained therein that those who have granted the Nihil Obstat or Imprimatur agree with the contents, opinions, or statements expressed.

Scripture excerpts in this work are taken from the *New American Bible with Revised New Testament*, copyright © 1986, 1970 by the Confraternity of Christian Doctrine, and used with permission. The publisher and author are grateful to all copyright holders without whose material this could not have been completed. If any copyrighted materials have been inadvertently used in this book without proper credit being given in one form or another, please notify Our Sunday Visitor in writing so that future printings of this work may be corrected accordingly.

ISBN: 0-87973-683-6
LCCCN: 00-130461

Cover design by Monica Haneline
PRINTED IN THE UNITED STATES OF AMERICA

To my students, past and present, at
The Catholic University of America
and at the
John Paul II Institute for Studies on Marriage and Family.

Contents

Foreword

I am delighted to offer a few words of introduction to Dr. William E. May's latest book, *Catholic Bioethics and the Gift of Human Life*. The reasons for my delight are many.

First, I deeply appreciate Professor May as both teacher and friend. Indeed, I have known Dr. May for well over two decades. I first met him in the early 1970s, when I was a student at Mount Saint Mary's Seminary in Emmitsburg, Maryland. Then a professor at The Catholic University of America, Dr. May came to Emmitsburg each week to conduct a seminar on ethical issues. His strong Catholic faith, his insightful courses, combined with a wonderful sense of humor, greatly enriched the seminarians' experience.

Soon after priestly ordination, I was a doctoral student at Catholic University. There I came to know Professor May through informal visits to his office in Caldwell Hall where, with the aid of an old electric typewriter, he produced an amazing output of scholarly books and articles. In 1979, I collaborated with Dr. May in organizing a symposium on moral theology at Catholic University — an experience I remember with much fondness. That symposium produced a volume entitled *Principles of Catholic Moral Life*, which Professor May edited.

Through the years. Dr. May has been a good friend and advisor to Cardinal Hickey and to those of us who work with the Cardinal. On so many occasions, he provided sound and insightful advice regarding the many ethical problems and issues that inevitably cross a bishop's desk. For ready, wise, and faithful assistance, I shall always be most grateful.

For the past ten years Dr. May has served as the Michael J. McGivney Professor of Moral Theology at the John Paul II Institute for Studies on Marriage and Family here in Washington. I have the impression that these have been enormously productive and happy years — a time when Dr. May has wholly dedicated his life and talents to studying, analyzing, and transmitting the vision of Pope John Paul II regarding the human person and the human family. It has been a joy to see my teacher and friend flourish.

Second, throughout the years of my friendship and association with Dr. May, I have come to know first-hand his great fidelity to the Lord and to the

Church. A philosopher by training, Dr. May has allowed the voice of the Church's Tradition to take ever-greater hold on his mind and heart. Fully engaging his gifts of grace and nature, Dr. May has transmitted the Church's teaching with insight and has applied it to the problems and possibilities of our day. But he has been more than a teacher; he has also been a witness to the truth and beauty of what the Church believes and teaches. So often, his witness to the Gospel of Life has been costly.

Third, it is a pleasure to introduce a book of such high quality. It is a resource that is timely, accurate, and fully reflective of the Church's profound teaching on the dignity and worth of the human person revealed in Christ Jesus. It begins with a masterful summary of magisterial documents. Then, Dr. May proceeds to apply the Gospel of Life to important bioethical issues today. Faithful to the teaching and Tradition of the Church, imbued with the vision of Pope John Paul II, Professor May helps us to understand more profoundly the nature of moral judgments and then to grapple with the ethical questions arising both from our culture and medical technologies both new and old. He assists us in seeing the truth and life-giving wisdom of the Church's teaching regarding the generation of human life, contraception, abortion, euthanasia, and organ transplants. He raises necessary cautions about experimentation involving human beings.

At the outset of his papacy, Pope John Paul II warned that ethics must keep pace with technology. As we read daily of emerging medical technologies, we know what a daunting challenge lies before us all. Such technologies have great capacity for good, but also great capacity for evil. Professor May is among those who are in the forefront of the struggle to raise up ethical issues that are vitally important, not only for the well-being of the Church but indeed for the community and for individual human beings.

I see this book as a resource for bishops and priests seeking to be updated and informed about important medical-ethical questions. I see it also as valuable for serious students of moral theology, including those preparing for priestly ministry and other forms of service in the Church. Indeed, it is a helpful work for anyone interested in really knowing what the Church teaches regarding these critical ethical issues — as oppposed to a caricature of those teachings. Once again, Dr. May has done us a great service by offering an excellent book.

I sincerely hope that many will read and refer to this important book. May the Lord grant to Dr. May many more years of productive and faith-filled scholarship.

The Most Reverend William E. Lori
Auxiliary Bishop of Washington

Introduction

October 7, 1979, is one of the most memorable days in my life. It was the day that Pope John Paul II, on his first apostolic visit to the United States, was celebrating Mass on the Capitol Mall in Washington, D.C. An enormous number of people had gathered to participate in the Mass and listen to his homily. I was there with several of my children. My wife, Patricia, was unfortunately not able to be with us because she had the flu, and my two oldest children, Michael and Mary, at that time college students, were not able to come either. (Mary, who was studying in Cambridge, Mass., had been thrilled a week earlier when she was able to participate in a Mass John Paul II had celebrated for young people on the Boston Commons.) But my other children were with me: Thomas, Timothy, Patrick, Susan, and Kathleen. It was for us an unforgettable experience.

The Holy Father's homily that wonderful day was called " 'Stand Up' for Human Life."* The Gospel of the day, on which Pope John Paul based his homily, was the Gospel according to Mark, 10:6-9, where Jesus, in replying to a question posed to him by the Pharisees in an effort to entrap him, reaffirmed the teaching of Scripture that God is the author of marriage, that marriage makes a man and a woman one flesh, and that no one can separate what God has joined. He then went on to say that in his Gospel Mark immediately afterwards describes the scene where Jesus becomes indignant when his own disciples tried to stop the people from bringing their children to him, declaring: "Let the little children come to me and do not hinder them" (Mark 10:14). It pains me to say that, sadly, some people walked out on the Holy Father's homily when he reaffirmed the indissolubility of marriage and declared that marriage should be "open to new life."

After beginning his homily by referring to these text of Mark's Gospel, the Holy Father invited all to reflect on the nature of marriage, the family, and the value of human life, three closely interconnected themes.

This homily, I believe, is one of the most eloquent and powerful that this great pope has ever given, and the key theme sounded in it — the preciousness of *all* human life as a great and precious gift of God — has been *the* major theme of his entire pontificate. In this inspiring homily, the Holy Father had no hesitation in declaring that "all human life — from the moment of conception and through all subsequent stages — is sacred, because human life is created in the image and likeness of God. Nothing," he went on, "surpasses the greatness or dignity of a human person. Human life is not just an idea or an abstraction; human life is the concrete reality of a being that lives, that acts, that grows and develops; human life is the concrete reality of a being that is capable of love, and of service to humanity."

Later on, he said that "Human life is precious because it is the gift of a God whose love is infinite; and when God gives life, it is for ever. Life is also precious," he went on to say, because "it is the expression and fruit of love. This is why life should spring up within the setting of marriage, and why marriage and the parents' love for one another should be marked by generosity in self-giving." Toward the conclusion of his homily, John Paul II committed himself to the defense of human life and challenged all those present to " 'Stand Up' for Human Life." In an eloquent passage, he declared:

> And so, we will stand up every time that human life is threatened. When the sacredness of life before birth is attacked, we will stand up and proclaim that no one ever has the authority to destroy unborn life. When a child is described as a burden or is looked upon only as a means to satisfy an emotional need, we will stand up and insist that every child is a unique and unrepeatable gift of God, with the right to a loving and united family. When the institution of marriage is abandoned to human selfishness or reduced to a temporary, conditional arrangement that can easily be terminated, we will stand up and affirm the indissolubility of the marriage bond. When the value of the family is threatened because of social and economic pressures, we will stand up and reaffirm that the family "is necessary not only for the private good of every person, but also for the common good of every society, nation, and state" (General Audience, January 3, 1979). When freedom is used to dominate the weak, to squander natural resources and energy, and to deny basic necessities to people, we will stand up and reaffirm the demands of justice and social love. When the sick, the aged or

the dying are abandoned or in loneliness, we will stand up
and proclaim that they are worthy of love, care, and respect.

In very many ways, this homily of Pope John Paul II, delivered early
in the second year of his pontificate, has set the agenda for his entire
pontificate, which has had as its hallmark the defense of innocent human life, of marriage, marital love, and the family. His homily has also,
as it were, set the agenda for this book.

This book, rooted in the conviction that human life, even when heavily
burdened, is always a great and precious gift of God, treats of many of
the most serious issues regarding human life and its value facing men
and women today. My hope is that it may prove useful to many in their
efforts to " 'stand up' for human life," as Pope John Paul II has challenged us to do.

I am grateful to many people for their help in preparing this book. In
particular, I owe a debt of gratitude to two of my former students, Mark
Latkovic and Paul deLadurantaye. Mark, a layman, married, and now
the father of four children, is currently professor of moral theology at
Sacred Heart Seminary, Detroit, Mich. Father Paul deLadurantaye, a
priest of the diocese of Arlington, is diocesan secretary for religious
education and adjunct professor of moral theology in the Notre Dame
Institute of Christendom College. Professor Latkovic and Father
deLadurantaye read a previous draft of this work, offered many excellent suggestions to me, and made several important corrections. Basil
Cole, O.P., an excellent Dominican theologian whose office is near mine,
generously read an earlier version of this book and made numerous recommendations, calling my attention frequently to relevant magisterial
texts. I am most grateful to the help these persons have given me. I also
want to thank His Excellency, the Most Reverend William Lori, auxiliary bishop of Washington, for his kindness in preparing a foreword.

To my students at the John Paul II Institute for Studies on Marriage
and Family in Washington D.C. I am also grateful. Many of them took
part in a course on bioethics that I teach at the Institute; their questions,
insights, and recommendations have been of real help to me in deciding
which issues to consider, lines of reasoning to be developed, etc. For the
past thirty years I have had the pleasure of teaching moral theology, for
the first twenty at The Catholic University of America and for the last
ten at the John Paul II Institute. I truly love teaching and thank God that
he has given me the opportunity to teach and to have as my students
outstanding young men and women, lay, clerical, and religious.

God has also been very good to me and my wife, Patricia. He has blessed our marriage with seven wonderful children — Michael, Mary, Thomas, Timothy, Patrick, Susan, and Kathleen — and he is now blessing us richly with the gift of grandchildren, nine thus far: Christopher, Elizabeth, Alexandra (Sasha), Anastasia (Anna), Kathryn (Katya), Megan, Peter, Margaret Mary, and Katherine Ann. Our hearts go out to couples who have not, despite their ardent desires, been blessed with children. They also go out to couples whose children suffer from serious illnesses and whose lives are thus in many ways heavily burdened. We have learned much from couples like this, wives and husbands who have at great sacrifice given themselves generously to the care of their children, whose lives, however burdened, are precious, good gifts of a loving God.

As John Paul said in " 'Stand Up' for Human Life!": "Human life is precious because it is the gift of a God whose love is infinite." May this book help foster respect and love for this great and surpassing gift.

William E. May
February 22, 2000

*Here I use the text of " 'Stand Up' for Human Life" found in *Enchiridion Familiae,* eds. Augusto Sarmiento and Javier Escriva Ivars (Madrid: Ediciones Rialp, 1992) 3.2378-2387.

Chapter One

CHURCH TEACHING AND MAJOR ISSUES IN BIOETHICS

It is important and helpful to begin this book by summarizing the teaching of the Church on major issues in bioethics. I believe that the most important magisterial documents relevant to the topics to be considered in this book are: (1) Pope John Paul II's 1995 Encyclical *Evangelium vitae* ("The Gospel of Life"); (2) The Congregation for the Doctrine of the Faith's 1987 *Instruction on Respect for Human Life in Its Origins and on the Dignity of Procreation* (entitled *Donum vitae* in Latin); (3) the same Congregation's 1974 *Declaration on Procured Abortion*; and (4) the same Congregation's 1981 *Declaration on Euthanasia*.

Other magisterial documents, in particular the *Catechism of the Catholic Church* and many addresses of Popes Pius XII and John Paul II, are also quite relevant to matters taken up in this book. In addition, the 1994 *Charter for Health Care Workers* prepared by the Pontifical Council for Pastoral Assistance to Health Care Workers, the 1994 *Ethical and Religious Directives for Catholic Health Care Services* promulgated by the Bishops of the United States, and pastoral letters of individual bishops and episcopal conferences bear on topics to be considered. Thus, in chapters to follow, reference will be made to these sources of Church teaching when it is relevant to do so. But the four documents singled out above are of such paramount importance that an exposition of their content and significance will provide a substantive introduction to the major issues in bioethics. In addition, the teaching found in these documents will be referred to time and again in the following chapters; hence presentation of their principal ideas here will eliminate the need for doing so in later chapters where specific topics taken up in these documents are examined. A simple reference to the matter found in this chapter will suffice.

Rather than consider the four documents chronologically, I will first take up John Paul II's *Evangelium vitae* because it is by far the most comprehensive and important of the documents. I will then consider the lengthy *Instruction* of the Congregation for the Doctrine of the Faith on issues surrounding the generation of human life, and then that Congregation's declarations on abortion and euthanasia.

1. JOHN PAUL II'S ENCYCLICAL *EVANGELIUM VITAE*

Pope John Paul II's encyclical is a wonderful manifesto eloquently presenting the reasons why human life is of incomparable dignity and, indeed, sanctity. It is also an incisive analysis and critique of the various factors and ideologies underlying the terrible threats menacing human life today, in particular, the life of the weakest members of the human family: the unborn, the severely impaired, the sick, and the dying. It is, above all, an impassioned plea to all people of good will to recognize the dignity and sanctity of human life, to defend it from the vicious and at times subtle attacks launched against it today, and to love it as a precious gift from the God whose only-begotten-Son-made-man poured forth his life on the Cross precisely so that everyone might have life in abundance and in union with him conquer death and rise to everlasting life in fellowship with the Triune God, the Giver of Life and Love.

A. Chapter One: "Present-Day Threats to Human Life"

This chapter begins with a meditation on the story of Cain and Abel in Genesis (nos. 7-9) and goes on to take up in detail the threats menacing human life today. John Paul II goes to the root causes of these threats, zeroing in on the emergence of a perverse idea of human freedom, understood as the autonomous freedom of individuals to be the arbiters of good and evil, right and wrong. This has blinded them to the value of human life, has eclipsed the sense of God and of man as a being of incomparable worth, and has led to the claim that *some* members of the human family, the strong and the able, have the *right* to dispose of the lives of the weak and vulnerable, in particular, the unborn, the "useless," the suffering, and the dying.

John Paul II, mincing no words, correctly claims that today we are confronted "by a culture which denies solidarity and in many cases takes the form of a veritable 'culture of death,'" one "actively fostered by powerful cultural, economic, and political currents which encourage an idea of society excessively concerned with efficiency." It is thus possible, he continues, "to speak in a certain sense of a *war of the powerful against the weak"* which unleashes a *"conspiracy against life,"* a conspiracy involving "not only individuals in their personal, family or group relationships, but go[ing] far beyond, to the point of damaging and distorting, at the international level, relations between peoples and States" (no. 12).

This "culture of death" has its roots in "the mentality which *carries the concept of subjectivity to an extreme* and even distorts it, and recognizes as a subject of rights only the person who enjoys full or at least incipient autonomy and who emerges from a state of total dependence on others" (no. 19). It is likewise rooted in a *"notion of freedom* which exalts the isolated individual in an absolute way, and gives no place to solidarity, to openness to others and service of them" (no. 19), a misunderstanding of freedom which *"leads to a serious distortion of life in society"* (no. 20). This "culture of death" results ultimately in an *"eclipse of the sense of God and of man* typical of a social and cultural climate dominated by secularism" (no. 21). Citing Vatican Council II's Pastoral Constitution on the Church in the Modern World, *Gaudium et spes* (no. 36), which affirmed: "Without the Creator the creature would disappear.... But when God is forgotten the creature itself grows unintelligible," John Paul II continues:

> Man is no longer able to see himself as "mysteriously different" from other earthly creatures; he regards himself merely as one more living being, as an organism which, at most, has reached a high stage of perfection. Enclosed in the narrow horizon of his physical nature, he is somehow reduced to being "a thing," and no longer grasps the "transcendent" character of his "existence as man." He no longer considers life as a splendid gift from God, something "sacred," entrusted to his responsibility, and thus also to his loving care and "veneration" (no. 22).

After this incisive critique of the "culture of death," its root causes and effects, John Paul II concludes the first chapter by reviewing "signs of hope" which invite all to commit themselves to welcoming, loving, and serving human life (nos. 26-28). Among these "signs of hope" are many married couples who generously accept children as the supreme gift of marriage; families which serve life and give themselves to the least of their brothers and sisters (abandoned children and elderly persons, handicapped people, teenagers in difficulty); people who generously volunteer to offer hospitality and a supportive environment to the weak; medical scientists, agencies and organizations mobilizing efforts to bring the benefits of modern medicine to the poor and needy (no. 26); movements and initiatives to raise social awareness to defend human life, particularly the life of the unborn and the sick and dying; the daily struggle of countless people to care for others; a new sensitivity ever more opposed to war as an instrument for resolving conflicts and to the use of capital punishment; concern for the quality of life and the ecology (no. 27). In concluding this chapter, the Holy Father points out that "the unconditional choice for life reaches its full religious and moral meaning when it flows from, is formed by, and nourished by *faith in Christ*" (no. 28).

B. Chapter Two: "The Christian Message Concerning Life"

This chapter first focuses our gaze on Christ, "the Word of Life" (1 Jn 1:1), in order to show us that the Gospel of Life is "something concrete and personal, for it consists in the proclamation of the *very person of Jesus*" (no. 29), the One who has come to reveal to us the complete truth about man and human life. Jesus through word and deed served life, in particular, the life of the poor and the weak. His words and deeds, John Paul II points out, "are not meant only for those who are sick or suffering or in some way neglected by society. On a deeper level they affect the *very meaning of every person's life in its moral and spiritual dimensions*" (no. 32). Jesus himself fully experienced life's contradictions and risks, living poverty throughout his life "until the culminating moment of the Cross: 'he humbled himself and became obedient unto death, even death on a cross. Therefore, God has highly exalted him and bestowed on him the name which is above every name' (Phil 2:8-9)." "It is precisely," the Pope continues, "*by his death* that *Jesus reveals all the splendor and value of life,* inasmuch as his self-oblation on the Cross becomes the source of a new life for all people (cf. Jn 12:32)" (no. 33).

Human life is surpassingly good because "the life which God gives man is quite different from the life of all other living creatures, inasmuch as man, although formed from the dust of the earth (cf. Gn 2:7, 3:19; Jb 34:15; Ps 103:14; 104:29), *is a manifestation of God in the world, a sign of his presence, a trace of his glory* (cf. Gn 1:26-27; Ps 8:6)" (no. 34). Jesus brings human life, which is always a precious gift from God, to fulfillment. For Jesus shows us that God, in giving us life, shares something of himself with us precisely so that we can, in union with Jesus, fully participate in the life of the "Eternal One" by literally becoming his very own children (nos. 37-38). "Eternal life is ... the life of God himself and at the very same time the *life of the children of God* (cf. 1 Jn 3:1-2).... *Here the Christian truth about life becomes most sublime.* The dignity of this life is linked not only to its beginning, to the fact that it comes from God, but also to its final end, to its destiny of fellowship with God in knowledge and in love of him" (no. 38). Human life thus becomes the " 'place' where God manifests himself, where we meet him and enter into communion with him" (no. 39). The life of every human being is sacred and inviolable because God himself personally treasures and cares for it. His commandment that we are not to kill is rooted in the love and reverence due to the life he has given and confided to our trust (nos. 39-41).

Because he loves and trusts us, God allows us to share in his lordship by taking responsibility for human life. Husbands and wives, in particular, are privileged to "become partners in a divine undertaking: through the act of procreation, God's gift [of life] is accepted" lovingly and given the home where it is to take root and grow (no. 43). But "the task of accepting and serving life involves everyone; and this task must be fulfilled above all towards life when it is at its weakest," for Christ himself has told us that what we do to his littlest ones we do to him (cf. Mt 25:31-46) (no. 43).

Human life, God's precious gift, is most vulnerable when it comes into the world and when it leaves the realm of time to embark upon eternity (no. 44). When it comes into the world it comes from the hand of God himself: "Before I formed you in the womb I knew you" (Jer 1:5; cf. Jb 10:8-12; Ps 139: 13-14; 2 Mc 7:22-23). Thus the life of every individual, from its very beginning, is part of God's loving plan for human existence, a truth confirmed and deepened by the incarnation of God's only-begotten Son, who while still in his mother's womb was greeted with joy by his cousin John, an unborn child himself, who leapt for joy in Elizabeth's womb when Mary came to visit her cousin, who, despite her advanced age, was "with child" (cf. Lk 2:22-23) (nos. 40-45).

Human life, inescapably bodily in nature, is precious, in itself and to God, at every moment of its existence, even and especially when it is weak, when it suffers, when it draws near to death (nos. 47-48). God's command "You shall not kill" (Ex 20:13; Dt 5:17) is a specific command intended to protect the dignity and sanctity of human life; indeed, the whole of God's law, his wise and loving plan for human existence, fully protects human life. This law finds its fulfillment in Jesus, who shows us the authentic meaning of human life, namely, "that of being a *gift which is fully realized in the giving of self,*" in the *"gift of self in love for one's brothers and sisters"* (no. 49).

The Gospel of Life is ultimately fulfilled on the tree of the Cross. From the pierced side of our Redeemer we have given to us "the very life of God." Jesus "proclaims that *life finds its center, its meaning, and its fulfillment when it is given up"* in love (no. 51).

C. Chapter Three: "God's Holy Law"

This chapter is devoted to the intimate bond between the Gospel of Life and the commandment, grounded in self-giving love, that we are not to kill. In this chapter, as he did in the first chapter of his Encyclical *Veritatis splendor*, John Paul II begins with a meditation on the Gospel story of the rich young man who asked our Lord what he must do to enter into eternal life and was told that to do so he must keep the commandments (cf. Mt 19:6ff) (no. 52). The Gospel of Life is both a great gift of God and an exacting task for humanity: "In giving life to man God *demands* that he love, respect, and protect life. The *gift* has become a *commandment*, and the *commandment is itself a gift"* (no. 52).

Because it is God's precious gift and is thus sacred and inviolable, human life, particularly when weak and helpless, has God as its *"goel,"* its defender (no. 53). The negative commandment "You shall not kill" simply indicates an extreme that can never be exceeded; but it implicitly encourages a positive attitude toward human life. This attitude, deepened and immeasurably enriched by the command that we are to love our neighbor as ourselves, helps to show us the enormity of the crime of murder, the intentional killing of innocent human beings (nos. 53-54).

The Pope, noting that "Christian reflection has sought a fuller and deeper understanding of what God's commandment prohibits and prescribes," reaffirms the Catholic tradition's teaching on the right to self-defense and on the right, and at times the duty, "for someone responsible for another's life, the common good of the family or of the State" to defend life even if one forsees that as a result of legitimately defending one's own or another's life from an unprovoked attack the life of the aggressor may be taken (no. 55). In such instances, one is not violating God's command, nor is one engaging in an act of killing. Rather, one's human act, as specified by the object chosen,[1] is rightly described as an act of legitimate defense and not as an act of killing.

It is in this context that the Pope takes up the question of capital punishment or the death penalty. Here it is important to note that he does not condemn capital punishment as intrinsically evil. Nonetheless, he teaches that, in order to defend the common good from criminal attacks and to punish evildoers for their unjust actions, society "ought not go to the extreme of executing the offender except in cases of absolute necessity; in other words, when it would not be possible otherwise to defend society." He concludes that today, "as a result of steady improvements in the organization of the penal system, such cases are very rare, if not practically non-existent" (no. 56). In other words, he is saying that under contemporary conditions one ought not to inflict the death penalty. Those wishing to do so have the burden of proving that doing so is absolutely necessary, and John Paul II seriously doubts that this can be so today.

The command "You shall not kill" is absolute, i.e., without exceptions, when it refers to innocent human life, "and all the more so in the case of weak and defenseless human beings, who find their ultimate defense against the arrogance and caprice of others only in the absolute binding force of God's commandment" (no. 57).

In developing this central truth, John Paul II makes it clear that the Church's teaching on the absolute inviolability of innocent human life and on the intrinsic evil of every freely chosen act of deliberately killing innocent human beings has been infallibly proposed by the ordinary Magisterium of the Church. He is *not* solemnly defining this truth by an *ex cathedra* pronouncement, but he definitely claims that this truth pertains to the patrimony of faith as proclaimed by the ordinary and universal Magisterium. He introduces the subject by writing as follows:

> Faced with the progressive weakening in individual consciences and in society of the sense of the absolute and grave moral illicitness of the direct taking of all innocent human life, especially in its beginning and its end, *the Church's Magisterium* has spoken out with increasing frequency in defense of the sacredness and inviolability of human life. The Papal Magisterium, particularly insistent in this regard, has always been seconded by that of the bishops, with numerous and comprehensive doctrinal and pastoral documents issued either by Episcopal Conferences or by individual bishops. The Second Vatican Council also addressed this matter forcefully, in a brief but incisive passage[2] (no. 57).

Continuing, he then goes on to say:

> Therefore, by the authority which Christ conferred upon Peter and his Successors, and in communion with the Bishops of the Catholic Church, *I confirm that the direct and voluntary killing of an innocent human being is always gravely immoral.* This doctrine, based upon that unwritten law which man, in the light of reason, finds in his own heart (cf. Rom 2:14-15) is reaffirmed by Sacred Scripture, transmitted by the Tradition of the Church, and taught by the ordinary and universal Magisterium (no. 57).

Since John Paul II explicitly refers, at the conclusion of the passage just cited, to the teaching of Vatican Council II in *Lumen gentium,* no. 25, it is both useful and necessary, properly to understand the significance of this centrally important passage, to see what the Council Fathers said in the passage referred to. It reads:

> Although the bishops, taken individually, do not enjoy the privilege of infallibility, they do, however, *proclaim the doctrine of the Church infallibly on the following conditions: namely, when, even though dispersed throughout the entire world but preserving for all that amongst themselves and with Peter's successor the bond of communion, in their authoritative teaching concerning matters of faith or morals, they are in agreement that a particular teaching is to be held definitively and absolutely (Lumen gentium*, no. 25, emphasis added).

Note that John Paul II, before invoking the authority conferred upon Peter and his successors, made it a point to call attention to the universal teaching of the bishops and to the teaching of Vatican Council II on the intrinsic and grave malice of every direct and voluntary killing of innocent human beings. Surely this is a teaching on a matter of "morals," and the universal Magisterium agrees in judging that this teaching is to be held definitively and absolutely. Consequently, one can legitimately conclude that here John Paul II is asserting that this truth of Catholic moral teaching has been infallibly proposed by the ordinary and universal Magisterium of the Church, according to the criteria set forth in Vatican Council II's Dogmatic Constitution on the Church, *Lumen gentium.*[3]

Later in this chapter, in condemning the intrinsic evil of direct abortion, John Paul II first reviews the teaching of Scripture (no. 61), the two-thousand-year Tradition of the Church (no. 61), recent papal teaching (no. 62), and the Church's canonical discipline from the earliest times to the present on this question. He then writes:

> Given such unanimity in the doctrinal and disciplinary tradition of the Church, Paul VI was able to declare that this tradition is unchanged and unchangeable (cf. Encyclical Letter *Humanae vitae*, no. 14). Therefore, by the authority which Christ conferred upon Peter and his Successors, in communion with the Bishops — who on various occasions have condemned abortion and who in the aforesaid consultation [which preceded publication of *Evangelium vitae*], albeit dispersed throughout the world, have shown unanimous agreement concerning this doctrine — *I declare that direct abortion, that is, abortion willed as an end or as a means, always constitutes a grave moral disorder,* since it is the deliberate killing of an innocent human being. This doctrine is based upon the natural law and upon the written Word of God, is transmitted by the Church's Tradition and taught by the ordinary and universal Magisterium [here again John Paul II explicitly refers to *Lumen gentium,* no. 25] (no. 62; emphasis in original).

Clearly, here John Paul II affirms that the teaching on the grave immorality of direct abortion has been infallibly proposed by the ordinary and universal Magisterium.

Later, in unequivocally condemning euthansia or mercy killing as always gravely immoral, John Paul II uses similar language:

> In harmony with the Magisterium of my Predecessors [here a note refers to the teaching of Popes Pius XII and Paul VI and to *Gaudium et spes*] and in communion with the Bishops of the Catholic Church, *I confirm that euthanasia is a grave violation of the law of God,* since it is the deliberate and morally unacceptable killing of a human person. This doctrine is based upon the natural law and upon the written Word of God, is transmitted by the Church's Tradition and taught by the ordinary and universal Magisterium [again a

note refers to *Lumen gentium*, no. 25] (no. 65; emphasis in original).

The Pope thus affirms here that this truth of Catholic moral teaching has been infallibly proposed by the ordinary and universal Magisterium.[4]

In this chapter John Paul II also insists that we must have the courage "to look truth in the eye and to call things by their proper names" (no. 58). Truth requires us to say that procured abortion is "the deliberate and direct killing, by whatever means it is carried out, of a human being in the initial phase of his or her existence, extending from conception to birth" (no. 58). The legalization of abortion is "a most serious wound inflicted on society and its culture by the very people who ought to be society's promoters and defenders" (no. 59).

It is also an affront to the dignity of human life to perform experiments on human embryos that are not intended to benefit them. Human life, even in its earliest stages of development, can never be regarded as "biological material" for research or as a source of organs or tissues for transplants: "the killing of innocent human creatures, even if carried out to help others, constitutes an absolutely unacceptable act" (no. 63).

The temptation "to have recourse to euthanasia, that is, to take control of death and bring it about before its time, 'gently' ending one's own life or the life of others" must be totally rejected (no. 64). Although it is morally licit to forgo medical procedures which "no longer correspond to the real situation of the patient, either because they are by now disproportionate to any expected results or because they impose an excessive burden on the patient and his family," "euthanasia is a grave violation of the law of God, since it is the deliberate and morally unacceptable killing of a human person" (no. 65). The same is true of suicide and "assisted suicide." Euthanasia and assisted suicide must be recognized as a *"false mercy,"* and indeed a disturbing 'perversion' of mercy. True 'compassion' leads to sharing another's pain; it does not kill the person whose suffering we cannot bear" (no. 66). The quite different *"way of love and true mercy"* leads us to recognize, in the pleas of the dying and the suffering, a "request for companionship, sympathy and support in the time of trial … a plea for help to keep on hoping when all human hopes fail" (no. 67).

Today, some, at times many, claim that abortion and euthanasia must be regarded as human rights, or at least as legally permissible options if approved by the majority. Unfortunately, the civil law of far too many societies has given legal sanction to such claims (nos. 68-69). When ethical relativism, the root of these tendencies, prevails, it perverts democratic societies. Democracy "cannot be idolized to the point of making it a substitute for morality or a panacea for immorality." The moral value of a democracy depends on conformity to the moral law, whose truths do not depend on changeable "majority" opinions (no. 70).

If sound democracy is to develop, there is urgent need to "rediscover those essential and innate human and moral values which flow from the very truth of the human being and express and safeguard the dignity of the person: values which no individual, no majority and no State can ever create, modify or destroy, but must only acknowledge, respect and promote" (no. 71). Public authority at times can tolerate moral evils in order to prevent more serious harms to human persons, but "it can never presume to legitimize as a right of individuals ... an offense against other persons caused by the disregard of so fundamental a right as the right to life." Nor can the legalization of abortion or euthanasia be justified by appeals to respect for the consciences of others, "precisely because society has the right and the duty to protect itself against the abuses which can occur in the name of conscience and under the pretext of freedom" (no. 71). Thus civil laws legalizing the direct killing of innocent human beings through abortion and euthanasia are totally opposed to "the inviolable right to life proper to every individual and thus deny the equality of everyone before the law" (no. 72). Since no human law can authorize such evils, there is a grave obligation in conscience to oppose them; it is never right to obey them or take part in propaganda campaigns in favor of them or to vote for them (no. 73).

John Paul II recognizes that "a particular problem of conscience can arise in cases where a legislative vote would be decisive for the passage of a more restrictive law, aimed at limiting the number of authorized abortions, in place of a more permissive law already passed or ready to be voted on." In such cases,

> when it is not possible to overturn or completely abrogate a pro-abortion law, an elected official, whose absolute personal opposition to procured abortion was well known, could licitly support proposals aimed at *limiting the harm* done by such a law and at lessening its negative consequences at the level of general opinion and public morality. This does not ... represent an illicit cooperation with an unjust law, but rather a legitimate and proper attempt to limit its evil aspects (no. 73).

A grave obligation of conscience requires persons not to cooperate formally in practices which, even if permitted by civil law, are contrary to "God's law." Such cooperation, which can never be justified, occurs "when an action, either by its very nature or by the form it takes in a concrete situation, can be defined as a direct participation in an act against innocent human life or a sharing in the immoral intention of the person committing it" (no. 74).

The commandment "You shall not kill," by absolutely excluding in-trinsically evil acts such as the deliberate killing of innocent human be-ings, is the point of departure for true freedom because "it leads us to promote life actively, and to develop particular ways of thinking and acting which serve life" (nos. 75-76). The new law of love immeasur-ably enriches and deepens this commandment: "for the Christian it in-volves an absolute imperative to respect, love, and promote the life of every brother and sister, in accordance with the requirements of God's bountiful love in Jesus Christ" (no. 77).

D. Chapter Four: "For a New Culture of Human Life"

This chapter is an appeal to proclaim the good news of the "Gospel of Life" and to carry out the work of evangelization, "an all-embracing, progressive activity through which the Church participates in the pro-phetic, priestly and royal mission of the Lord Jesus"(no. 78). Ransomed by the "Author of life" (Acts 3:15) at the price of his blood (cf. 1 Cor 6:30), and made his members by baptism, we are now *the people of life and we are called to act accordingly*," sent into the world as a people to celebrate and serve life (no. 79). To proclaim Jesus is to proclaim life because he is "the word of life" (1 Jn 1:1). Because of our union with Jesus we are adopted children of God, members of the divine family (no. 80). We are thus called to proclaim the "living God who is close to us, who calls us to profound communion with himself, who awakens in us the certain hope of eternal life"; we are summoned to affirm "the in-separable connection between the person, his life and his bodiliness" (no. 81).

Teachers, catechists, and theologians must show the anthropological reasons on which respect for every human life is based and help every-one discover how the Christian message "fully reveals what man is and the meaning of his being and existence." The task of proclaiming the Gospel of Life is primarily entrusted to bishops (no. 82).

To carry out our mission we must foster in ourselves "a contempla-tive outlook," that "of those who see life in its deeper meaning, who grasp its utter gratuitousness, its beauty and its invitation to freedom and responsibility," accepting reality as a gift and with deep religious awe in order to "rediscover the ability to *revere and honor every person"* (no. 83).

Celebrating the Gospel of Life means celebrating the God of life, the God who gives life (no. 84). It requires us to *"appreciate and make good use of the wealth of gestures and symbols present in the traditions and customs of different cultures and peoples"* (no. 85). Above all, the Gospel of Life must be celebrated in our daily lives, filled with self-giving love for others. Only in this way can we provide the context within which *"heroic actions … are born,"* actions proclaiming the Gospel of Life *"by the total gift of self."* Such heroism is reflected quietly in the lives of brave mothers "who devote themselves to their own families without reserve, who suffer in giving birth to their children, and who are ready to make any effort, to face any sacrifice, in order to pass on to them the best of themselves" (no. 86).

The Gospel of Life must be proclaimed by works of charity, a pressing need today. In carrying out these works, our attitude must be to "care for the other as a person for whom God has made us responsible." Appropriate and effective programs to support new life in particular must be implemented (no. 87).

A tremendous educational effort is needed to proclaim the Gospel of Life, including the development of centers for natural methods of regulating fertility, for marriage preparation and support, for helping unwed mothers welcome new life and care for it. Needed too are communities to help treat people suffering from drug addiction, from AIDS; and for all who are disabled. The elderly and terminally ill must be given the support necessary to sustain them in their final days. This requires a reconsideration of the role of hospitals, clinics, and convalescent homes, which must be "places where suffering, pain and death are acknowledged and understood in their human and specifically Christian meaning" (no. 88).

In proclaiming the Gospel of Life, a unique responsibility belongs to health-care personnel: doctors, pharmacists, nurses, chaplains, men and women religious, administrators, and volunteers (no. 89). Effective works of charity need certain forms of social activity and commitment in the political field. Civil leaders have a grave obligation to serve human life through legislative measures. Political leaders must not enact laws "which by disregarding the dignity of the person, undermine the very fabric of society." It is not enough to remove unjust laws; it is necessary to root out the underlying causes of attacks on life, "especially by ensuring proper support for families and motherhood. A *family policy must be the basis and driving force of all social policies"* (no. 90).

The issue of population growth must be addressed by respecting the primary and inalienable responsibility of married couples and families and "cannot employ methods which fail to respect the person and fundamental human rights, beginning with the right to life of every innocent human being" (no. 91).

The family has a decisive responsibility with respect to the Gospel of Life. "This responsibility flows from its very nature as a community of life and love, founded on marriage, and from its mission to 'guard, reveal and communicate love.' " The family is the true "sanctuary of life." It is indeed the "domestic church," summoned to proclaim, celebrate and serve the Gospel of Life. Married couples are called upon to be givers of life; they must recognize that procreation is "a unique event which clearly reveals that human life is a gift received in order to be given as a gift." They must raise their children in the love and service of God and neighbor (no. 92). To carry out its mission the family must pray daily, practice solidarity within the home, and extend hospitality and solidarity to others (no. 93).

The neglect or, worse yet, the rejection of the elderly, who have a valuable contribution to make to the Gospel of Life, is an intolerable offense (no. 94).

Because the future of humanity passes through the family, the sanctuary of life, "the *family urgently needs to be helped and supported."* Tragically today, social, economic and cultural conditions, far from serving the family, make its tasks more difficult. This must change (no. 94).

There is an urgent need for *"general mobilization of consciences and* a *unified ethical effort* to activate a *great campaign in support of life. All together, we must build a new culture of life"* (no. 95). To do this, the first and fundamental step is to form consciences rightly about the incomparable and inviolable worth of every human life and to reestablish the essential link between life and freedom, inseparably related goods of the human person. Of crucial importance in forming consciences is *"the rediscovery of the necessary link between freedom and truth."* Men must acknowledge that they are God's creatures: "Where God is denied and people live as though he does not exist, or his commandments are not taken into account, the dignity of the human person and the inviolability of human life also end up being rejected or compromised" (no. 96).

Education for life must emphasize its inherent value from its beginning. This demands that young people learn to value their sexuality and come to see the intimate bond between sexuality and authentic human love. Education in sexuality is education in chastity, a virtue enabling persons to respect the "spousal" meaning of the body, the responsibility of married couples to respect the beauty of human procreation and to be open to the gift of life by using natural methods of regulating fertility. Education for life also requires an education in the true meaning of suffering and death (no. 97).

In short, to develop a new culture of life we must have the courage "to *adopt a new life-style"* based on a correct scale of values: *"the primacy of being over having, of the person over things"*; it requires passing from indifference to concern for others, from rejection to acceptance. In developing this culture everyone has a role. An indispensable one belongs to intellectuals, in particular Catholic intellectuals; likewise universities, especially Catholic universities, and centers, institutes, and committees of bioethics have an indispensable role. So too do those involved in the mass media, who should "present the positive values of sexuality and human love, and not insist on what defiles and cheapens human dignity" (no. 98). Women play a particularly important role in developing a new culture of life. They are to bear witness to the meaning of genuine love, especially of love for human life at its inception. Women who have had abortions should remember that the "Father of mercies is ready to give [them] forgiveness and peace," and enable them to recommit themselves to the service of life (no. 99).

In developing a new culture of life we must always remember that God, the Giver of Life, is our greatest friend and helper. We need to ask for his help in prayer and fasting "so that the power from on high will break down the walls of lies and deceit: the walls which conceal from the sight of so many of our brothers and sisters the evil of practices and laws which are hostile to life" (no. 100). The Gospel of Life, finally, is not for believers only, but for *everyone.* The value at stake, the value of human life, "is one which every human being can grasp by the light of reason." To be actively pro-life is "to contribute to the renewal of society through the promotion of the common good"; no genuine democracy can exist "without a recognition of every person's dignity and without respect for his or her rights." Nor can true peace exist unless *"life is defended and promoted"* (no. 101).

Conclusion

In the conclusion of his encyclical, Pope John Paul II turns to gaze on

Mary, the Virgin Mother so intimately and personally associated with the Gospel of Life (nos. 102-104). She helps the Church to *"realize that life is always at the center of a great struggle* between good and evil, between light and darkness." She helps us realize that "it is precisely in the 'flesh' of every person that Christ continues to reveal himself and to enter into fellowship with us, so that *rejection of human life...is really a rejection of Christ"* (no. 104). She is the one who helps us face our mission to proclaim life. Like her, we are not "to be afraid," for "with God nothing is impossible" (Lk 1:30, 37) (no. 105).

2. THE VATICAN INSTRUCTION ON RESPECT FOR HUMAN LIFE IN ITS ORIGIN AND ON THE DIGNITY OF PROCREATION (DONUM VITAE)

On February 22, 1987 the Congregation for the Doctrine of the Faith issued this document, which is divided into an introduction and three principal parts. I will now summarize its contents.

A. Introduction

The Introduction contains five sections. Section 1 deals with biomedical research and Church teaching. The purpose of the document is to put "forward the moral teaching corresponding to the dignity of the person and to his integral vocation" with reference to issues posed by contemporary biomedical research. Section 2 takes up the contributions science and technology can make to the human person. But science and technology are not morally neutral. They require respect for the "fundamental criteria of the moral law," the service of the human person, of his inalienable rights and his integral good according to God's design. Section 3 relates truths about human anthropology to procedures in the biomedical field. Interventions upon the human body affect the human person, especially in the field of sexuality and procreation, where "the fundamental values of life and love are actualized." Biomedical interventions must be morally evaluated in light of the dignity of the human person and his divine vocation. Section 4 proposes two basic criteria for moral judgment in this area, namely (1) the inviolability of innocent human life "from the moment of conception until death," and (2) the special character of the transmission of human life which has been "entrusted by nature to a personal act." Section 5 recalls the teaching of the Magisterium, which offers human reason the light of revelation on these two points, holding (1) that human life, from the moment of conception, must be absolutely respected because man is the only creature on earth that God "has wished for himself" and because the spiritual soul of man is "immediately created by God"; and (2) that human procreation requires the responsible collaboration of spouses with God's fruitful love. Human procreation must be realized in marriage through the acts proper and exclusive to spouses.

B. Part I: Respect for Human Embryos

This part has six major sections. Section 1, on respect due to the human embryo, reminds us that "the human being is to be respected as a person from the first moment of his existence." Modern science recognizes that the biological identity of a new human individual is already constituted in the zygote resulting from fertilization. This scientific conclusion gives a valuable indication for discerning by the use of reason a personal presence at the moment of the first appearance of human life: how could a human individual not be a human person?

The moral condemnation of procured abortion is reaffirmed. "Since the human embryo must be treated as a person, it must also be defended in its integrity, tended and cared for, to the extent possible, in the same way as any other human being." This is the principle determining the answers to the moral questions that will follow.

Section 2 deals with prenatal diagnosis. This is licit if the methods used with the informed consent of parents respect the life and integrity of the embryo and the mother without subjecting them to disproportionate risks. It is gravely immoral when the diagnosis is done with the thought of possibly inducing an abortion depending on its results. One must deny to the State or any other authority the right to link in any way prenatal diagnosis and procured abortion.

Section 3, concerned with *therapeutic* procedures on human embryos, affirms that they are licit if they respect the embryo's life and integrity and do not involve disproportionate risks. Procedures menacing the life or integrity of human embryos are illicit.

Section 4 takes up medical *research and experimentation* on human embryos. If the research is intended to benefit the embryo, it can be undertaken provided there is certainty that it will not harm the embryo's life or integrity and provided that proper consent has been given. Research and experimentation not directly therapeutic is absolutely illicit. Moreover, the corpses of human embryos and fetuses must be respected.

Section 5 affirms that it is absolutely immoral to produce human embryos *in vitro* as research material.

Section 6, which deals with procedures for manipulating human embryos engendered by new reproductive technologies, brands as absolutely immoral efforts to obtain a human being asexually through "twin fission," cloning, or parthenogenesis. It likewise brands as immoral efforts to make animal-human hybrids or to gestate human embryos in artificial or animal uteruses, as well as the freezing of embryos, attempts to engineer the "sex" of embryos, etc.

C. Part II: Interventions Upon Human Procreation

Here concern is with "artificial procreation and insemination," i.e., different technical procedures directed toward obtaining a human conception in a manner other than the sexual union of man and woman. This part begins by noting the ideological link between procured abortion and *in vitro* fertilization. This deathly dynamic, however, does not exempt us from a further and thorough ethical study of artificial fertilization, whether heterologous (when the gametic cells used come from persons not married to each other) or homologous (when these cells come from persons married to each other).

(1) Heterologous Artificial Insemination

Section 1 deals with the intimate link between marriage and human procreation. From the moral point of view human procreation must be the fruit of marriage: this is the key principle. Every human being must be accepted as a gift and blessing. The procreation of a new human person must be "the fruit and sign of the mutual self-giving of the spouses." The child has a right to be conceived, carried in the womb, brought into the world and brought up within marriage. The good of society as well demands this. This is the only truly *responsible* way of generating human life.

Thus Section 2 repudiates heterologous artificial fertilization as immoral because it is contrary to the unity of marriage, to the dignity of the spouses, to the right of the child to be conceived and brought into the world in marriage and from marriage. Moreover, the fertilization of a woman who is unmarried or widowed, whoever the donor may be, is not morally justified.

Section 3 rejects "surrogate" motherhood as unacceptable for the reasons given already in repudiating heterologous artificial fertilization.

(2) Homologous Artificial Insemination

The key moral principle here is the intimate connection between procreation and the marital act. Three arguments are then given in Section

4, concerned with the connection between procreation and the marital or conjugal act.

(a) There is an inseparable connection, willed by God and unlawful for man to break on his own initiative, between the unitive and procreative meanings of the conjugal act. But artificial fertilization and procreation, even if the gametic cells used come from husband and wife, severs this bond. Fertilization is licitly sought when it is the result of a "conjugal act which is per se suitable for the generation of children to which marriage is ordered by its nature and by which the spouses become one flesh." From the moral point of view, procreation is deprived of its proper perfection when it is not desired as the fruit of a conjugal act, of the one-flesh unity of the spouses.

(b) The "language of the body" likewise shows that it is immoral for spouses to generate human life outside of their marital union, an act inseparably corporeal and spiritual. The origin of a new human person should be "linked to the union, not only biological but spiritual," of husband and wife.

(c) Respect for a human person in his origin requires that he not be treated as a product. When a child is begotten through the conjugal act, he comes to be as a gift from God, a gift crowning the spouses' mutual gift of themselves to each other. When a child is "produced" it comes to be, not as a gift from God, which in truth it is, but as a product of human control.

Section 5 specifically addresses the morality of homologous *in vitro* fertilization and embryo transfer. Even if we prescind from the ideological link between these procedures and procured abortion, the conclusion must be that these ways of generating human life are immoral. They dissociate the begetting of human life from the conjugal act and in fact establish the dominion of technology over the origin and destiny of the human person. Conception *in vitro* is not achieved or positively willed as the expression and fruit of a specific conjugal act; in homologous *in vitro* fertilization and embryo transfer, the generation of human persons is objectively deprived of its proper perfection, namely, that of being the result and fruit of a conjugal act expressing the love of husband and wife. The child so obtained has not been respected in his origin.

However a child comes into the world, whether as the fruit of a conjugal act or through these technologies, he must be respected as a person and as a gift from God.

Section 6 deals with homologous artificial insemination. This is rejected because it dissociates the two meanings of the conjugal act. The basic principle is this: if the procedure *replaces* or *substitutes* for the conjugal act, it is immoral; if, however, it *assists* or *helps* the conjugal act to achieve its purpose, it may be morally licit. Masturbation is repudiated as a morally illicit means of obtaining human sperm.

Section 7 treats of the moral criteria for medical intervention in human procreation. The physician is at the service of the person and of human procreation. He does not have the authority to dispose of them or to decide their fate. He is to aid the spouses and not, by his technique, substitute for them.

Section 8 concerns the suffering of spouses who cannot have a child or fear to bring a handicapped child into the world. The desire of spouses for children is natural and legitimate. But they do not have "right" to a child because the child is not an object but a gift from God. Spouses suffering from sterility must bear their cross.

D. Part III: Moral Law and Civil Law

The inviolable right of every innocent human person and the institution of marriage are moral values and constitutive elements of the civil society and its order.

New technological possibilities require the intervention of political authorities and of legislators. Such intervention should be directed to ensuring the common good of the people through respect for their fundamental rights, the promotion of peace, and public morality. It furthermore ought to preserve the human community from temptations to selfishness and from discrimination and prejudice.

Among fundamental rights are these: (a) every human being's right to life and physical integrity and (b) the rights of the family and of the child.

Political authority may not approve making human beings through procedures exposing them to the grave risks noted in the document. The recognition by positive law of techniques of artificial transmission of human life would widen the breach already opened by the legalization of abortion. The law cannot tolerate, and in fact must forbid, that human beings, even at the embryonic stage of development, be treated as objects of experimentation, mutilated, or destroyed.

Civil law cannot approve techniques of artificial procreation which, for the benefit of third parties, take away what is a right inherent in the spousal relationship; therefore, civil law cannot legalize donation of gametes between persons who are not united in marriage. Legislation ought also prohibit embryo banks, post mortem insemination, and surrogate motherhood.

Conclusion

In its conclusion the document issues an invitation to all who can to exercise a positive influence and ensure that, in family and society, due respect is accorded to human life and love. In particular, it invites theologians, above all moralists, to study more deeply and make ever more accessible to the faithful the teaching of the Magisterium in the light of a valid anthropology of human sexuality and marriage.

All are invited to act responsibly in the area proper to each and, like the Good Samaritan, to recognize as a neighbor even the littlest among the children of men.

3. DECLARATION ON PROCURED ABORTION

This document was issued by the Congregation for the Doctrine of the Faith on November 18, 1974, during the pontificate of Pope Paul VI.

Consisting of 27 numbered sections, it is structured as follows: (1) an Introduction (nos. 1-4); (2) In the Light of Faith (nos. 5-7); (3) In the Additional Light of Reason (nos. 8-14); (4) Reply to Some Objections (nos. 15-18); (5) Morality and the Law (nos. 19-23); and (6) a Conclusion (nos. 24-27).

Introduction

This stresses that the Church cannot remain silent about the question of abortion because of her obligation to defend man against whatever destroys or degrades him and because the issue is so grave, concerned as it is with human life, the most basic of all man's goods (no. 1). The claim that abortion should be legalized since it does not violate anyone's conscience and reflects legitimate ethical pluralism is specious, because no one can claim freedom of thought as a pretext to attack the rights of others, especially the right to life (no. 2). Thus Christians, both clerical and lay, and notably bishops, have rightly resisted efforts to legalize abortion (no. 3). It is appropriate and necessary for the Congregation for the Doctrine of the Faith, charged with protecting and fostering faith and morals in the Church, to speak out on this matter; all the faithful must realize the need to assent to the truths of faith and morals proposed by the Magisterium. The *Declaration's* teaching, therefore, lays a serious obligation on the consciences of the faithful (no. 4).

In the Light of Faith

Here the document stresses that God is the God of life, not death (no. 5), that the Church's Tradition from earliest times (e.g., the *Didache* of the second century) has always taught that human life must be protected at every stage in its course, including the beginnings (no. 6), despite different opinions regarding the precise time when a spiritual soul is infused. The teaching condemning abortion as gravely sinful, even by those who thought that the soul was not infused at conception, has been consistent throughout Church history and has been forcefully proclaimed by the Magisterium, especially in our day. As Pope Paul VI has said, the teaching of the Church on this matter is "unchanged and immutable" (no. 7).

In the Additional Light of Reason

Key points made here are: (1) human beings are persons because they have a rational nature and are radically capable of knowing the truth and making free choices; as a person, a human being is the subject of inviolable rights, among them the right to life (no. 8); (2) as a person, a human being is not subordinate to society but only to God, although a person must subordinate individual interests to the common good of society; his bodily life is a fundamental good (no. 9); (3) conscience must be enlightened to recognize that society is not the source of fundamental human rights but rather is obligated to respect and protect them (no. 10); the first right is the right to life, and society must respect this (no. 11); human life must be respected at all stages of development from fertilization until natural death (no. 12).

Number 13 of this section is particularly interesting. It declares that modern genetic science confirms belief that all the characteristics of the person are fixed at conception. However, in footnote 19 of this Number, the *Declaration* says that it deliberately leaves untouched the question, philosophical in nature, of when the spiritual soul is infused. It does so because "the tradition is not unanimous in its answer and authors hold different views: some think that animation occurs in the first moment of life, others that it occurs only after implantation." But it insists that the moral position it takes on abortion does not depend on the answer to that question, and this for two reasons: (1) Even if one supposes that animation occurs after conception, the life in question is incipiently human, preparing for and calling for a soul in which the nature received from the parents is completed. (2) It is enough that the presence of a soul is at least probable — and the contrary cannot be established with certainty

— to show that taking the life of the fetus at least runs the risk of killing a person already in possession of a soul.

It is very important, I believe, to note that in *Evangelium vitae* Pope John Paul II addressed this question when he considered the view of those who "try to justify abortion by claiming that the result of conception, at least up to a certain number of days, cannot yet be considered a personal human life" (no. 60). After explicitly referring to no. 13 of the *Declaration on Procured Abortion*, he then said:

> What is at stake is so important that, from the standpoint of moral obligation, the mere probability that a human person is involved would suffice to justify an absolutely clear prohibition aimed at killing a human embryo. Precisely for this reason, over and above all scientific debates and those philosophical affirmations to which the Magisterium has not expressly committed itself, the Church has always taught and continues to teach that the result of human procreation, from the first moment of existence, must be guaranteed that unconditional respect which is morally due to the human being in his or her totality and unity as body and spirit.

He then concluded by making his own the teaching of *Donum vitae,* namely, that " 'The human being is to be respected and treated as a person from the moment of conception; and therefore from that same moment his rights as a person must be recognized, among which in the first place is the inviolable right of every innocent human being to life' " (no. 60).

Reply to Some Objections

There can be serious reasons or motives for having an abortion (e.g., dangers to the mother's life and health, abnormal condition of the unborn child, extreme poverty, etc.). But life is too fundamental a good to be weighed against even very serious disadvantages. No reason can justify deliberately killing the unborn (no. 14). Women's liberation does not justify abortion (no. 15), nor does sexual freedom (no. 16), nor technological advance, which must be ruled by morality (no. 17), nor is birth control the answer (no. 18).

Morality and the Law

Cannot a legitimate pluralism legalize abortion, particularly to avoid harm to desperate women who seek abortion clandestinely (no. 19)?

While civil law must tolerate some evils, it cannot accept the killing of the unborn (no. 20); civil law is subordinate to natural law, and the state has the obligation to protect the weak from the strong (no. 21). No one can rightly obey a law immoral in itself, nor can anyone take part in campaigns in favor of such laws, nor vote for them, nor collaborate in their application, etc. (no. 22). Law must reform society so that children will be welcomed and received worthily (no. 23).

Conclusion

At times heroism is needed to follow conscience and obey God's law, but fidelity to truth is necessary for true progress of human persons (no. 24). A Christian, whose outlook cannot be confined to this world, knows that he cannot measure happiness by the absence of sorrow and misery here below (no. 25). Every Christian must attempt to remedy such sorrows and miseries; while never approving abortion, Christians must work to combat its causes by effective means, including political action and development of suitable institutions to help pregnant women (no. 26). Action will never change unless hearts and minds are changed so that people will consider fertility a blessing, not a curse, and responsible cooperation with God in giving life a privilege and honor. Christians know that in facing these tasks Jesus will help them (no. 27).

4. THE DECLARATION ON EUTHANASIA

This *Declaration,* promulgated by the Congregation for the Doctrine of the Faith on May 5, 1981, contains an Introduction, four parts (I. The Value of Human Life; II. Euthanasia; III. The Meaning of Suffering for Christians and the Use of Painkillers; IV. Due Proportion in the Use of Remedies), and a Conclusion.

A. Introduction

Here the document reminds readers of Vatican II's reaffirmation of the dignity of the human person and its unequivocal condemnation of crimes such as abortion, euthanasia, and willful suicide, and also of the Congregation's earlier *Declaration on Procured Abortion.* The Congregation now judges it opportune to set forth Church teaching on euthanasia, particularly in view of progress in medical science and issues this has raised.

B. Part I: The Value of Human Life

This part reaffirms that human life is the basis of all human goods. Most people regard it as sacred; no one may dispose of it at will; and believers regard it even more highly as a precious gift of God's love "which they are called upon to preserve and make fruitful." It then declares:

> 1. No one can make an attempt on the life of an innocent person without opposing God's love for that person, without violating a fundamental right, and therefore without committing a crime of the utmost gravity. 2. Everyone has the duty to lead his or her life in accordance with God's plan. That life … must bear fruit already here on earth, but … finds its full perfection only in eternal life. 3. Intentionally causing one's own death, or suicide, is therefore equally as wrong as murder…. however, one must clearly distinguish suicide from that sacrifice of one's life whereby for a higher cause … a person offers his or her own life or puts it in danger.

C. Part II: Euthanasia

The document defines euthanasia or mercy killing as "an action or an omission which of itself or by intention causes death, in order that all suffering may in this way be eliminated. Euthanasia's terms of reference, therefore, are to be found in the intention of the will and in the methods used." **NB:** one can kill a person mercifully or commit euthanasia by an act of *omission* as well as by one of commission.

It then articulates the *basic principle*, namely, "nothing and no one can in any way permit the killing of an innocent human being, whether a fetus or an embryo, an infant or an adult, an old person, or one suffering from an incurable disease, or a person who is dying." This is a "question of the violation of the divine law, an offense against the dignity of the human person, a crime against life, and an attack on humanity."

Some people, because of pain, suffering, etc., may ask to be killed mercifully; but many times when they ask for death they are really giving an anguished plea for help and love. What they need, besides medical care, is love.

D. Part III: The Meaning of Suffering for Christians and the Use of Painkillers

Physical suffering is an inevitable part of the human condition; it serves a useful purpose but so affects human psychology that it can become so severe that one wishes to remove it at any cost. Christians recognize that suffering has a special place in God's saving plan as a sharing in Christ's passion and union with his redemptive work. But there is nothing wrong in using painkillers as such so long as their use does not prevent one from carrying out religious and moral duties, even if one foresees that their use may shorten life. Painkillers that cause unconsciousness need special consideration because it is not right to deprive a person of consciousness without a serious reason for permitting this to happen.

E. Part IV: Due Proportion in the Use of Remedies

This is a very important part. The *Declaration* recalls the use in the past Catholic tradition of the distinction between "ordinary" and "extraordinary" means and notes that today — although the principle behind this distinction is good — it is sometimes difficult to understand because of the imprecision of these terms. Thus some today distinguish between "proportionate" and "disproportionate" means. The *Declaration* says that in any event one can make a "correct judgment as to means by studying the type of treatment to be used, its degree of complexity or risk, its cost and the possibilities of using it, and comparing these elements with the result that can be expected, taking into account the state of the sick person and his or her physical and moral resources."

This means that, although it is always gravely immoral to kill a person because of his or her alleged bad quality of life, the condition of a person's life can be used in judging whether a particular medical treatment is "proportionate" or "disproportionate."

In saying this the *Declaration* in no way supports the proportionalist method of making moral judgments (as some proportionalists have claimed). First of all, the *Declaration* had previously affirmed unambiguously the existence of an absolute moral norm prohibiting an intrinsically evil act, namely, the norm absolutely proscribing the intentional killing of an innocent human being. No proportionalist affirms but rather denies this truth. Second, there are contexts in which judgments of proportionality can be made, *when there is some measure that can be used to compare measurable things*. Here the things to be measured are medical treatments of different types, each with their own risks, hazards, pains, costs, etc., and with their benefits. The judgment to be made in such cases is basically a technical one requiring some help from the medical profession. Moreover, although it is always wrong to kill a person because of the alleged bad quality of his life, a person's physical and moral resources will be such that some can accept treatments that other persons cannot because for some the treatment would be useful and not unduly burdensome whereas for others the treatments would not be useful and would be unduly burdensome. This topic will be considered at length in a later chapter.

The document then notes that it is not always wrong for patients to undergo perhaps hazardous and untried treatments if they so desire, and they can also forgo their use when they are seen not to do what they were supposed to do. Doctors can help greatly in judging whether the investment in instruments, personnel, etc. is just in proportion to the results achieved. No one can force a person to accept a risky or burdensome treatment, etc. If death is imminent, only normal care is required.

Conclusion

This chapter has reviewed in depth the teaching found in four major documents of the Magisterium relevant to the issues to be taken up in this book. The teaching found in Pope John Paul II"s Encyclical *Evangelum vitae* is pertinent to almost every topic that will be considered, while the teaching set forth in *Donum vitae* is crucially important relative to questions concerning the generation of human life, that presented in the *Declaration on Procured Abortion* is central to the problem of abortion, and that given in the *Declaration on Euthanasia* is, naturally, quite pertinent to issues regarding the care of the dying. In our subsequent study of these specific issues, reference will be made to the documents examined here as well as to other relevant sources of magisterial teaching.

ENDNOTES

1. On this see John Paul II, Encyclical *Veritatis splendor*, no. 78; see also St. Thomas Aquinas, *Summa theologiae*, 2-2, 64, 7.
2. Here the Pope refers to an incisive passage in *Gaudium et spes*, no. 27, where the Council Fathers had said: "all offenses against human life itself, such as murder, genocide, abortion, euthanasia, willful suicide ... are criminal; they poison civilization, and they debase their perpetrators more than their victims and militate against the honor of the Creator."
3. The truth of this conclusion is confirmed by what John Paul II subsequently declared in his *motu proprio, Ad tuendam fidem* ("To defend the faith") on May 1998 and by the "explanatory note" on this document prepared by the Congregation for the Doctrine of the Faith. In this note the Congregation *explicitly* includes the "doctrine on the grave immorality of the direct and voluntary killing of an innocent

human being" as an example of a truth proposed as divinely revealed, not through a "defining act," i.e., a truth "solemnly defined by an *ex cathedra* pronouncement of the Roman Pontiff or by the action of an ecumenical council, but through a "non-defining act," i.e., "by the ordinary and universal magisterium of the bishops dispersed throughout the world who are in communion with the Successor of Peter." The Congregation then notes: "Such a doctrine can be confirmed or reaffirmed by the Roman Pontiff, even without recourse to a solemn definition, by declaring that it belongs explicitly to the teaching of the ordinary and universal magisterium." The text of John Paul II's *Ad tuendam fidem* and of the Congregation's explanatory note, entitled "Commentary on the Profession of Faith's Concluding Paragraphs," is found in *Origins: CNS Documentary Service* 28.8 (July 16, 1998). The text of *Ad tuendam fidem* is given on pp. 114-116; that of the commentary on pp. 116-120. See in particular nos. 9 and 11 of the commentary.

4. In its explanatory note on John Paul II's *Ad tuendam fidem*, the Congregation for the Doctrine of the Faith explicitly recalls the teaching of *Evangelium vitae* and cites euthanasia as an example of a truth which, while not revealed, is connected by logical necessity to revealed truth and as one infallibly proposed by the ordinary and universal Magisterium of the Church. See no. 11 of "Commentary on the Profession of Faith's Concluding Paragraphs," in *Origins* (cf. endnote 3).

Chapter Two

MAKING TRUE MORAL JUDGMENTS AND GOOD MORAL CHOICES

Before considering, in the following chapters, major bioethical issues, it is fitting and useful to consider first of all the subject of making true moral judgments and good moral choices. It is so precisely because the principles in light of which true moral judgments and good moral choices can be made in our everyday lives as husbands and wives, students, business men and women, or what have you, are the very same principles in light of which true moral judgments and good moral choices can be made in matters pertaining to bioethics.

Upright, virtuous men and women make true moral judgments and good moral choices insofar as doing so has become, as it were, second nature to them. Moreover, faithful Catholics can be confident that they make such judgments and choices by conforming them to the teaching of the Church, which speaks in the name of Christ. But everyone, even the virtuous person, is at times perplexed about what to do, and frequently there is no firm teaching of the Church to which one can appeal in order to make a true moral judgment about some difficult moral problem, and at times it is very difficult to apply such teaching to some complex issues. It is thus worthwhile to reflect more systematically on this matter.

Moreover, it is good for virtuous persons and faithful Catholics to reflect in this way so that they can more intelligently explain both to themselves and to others why they regard some human actions as morally good and others as morally bad, and why the Church's teaching on moral matters is true.

I will proceed as follows: First, I will clarify the meaning of a "human act," its religious and existential significance, and the sources of its moral goodness or badness. I do so because moral judgments bear upon human acts, assessing them for their moral quality. Second, I will consider different kinds of human dignity to show how human freedom of choice is related to truth, to God's wise and loving plan for human existence. Third, I will consider the relationship between the "good" and human choice and action and the first principle of natural law. Fourth, I will consider the basic normative truths or principles of natural law, i.e., truths enabling us to distinguish between morally good and morally bad alternatives of choice and action. Fifth, I will outline briefly an intelligent way to go about making good moral judgments. Finally, I will consider how the natural law is fulfilled and perfected by the new law of love and what this means for Christians in making moral judgments and choices.[1]

1. THE MEANING OF A "HUMAN ACT"; ITS EXISTENTIAL AND RELIGIOUS SIGNIFICANCE; THE SOURCES OF ITS MORAL CHARACTER

A. The Meaning of a "Human Act"

Human acts are *not* physical events that come and go, like the falling of rain and the turning of leaves, nor do they "happen" to a person. They are, rather, the outward expression of a person's choices, for at the core of a human act is a free, self-determining choice, which as such is something spiritual which abides within the person, determining the very *being* of the person.

The Scriptures, particularly the New Testament, are very clear about this. Jesus taught that it was not what enters a person that defiles him or her; rather, it is what flows from the person, from his or her heart, from the core of his or her being, from his or her choice (cf. Mt 15:10-20; Mk 7:14-23).

Although many human acts have physical, observable components, what is central to them is the fact that they embody and carry out human choices; because they do, they abide within the person as dispositions to further choices and actions of the same kind, until a contradictory kind of choice is made. Thus I become an adulterer and remain an adulterer once that I freely adopt by choice the proposal to have sex with someone other than my wife. I commit adultery in the heart even before I engage in the outward, observable act. And I remain an adulterer, disposed to commit adultery again, until I make a contradictory choice, i.e., until I sincerely repent of my adultery, do penance, and commit myself to amending my life and being faithful to my wife. Even then, in a sense, I remain an adulterer because I freely gave myself that identity, but now I am a *repentant* adulterer, resolved to be a faithful, loving husband, and I am a repentant adulterer because I have given myself this identity by my freely chosen act (made, of course, with the help of God's grace) of repentance.

B. The Existential, Religious Significance of Human Acts as Freely Chosen

This great truth, namely, that human acts as freely chosen have an existential, religious significance, has already, to some extent, been brought out in our consideration of the meaning of a human act as a reality shaped by a free, self-determining choice. But this matter is so critically important — it is precisely because human acts as freely chosen have existential and religious significance that eternal life depends on our making *good* moral choices in the light of *true* judgments — that it merits further reflection.

John Paul II eloquently emphasizes this truth at the very beginning of his 1993 Encyclical *Veritatis splendor*, in meditating on the dialogue between Jesus and the rich young man who asked, "Teacher, what good must I do to have eternal life?" (Mt 19:16). Reflecting on this question, the Holy Father says: "For the young man the question is not so much about rules to be followed, but *about the meaning of life*…. This question is ultimately an appeal to the absolute Good which attracts and beckons us: it is the echo of a call from God, who is the origin and goal of man's life" (VS, no. 7). It is, he continues, *"an essential and unavoidable question for every man* for it is about the moral good which must be done, and about eternal life. The young man senses that there is a connection between moral good and the fulfillment of his own destiny" (VS, no. 8).

The rich young man's question has existential and religious significance precisely because it is in and through the actions we freely choose to do that *we determine ourselves* and establish our identity as moral beings. "It is precisely through his acts," the Pope writes, "that man attains perfection as man, as one who is called to seek his Creator on his own accord and freely to arrive at full and blessed perfection by cleaving to him." Our freely chosen deeds, he continues, "do not produce a change merely in the state of affairs outside of man, but, to the extent that they are deliberate choices, they give moral definition to the very person who performs them, *determining his most profound spiritual traits"* (VS, no. 71). Each choice involves a *"decision about oneself* and a setting of one's own life for or against the Good, for or against the Truth, and ultimately for or against God" (VS, no. 65).

To recapitulate: we *determine ourselves, make ourselves to be the kind of persons we are in and through the actions we freely choose to do.* We are free to choose what we are to do and through our choices make ourselves to be the kind of persons we are. But we are *not* free to make what we choose to do to be good or bad, right or wrong. We know this from our own experience, for we know that at times we have freely chosen to do things that we knew, at the very moment we chose to do them, were *morally wrong*. We can, in short, choose badly or well; and if we are to be fully the beings we are meant to be we need to choose well, i.e., in accordance with the truth. We will take this matter up in detail later this chapter.

C. The Sources of the Morality of a Human Act

The morality of a human act depends on three factors: the *object* of the act, its *end*, and the *circumstances* in which it is done (cf. CCC, nos. 1750-1754; ST, I-II, 18). Of these the *primary* source of the morality of a human act is the *object*, and no wonder, because the object of the act is precisely what the acting person *chooses to do*. This object is not some physical event in the external world. Since it is precisely what the acting person is choosing to do here and now, he or she ratifies this object in his or her heart and makes himself or herself to be the kind of person willing to do *this*. Thus, if I choose to lie, lying is the object of my act specifying it as an act of lying, and, because I freely choose to lie, I make myself *to be* a *liar*, no matter how I may want to describe myself to others or even to myself.

Pope John Paul II, rejecting some contemporary moral theories utterly incompatible with Catholic faith, has emphasized this great truth. Thus he wrote: *"the morality of the human act depends primarily and fundamentally on the 'object' rationally chosen by the deliberate will"* (VS, no. 78; emphasis in the original). In a very important passage which not only well summarizes the Catholic tradition but also bears witness to the truth that a human act is no mere physical happening but rather a reality flowing from the inner core of the person insofar as it is a freely chosen deed, John Paul II goes on to say:

> In order to be able to grasp the object of an act which specifies that act morally, it is therefore necessary to place oneself *in the perspective of the acting person.* The object of an act of willing is in fact a freely chosen kind of behavior. To the extent that it is in conformity with the order of reason, it is the cause of the goodness of the will; it perfects us morally.... By the object of a given moral act, then, one cannot mean a process or an event of the merely physical order, to be assessed on the basis of its ability to bring about a given state of affairs in the outside world. Rather that object is the proximate end of a deliberate decision which determines the act of willing on the part of the acting person (VS, no. 78; cf. ST, I-II, 18).

Note that in this passage John Paul II affirms that the object freely chosen, if it is "in conformity with the order of reason," is the "cause of the goodness of the will" and "perfects us morally." Obviously, if this object is *not* in conformity with the order of reason and is known not to be, then it will be the cause of the badness of the will and will debase us morally. The "order of reason" to which John Paul II refers will occupy us below, in considering the "natural law" or set of truths intended to guide human choices and enable human persons to distinguish between morally good and morally bad alternatives of choice/action.

Note too that in this passage John Paul II says that the "object" is also the "proximate end of a deliberate decision which determines the act of willing on the part of the acting person." The "object" is the "proximate" or "immediate" end of an act of willing because it is what one chooses to do here and now. There is also a further or ulterior end of most human actions, the end for whose sake one chooses to do this here and now. This further or ulterior end is a distinct source of the morality of a human act different from the "object" or "proximate end." But both the object or proximate end, and the further or ulterior end must be good or in conformity with the order of reason if the human act in its totality is to be morally good. One can choose to do something morally good and in conformity with the order of reason for very bad ulterior ends. Thus one can choose to help carry an elderly widow's groceries into her house in order to gain entry to the house and steal her silverware or computer. The whole action is vitiated by the bad end toward which it is ordered and for whose sake one chose to carry in the groceries.

Frequently people seek to justify their actions in terms of the further or remote end for whose sake they are done, and at times they even try to re-describe the "object" of their act in terms of its hoped-for benefits. Thus some may seek to justify an abortion by saying that what they are doing — their moral object — is to prevent human suffering (e.g., the suffering that a child afflicted by cystic fibrosis and his family might experience if he is allowed to be born). But this alleged justification is patently false, for the true "object" specifying their act of choice is aborting the unborn child. This is the means chosen, the act done, in order to bring about the remote or further end motivating the act.

The morality of an act also depends on the *circumstances* in which it is done. These too can be either good or bad. For instance, it is good to offer charitable correction to a friend, but to do so in front of his children rather than in private is a circumstance affecting the act, turning one otherwise morally good into one morally bad.

Because the morality of a human act, considered in its totality, depends on object (= proximate end), end (further or ulterior end), and circumstances, the act is morally good *only if all* these factors are morally good, i.e, in conformity with the order of reason. This is what can be called the principle of plenitude or perfection, expressed in Latin by the dictum *bonum ex integra causa,* which means that the act is morally good if and only if all the factors contributing to its moral quality are good. If *any* of these morally relevant factors is contrary to the order of reason, then the act is morally bad: *malum ex quocumque defectu* — an act is bad if it has any moral defect whatsoever (cf. CCC, nos. 1755-1756; ST, I-II, 18, 1; 18, 4, ad 3; 19, 6, ad 1).

Of these three sources of the morality of a human act, the "object," understood precisely as John Paul II has described it, is primary. An act morally bad by reason of the object freely chosen can never be made good by reason of any end, no matter how noble, or any circumstances, whatever they may be.

2. KINDS OF HUMAN DIGNITY; HUMAN FREEDOM AND GOD'S WISE AND LOVING PLAN FOR HUMAN EXISTENCE

A. Kinds of Human Dignity

According to Catholic tradition, there is a threefold dignity predicable of human persons: (1) the first is intrinsic, natural, inalienable, and an endowment or gift; (2) the second is also intrinsic, but it is an achievement, not an endowment, an achievement made possible, given the reality of original sin and its effects, only by God's unfailing grace;

(3) the third, again an intrinsic dignity, is also a gift, not an achievement, but is a gift far surpassing man's nature and literally divinizing him.

The first dignity proper to human beings is the dignity that is theirs simply as living members of the human species, which God called into being when, in the beginning, he "created man in his own image and likeness … male and female he created them" (Gn 1:27). Every human being is a living image of the all-holy God and can therefore rightly be called a "created word" of God, the created word that his Uncreated Word became and is precisely to show us how much God loves us.

When we come into existence we *are,* by reason of this intrinsic dignity, *persons.* As God's "created words," as persons, we are endowed with the capacity to know the truth and the capacity to determine our lives by freely choosing to conform our lives and actions to the truth.[2] Yet when we come into existence we are *not yet* fully the beings we are meant to be. And this leads us to consider the second sort of dignity proper to human persons, a dignity that is intrinsic but an achievement (made possible only by God's never-failing grace), not an endowment.

This second kind of dignity is the dignity to which we are called as intelligent and free persons capable of determining our own lives by our own free choices. This is the dignity we are called upon to *give to ourselves* (with the help of God's unfailing grace) by freely choosing to shape our choices and actions in accord with the truth. In other words, we give ourselves this dignity and inwardly participate in it by making good moral choices, and such choices are possible only in the light of true moral judgments. We give this dignity to ourselves by being true to our natural dignity as persons created in God's image and likeness.

The third kind of dignity is ours as "children of God," brothers and sisters of Jesus, members of the divine family. This kind of dignity is a pure gratuitous gift from God himself. He made us to be the *kind* of beings we are, i.e., persons made in his image and likeness, because he willed that there be beings inwardly capable of receiving, should he choose to grant it, the gift of divine life. And God has chosen to give this utterly supernatural gift to us in and through his Son become man, Jesus Christ. Just as Jesus truly shares our human nature, so too do human persons who are re-generated in the waters of baptism share in Jesus' divine nature. As true children of God and brothers and sisters of Jesus, we are called to walk worthily of our vocation *to be* co-workers with Christ, his collaborators in redeeming the world. I will take up the relevance of this dignity for making true moral judgments and good moral choices in section 6, below. My concern here and in the next two sections is with the second kind of dignity proper to human persons, the dignity that, as intelligent and free persons made in God's image and likeness, they are to give themselves by choosing in accordance with the truth.

B. Human Freedom of Choice and God's Wise and Loving Plan for Human Existence

The nature of this dignity and the relationship between human freedom and God's wise and loving plan for human existence was beautifully developed by Vatican Council II. According to the Council, "the highest norm of human life is the divine law — eternal, objective, and universal — whereby God orders, directs, and governs the entire universe and all the ways of the human community according to a plan conceived in wisdom and in love" (DH, no. 3). Immediately afterwards, the Council went on to say: "Man has been made by God to participate in this law, with the result that, under the gentle disposition of divine providence, he can come to perceive ever increasingly the unchanging truth" (DH, no. 3). Precisely because he can do this, man "has the duty, and therefore the right, to seek the truth" (DH, no. 3). The truth in question here is the truth that is to inwardly shape and guide human choices and actions — moral truth.

The passage concludes by saying: "on his part man perceives and acknowledges the imperatives of the divine law through the mediation of conscience" (DH, no. 3). Another Council document, the Pastoral Constitution on the Church in the Modern World *Gaudium et spes*, develops this thought in a very significant passage:

> Deep within his conscience man discovers a law which he has not laid upon himself but which he must obey. The voice of this law, ever calling him to love and do what is good and to avoid evil, tells him inwardly at the right moment, do this, shun that. For man has in his heart a law written by God. *His dignity lies in obeying this law*, and by it he will be judged. His conscience is man's most secret core, and his sanctuary. There he is alone with God, whose voice echoes in his depths. By conscience, in a wonderful way, that law is made known which is fulfilled in the love of God and of one's neighbor (GS, no. 16; emphasis added).

These passages make it clear that human persons give to themselves the dignity to which they are called only by choosing in accord with the truth. They likewise make it clear that God's divine, eternal law, his "wise and loving plan for human existence," is the highest norm of human life. They also affirm that human persons have been so made by God that they can inwardly participate in his divine, eternal law. Although these passages do not explicitly use the expression "natural law" to refer to our intelligent participation in God's eternal law, this is precisely what the expression "natural law" does mean in the Catholic tradition, and the Council Fathers, through official footnotes appended to the text, show that this is precisely how they understand natural law.[3]

3. THE RELATIONSHIP BETWEEN THE "GOOD" AND HUMAN CHOICES AND ACTION; THE FIRST PRINCIPLES OF NATURAL LAW

Human choices and actions, whether morally good or morally bad, are intelligible and purposeful. Sinful choices, although *unreasonable* and opposed to the "order of reason," are not *irrational, meaningless, absurd.* All human choice and action is directed to some end or purpose, and the ends of purposes to which human choices and actions are ordered are considered as "goods" to be pursued. The "good" has the meaning of what is perfective of a being, constitutive of its flourishing or well-being. Consequently, the proposition *good is to be done and pursued and its opposite, evil, is to be avoided* is a proposition to which every human person, as intelligent, will assent (ST, I-II, 94, 2). It is a "principle" or "starting-point" for intelligent, purposeful human choice and action. If human persons are to do anything, whether *morally* good or *morally* bad, there must be some "point" in doing it, something promising a benefit to the acting person. The principle that good is to be done and pursued and evil is to be avoided is the first principle or truth of the natural law, and everyone can understand it.

Moreover, this is not an empty principle. It can be specified by identifying the real goods perfective of human persons, aspects of their flourishing or full-being, and these goods are grasped by our practical reason as purposeful ends of human choice and action. St. Thomas identified a triple-tiered set of such human goods which, when grasped by our reason as ordered to action ("practical reason"), serve as first principles or starting-points for intelligent human activity, as starting-points for practical deliberation — "what am I to do?" The first set includes being itself, a good that human persons share with other entities; and since the being of living things is life itself, the basic human good at this level is that of life itself, including bodily life, health, and bodily integrity. The second set includes the bodily union of man and woman in order to hand life on to new human persons who need education and care if they are to flourish, and this is a set of goods that human persons share with other animals, but, of course, in a distinctively human way. The third set includes goods unique to human persons, such goods as knowledge of the truth, especially truth about God, fellowship with other persons in a human community (friendship and justice, peace), and the good of being reasonable in making choices (cf. ST, I-II, 94, 2).

To sum up: the first principles—the "starting-points"—or first truths of natural law are the truths (a) that *good is to be done and pursued and evil is to be avoided* and (b) propositions identifying real goods of human existence as the goods that are to be pursued and done and whose opposites are evils to be avoided, propositions such as *life is a good to be pursued and protected, knowledge of the truth is a good to be pursued, friendship is a good to be pursued,* etc. These propositions articulate truths, practical in nature (i.e., relevant to human action), that do not need to be demonstrated as true — their truth is immediately evident for anyone who knows what they mean.

None of these goods is the highest or greatest good, the *Summum Bonum*. God alone is this good. But each of these goods is a real good of human persons, inwardly perfective of them; each is a created participation in the uncreated goodness of God himself. The propositions directing that good is to be done and identifying these as the goods which authentically perfect human persons and which are, consequently, the goods to be pursued in and through human action do not, however, enable us to distinguish, prior to choice, between alternatives of action that are morally good and those that are morally bad. Indeed, even sinners appeal to these goods and the principles directing that they be protected in order to "justify" or, rather, rationalize their immoral choices. Thus a research scientist who unethically experiments on human subjects, failing to secure their free and informed consent because he knows that they will not give it should they be aware of the risks his experiment entails, may try to rationalize his immoral behavior both to himself and others by appealing to the good of knowledge to be gained through his experiments and its benefits for the life and health of other persons.

But in addition to these *practical* principles of natural law there are also practical principles that are *moral* in function, i.e., truths that enable human persons to distinguish, prior to making choices, which alternatives are morally good and which are morally bad. I shall now turn to a consideration of these moral or normative truths of the natural law.

4. NORMATIVE TRUTHS OF NATURAL LAW

St. Thomas, in an article devoted to showing that all of the moral precepts of the Old Law can be reduced to the ten precepts of the Decalogue, taught that the twofold law of love of God and neighbor, while not among the precepts of the Decalogue, nonetheless pertained to it as the "first and common precepts of natural law." Consequently, all the precepts of the Decalogue must, he concluded, be referred to these two love commandments as to their "common principles" (ST, I-II, 100, 3 and ad 1). In other words, for St. Thomas the very first *moral* principle or normative truth of natural law can be properly expressed in terms of the twofold command of love of God and neighbor. St. Thomas held this view, obviously, on the authority of Jesus himself, who, when asked, "Teacher, which is the greatest commandment in the law?," replied, citing two Old Testament texts (Dt 6:5 and Lv 19:18), "You shall love the Lord your God with all your heart, and with all your soul, and with all your mind. This is the great and first commandment. And a second is like it, You shall love your neighbor as yourself. On these two commandments depend all the law and the prophets" (Mt 22:36-40; cf. Mk 12:28-31; Lk 10:25-28; Rom 13:10; Gal 5:14).

In short, for St. Thomas — and the entire Catholic tradition — the very first moral principle of natural law is that we are to love God and our neighbor as ourselves. Moreover, and this is very important, there is an inseparable bond uniting this first *moral* principle of natural law to the first *practical* principle of natural law which directs us to do and pursue the good and the principles specifying the real goods of human persons that are to be pursued and done. For the goods that are to be done and pursued in human action — the goods perfecting human persons — are in truth *gifts* from a loving God that we are to welcome and cherish, and it is obvious that we can love our neighbors *only* if we are willing to respect fully the goods perfective of them, only by willing that these goods flourish in them, and by being *unwilling* intentionally to damage, destroy, or impede these goods, to ignore them or slight them or put them aside, substituting pseudo-goods for them.

Pope John Paul II has well expressed the indissoluble bond between love for the goods of human existence and love for our neighbor. Commenting on the precepts of the second tablet of the Decalogue, i.e., those concerned with actions regarding our neighbor, he reminds us (as did Aquinas before him) that these precepts are rooted in the commandment that we are to love our neighbor as ourselves, a commandment expressing *"the singular dignity of the human person,* 'the only creature that

God has wanted for its own sake' " (VS, no. 13, with an internal citation from GS, no. 22).

After saying this, the Holy Father continues, in a passage of singular importance for grasping the *truth* that is meant to guide our choices and actions, by emphasizing that we can love our neighbor and respect his dignity as a person only by cherishing the real goods perfective of him and by refusing intentionally to damage, destroy, impede, ignore, neglect or in any other way shut ourselves off from what is truly good. Appealing to the words of Jesus, he highlights the truth that "the different commandments of the Decalogue are really only so many reflections on the one commandment about the good of the person, at the level of the many different goods which characterize his identity as a spiritual and bodily being in relationship with God, with his neighbor, and with the material world.... The commandments of which Jesus reminds the young man *are meant to safeguard the good of the person, the image of God, by protecting his goods"* (VS, no. 13). The negative precepts of the Decalogue — "You shall not kill; You shall not commit adultery; You shall not steal; You shall not bear false witness" — all these precepts, he concludes, "express with particular force the ever urgent need to protect human life, the communion of persons in marriage," and so on (VS, no. 13).

Here the Holy Father is simply articulating once more the Catholic moral tradition. Centuries ago St. Thomas Aquinas observed that "God is offended by us only because we act contrary to our own good" (SCG; 3.122).

In summary: the first *moral principle* of natural law, requiring us to love God and our neighbor as ourselves, directs us, in every one of our freely chosen deeds, to respect fully *every real good* perfective of human persons and to refrain from intentionally choosing to damage, destroy, impede, neglect, ignore, or in any other way fail to honor these goods and the persons in whom they are meant to flourish. This first moral principle of natural law, expressed fittingly in religious language by the twofold commandment of love of God and neighbor, can be expressed in more philosophical language, some contemporary Catholic authors convincingly argue, by saying that "in voluntarily acting for human goods and avoiding what is opposed to them, one ought to choose and otherwise will those and only those possibilities whose willing is compatible with integral human fulfillment" (CMP, p. 184).[4]

In other words, if we are to choose well, in accordance with the truth or order of reason, our basic attitude must be that of persons eager to embrace, revere, and honor the real goods perfective of human persons and the persons in whom these goods are meant to flourish because these goods are *gifts* from God himself, created participations in his own uncreated goodness, and constitutive aspects of the *full being* of the human persons made in his image.

This basic, first principle of morality logically entails various "modes of responsibility," i.e., moral principles specifying ways in which we can fail to love human persons and the goods meant to flourish in them. These are moral principles such as the Golden Rule — we are to do unto others as we would have others do unto us and not do unto others as we would not have them do unto us (cf. Mt 7:12; Lk 6:31; ST, I-II, 94, 4, ad 1) — and the principle that we are not to do evil so that good may come about (cf. Rom 3:8) (on this subject cf. May, pp. 77-79).

In light of the first moral principle of natural law and its modes of responsibility we can show the truth of more specific moral norms, such as the precepts of the Decalogue, and come to understand that some human acts, as specified by their moral objects, are intrinsically evil and hence absolutely forbidden. If we were willing to make these objects the end of our will act of choice, we would be willing that *evil be* and thus freely make ourselves *evil*-doers.

This truth will be grasped readily if we recall here what was said before about the "object" of a human act, namely, the "freely chosen kind of behavior." Morally good objects are compatible with a love for *all* the goods of human persons and for the God whose gifts these goods are. Human acts specified by such objects are capable of being ordered to God; they specify morally good kinds of human acts, whereas objects opposed to these goods and to the persons in whom they are meant to flourish are not capable of being ordered to God, and such objects specify morally bad kinds of human acts. As Pope John Paul II puts the matter: "reason attests that there are objects of the human act which are by their nature 'incapable of being ordered to God,' *because they radically contradict the good of the person made in his image"* (VS, no. 80). Acts so specified are *intrinsically evil* acts and the specific moral norms proscribing them are *absolute,* i.e., without any possible exceptions.

The Catholic moral tradition — and sound philosophical ethics as well — has recognized that there are human acts of this kind, i.e., human acts specified by "objects" which cannot be chosen by one with a will toward integral human fulfillment, by one who loves all the goods of human persons and the persons in whom these goods are meant to flourish, who regards these goods as precious gifts from God himself. Among

such intrinsically evil acts are the intentional (direct) killing of an innocent human being, having sexual relations outside of marriage (fornication, adultery), and the like; norms proscribing such intrinsically evil
acts are moral absolutes.

Precisely because the truth of these moral absolutes is so widely denied today, even by some theologians, John Paul II found it necessary to
devote his Encyclical *Veritatis splendor* to the defense of this truth. He
declared that "the central theme of this encyclical ... is the reaffirmation of the universality and immutability of the moral commandments,
particularly those which prohibit always and without exception intrinsically evil acts" (VS, no. 115). He clearly affirms that the truth of these
moral commandments is rooted in God's love and in his call to each one
of us to be holy as he is holy (cf. Lv 19:2), his commandment that we are
to be as perfect as he is perfect (cf. Mt 5:48). "The unwavering demands
of that commandment are based upon God's infinitely merciful love (cf.
Lk 6:36) and the purpose of that commandment is to lead us, by the
grace of Christ, on the path of that fullness of life proper to the children
of God" (VS, no. 115).

5. STEPS IN MAKING TRUE MORAL JUDGMENTS

In light of the normative truths of natural law, we can make true judgments regarding the morality of human acts as specified by their "objects," i.e., by *what* is proposed as an object of free choice. We have
already seen that there are certain kinds of human acts, as specified by
their moral objects, that we ought never freely choose to do: intentionally to kill an innocent human being, to commit adultery or fornication,
etc. Obviously, one cannot intentionally choose to kill an innocent human being without freely willing that a great evil *be*, namely, the death
of that person whose life, a good of incalculable value, one has chosen
to destroy. Similarly, one cannot freely choose to commit adultery without being willing to damage the incalculable human good of marital
fidelity and communion.

What this shows us is that, in considering the moral quality of any
proposed alternative of action — any "object" of a human act — one
must consider how this proposed action impinges on the *goods* of human persons. If the proposed action is specified by an object of choice
that one *cannot* will without being willing to damage, destroy, or impede some true good of human persons, or without being willing to
ignore, slight, or repudiate some real good of human persons, then this
proposed action is specified by a morally bad object and hence not re-

ferable to God because it contradicts the good of persons made in his image.

Moreover, since the morality of human acts, though primarily settled by the object freely chosen, also depends on the ends for whose sake they are chosen and done and on the circumstances in which they are done, these ends and circumstances must also be in accord with the order of reason, i.e., in accord with a love and respect for the goods of human persons. Actions good by reason of their object can become bad by reason of the end for which they are chosen or the circumstances surrounding them. Thus, while it is morally good in itself to sing a beautiful aria — by doing so one is participating in the good of beauty and perhaps enabling others to do so as well — it is not morally good to choose to do so in a dormitory at 3 a.m. and thus disturb the sleep of others. But one can never justify a human act morally bad by reason of its object (an intrinsically evil act) by *any* end, however noble (cf. CCC, no. 1756).

To put matters another way: Some proposals of choice (the "objects" of the act), while relevant to one or perhaps more human goods, are *compatible with a love and respect for all human goods.* Such moral objects are in accord with the order of reason, and thus acts specified by them can be rightly chosen. Other proposals of choice, while relevant to one or perhaps more human goods and compatible with a love and respect for *some* human goods, *are not compatible with love and respect for at least one human good,* that good, namely, whose destruction or injury is indeed the "object" of choice. Human acts specified by moral objects of this kind are not in accord with the order of reason and must be judged immoral.

6. THE "FULFILLMENT" OR "PERFECTION" OF NATURAL LAW THROUGH THE REDEMPTIVE WORK OF CHRIST

In his introduction to *Veritatis splendor,* John Paul II calls attention to a truth of supreme importance. This is the truth that "it is only in the mystery of the Word Incarnate that light is shed on the mystery of man.... It is Christ, the last Adam, who fully discloses man to himself and unfolds his noble calling by revealing the mystery of the Father and the Father's love" (VS, no. 2, citing GS, no. 22). Jesus, in his very person, "fulfills" the law and brings it to perfection and thereby reveals to man his noble calling. As a consequence, to live a moral life means ultimately to follow Christ.

We follow him not by any outward imitation but by "becoming conformed to him who became a servant even to giving himself on the Cross" (VS, no. 21; cf. Phil 2:5-8). Following Christ means "holding fast to the very person of Christ" (VS, no. 19).

But how can we "hold fast" to Christ? We do so by shaping our lives — by making moral judgments and choices — in accord with the sublime truths that Jesus makes known to us. Jesus not only reconfirms the truths of the old law given to Moses (which embodied truths of natural law), he also gives us a new command of love. The old law — as well as the natural law — commands us to love our neighbor as ourselves. The new commandment Jesus gives us still requires this but it goes beyond it, for Christians, Jesus' brothers and sisters, true children of God, are commanded by him to love one another even as he has loved us, with a healing, redemptive kind of love (cf. Jn 15:12; VS, nos. 18, 20), the kind of self-giving love that finds expression on the Cross.

In his Sermon on the Mount (Mt 5), Jesus specifies for us the nature of this self-giving love. Pope John Paul II, following St. Augustine, St. Thomas, and the Catholic tradition, regards our Lord's Sermon on the Mount as the *"magna charta* of Gospel morality" (VS, no. 15). The Beatitudes of this Sermon "speak of basic attitudes and dispositions in life and therefore they do not," John Paul II says, "coincide with the commandments…. [they are], above all, *promises* from which there also flow *normative indications* for the moral life…. They are a sort of self-portrait of Christ … invitations to discipleship and communion of life with Christ" (VS, no. 16).

The Beatitudes are not optional for the Christian, precisely because they describe the dispositions and attitudes that ought to characterize the followers of Christ. Here we must keep in mind the supreme truth about our existence as Christians and the sublime dignity (cf. the third kind of dignity described above) that is ours as children of God, brothers and sisters of Jesus, members of the divine family.

The Beatitudes of the Sermon on the Mount can be regarded — as Germain Grisez has so well presented matters — as "modes of Christian response." They specify ways of acting (including ways of making good moral judgments) that mark a person whose will, enlivened by the love of God poured into his or her heart, is inwardly disposed to act with the confidence, born of his or her Christian hope, that integral human fulfillment is *indeed* possible and realizable in union with Jesus (cf. CMP, pp. 653-655).

In bearing our cross daily and shaping our judgments, choices, and actions in accord with the truth — and ultimately the truth made known to us by Jesus — we can be confident that the burden he gives us is sweet and his yoke is light because *he is with us!!!* He is our Emmanuel. And he is, in truth, our Simon of Cyrene, who will help us bear our cross so that we can carry on his work of redemptive love.

ENDNOTES

1. The following sources are used for this chapter:
Documents of the Church's Magisterium:

(1) *Catechism of the Catholic Church,* abbreviated as CCC;

(2) Vatican Council II, Dogmatic Constitution on the Church, *Lumen gentium,* abbreviated as LG;

(3) Vatican Council II, Pastoral Constitution on the Church in the Modern World, *Gaudium et spes,* abbreviated as GS.

(4) Vatican Council II, Declaration on Religious Liberty, *Dignitatis humanae,* abbreviated as DH.

(5) Pope John Paul II, Encyclical *Veritatis splendor* ("The Splendor of Truth"), abbreviated as VS.

Other Sources:

(1) St. Thomas Aquinas, *Summa theologiae,* abbreviated as ST. The *Summa theologiae* is divided into parts, questions, and articles. There are three parts in the *Summa*, and the second part is in turn divided into two parts. The parts will be referred to by roman numerals, the questions and articles by arabic numerals. Thus ST, I-II, 94, 2 means: *Summa theologiae*, First Part of the Second Part, question 94, article 2. Frequently important material is contained in St. Thomas's responses to the objections he poses at the beginning of each article. These responses are indicated by "ad 1," "ad 2," etc., meaning "response to objection 1," "response to objection 2," etc.

(2) St. Thomas Aquinas, *Summa contra gentiles*, abbreviated as SCG. This work is divided into four books, and the books are divided into chapters. Both will be indicated by arabic numerals, with a period between the arabic numeral designating the book and the arabic numeral indicating the chapter. Thus SCG 3.111 means *Summa contra gentiles*, book 3, chapter 111. This work of St. Thomas has been translated into English as *On the Truth of the Catholic Faith* (New York: Doubleday Image Books, 1955), five volumes.

NB: Perhaps the finest presentation of St. Thomas's moral thought is to be found in John Finnis, *Aquinas: Moral, Political, and Legal Theory* (Oxford and New York: Oxford University Press, 1998), chapters II-V, pp. 20-186.

(3) Germain Grisez, *The Way of the Lord Jesus,* Vol. 1, *Christian Moral Principles* (Chicago: Franciscan Herald Press, 1983). This work will be abbreviated as CMP.

(4) William E. May, *An Introduction to Moral Theology* (revised ed.: Huntington, IN: Our Sunday Visitor, 1995). This will be referred to as May.

All the above references are placed in parentheses in the text at appropriate places.

2. A baby, born or preborn, does not, of course, have the *developed* capacity for deliberating and choosing freely, but he has the *natural* or *radical* capacity to do so becauses he is human and personal in nature. This matter will be taken up in more depth in a later chapter concerned with the moral status of the embryo.

3. Thus, in *Dignitatis humanae,* no. 3, after affirming that God has made man capable of sharing in his law and thus coming to know ever more the unchanging truth, the Council Fathers added an official footnote, in which they refer to three key texts of St. Thomas, namely, ST, I-II, 91, 1; 93, 1; and 93, 2, in which St. Thomas affirms, among other things, that "the eternal law is unchanging truth, and everyone somehow knows the truth, at least the *common principles of natural law* (even though in other matters some people share more and some less in the knowledge of the truth)" (ST, I-II, 93, 2). Unfortunately, the commonly used English translations of the Documents of Vatican Council II (the "Abbott" edition and the first "Flannery" edition) fail to include this official footnote, which is, however, in the Latin original. Fortunately, subsequent editions of the "Flannery" translation include the footnote.

4. In suggesting this way of formulating in non-religious and more philosophical language the first moral principle of natural law, Grisez and his associates (John Finnis, Joseph Boyle and myself) are in large measure simply following a suggestion made by the Fathers of Vatican II. As we have seen already, they clearly affirmed that the "highest norm of human life," i.e., the *ultimate norm of morality,* is God's divine, eternal law, in which we participate through the natural law (cf. DH, no. 3). But, in speaking of human action in this world, they also said that the "norm for human activity is this: that, in accord with the divine plan and will, *human activity should harmonize with the genuine good of the human race,* and allow men as individuals and as members of society to pursue their total vocation and fulfill it" (GS, no. 35).

Chapter Three

GENERATING HUMAN LIFE: MARRIAGE AND THE NEW REPRODUCTIVE TECHNOLOGIES

Introduction

If the human race is to continue, new human beings must come into existence. It is now possible to "make" human babies in the laboratory through an array of modern reproductive technologies. But, as we all know, the usual way for bringing new human persons into existence is for a man and a woman to engage in genital intercourse, either within marriage and through the marital act or outside of marriage through acts of adultery and fornication or, as the latter is euphemistically called today, "premarital" sex.

No matter how a new human being comes into existence, he or she is something precious and good, a person, a being of incalculable value, worthy of respect, a bearer of inviolable rights, a being *who ought to be loved.*[1] This is true no matter how the child comes to be: whether through the intimate and chaste embrace of husband and wives, through acts of adultery or fornication, or through use of modern reproductive technologies.

This chapter is divided as follows. Part One briefly considers moral issues raised by generating human life through acts of fornication and adultery. Part Two considers at greater length and in depth the bonds intimately uniting marriage, the marital act, and the gift of human life in order to show why, in God's loving plan for human existence, new human life is properly respected when it comes to be in and through the marital embrace and how the generation of human life in and through the marital act is an act of *procreation,* not one of *reproduction.* Part Three takes up in depth the new reproductive technologies; after describing them in some detail it will set forth ethical and theological arguments to show that it is intrinsically immoral to make use of technologies that generate new human life outside the marital act. Part Four presents criteria for distinguishing between technological interventions that "assist" the marital or conjugal act in being fruitful and those which substitute for it and replace it. Part Five considers the "rescuing" of frozen embryos produced by the new reproductive technologies.

1. PART ONE: FORNICATION, ADULTERY, AND THE GENERATION OF HUMAN LIFE

Here we can state straightforwardly that it is *not* good to generate human life through acts of adultery and fornication. It is not good because fornicators and adulterers have not made themselves *fit* to receive the great gift of human life. They do not have the moral capacity to receive this surpassingly great gift because they have not, through their own free and self-determining choices, capacitated themselves to cooperate with God in raising up new life and giving it the home where it can take root and grow.[2] Indeed, practically all civilized societies have, until recently, regarded as irresponsible the generation of new human life through the coupling of unattached males and females. Even today secular society judges fornicators and adulterers to be acting "responsibly" only if they take care to prevent unwanted pregnancies (and for the most part fornicators and adulterers do not want a pregnancy) by using contraceptives and, should contraceptives fail, abortion as a backup to prevent the birth of an unwanted child (the issues of contraception and abortion will be taken up in depth in later chapters).[3] It is, unfortunately, symbolic of a new barbarism — of the "culture of death"— that many today claim that unmarried individuals have the "right" to generate human life if they so choose, whether through freely chosen genital acts of fornication or adultery or through new laboratory methods of producing new human life.[4]

2. PART TWO: MARRIAGE AND THE GENERATION OF HUMAN LIFE

Two of the documents examined in Chapter One (*Evangelium vitae, Donum vitae*) testify to the Church's profound love and respect for marriage and the family. Married couples, as Pope John Paul II affirmed, are summoned to be givers of life and to recognize that procreating human life is "a unique event which clearly reveals that human life is a gift received in order to be given as gift" (*Evangelium vitae,* no. 92). The *Instruction on Respect for Human Life in its Origin and on the Dignity of Human Procreation (Donum vitae)* insisted that the procreation of new human life must be the fruit of marriage and the marital act. As we saw in Chapter One, this document gave three reasons why it is wrong to generate human life outside the marital act: the first was based on the inseparable connection, willed by God and not lawful for man to sunder on his own initiative, between the unitive and procreative meanings of the marital act; the second, on the "language of the body"; the third, on the obligation to regard the child always as a person and never as a product. When children are engendered through the loving embrace of husbands and wives, the "inseparable connection" and the "language of the body" are fully respected, nor is the child in any way treated as a "product." To show that this is true I will consider (A) how men and women, by getting married, give themselves rights and capacities that unmarried persons simply do not have. Next (B), I will reflect on the meaning of the marital act as inherently unitive and procreative, and I will then (C) show that the life given in and through the marital act is truly "begotten, not made."

A. Marriage, Marital Rights and Capacities

Fornicators and adulterers do not have the right either to "give" themselves to one another in genital sex nor to "receive" the great gift of human life. They do not have the right to do these things precisely because they have failed to capacitate themselves to do them, to make themselves *fit* to do them.

But husbands and wives, precisely because they have given themselves irrevocably to each other in marriage, have established each other as irreplaceable, nonsubstitutable, nondisposable persons and by doing so have *capacitated* themselves to do things that unmarried individuals simply cannot do, among them to "give" themselves to one another in the act proper and exclusive to spouses — the marital act — and to receive the gift of life.

In and through his act of marital consent — an act of free self-determination — the man, forswearing all others, has given himself irrevocably the identity of this particular woman's *husband*, while the woman, in and through her self-determining act of marital consent, has given herself irrevocably the identity of this particular man's *wife,* and together they have given themselves the identity of *spouses*. They have established each other as absolutely unique and irreplaceable.[5]

Moreover, in and through the choice that makes them to be husband and wife, a man and a woman give to themselves new capacities and new rights, and they freely take upon themselves new responsibilities. They are now able to do things that unmarried men and women simply cannot do, precisely because the latter have failed to capacitate themselves to do them by getting married. In short, men and women who give themselves irrevocably to one another in marriage have the right and capacity to do what husbands and wives are supposed to do. And among the things that married persons are supposed to do are (1) to give one another a unique kind of love, conjugal or spousal or marital love, (2) to engage in the marital act, and (3) to "welcome life lovingly, nourish it humanely, and to educate it religiously," i.e., in love and service of God and neighbor.

B. The Meaning of the Marital Act

The marital act is not simply a genital act between men and women who happen to be married. Husbands and wives have the capacity to engage in *genital* acts because they have genitals. Unmarried men and women have the same capacity. But husbands and wives have the capacity (and the *right*) to engage in the *marital* act only because they are married, i.e., husbands and wives, spouses. The marital act, therefore, is more than a simple genital act between people who just happen to be married. As marital, it is an act that inwardly participates in their marital union, in their one-flesh unity, a unity open to the gift of children.[6] The marital act, in short, is an act inwardly participating in the "goods" or "blessings" of marriage, i.e., the good of steadfast fidelity and exclusive conjugal love, the good of children, and, for Christian spouses, the good of the "sacrament."

The marital act expresses, symbolizes, and manifests the exclusive nature of marital love, and it does so because it is both a communion in being (the unitive meaning of the act) and the sort or kind of an act in and through which the spouses open themselves to the good of human life in its transmission, to the blessing of fertility (its procreative meaning).[7]

The marital act is unitive, that is, a communion in being or in an intimate, exclusive sharing of personal life because in and through it husband and wife come to "know" each other in a unique and unforgettable way, revealing themselves to each other as unique and irreplaceable persons of different but complementary sex.[8] In and through this act they become personally "one flesh," renewing the covenant they made with each other when they gave themselves to each other in marriage.[9] In the marital act husbands and wives "give" themselves to one another in a way that concretely expresses their sexual complementarity, for the husband gives himself to his wife in a receiving sort of way while she in turn receives him in a giving sort of way. His body, which expresses his person as a male, has a "nuptial significance," for it enables him to personally give himself to his wife by entering into her body-person and doing so in a receiving sort of way, while her body, which expresses her person as a female, likewise has a "nuptial significance," for it is so structured that she is uniquely equipped to receive his body-person into herself and in so receiving him to give herself to him.[10] The marital act thus indeed, as Pope John Paul II has said, speaks "the language of the body."

The marital act is also a procreative kind of an act. In giving themselves to each other in this act, in becoming "one flesh," husband and wife also become one complete organism capable of generating human life. Even if they happen to be sterile, their marital union is the sort or kind of act in and through which human life can be given should conditions be favorable: it is procreative in kind.[11] Moreover, precisely because husbands and wives are married, they have capacitated themselves, as nonmarried persons have not, to cooperate with God in bringing new human persons into existence in a way that responds to the dignity of persons. They have capacitated themselves to "welcome life lovingly, nourish it humanely, and educate it in the love and service of God and neighbor," to give this life the "home" it needs and merits in order to grow and develop.

The marital act, therefore, is not, as Pope Pius XII rightly said, "a mere organic function for the transmission of the germ of life." It is rather "a personal action, a simultaneous natural self-giving which, in the words of Holy Writ, effects the union in 'one flesh'... [and] implies a personal cooperation [of the spouses with God in giving new human life]."[12] Indeed, as Pope Paul VI put matters: "because of its intimate nature the conjugal act, which unites husband and wife with the closest of bonds, also *make them fit* [the Latin text reads: *eos idoneos facit*] to bring forth new human life according to laws inscribed in their very being as men and women."[13]

The marital act, therefore, precisely as marital, participates inwardly in the goods or blessings of marriage. It is inherently love-giving (unitive) and life-giving (procreative). And this is why the Church teaches that "there is an inseparable connection, willed by God and not lawful for man to break on his own initiative, between the unitive and procreative meaning of the marital act."[14] The bond inseparably uniting these two meaning of the marital act is the marriage itself, and "what God has joined together, let no man put asunder."

The marital act is thus an utterly unique kind of human act. It is a collaborative, personal act executing the choice of the spouses to actualize their marital union and participate in the goods proper to it. It is integrally unitive and procreative, and it speaks the "language of the body."

C. "Begetting" Human Life Through the Marital Act

When human life comes to be in and through the marital act, it comes as a "gift" crowning the act itself. The child is "begotten" through an act of intimate conjugal love; he or she is not "made," treated like a product. Husband and wife do not "make" a baby, just as they do not "make" love, for neither a human baby nor love are "products" one makes. In engaging in the marital act, husbands and wives are not "making" anything. They are, rather, "doing" something, i.e., *giving* themselves to each other as irreplaceable and nonsubstitutable persons complementary in their sexuality, and opening themselves to the gift of human life. They are rightly regarded as "procreating" or "begetting" a child through an act of love; they are *not* "producing" one, "making" one. Their act is properly one of "procreation" and not one of "reproduction."

Properly to grasp this truth, it is necessary to understand the difference between "transitive" and "immanent" human activity, between "making" and "doing." In the one mode of human activity, making, the action proceeds from the agent or agents to something produced in the external world by the use of various materials (e.g., cars, cookies, a poem). Such action is *transitive* insofar as it passes from the acting subject(s) to an object or objects fashioned by him or her or them. In this mode of human activity, which is governed by the rules of art, interest centers on the product made, and those that do not measure up to standards are frequently discarded. Thus autoworkers produce cars, cooks bake cakes, novelists write books, and college and university teachers produce lectures and texts. In this mode of human activity, the action perfects (or fails to perfect) the object made, not the agent producing the object — and I would rather have delicious cookies baked by a culinary artist who might, for all I know, be a morally bad person, than inedible ones produced by a saint.

In another mode of activity, doing, the action abides in the acting subject(s). The action is *immanent* (i.e., within the subject) and is governed by the requirements of the virtue of prudence, not by the rules of art. If the action is morally good, it perfects the agent(s); who in and through it "make" himself (herself; them) *to be* the kind of person he or she is (or they are), i.e., morally good.[15]

It is important to note that every making involves a doing, for one *chooses* to make something, and the act of choice, whereby we determine ourselves and give ourselves our identity as moral beings, is something we "do." And there are some things that we *can* make that we know we *ought not* to make because a choosing to make them is a morally bad kind of choice, e.g., pornographic films.

The marital act is *not* an act of making or producing. It is not a transitive act issuing from spouses and terminating in some object distinct from them. It is something that they "do." In it they do not "make" love or "make" babies. They *give* love to one another by giving themselves bodily to one another and they open themselves to the gift of human life. The life begotten through their one-flesh union is not the product of their art, but "a gift supervening on and giving permanent embodiment to" the marital act itself.[16] Thus, when human life comes to be in and through the marital act we can rightly say that the spouses are procreating or begetting. Their child is "begotten, not made."

3. PART THREE: GENERATING HUMAN LIFE THROUGH NEW REPRODUCTIVE TECHNOLOGIES

Chapter One provided an extended account of the teaching on this matter found in the Vatican *Instruction on Respect for Human Life in its Origin and on the Dignity of Procreation (Donum vitae)*. Hence there is no need here to repeat this teaching. But I will, prior to describing and offering a moral evaluation of the various methods of generating human life outside the marital act, summarize the teaching of Pope Pius XII on this matter and also the teaching found in the 1997 document issued by the Pontifical Academy for Life on cloning, an issue not treated in *Donum vitae*.

A. The Teaching of Pius XII and the Pontifical Academy for Life

Pius XII died in 1958, twenty years before the birth of Louise Brown, the first baby conceived *in vitro* to be born. Yet he was quite farsighted and in several of his addresses took up the artificial generation of human life.[17] In one address, concerned with artificial insemination either by a third party or by the husband, he articulated the "inseparability principle." His teaching is quite clear, as the following passage shows:

> The Church has ... rejected the ... attitude which pretended to separate in procreation the biological activity from the personal relations of husband and wife. The child is the fruit of the marriage union, when it finds full expression by the placing in action of the functional organs, of the sensible emotions thereto related, and of the spiritual and disinterested love which animates such a union; it is in the unity of this human act that there must be considered the biological condition of procreation. Never is it permitted to separate these different aspects to the point of excluding positively either the intention of procreating or the conjugal relation.[18]

Referring specifically to artificial insemination by the husband, he put matters very eloquently:

> To reduce the common life of a husband and wife and the conjugal act to a mere organic function for the transmission of seed would be but to convert the domestic hearth, the family sanctuary, into a biological laboratory. Therefore, in our allocution of September 29, 1949, to the International Congress of Catholic Doctors, We expressly excluded artificial insemination in marriage. The conjugal act in its natural structure is a personal action, a simultaneous and immediate cooperation of husband and wife, which by the very nature of the agents and the propriety of the act, is an expression of the reciprocal gift, which, according to Holy Writ, effects the union "in one flesh." That is much more than the union of two germs, which can be effected even by artificial means, that is, without the natural action of husband and wife. The conjugal act, ordained and designed by nature, is a personal cooperation, to which husband and wife, when contracting marriage, exchange the right.[19]

In another address he condemned *in vitro* fertilization, at that time only a possibility. In no uncertain terms he declared: "As regards experiments of human artificial fecundation 'in vitro,' let it be sufficient to observe that they must be rejected as immoral and absolutely unlawful."[20]

Although condemning artificial insemination/fecundation by a husband as intrinsically immoral, he declared that "this does not necessarily proscribe the use of certain artificial means destined solely to facilitate the marital act, or to assure the accomplishment of the end of the natural act normally performed."[21] As we have seen, the Vatican *Declaration on Respect for Human Life in Its Origin and the Dignity of Procreation* some thirty years later affirms the legitimacy of technological interventions that "assist" the marital act and do not "replace" it or "substitute" for it.

In June 1997 the Pontifical Academy for Life issued its *Reflections on Cloning.* The document was issued after the success of Scottish scientists in cloning the sheep "Dolly." After noting that cloning "represents a radical manipulation of the constitutive relationality and complementarity which is at the origin of human procreation in both its biological and strictly personal aspects," the Academy pronounces on the morality of cloning: "All the moral reasons which led to the condemnation of *in vitro* fertilization as such and to the radical censure of *in vitro* fertilization for merely experimental purposes must also be applied to human cloning."[22]

B. The New Reproductive Technologies

These include two broad categories: (1) artificial fertilization, which embraces (a) artificial insemination, (b) *in vitro* fertilization and embryo transfer, (c) alternative technologies using male and female gametic cells; and (2) cloning or agametic reproduction.

(1) Artificial Fertilization

Fertilization naturally occurs when male sperm (male gametic cells) are introduced into a woman's body through an act of sexual coition and one of the sperm succeeds in penetrating the woman's ovum (female gametic cell) and fertilizing it. Artificial fertilization is brought about when male sperm are not united with the female ovum through an act of sexual coition but by some other means. In artificial *insemination,* male sperm are introduced into the female reproductive tract by the use of a cannula or other instruments, with fertilization occurring when one of the sperm so introduced fuses with the woman's ovum. Fertilization occurs within the woman's body. In *in vitro* fertilization male sperm and female ova are placed in a petri dish (hence the name *in vitro,* "in a glass") and subsequent fusion of sperm and ovum and fertilization occur outside the woman's body.

Both these forms of artificial fertilization can be either homologous or heterologous. *Homologous* artificial fertilization uses gametic cells of a married couple, whereas *heterologous* artificial fertilization uses the gametic cells of individuals not married to each other (although one or both of the parties may be married to another person).[23]

(a.) Artificial Insemination

Homologous artificial insemination or artificial insemination by husband (AIH) introduces the husband's sperm into the wife's body by use of a cannula or other instruments. Ordinarily the husband's sperm are obtained through masturbation, although an alternative is intercourse using a perforated condom or, in cases of obstruction of the vas deferens, which serves a conduit for spermatozoa, the surgical removal of sperm from the epididymis, where the sperm are stored.[24]

Some married couples resort to AIH in order to achieve pregnancy when, for whatever reason, the husband is not able to ejaculate within the vagina. It is also used when the husband suffers from oligospermia (when his sperm production is very low and thus makes conception less likely through sexual union) or when some allergy exists that cannot be treated hormonally. Today AIH involves "washing" the sperm in a laboratory procedure to remove antibodies and prostaglandins and to capacitate the sperm for fertilizing the ovum. [25]

With the ability to freeze and store sperm (the cryopreservation of sperm) AIH can also be used to help a widow conceive a child by her own husband's sperm after his death.

Heterologous artificial insemination is usually referred to by the acronym AID, signifying "artificial insemination by a donor." But, as Walter Wadlington correctly observes, "the term 'sperm donor' is a misnomer because compensation of persons supplying semen has been a long-standing practice."[26] It is thus far more accurate to call this form of artificial insemination "artificial insemination by a vendor."[27]

Traditionally this form of artificial insemination was used by married couples so that the wife could bear a child genetically her own if her husband were infertile or if there was "genetic incompatibility" between the couple; i.e., when the couple were bearers of a recessive genetic defect and there was the likelihood that any child they might conceive might be actually afflicted by this genetic impairment. Today the procedure is still commonly used for these purposes, but it is now also used by single women who want to bear a child and who, as Wadlington puts it, "do not have a marital or other stable heterosexual partner or by a woman in a life partnership with another woman."[28] It is also used in implementing surrogacy agreements under which a woman will conceive and bear a child who will then be turned over to the sperm provider or another person or other parties after birth.

Because of the danger that the sperm provided by the "vendor" may carry the human immuno-deficiency virus (H.I.V.) and thus threaten the woman and child with AIDS (acquired immune deficiency syndrome), today most doctors engaging in this form of artificial insemination use only frozen sperm from commercial sperm banks which have quarantined the samples long enough to test for H.I.V.[29]

(b.) In Vitro *Fertilization and Embryo Transfer*

Until the late 1970s artificial insemination was the only alternative to sexual union for effecting conception. But in the late 1970s Patrick Steptoe and Paul Edwards succeeded in bringing to birth a child conceived *in vitro* and transferred a few days after fertilization to her mother's womb. Thus, with the birth of Louise Brown on July 25, 1978, a new mode of human reproduction became a reality: *in vitro* fertilization. It is ironic to note that Louise was born precisely ten years after Pope Paul VI signed his Encyclical *Humanae vitae*, which affirmed the "inseparable connection willed by God and unlawful for man to break on his own initiative, between the unitive and procreative meanings of the marital act." *In vitro* fertilization makes it possible for human life to be conceived outside the body of the (genetic) mother, but it is still a form of generating human life that is gametic, i.e., possible only by uniting a male gametic cell, the sperm, with a female gametic cell, the ovum. The new human life is conceived in a petri dish using sperm provided by a man and an ovum provided by a woman. Approximately two days after the fertilization process has been completed, the embryo, which by then has developed to the four-to-eight cell stage, is ready for transfer into a woman's uterus, where it can implant and, if implantation is successful, continue intrauterine development until birth.

Initially *in vitro* fertilization and embryo transfer (hereafter IVF-ET) was carried out by obtaining a single egg (ovum) from a woman through a laparoscopy, a procedure requiring general anesthesia. When a laparoscopy is performed, the physician aspirates the woman's egg through a hollow needle inserted into the abdomen and guided by a narrow optical instrument called a laparoscope. The first time IVF-ET succeeded, it was carried out in a normally ovulating woman, Louise Brown's mother, whose fallopian tubes had been surgically removed. After a single egg was obtained through laparoscopy, it was fertilized by her husband's sperm *in vitro* and the resulting embryo was then transferred to her womb two days after the fertilization process was completed.

Today the standard procedure is to overstimulate the ovaries with ovulatory drugs such as Clomid, Pergonal, and Metrodin so that the woman will produce several oocytes for retrieval and subsequent fertilization. Oocytes (ova) produced are retrieved not by laparoscopy with its requirement of general anesthesia but by ultrasound-guided transvaginal aspiration, which does not require general anesthesia. This greatly simplifies the procedure. Standard practice today also includes fertilization of many ova, mixing them in the petri dish with sperm (usually collected by masturbation) that have been "washed" to make them more apt to fertilize. Thus several new human zygotes (human beings at the earliest stage of development) are produced and allowed to grow to the early embryo stage. It is now customary to transfer two to four of these early embryos to the womb to increase probability of implantation and subsequent gestation until birth and to freeze and store the others so that they can be used for implantation later if the first attempts are unsuccessful. These "spare" frozen embryos can also be "donated" for research purposes. Eventually, if not claimed by the persons responsible for their manufacture or used in research, the frozen embryos will be destroyed.[30]

IVF-ET can be either homologous or heterologous. Initially homologous IVF-ET was used almost exclusively for wives whose fallopian tubes had been damaged, to enable them and their husbands to have children of their own. But now this procedure has been extended to include male-factor infertility (oligospermia, for instance) and other cases in which no precise cause for the couple's infertility has been determined.[31] It can also be used, it is now increasingly possible, to help a married couple avoid conceiving a child who could be affected by a genetically inherited pathology. For example, in the summer of 1998 scientists succeeded in identifying and separating male sperm responsible for the conception of female and male children. Male children alone are afflicted by hemophilia. Hence a married couple legitimately worried about conceiving a male child so afflicted can now choose to conceive the child *in vitro*, fertilizing the wife's ovum with sperm provided by her husband but with the assurance that the sperm provided are female-producing and not male-producing sperm. In the future it is likely that more gametic cells, both male and female, carrying the genes responsible for genetically induced pathologies will be identified and separated, and then only those identified as not carrying the genes causing the maladies can be used for fertilization *in vitro*.

Heterologous IVF-ET can now be used instead of artificial insemination in instances when the husband is completely infertile or when the wife lacks ovaries or when there is genetic incompatibility between the spouses. Sperm "donation" is easier than ova "donation," inasmuch as the latter is complicated by the need to synchronize the menstrual cycles of the woman who "donates" the ova and the wife into whom the embryo is to be implanted. Embryos conceived *in vitro* as well as sperm and ova can also be "donated," and embryo donation, like sperm donation, does not require synchronizing the menstrual cycles of different women. Both homologous and heterologous IVF can include implanting the resulting embryo into the womb of a woman other than the one who supplied the ovum, a so-called "surrogate" mother.[32]

As this makes evident, many permutations and combinations of generating human life are now technically feasible as a result of *in vitro* fertilization, among them such procedures as ZIFT (zygote intrafallopian tube transfer), which occurs when the zygote resulting from IVF is inserted into the fallopian tube rather than having the embryo transferred into the womb; and PROST (pro-nuclear tubal transfer), which transfers the very early embryo by use of a laparascope into the fallopian tube.[33]

(c.) Alternative Technologies Using Male and Female Gametic Cells

Certain contemporary techniques are not, strictly speaking, variants of *in vitro* fertilization inasmuch as fertilization itself occurs, not outside the woman's body in a petri dish, but within a woman's body. Thus these techniques are more closely related to artificial insemination than to *in vitro* fertilization as methods of artificial fertilization. But their development was stimulated by research into *in vitro* fertilization and embryo transfer. In these procedures sexual union is not required in order to unite male and female gametic cells.

One such technique is called SIFT or sperm intrafallopian tube transfer. This is sometimes used as an option for infertile couples who have not conceived following AIH. In this procedure the woman's ovaries are hyperstimulated; this is coupled with a laparoscopy under general anesthesia to inject a "washed" or prepared concentrate of the husband's sperm (or that of a "donor" if necessary) into the fallopian tubes so that conception can occur there.[34]

Another procedure of special interest is GIFT or gamete intrafallopian tube transfer. This is similar to IVF in that the woman's ovaries are hyperstimulated to produce multiple eggs, which are retrieved either by laparoscopy or ultrasound-guided transvaginal procedures. An egg (or goup of eggs) is placed into a catheter with sperm (provided either by masturbation or by the use of a perforated condom during intercourse) that have been treated and "capacitated," with an air bubble separating ova from sperm to prevent fertilization from occurring outside the woman's body. The catheter is then inserted into her fallopian tube, the ovum (ova) and sperm are released from the catheter, and fertilization can then occur within the body of the woman, who can, of course, be the wife of the man whose sperm are used and who could have provided the ovum (ova).[35]

There is currently a debate among theologians over GIFT and some similar procedures, such as LTOT (low tubal ovum transfer) and TOT (tubal ovum transfer). Some hold that GIFT and other procedures can, if used by married persons in a way that avoids procuring sperm through masturbation, be regarded as "assisting" the marital act and not replacing it and hence morally permissible. Others hold that GIFT is definitely a procedure that replaces or substitutes for the marital act and that, therefore, its use is immoral. I will take up this question in the Part 4 of this chapter.

(2) Cloning or Agametic Reproduction

The February 27, 1997 issue of the journal *Nature* carried the news of the birth of the sheep Dolly through the work of Scottish researchers Ian Wilmut and K. H. S. Campbell and their associates at Edinburgh's Roslin Institute. They succeeded in generating a new sheep by a process called "cloning," or more technically "somatic-cell nuclear transfer."[36] What they did was to produce "Dolly" by fusing the nucleus of a somatic (body) cell of an adult sheep with a denucleated oocyte, that is, an oocyte deprived of the maternal genome. The genetic identity of the new individual sheep, Dolly, was derived from only one source, namely, the adult sheep whose somatic cell nucleus was inserted into the denucleated oocyte to "trigger" development into a new individual of the species. This procedure can, in principle, be used to generate new human beings whose genetic endowment would be identical to that of the human beings whose somatic cells were inserted into a denucleated human ovum.

A somewhat different procedure, developed by Ryuzo Yanagimachi and his team at the John A. Burns School of Medicine at the University of Hawaii, was used to clone mice and reported in the July 24, 1998, issue of *Nature* magazine. But their work, too, produced a new member of a mammalian species by a procedure that is asexual or agametic in nature inasmuch as it does not require fertilization of the female gametic cell, the ovum, by the male gametic cell, the sperm. Thus, even from a biological perspective, cloning is a far more radical mode of reproduction than artificial insemination or *in vitro* fertilization and their permutations and combinations. As the Pontifical Academy for Life noted in the document previously referred to, cloning "tends to make bisexuality a purely functional leftover, given that an ovum must be used without its nucleus in order to make room for the clone-embryo."[37]

C. An Ethical and Theological Evaluation of the New Reproductive Technologies

(1) Ethical Reasons Why Non-Marital Ways of Generating New Human Life Are Intrinsically Immoral

As we saw in Chapter One, the *Vatican Instruction on Respect for Human Life in Its Origin and on the Dignity of Procreation (Donum vitae)* briefly sets forth three lines of reasoning to support the conclusion that it is always immoral to generate human life outside the marital act. The first is based on the "inseparability principle," which claims that it is not lawful for man on his own initiative to separate the unitive and procreative meanings of the conjugal act. The second is rooted in the "language of the body," and the third is that non-marital ways of engendering human life change its generation from an act of procreation to one of reproduction, treating the child as if he or she were a product.

I believe that in the first part of this chapter, in reflecting on the meaning of marriage and the marital act, I provided evidence to show that the bond uniting marriage, the marital act, and the generating of new human life is intimate, that the marital act, precisely *as* marital, is inherently both unitive and procreative, and that it speaks the language of the body. Thus I think that in that part of the chapter I offered good reasons to support the first two lines of argument used by *Donum vitae*. There I also emphasized that when a child comes to be in and through the marital act, he or she is "begotten, not made," and that in engaging in the marital act husbands and wives are not "making" anything, either love or babies, but are rather "doing" something, i.e., *giving* themselves to one another in an act that actualizes their marital union and expresses their sexual complementarity, and *opening* themselves to the gift of human life. I thus touched on the third line of reasoning used by *Donum vitae* to show that it is wrong to generate human life outside the marital act, because doing so treats the child as if he or she were a product.

Here I wish to develop this third line of reasoning because I think that it is the one that more clearly shows how seriously wrong it is to generate human life outside the marital act.

In what follows I will focus attention on *homologous* artificial insemination and IVF-ET, i.e., ways of bringing new human life into existence by uniting the gametic cells of husband and wife outside the marital act. I do so because although some people in our society — and perhaps their number is increasing — find the Church's teaching on heterologous fertilization too restrictive of human freedom, most people, Catholic and non-Catholic alike, can understand and appreciate this teaching even if, in some highly unique situations, they might justify heterologous insemination and fertilization. Nonetheless, most people recognize that when a man and a woman marry, they "give" themselves exclusively to each other and that the selves they give are sexual and procreative persons. Just as they violate their marital covenant after marriage by attempting to "give" themselves to another in sexual union, so too they dishonor their marital covenant and the uniqueness and exclusiveness of their love and marital union by choosing to exercise their procreative powers with someone other than their spouse, the one to whom they have given themselves, including their power to procreate, irrevocably, "forswearing all others."

But many of these people, including Catholics, find the Church's judgment that *homologous* artificial insemination and IVF-ET are *always* wrong, intrinsically evil, difficult to understand and accept. This is a "hard" teaching, and strikes many as harsh, insensitive, and cruel. They ask, and not without reason, why *must* human life be given *only* in and through the marital act? What evil is being done by a married couple, unable to have children by engaging in the marital act, if they make use of the new reproductive technologies to overcome the obstacles preventing their marriage from being blessed with the gift of children?

It seems obvious that, if homologous artificial fertilization (whether artificial insemination or IVF-ET) is intrinsically immoral, it follows *a fortiori* that this is true of heterologous fertilization and cloning.

To show that even homologous artificial fertilization is intrinsically immoral, I will, as noted earlier, focus on the argument that generating children outside of the marital act, even by procedures making use of gametic cells of husband and wife, changes the generation of human life from an act of "procreation" to one of "reproduction," treating the child as if he or she is a product. I will argue that this is indeed the case and that it is always gravely immoral to treat a human being, even in his or her initial stages of existence, as a product and not as a person.

The argument to be advanced is intelligible in the light of the distinction, made previously, between "making" and "doing." We have seen already that in engaging in the marital act husbands and wives are not "making" anything, but are rather "doing" something, and that any human life brought into being in and through this act is begotten, not made.

In "making," as we have seen already, the action proceeds from an agent or agents to something in the external world, to a product. In making, interest centers on the product made, and ordinarily products that do not measure up to standards are discarded or, at any rate, are little appreciated and for this reason are frequently called "defective." In making, moreover, the logic of manufacturing is validly applied: one should use the most efficient procedures available, keeping costs as low as possible, etc.

When new human life comes to be as a result of homologous artificial insemination or homologous IVF-ET, it comes to be as the end product of a series of actions, transitive in nature, undertaken by different persons in order to make a particular product, a human baby. The spouses "produce" the gametic materials which others then manipulate and use in order to make the final product. When these new reproductive technologies are employed, one cannot deny that the child "comes into existence … in the manner of a product of making (and, typically, as the end product of a process managed and carried out by persons other than his parents)."[38] With use of these technologies, it is true to say that the child is "made," not "begotten."

Precisely because homologous artificial insemination/IVF-ET — like heterologous artificial insemination/IVF-ET — is an act of "making," it is standard procedure, as we have seen in surveying the literature describing the technologies, to overstimulate the woman's ovaries so that she can produce several ova for fertilization by sperm, usually obtained most economically through masturbation and then washed and "capacitated" so that they can better do their job; of the resulting new human embryos, some are frozen and kept on reserve for use should initial efforts to achieve implantation and gestation to birth fail; it is also common to implant several embryos (two to four) in the womb to enhance likelihood that at least one will implant and, should too large a number of embryos successfully implant, to discard the "excess" number through a procedure some euphemistically call "pregnancy reduction." Finally, it is common practice to monitor development of the new human life both prior to being transferred to the womb and during gestation to determine whether it suffers from any defects, and, should serious defects be discovered or thought likely, to abort the product that does not measure up to standard. As a form of "making" or 'producing," artificial insemination/fertilization, homologous as well as heterologous, leads to the use of these methods, for they simply carry out the logic of manufacturing commodities: one should use the most efficient, time-saving, and cost-effective means available to deliver the desired product under good quality controls.

One readily sees how dehumanizing such "production" of human babies is. It obviously treats them as if they were products inferior to their producers and subject to quality controls, not persons equal in dignity to their parents.

But some people, including some Catholic theologians, note — correctly — that homologous insemination/fertilization does not *require* hyperovulating the woman, creating a number of new human beings in a petri dish, freezing some, implanting others, monitoring development with a view to abortion should "defects" be discovered, etc. They think that if these features commonly associated with homologous insemination/fertilization are rejected, then a limited resort by married couples to artificial insemination/IVF-ET does not really transform the generation of human life from an act of procreation to one of reproduction.

A leading representative of this school of thought, Richard A. McCormick, S.J., argues that spouses who resort to homologous *in vitro* fertilization do not perceive this as the " 'manufacture' of a 'product.' Fertilization *happens* when sperm and egg are brought together in a petri dish," but "the technician's intervention is a condition for its happening, not a cause."[39] Moreover, he continues, "the attitudes of the parents and the technicians can be every bit as reverential and respectful as they would be in the face of human life naturally conceived."[40] In fact, in McCormick's view and in that of some other writers as well, for instance, Thomas A. Shannon, Lisa Sowle Cahill, and Jean Porter,[41] homologous *in vitro* fertilization can be considered an "extension" of marital intercourse, so that the child generated can still be regarded as the "fruit" of the spouses' love. While it is preferable, if possible, to generate the baby through the marital act, it is, in the cases of concern to us, impossible to do this, and hence their marital act — so these writers claim — can be, as it were, "extended" to embrace *in vitro* fertilization.

Given the concrete situation, any disadvantages inherent in the generation of human lives apart from the marital act, so these authors reason, are clearly counterbalanced by the great good of new human lives and the fulfillment of the desire for children of couples who otherwise would not be able to have them. In such conditions, they contend, it is not unrealistic to say that homologous IVF-ET is simply a way of "extending" the marital act.

I believe that it is evident that this justification of homologous insemination/IVF-ET is rooted in the proportionalistic method of making moral judgments. It claims that one can rightly intend so-called "premoral" or "nonmoral" or "ontic" evils (the "disadvantages" referred to above) in order to attain a proportionately greater good, in this case, helping a married couple otherwise childless to have a child of their own. But this method of making moral judgments is very flawed and was explicitly repudiated by Pope John Paul II in *Veritatis splendor*.[42] It comes down to the claim that one can never judge an act to be morally bad only by taking into account the "object" freely chosen and that it is necessary, in order to render any moral judgment of an action, to consider it in its totality, taking into account not only its object but the end and circumstances as well. If the end for whose sake something is chosen and done is a "proportionately greater good" than the evil one does by choosing this object (e.g., making a baby in a petri dish), then the act as a whole can be morally good. In chapter two, above, this flawed method of making moral judgments was briefly criticized.[43]

Moreover, the reasoning advanced by McCormick and others is rhetorical in character and not based on a realistic understanding of what is involved. Obviously, those who choose to produce a baby make that choice as a means to an ulterior end. They may well "intend" — in the sense of their further intention — that the baby be received into an authentic child-parent relationship, in which he or she will live in a communion of persons which befits those who share personal dignity. If realized, this intended end for whose sake the choice is made to produce the baby will be good for the baby as well as for the parents. But, even so, and despite McCormick's claim to the contrary, their "present intention," i.e., the choice they are making here and now, is precisely "to make a baby" — this is the "object" specifying their freely chosen act. The baby's initial status is the status of a product. In *in vitro* fertilization the technician does not simply *assist* the marital act (that would be licit) but, as Benedict Ashley, O.P., rightly says, he *"substitutes* for that act of personal relationship and communication one which is like a chemist making a compound or a gardener planting a seed. The technician has thus become the principal cause of generation, acting through the instrumental forms of sperm and ovum."[44]

Moreover, the claim that *in vitro* fertilization is an "extension" of the marital act and not a substitution for it is simply contrary to fact. "What is extended," as Ashley also notes, "is not the act of intercourse, but the intention: from an intention to beget a child naturally to getting it by IVF, by artificial insemination, or by help of a surrogate mother."[45] Since the child's initial status is thus, in these procedures, that of a product, its status is subpersonal. Thus, the choice to produce a baby is, inevitably, the choice to enter into a relationship with the baby, not as its equal, but as a product inferior to its producers. But this initial relationship of those who choose to produce babies with the babies they produce is inconsistent with and so impedes the communion of persons endowed with equal dignity that is appropriate for any interpersonal relationship. It is the choice of a bad means to a good end. Moreover, in producing babies, if the product is defective, a new person comes to be as *unwanted.* Thus, those who choose to produce babies not only choose life for some, but — and can this be realistically doubted? — at times quietly dispose of at least some of those who are not developing normally.[46]

I think that the reasons advanced here to show that it is not morally right to generate human life outside the marital act can be summarized in a syllogism, which I offer for consideration:

> *Major:* Any act of generating human life that is non-marital is irresponsible and violates the respect due to human life in its generation.

> *Minor:* But artificial insemination, *in vitro* fertilization, whether homologous or heterologous, and other forms of generating human life outside the marital act, including cloning, are non-marital.

> *Conclusion:* Therefore, these modes of generating human life are irresponsible and violate the respect due to human life in its generation.

I believe that the minor of this syllogism does not require extensive discussion. However, McCormick, commenting on an earlier essay of mine in which I advanced a syllogism of this kind, claims that my use of the term "non-marital" in the minor premise is "impenetrable," because the meaning of a "non-marital" action is not at all clear.[47] This objection simply fails to take into account all that I had said in my previous essay and in the earlier part of this chapter about the *marital* act.[48]

It is obvious that heterologous insemination/fertilization and cloning are "non-marital." But "non-marital" too are homologous artificial insemination and IVF. Even though married persons have collaborated in these procedures and even though these procedures make use of gametic cells supplied by husband and wife, the procedures are "non-marital" because the marital status of the man and the woman participating in them is accidental and not essential, whereas, as we saw in the first part of this chapter, the marital status of man and woman *is essential* for a *marital* act. Indeed, the marital status of the parties involved in homologous artificial insemination/IVF is utterly irrelevant to the procedures as such. What makes husband and wife capable of participating in these procedures is definitely *not* their marital union, whereas the *marital act* is possible only by reason of their marital union. Their marital status is irrelevant to artificial insemination/IVF because they are able to take part in these procedures simply because, like *unmarried* men and women, they are producers of gametic cells that other individuals can then use to fabricate human life. Just as spouses do not generate human life *maritally* when this life (which is *always* good and precious, no matter how engendered) is initiated as a result of an act of spousal abuse, so they do not generate new human life maritally when what they do is simply provide the materials to be used in making a baby.

The foregoing reflections should suffice to clarify the meaning of the minor premise of the syllogism and to show its truth.

The truth of the major premise is supported by everything said about the intimate bonds uniting marriage, the marital act, and the generation of human life. Those bonds are the indispensable and necessary means for properly respecting human life in its origin. To sunder them is to break the inseparable bond between the unitive and procreative meanings of the conjugal act, to refuse to speak the "language of the body," and above all to treat a child in its initial stage of existence as a product, as something "made," not "begotten." We have seen already that non-marital modes of generating human life change the act generating such life from one of "procreation" or "begetting" to one of "reproducing." Such reproductive modes of generating human life are indeed instances of "making."

(2) The Basic Theological Reason Why Human Life Ought To Be Generated Only in and Through the Marital Act

There is a very profound theological reason that offers ultimate support for the truth that new human life ought to be given *only* in and through the marital act — the act proper and unique to spouses, the act made possible only by marriage itself — and not through acts of fornication, adultery, spousal abuse, or new "reproductive" technologies.

The reason is this: human life ought to be "begotten, not made." Human life is the life of a human person, a being inescapably male or female, made in the image and likeness of the all-holy God. A human person, who comes to be when new human life comes into existence, is, as it were, an icon or "created word" of God. Human beings are, as it were, the "created words" that the Father's Uncreated Word became and is,[49] precisely to show us how deeply God loves us and to enable us to be, like him, children of the Father and members of the divine family.

But the Uncreated Word, whose brothers and sisters human persons are called to be, was "begotten, not made." These words were chosen by the Fathers of the Council of Nicaea in A.D. 325 to express unambiguously their belief that the eternal and uncreated Word of God is indeed, like the Father, true God. This Word, who personally became true man in Jesus Christ while remaining true God, is not inferior to his Father; he is not a product of his Father's will, a being made by the Father and subordinate in dignity to him. Rather, the Word is one in being with the Father, equally a divine person. The Word, the Father's Son, was begotten by an immanent act of personal love.

Similarly, human persons, the "created words" of God, ought, like the Uncreated Word, to be "begotten, not made." Like the Uncreated Word, they are one in nature with their parents, persons like their mothers and fathers; they are not products inferior to their producers. Their personal dignity is equal to that of their mothers and fathers, just as the Uncreated Word's personal dignity is equal to the personal dignity of the Father. That dignity is respected when their life is "begotten" in an act of self-giving spousal union, in an act of conjugal love. It is not respected when that life is "made" as the end product of a series of transitive acts of making. Nor is it respected when generated by acts of fornication, adultery, or spousal abuse.

4. PART FOUR: "ASSISTED" INSEMINATION/FERTILIZATION

The Church's Magisterium, as we have seen, distinguishes between technological procedures, such as artificial insemination and *in vitro* fertilization, whether homologous or heterologous, which *substitute for or replace the marital act* and procedures which *assist* the marital act in being crowned with the gift of human life. Although married couples ought never to use techniques which replace the marital act, they can legitimately use those that assist it in generating new human life. As Pope John Paul II has said, "infertile couples ... have a right to whatever legitimate therapies may be available to remedy their infertility."[50]

But there is serious controversy, even among Catholics who defend the truth of the Church's teaching on the generation of human life, regarding the kinds of procedures which assist rather than replace the marital act. After presenting basic criteria to help distinguish procedures that "assist" the conjugal act from those replacing it, I will then examine some specific techniques. We will find that there is a consensus among Catholic theologians regarding some of these procedures, whereas over others there is controversy.

A. Basic Criteria

The basic principle operative here is accurately formulated in the following text from *Donum vitae*:

> The human person must be accepted in his parents' act of union and love; the generation of a child must therefore be the fruit of that mutual giving which is realized in the conjugal act wherein the spouses cooperate as servants and not as masters in the work of the Creator who is love.[51]

If the child is to be the "fruit" of the marital act, the marital act must be directly related (=have a direct causal relationship) to the origin of new human life. The marital act, in other words, must be the "principal" cause of the conception of the child. It is so because the marital act not only unites husband and wife in an intimate "one-flesh" unity but also directly and personally introduces into the wife's body the sperm of her husband which then actively seek an ovum in order to fertilize it and cause the conception of the child.. Given that the marital or conjugal act is and must be the principal cause of the child's conception if the dignity of human life in its origin is to be respected, then what basic criteria will enable us to determine whether a techno-logical intervention "assists" the marital act rather than "replaces" it or "substitutes" for it?

In an excellent study of this issue[52] John Doerfler offers a thorough review of relevant literature, offering perceptive critiques of several essays and judging as one of the most helpful an insightful (but ne-glected) essay by Josef Seifert.[53] Doerfler proposes that the marital act is and remains the principal cause of conception only if the techni-cal procedure either enables it to be performed by removing obstacles preventing the conjugal act from being effective or enables it to be performed by providing active condition(s) for it to exercise its own principal causality (technical procedures of this type will be illustrated below). But the conjugal act is not or does not remain the principal cause of conception if the natural causal process initiated by the mari-tal act and leading to conception is interrupted by the technical means, and it is so interrupted if the technical means terminates or stops the natural causal process, if these means require the husband's sperm to be removed from her body after the marital act has taken place, if conception occurs outside the wife's body, or if the technical means initiates the process anew once it has been stopped. Obviously, too, the conjugal act is not the principal cause of conception if it merely serves as a means for obtaining sperm. These are the major criteria developed by Doerfler[54] (I have in some measure modified and sim-plified them for presentation here), and in my opinion these are very helpful in enabling us to determine whether a given technical inter-vention assists or replaces the conjugal act.

From this it follows, I believe, that a procedures assists the marital act if and only if a marital act takes place and the procedure in question either circumvents obstacles preventing the specific marital act from being fruitful or supplies condition(s) needed for it to become effective in causing conception.

With these criteria in mind I will now examine some specific proce-dures claimed by Catholic theologians to be licit examples of techniques that "assist" rather than "replace" the conjugal act. As will be seen, there is sharp disagreement among these theologians over some of the proce-dures to be examined. I will begin with techniques which all commenta-tors, so far as I know, regard as instances of "assisted" insemination or fertilization, and then take up techniques over which controversy exists, offering my own assessment, guided by the criteria developed by Doerfler in his comprehensive study.

B. Acknowledged Instances of Assisted Insemination or Fertilization

(1) Use of Perforated Condom to Circumvent Hypospadias

Hypospadias is an anomaly of the male penis in which the urethra does not open at the distal end of the penis but on its underside, close to the man's body. This frequently prevents the husband from ejaculating sperm into his wife's vagina during the marital act. The use of a perforated condom would prevent the husband's sperm from being emitted outside his wife's body and facilitate their entrance into her vagina. This would thus be an instance of a technical means that would *remove an obstacle* to the fruitfulness of the conjugal act; all Catholic theologians who have discussed this procedure agree that it assists and does not replace the marital act and that, consequently, it is morally licit. It surely meets the criteria developed by Doerfler.[55]

(2) Low Tubal Ovum Transfer (LTOT)

This procedure, originally designed for women whose infertility was caused by blocked, damaged, or diseased fallopian tubes, relocates her ovum, bypassing and circumventing the area of tubal pathology in order to place the ovum into the fallopian tube below the point of damage, disease or blockage so that her own husband's sperm, introduced into her body by the marital act, can then effect fertilization. It is called *"low tubal ovum transfer"* because ordinarily the ovum is relocated in the lower part of the fallopian tube (or at times in the uterus itself).

This procedure evidently "removes an obstacle" preventing conception from occurring after the marital act has taken place or provides the conditions necessary if the marital act is to be fruitful. All the procedure does is to relocate the wife's ovum within her body prior to the marital act. The sperm that fertilize the ovum are introduced into her body-person directly as a result of the marital act. This technique clearly meets the criteria set forth by Doerfler.

All Catholic theologians who have addressed this technique agree that LTOT is a morally legitimate way of assisting the marital act.[56]

(3) Moving Sperm Deposited in the Vagina into the Uterus and Fallopian Tubes

Apparently the fruitfulness of some marital acts is impeded because the husband's sperm do not migrate far enough or rapidly enough into the reproductive tract of his wife, but linger in the vagina or at most migrate only very slowly to those portions of the wife's reproductive tract where conception is most likely to occur, with the result that most of the sperm die before they are able to unite with an ovum and fertilize it.

This obstacle to the fruitfulness of the marital act is removed and the conditions favorable for it to bear fruit can be fulfilled if the physician, after husband and wife have completed the marital act, uses some instrument(s) to propel the sperm deposited in the vagina into the uterus and fallopian tubes. If this is the way the technical intervention occurs, then it seems evident that it merely removes an obstacle preventing the marital act from being fruitful, supplying condition(s) necessary for it to be effective. It thus meets the criteria we have noted before and can rightly be said to assist and not replace the marital act.[57]

C. Controverted Technologies

(1) Temporary Removal of Sperm or of Ova to "Wash" and "Capacitate" Them

The procedure just discussed, namely, moving and relocating within the wife's body sperm deposited by her husband during the marital act may be modified somewhat, requiring the sperm to be removed temporarily from the wife's body or perhaps having her ovum temporarily removed and treated for some pathological condition, and then relocating one or both elements to the fallopian tube where they can unite. Many Catholic theologians who have discussed this procedure believe that it too can be regarded as a legitimate assistance of the marital act.[58] This procedure, too, so it seems to them, assists the marital act by removing an obstacle to its fruitfulness or by supplying the conditions under which it can be effective.

Despite my respect for this opinion, I believe that the procedure in question does not truly assist the marital act but rather substitutes for it. One of the criteria developed by Doerfler in his well-reasoned study and supported by the analysis given by Seifert is that a technical means which stops or terminates the natural causal process initiated by the marital act and then initiates the process anew after its termination can hardly be designated as assisting the conjugal act or the causal process initiated by it.[59] It seems to me quite clear that distinct human acts, specified by their objects, are being chosen and done, and that one of them definitely *stops* or *terminates* a causal process initiated by the other. One of the acts is the marital act; the other is the technical intervention of removing and treating either the sperm introduced into the wife's body by the marital act or the ova present within her body when the marital act occurred, treating them in some fashion. This act is not marital, nor does it assist the causal process initiated by the marital act to be fruitful. It does not assist because it terminates the act in order to do something else, i.e., to treat sperm or ova. A third human act is then required to initiate the causal process that leads to conception, since a new human choice is needed for the reintroduction of sperm and/or ovum into the wife's body. It thus seems clear to me that this procedure substitutes for the marital act and does not assist it.

(2) Accumulating Sperm from a Series of Marital Acts and Introducing Them Into the Wife's Vagina in Conjunction With a Marital Act

In order to cope with infertility caused by oligospermia (a condition causing relatively low sperm production by the husband), some theologians propose that the physician collect amounts of sperm from the husband's ejaculate (by morally permissible means, such as use of a perforated condom), conserve and centrifuge such accumulated sperm and then place this concentrate into the wife's generative tract in association with a marital act (usually prior to one) in order to mix with and fortify the husband's ejaculate during the marital act.

Although some Catholic theologians who accept the teaching of *Donum vitae* think that this procedure assists the marital act, [60] I believe that a proper assessment of what is going on shows that this technique replaces the marital act and does not assist it.

First of all, in this procedure one does not know whether the sperm that fertilize the ovum are sperm introduced into the wife's body by the husband during the marital act or sperm contained in the concentrate obtained by collecting sperm into a perforated condom during previous marital acts. But if the sperm that fertilize the ovum derive from that concentrate, then they simply *cannot* and *must not* be considered as part of the marital act. They cannot and must not be so considered precisely because they have been *intentionally withheld* from prior marital acts in order to procure sperm in a nonmasturbatory way. The marital act merely serves as an instrument for obtaining sperm. And since one cannot say whether fertilization is caused by sperm introduced into the wife's body by the specific marital act in question or by sperm contained in the concentrate resulting from *deliberately withholding sperm* from prior marital acts, one cannot truly say that the procedure "assists" the specific marital act in question. This procedure clearly violates one of the criteria developed by Doerfler.[61]

(3) Gamete Intrafallopian Tube Transfer (GIFT) and Tubal Ovum Transfer with Sperm (TOTS)

GIFT has already been described: the wife's eggs are removed by laparoscopy or ultrasound-guided transvaginal procedures. An egg (or group of eggs) is placed in a catheter with sperm (provided either by masturbation or by using a perforated condom during previous marital acts) that have been treated and "capacitated," with an air bubble separating ovum (ova) from sperm in the catheter while outside the wife's body. Thus fertilization does not take place outside the wife's body. The catheter is then inserted into the wife's body (and this can be done either prior to or immediately following a marital act), the ovum and sperm are released from the catheter and fertilization and conception can then take place within the wife's body, caused by the concentrate of sperm placed in the catheter and released after its insertion into the wife's body or perhaps by sperm released into her body by the marital act in association with which the catheter is inserted.

Several Catholic theologians—among them, Donald McCarthy, Orville Griese, Peter Cataldo, and John W. Carlson—strongly defend GIFT as a procedure that assists the marital act in being fruitful.[62]

With many others, I disagree completely with this approval of GIFT. First of all, the procedure was originally developed as an offshoot of IVF and the husband's sperm was collected by masturbation. Informed that the Catholic Church condemns masturbation, even as a way of obtaining a husband's sperm, the doctors who used the method suggested that sperm be obtained by using a perforated condom during the marital act. This shows definitely that with GIFT the marital act is merely incidental to the entire procedure, used only as a way of obtaining sperm in a nonmasturbatory way. These sperm, since they have been *deliberately, intentionally withheld from a marital act or series of marital acts*, can then not be said truly to be integral to the marital act when the catheter containing these sperm and the wife's ovum are inserted into her body. Although subsequent fertilization of her ovum *may* be caused by sperm introduced into her body during the accompanying marital act, such fertilization would be *per accidens* and not *per se*. Thus with many others, including Doerfler, Seifert, DeMarco, Tonti-Filippini, Grisez, and Ashley-O'Rourke, I believe that GIFT definitely substitutes for or replaces the marital act and does not assist it; and that, therefore, it is immoral to make use of it.[63]

TOTS is similar to GIFT. In this procedure sperm are procured from the husband either by masturbation or use of a perforated condom. Sperm are then placed in a catheter along with the wife's ovum (ova) and separated by an air bubble, and the catheter is then inserted into the fallopian tube (hence the name Tubal Ovum Transfer With Sperm), where ovum (ova) and sperm are released and fertilization can then occur. As can be seen, TOTS is quite similar to GIFT and not similar to LTOT or low tubal ovum transfer. Like GIFT, it substitutes for the marital act and does not assist it since the marital act is only incidental to retrieval of sperm and sperm so retrieved are intentionally withheld from a marital act and hence cannot be regarded as part of a marital act.

Someone might say that with respect to procedures where reputable Catholic theologians disagree, and since there is no specific magisterial teaching on them, Catholics are at liberty to follow whatever view they prefer as a "probable opinion." This way of looking at the issue is quite legalistic in my opinion. What one ought to do is examine the arguments and reasons given by theologians to support their claims to see which is true and takes into account the realities involved.

D. Conclusion to Part Four; A Word About Fertility Drugs

Some may think that the preceding analysis of procedures to determine which assist and which replace the marital act may be a bit nit-picking. Nonetheless, it deals with a real situation. The proper way to "assist" the conjugal act, I think, is to do more research to discover the root causes of female/male infertility and cure these underlying pathologies. At present the usual recommendation to overcome problems posed by blocked fallopian tubes (not an uncommon cause of inability to conceive) is to have recourse to IVF-ET. Yet such recourse does not cure the underlying pathology but rather responds to a human desire. It would be more in line with true medical research to reconstruct the fallopian tubes surgically or perhaps to attempt a tubal transplant. Why can't fallopian tube be transplanted from cadavers just as kidneys are? This would permanently cure the pathological condition.

Moreover, efforts to overcome infertility through use of hormones are gradually meeting with more and more success. Hormone treatment, to which I will return briefly below, is a type of infertility treatment by drugs, but it does not cause the problems associated with use of hyperovulatory drugs. Although use of hyperovulatory drugs is not intrinsically immoral, their use raises very serious problems. Ordinarily they cause the wife to produce a large number of ova (more than four) which could be fertilized by her husband as a result of the marital act. If all are fertilized and implanted, this can cause serious problems affecting the life and health both of the mother and of the unborn children during pregnancy, leading some doctors who use such drugs to recommend "pregnancy reduction" — a euphemism for injecting potassium chloride into the hearts of some unborn children to kill them — as a means of protecting the health and life of some of the unborn babies. Usually, too, children conceived in this way are born prematurely and must thus spend long periods in the neonatal intensive care unit. This is obviously burdensome to them, and the costs involved are extremely high. The burdens that these children will likely suffer and the extreme expenses involved are likely consequences of using hyperovulatory drugs in an effort to overcome infertility. It seems to me that one ought to avoid these foreseen consequences by not resorting to use of such drugs.

As noted before, hormonal treatments of some causes of infertility have had success. Such treatments and other alternatives have been developed and are being further developed by Thomas W. Hilgers, M.D., at his Pope Paul VI Institute. Dr. Hilgers, a member of the Pontifical Academy for Life, resolutely refuses to use IVF-ET, AIH, GIFT, TOTS and other technologies that substitute for the marital act, but has been able to be of help to many married couples through the programs he has developed.[64] There is hope for couples who have difficulty in conceiving. But all married couples must remember that they do not have a "right" to a child, and God may give them the cross of childlessness to carry. If he does, they must remember that he will be their Simon of Cyrene, ready to help them bear the cross he gives them.

5. PART FIVE: "RESCUING" FROZEN EMBRYOS[65]

As we have seen, *in vitro* fertilization requires that an ovum be removed from the body of a woman and then fertilized by male sperm in a petri dish. Because the procedure may fail or the newly conceived embryo may not implant in the womb, standard procedure is to retrieve several ova and fertilize them all. One or several may be immediately implanted, but others may be held in a state of virtual suspended animation through the process of *cryopreservation.* In this procedure an embryo — a living human person at the earliest stages of his/her life, we must not forget — is "frozen" by being put into a reservoir of liquid nitrogen. Because of various circumstances, some — in fact many — embryos frozen in this way will be left stranded in this absurd state, prisoners in what the late and great French geneticist Jerome Lejeune appropriately called "concentration cans."[66] As a result, today thousands of embryonic human beings are now so imprisoned, left orphans even before their birth. The question thus arises, what can be done on behalf of these human persons?[67]

There is currently a debate among Catholic theologians and philosophers regarding the liceity of "rescuing" frozen embryos. Some claim that there are, unfortunately, no morally licit ways of doing so; others argue that it is morally licit for a woman, preferably a married woman, to have a frozen embryo transferred from its "concentration can" to her womb, to be nurtured until birth. I will first consider the reasons given by Msgr. William B. Smith and Mary Geach to support the conclusion that there is no morally licit way to "rescue" frozen embryos, offering comments on the reasons they advance. Next the arguments developed by Germain Grisez, Geoffrey Surtees, and Helen Watts to support their conclusion that such "rescuing" can be morally undertaken will be set forth. Finally, I will offer my conclusions.

A. There Are No Morally Licit Ways of "Rescuing" Frozen Embryos

This position, as already noted, is defended by Msgr. William B. Smith, professor of moral theology at St. Joseph's Seminary, Dunwoodie, N.Y., and by Mary Geach, an English philosopher, wife, and mother. Smith's view is based primarily on his understanding of the text of *Donum vitae*, whereas Geach, whose position is essentially the same as Smith's, develops in some detail a philosophical argument in its support.

Smith presented his view in answering the question whether it would be permissible for a couple, who are opposed to *in vitro* fertilization, to rescue and adopt an unborn frozen child and raise it.[68] Smith based his negative answer both on a specific passage in *Donum vitae*, on its teaching regarding "surrogate motherhood," and on the "principled conclusion" of the document.

The specific passage on which Smith relies states: "In consequence of the fact that they have been produced *in vitro,* those embryos which are not transferred into the body of the mother and are called 'spare' are exposed to an absurd fate, with no possibility of their being offered safe means of survival which *can be licitly pursued.*"[69] Smith then writes: "No safe means that *can licitly be pursued!* Perhaps the CDF did not intend to address this precise case, but I read here a first principled insight indicating that this volunteer 'rescue' is *not* a licit option."[70]

Smith also contends that the document's teaching on surrogate motherhood excludes this option. He acknowledges that the "surrogacy" condemned in *Donum vitae* is the "surrogate who plans to carry the pregnancy but plans to surrender the baby once born, whereas the questioner plans to accept and adopt … the child," but he argues that the "foundational reasons for rejecting 'surrogacy' as licit also apply to this project," namely, "a failure to meet the obligations of maternal love, conjugal fidelity and responsible motherhood."[71]

The "principled conclusion" of *Donum vitae* to which Smith appeals is its teaching on the moral relevance of the bond uniting the procreative and unitive meanings of the conjugal act and between the goods of marriage, along with the unity and dignity of the human person which requires that "the procreation of a human person be brought about as the fruit of the conjugal act specific to the love between spouses."[72] Since the projected "rescue" of the frozen embryo is not procreation of this kind, Smith concludes that it cannot be morally licit.[73]

Geach, writing independently of Smith, does not explicitly refer to *Donum vitae*, but rather argues that a woman should allow herself to become pregnant *only* through normal marital relations, not by implanting a frozen embryo into her womb. She claims that if a woman makes her womb available to the child of strangers and allows herself to be made pregnant by means of a technical act of impregnation, she shares in the evil of *in vitro* fertilization and unchaste acts. A woman does so because she ruins reproductive integrity: what is meant to be the result of a marital act — a pregnancy — is now the result of a merely technical procedure.[74]

This, in brief, is Geach's principal argument: a woman who allows herself to become pregnant by having a frozen embryo implanted in her womb is acting unchastely, and, in fact, in a more perversely unchaste way than a woman who masturbates herself. It is worth examining in some detail the reasoning Geach employs to support this argument.

Unchaste bodily acts, she notes quite correctly, are objectionable because in committing them one does something that is enough like a marital act to carry some of its significance but is nonetheless *not* marital. Through unchaste actions, a person dissociates the parts of the marriage act from one another and in doing so destroys in oneself the full meaning of man as a unity of soul and body, as an animal whose life is spiritual. She emphasizes that "the life begun through human procreation is this spiritual life of an animal" and that "one's sense of this is kept intact if one's act of generation is not resolved into its component elements, but is itself one act … defined by the conjoint end, which is to perform a unitive act of procreative kind."[75] Moreover, in this act the woman's laying herself open to an impregnating intromission "is a vital part of the self-giving involved in the woman's part of the marriage act," and "this self-giving is not just a self-giving to the possible child, but to the father, since it would be his child that she would be bearing."[76] But, Geach argues, a woman's act of admitting a frozen embryo into her womb whereby she allows herself to become pregnant "is profoundly like such an act of generation." Continuing, she writes:

> This similarity is more profound than the similarity of a woman's perverse sexual act [masturbation] to the female act of generation A woman could perform a complete marriage act without having any of those motions of the flesh some of which usually occur and make the act more efficacious and pleasurable. But a complete marriage act is *always* an act of admission which is of a kind to make one pregnant, nor would it be a true marriage act if one was unaware of this fact. To separate it [the act of admission of a kind to make one pregnant] from the other parts of the marriage act would be to destroy in oneself that same reproductive integrity which is destroyed by unchaste actions.[77]

Thus, she argues, if it is seriously wrong for a woman to excite within herself through solitary sexual acts the sensations properly associated with and accompanying the self-giving involved in the conjugal act, then

> How much worse must it be to isolate the spiritual component of the marriage act, the giving up of the body to the impregnator, dissociating oneself from the parents of the child, and substituting for the relation to the father a mere arrangement with a technician.... If solitary vice is objectionable as part of the marriage act taken out of context, much more so is this giving up of one's body to an impregnating intromission.[78]

Comments on the Smith and Geach Positions:
Grisez and Surtees argue, correctly, I believe, that Smith has taken the passage in *Donum vitae* to which he appeals to support his conclusion that there is "no possibility of their [=frozen embryos'] being offered safe means of survival which can be licitly pursued," out of con-

text. It occurs in a section in which the document is concerned with using embryos produced *in vitro* as subjects of experimental research. Thus, Grisez concludes that the "sentence Smith quotes should not be understood as referring to the action of a rescuer who has in no way participated in the wrongs that have brought the embryonic persons to be and left them to their absurd fate, but to the options available to those wrongly involved in IVF."[79]

Smith's second claim — that rescuing frozen embryos by having them transferred to the womb of a woman who volunteers to rescue them is excluded by *Donum vitae's* condemnation of surrogate motherhood — is also effectively answered by both Grisez and Surtees. Grisez simply points out that Smith "ignores the fact that bearing [a child] *on another's behalf* is part of the very definition of surrogacy."[80] Since Surtees' critique of Smith on this point is intimately related to his own defense of the legitimacy of a married couple's "adoption" of a frozen embryo prenatally, I will take up his critique of Smith on this point below, in presenting his position.

Surtees clearly shows the irrelevance of the "principled conclusion" of *Donum vitae* to which Smith appeals regarding the bonds uniting the meanings of the conjugal act which, together with respect for the dignity of the human person in his origins, require that the procreation of a human person "be the fruit of the conjugal act specific to the love between spouses." The "principled conclusion" of *Donum vitae* is true. But, as Surtees notes, the proposal to rescue frozen embryos "is not about a perversion or abuse of the conjugal act because this project has *nothing to do with the conjugal act.* The conjugal act, or rather the perversion thereof, has already taken place ... the child is [already] in existence."[81] Those seeking to rescue the child are in no way sundering the bonds uniting the procreative and unitive meaning of the conjugal act, nor are they the ones who deprive the new human person of his/her proper origin through an act of procreative love of a husband and wife. *Other persons* have done all this; these are the ones who have acted contrary to the "principled conclusion" of *Donum vitae,* but those seeking to save that child's life have in no way done so. Smith simply misapplies the teaching of *Donum vitae* here.

With reference to Geach's argument, Helen Watt argues that she fails to distinguish adequately ways whereby a woman "allows herself to become pregnant." Watt argues that the "term 'allowing oneself to be made pregnant' covers two quite different intentions, which affect in different ways the morality of what is being done." Continuing, she writes:

The first intention is the intention to allow a child *to come to be* — to be created — inside one's body. Such an intention can exist in combination either with the intention to have intercourse or with the intention to have artificial insemination. Intercourse and AID or AIH are different ways of achieving the result that a child is created inside the body of a woman. For this reason, artificial insemination can be seen as wrongfully displacing the marital act....

Quite different from the intention to have a child *come to be* inside one's body is the intention to have a child *put* inside one's body.... It is ... not the case that uterine pregnancy — that is, pregnancy after implantation — is directly caused by intercourse. If this is so, should it still be said that intercourse must *always precede* uterine pregnancy? What I want to argue is that whereas ideally intercourse *should* precede uterine pregnancy, the only *absolute* moral requirement is that intercourse precede — and indeed directly cause — *in vivo* conception.[82]

I believe that the distinctions Watt makes are relevant to the issue. In many ways her criticism of Geach is similar to Surtees' criticism of Smith noted above, distinguishing a perversion of the *marital act* from the choice to rescue a child *already conceived.* Thus, in the earlier draft of this part noted previously, I claimed that Watt had provided an adequate critique of Geach's position. But in a personal communication to me, Geach maintains that Watt and I (erroneously) treat her argument as if she claimed that embryo transplantation (even to rescue the embryo) wrongly *displaces* the marital act, whereas her major argument, as summarized above (far more accurately than in the earlier draft), is that by allowing herself to be made pregnant by the technician's art a woman engages in a highly defective version of the marital act.[83]

I do not believe that Geach's claim is true, primarily because I think that she fails to take adequately into account that human acts, as John Paul II reminds us in no. 78 of *Veritatis splendor,* receive their primary moral specification from the "object" freely chosen by the acting person. In the case at hand, Geach seems to hold that the rescuing woman's moral object is to "substitute for the relation to the father a mere arrangement with a technician" as the chosen means for getting pregnant. I believe that in the case at hand the moral object specifying the woman's choice is to transfer the embryo from its concentration can to her own womb, and that this choice is not intrinsically evil.

In a further personal communication to me, Geach maintains that my critique is arbitrary, since it claims (in her opinion) that

> one can decide about one of the many descriptions of one's action in doing something, that it, and it alone, gives one's act its "moral specification." Anyone who wishes to kill his old uncle to get money could say that his *not* intrinsically evil object is that he inherit money under his uncle's will. But he wishes to kill in order to do this, and he cannot choose the description "act liable to lead to my inheriting money" and say that that specifies his action morally…. "The object of the act of willing," says the Pope in the passage cited by May, "is in fact a freely chosen kind of behavior." So, one is morally responsible for one's actions under all descriptions under which one freely chooses them. In the case at hand, the woman freely chooses to admit an insertion of a kind to make her pregnant without generating…. It is under this description that her action is unacceptable, since it follows from this description that she is performing an act which is centrally and importantly like the marriage act, but which is not the marriage act or a part of it.[84]

First of all, with Geach I agree completely about the man who kills his uncle and attempts to justify it in the way he does. He is *redescribing his action in terms of its hoped-for benefits,* a common enough way of rationalizing evil deeds. But such redescribing of an act is *not* being done in the rescuing of frozen embryos. In saying that the woman rescuing the embryo is *transferring a frozen embryo to her womb,* one is in no way redescribing *what* she is doing (i.e., the object of her free choice). The end for whose sake she does this is good, namely, the preservation of this orphaned child's life, and the means she chooses — having the embryo transferred to her womb — is *not* intrinsically evil. *As a result of her choice*, she allows herself to become pregnant and foresees that she will, but the precise object of her choice — *what she is freely choosing to do* — is not to make herself pregnant independently of a marital act. What she does is analogous to what a doctor does who removes cancerous eyes, foreseeing that by doing so he will deprive his patient of his sight. The object morally specifying this doctor's act is surely not the *blinding of his patient,* but rather the *protecting of his life by removing dangerous cancer.* Thus, I acknowledge that the woman who freely chooses to have a frozen embryo transferred from its concentration can to her womb foresees and is responsible for her becoming pregnant without generating, but that this is not the precise object freely chosen. That object is rather, as we have seen, the *transferring of the frozen embryo to her womb.* As John Paul II makes clear in the passage cited, "in order to grasp the object of an act which specifies that act morally, it is therefore necessary to place oneself *in the perspective of the acting person*" (*Veritatis splendor,* no. 78; emphasis in the original). This issue will be considered further below, in examining the positions of Grisez, Surtees, and Watt.

B. It Can Be Morally Licit for a Woman to Have a Frozen Embryo Transferred to Her Womb and Nurtured

This position, as noted previously, is defended by Geoffrey Surtees, Germain Grisez, and Helen Watt. It should be noted that the view, defended philosophically and theologically by these authors, is held by many in the pro-life movement.[85]

Surtees accepted Msgr. Smith's invitation to offer reasons challenging his conclusion that nothing could be rightly done to "rescue" frozen embryos.[86] We have already seen some of Surtees' major criticisms of Smith's position. I will now focus on the central argument Surtees advances to justify the prenatal adoption of a frozen embryo by a married couple. Surtees introduces his argument in countering Smith's claim that a couple who volunteer to adopt a frozen embryo prenatally are acting like those who participate in the *in vitro* production of human life (and, analogously, that a wife who volunteers to "adopt" a frozen embryo prenatally and have it implanted in her womb is immorally acting as a "surrogate" mother). Surtees argues that the *human act* willed and done by a couple who adopt a frozen embryo prenatally and by the wife who has this embryo transferred into her womb differs profoundly from artificially producing a child and from serving as a surrogate mother. Commenting on the passage from John Paul II's *Veritatis splendor,* no. 78 on the moral specification of human acts (noted above in my comments on Geach's position), Surtees writes as follows: "From the perspective of the acting persons cooperating in artificial reproduction there are … no licit means to offer safe survival for the embryo(s). It would be wrong to conclude, however, that the embryo must, per logical force, waste away in deep freeze because of the sins of his parents. The couple who would rescue this embryo through adoption are choosing another moral object entirely different and distinct from what the couple using artificial reproduction [or the woman serving as a surrogate] has chosen."[87]

The following passage provides a good summary of Surtees' principal argument:

> That the adoption of a frozen embryo cannot be compared with surrogate motherhood, *in vitro* fertilization, and "other means of artificial reproduction" repudiated by the Church, is made most manifest when we consider what constitutes the object of choice for the adopting couple and the object of choice for the couple using methods of artificial reproduction... .The intelligible proposal of action being freely adopted by choice by the rescuing, adopting couple is ... *adoption* — an action ... entirely licit and moral, an action which involves a child already conceived but rejected, an action never condemned by the magisterium of the Church. Though the embryo's first adoptive "home," as it were, would be the womb of his new mother, I can see no reason by such a "home" should not be made available. On the other hand, the intelligible proposal being freely adopted by choice by the artificial reproduction couple is *artificial reproduction*....[89]

Surtees believes that prudence demands that only a married couple ought to adopt a frozen embryo — tiny human child — prenatally. Since "any child who is to be adopted should be adopted into a state of life becoming of the spiritual, mental, and physical well-being of the child," and since "the only state of life intrinsically ordered to do this is that of marriage and the family," Surtees concludes that single women, including nuns, are not properly capacitated to undertake the duties of parenthood and that, therefore, it would not be prudent for single women to attempt to "rescue" frozen embryos by having them transferred into their wombs to be nurtured until birth and then given up for adoption.[89] In fact, Surtees claims that although single women volunteering to rescue frozen embryos in this way "mean well," their actions would to some degree "perpetuate the 'absurd fate' of the child," who is "not an object or item to be transferred about as a mere temporary possession ... [but is rather] entitled to be adopted into a family which vows to meet the obligations, responsibilities, and duties that any family must live up to."[90]

Despite saying all this, Surtees does not consider the "rescuing" of frozen embryos by single women who would nurture them until birth and then give them up for adoption *intrinsically* immoral, but rather contrary to prudence.[91]

Comment: Smith, in replying to Surtees' essay, asserts that the *end* motivating the couple is the adoption of the child and that this a good end. But, Smith contends, the *means* chosen to attain that end is immoral, because, in his view, *what* they do — the object of their choice — is to "have the wife become a nine-month surrogate *in order to adopt* the child upon birth." Smith does "not question the goodness of that generous goal and intention, but" he is not persuaded "that the chosen *means* to that good *end* is a licit means."[92]

Smith's response seems to me simply to reaffirm his claim that the effort to rescue a frozen embryo by having it transferred into the womb of a wife who, with her husband, adopts the child prenatally is an instance of "surrogacy" For Smith, the *object chosen* (and thus specifying the act morally) is "surrogacy," whereas Surtees has argued that the freely *chosen object* specifying the act morally is precisely the prenatal adoption of the child and giving it a home, first of all within the wife's womb. Their argument, consequently, is over the proper way of describing the object freely chosen and giving the human act its moral specification. It seems to me that Smith has not properly identified this object. As noted above, in commenting on Smith's position, we saw that he can rightly be criticized here. A surrogate is impregnated either by transferring to her an embryo resulting from IVF or by fertilizing her own ovum with sperm from a man who is not her husband, and she bears the child as part of an arrangement with someone to whom she will surrender the baby after birth. This is the object freely chosen by a surrogate, and it is surely *not* the object freely chosen in this instance of "rescuing" a frozen embryo. Thus I do not think that Smith's criticism of Surtees is valid. But is Surtees' description of the object accurate?

Germain Grisez thinks that Surtees is incorrect in saying that adoption is the object freely chosen and specifying the act. According to him, the precise object of the act in question is to *transfer the embryo from the freezer to the woman's womb.* With Smith, he believes that adoption is the *end* for whose sake the transfer of the embryo may be chosen as a means, but that adoption cannot be regarded as the object freely chosen.[93] But Grisez does not, like Smith, believe that the object specifying the act is one of surrogacy. Here he is in agreement with Surtees.

Before taking up Grisez's own position I want first to suggest that

Surtees' argument needs to be clarified and strengthened by making some distinctions. I believe that it can be argued that *one moral* object chosen by a married couple is, as Surtees maintains, to *adopt* a frozen embryo, a child "orphaned" before birth. By freely choosing to do so, they freely give to themselves the *identity* of that child's adoptive parents. This choice, however, *commits* them to further choices in harmony with the choice to be the child's adoptive parents. And one central choice to which they are committed is *to rescue the frozen embryo by having it transferred from the freezer to the wife's womb,* to give the child the home it needs and merits in order to grow and develop. The wife then, in carrying out this commitment, chooses to *give the frozen embryo its first home within her womb* by having the frozen embryo transferred into her womb. After she has given birth to the child she, with her husband, gives the child the home she and her husband both provide. I think that Surtees' argument can be more clearly expressed in this way. There is *first* the choice by the married couple to adopt the child and subsequently the choice, made by the wife and to which she and her husband have committed themselves, *to transfer the frozen embryo to the woman's womb.* In short, I think that Surtees' argument is substantively correct, but that it needs to distinguish between two intimately related moral choices, first the choice to adopt and then, in serving the good to which the choice of adoption has committed them (or, better, to serve the good to which they have *committed themselves* by becoming adoptive parents), the choice to give their adopted child a home, first within the womb of the wife (=to have the frozen embryo transferred into her womb).

I now take up Grisez's view. As noted, Surtees argues for the "prenatal" adoption of a frozen embryo by a married couple. Although he does not think that it would be intrinsically evil for a single woman to have a frozen embryo transferred to her womb for nurture until birth and then have it adopted by a married couple, he believes that this would be highly imprudent (and, therefore, so it would seem, morally wrong, since we ought not to act imprudently).

C. Even Single Women Can Rightly Nurture and Bear Frozen Embryos

Grisez defends the rescuing of a frozen embryo by unmarried women. Grisez develops his view in answering a single woman whose sister had committed suicide after her husband abandoned her for his secretary, leaving behind a frozen embryo. The woman, firmly opposed to IVF, surrogacy, and all forms of artificial reproduction, wanted to act in conformity with Church teaching and wondered whether she would be acting rightly if she had the frozen embryo transferred to her womb, nurturing and caring for it until birth, and then giving it up for adoption.

Grisez clearly distinguishes her object of choice from that of those responsible for producing the child artificially. The object of her choice is to transfer the frozen embryo to her womb — this aspect of his argument will be taken up in more detail below. He likewise points out that the woman is proposing "to bear the child not on anyone else's behalf but simply to save his or her life." Thus, if her proposal succeeds, and even if she gives the child up for adoption, Grisez argues that she is "not acting as a surrogate mother" but rather would be "acting in much the same way as a mother who volunteers to nurse at her own breast a foundling conceived out of wedlock, abandoned by his or her natural mother, and awaiting adoption by a suitable couple. Like that mother's nursing, the nurture [she hopes] to give will in no way involve [her] in the wrongs previously done to the baby and will be offered to him or her for his or her own sake, not done as a service to anyone else. Therefore," Grisez concludes, the woman "certainly can try to save the baby without acting contrary to what the Church has taught regarding IVF and surrogate motherhood."[94]

According to Grisez, the *end* for whose sake the woman has the frozen embryo transferred is good, namely, to attempt to save the baby's life, and the *means* chosen to pursue this end is to *transfer the embryo from the freezer to her womb as any upright woman nurtures her child.* Grisez summarizes his analysis of the means chosen in the following way:

> nurturing the baby in your womb surely will not be wrong; if someone transferred an embryo to your womb without your consent, abortion would be wrong, and it would be your duty to nurture the baby, just as it is the duty of a woman who has been raped and finds herself pregnant. Thus, if anything makes your project intrinsically wrong, it must be having the embryo moved from the freezer into your womb. But that is not at odds with any basic human good. It protects life rather than violates it; since the new person already exists, it does not violate the transmission of life; and it has nothing to do with the good of marriage, because it is not a sexual act, and the relationship between you and the baby is neither marital nor a perverse alternative to the marital relationship.[95]

Although embryo transfer is integral to IVF, an immoral procedure, in this case the transfer of the embryo is part of an entirely different proposal, of an entirely different project: rescuing a person in distress.

Although he defends the rescuing of a frozen embryo by a single woman, Grisez believes that it would be better for a married woman to rescue the frozen embryo by having it transferred to her womb and then, with her husband, adopting it.[96]

Finally, there is the view developed by Helen Watt. We have already seen how Watt, in criticizing Geach, distinguishes between intending to have a child *come to be* within one's body and intending to have an already existing child *put* within one's body, and the moral significance of this distinction. Watt also considers motherhood under three distinct aspects: genetic, gestational, and social, emphasizing that *ideally* all three aspects should be together, committed to and experienced by one woman, and she argues that "it is only *genetic* motherhood one should *never* seek to achieve by a purely technical procedure."[97]

But the three aspects are not always found together, and the *social* motherhood established by the adoption of an already born child is surely not immoral. In post-natal adoption, the child of one set of individuals is raised by another (genetically different) set of individuals. Thus there need be no necessary and intrinsic link between genetic and social motherhood. Nor is there an intrinsic link between gestational and social motherhood, since a woman who has conceived as a result of rape can rightly have the child so conceived adopted by others after birth. But is there a necessary or intrinsic link between genetic and gestational motherhood? Watt answers "no," and uses the analogy between embryo implantation and giving birth to support her argument. She states that normally, if a woman chooses to have intercourse open to life, she makes herself available not only to conceive but also to give birth to any new life that might result. However, some women do not give birth themselves, but need Caesarian sections. What is morally required, as a minimum, is only conception; giving birth is the end result of a series of natural processes begun by an act of marital union. Hence her analogy: "Just as a Caesarian section is a non-ideal, but sometimes permissible way of *completing* a pregnancy, so embryo transfer is a non-ideal, but sometimes permissible way of *beginning* a pregnancy."[98]

Watt's argument shows that there is nothing intrinsically wrong with gestational motherhood even if it not connected to genetic motherhood. Watt's notion of gestational motherhood seems equivalent to Grisez's idea of transferring a frozen embryo to a womb; i.e., the moral object specifying the woman's choice is for both Watt and Grisez the same, or so it seems to me. This gestational motherhood (or transferring of the frozen embryo to the gestational mother's womb) is precisely the choice to give the embryonic child his or her first home in the womb of a wife or single woman. I thus find Watt's view quite analogous to that of Grisez, although expressed differently.

D. Conclusion to the "Rescuing of Frozen Embryos"

With Surtees and Grisez I believe that the moral object specifying the human act of a woman who seeks to rescue a frozen embryo is *not,* as Smith holds, an act of surrogacy. Nor is it, as Geach seems to claim and Watt contests, precisely to "substitute for the relation to the father a mere arrangement with a technician." But what precisely is the object? It seems to me that Surtees is on the right path. A married couple can licitly have as their moral object the *adoption* of a frozen embryo, a human child abandoned by those who have generated it. This freely chosen act *commits* them to further actions, of which the basic one is *to give their adopted child a home,* which they do, first, when the wife/mother *chooses* to have the frozen embryo transferred into her womb, and which they continue to carry out by giving their adopted child, once born, the home provided by both wife and husband. I thus conclude that Surtees' argument is basically sound, although it needs to be strengthened by making the distinctions I have made between the choice to *adopt* and the choice to give the child a home, first by choosing *to transfer it to the womb of the wife/mother.* The precise object in *rescuing the frozen embryo*, is thus more properly identified as *transferring it from the freezer to the woman's womb.*

Although it is preferable for frozen embryos to be rescued by being adopted by a married couple prenatally and, in meeting their obligations as adoptive parents by having it transferred to the wife's womb rather than having it rescued by first being transferred to the womb of a single woman and then, after birth, adopted by a married couple, it would not be intrinsically evil for a single woman to rescue a frozen embryo by having it transferred to her womb (the moral *object* is the transfer of the frozen embryo to her womb, or, to use the equivalent terminology of Watt, the object is *gestational mothering*; the *end* is protecting his/her life). Earlier, in thinking about this problem, I held that it would be *wrong* for a single woman to have the embryo transferred and to give the child up for adoption after birth. But I have changed my mind on this. Grisez's example of a woman who becomes pregnant after rape convinced me that it cannot be intrinsically evil for a mother who nurtures a child within her womb to give it up for adoption after birth (and the same would be true of single women who become pregnant after fornication — their fornication was wrong, but they have an obligation not to abort but rather to nurture within their womb the life they have conceived, and they may well have an obligation to allow the child to be adopted). Hence, it cannot be intrinsically immoral for a single woman to rescue an abandoned frozen embryo — a little baby in its earliest stages of development—by having it transferred to her womb in order to protect its fragile life at this stage of its development and then giving it up for adoption after birth.[99]

ENDNOTES

1. This truth, a matter of Catholic faith, will be discussed in more detail below in the chapter on abortion. In his book *Love and Responsibility*, trans. H. T. Willetts (New York: Farrar, Straus, Giroux, 1981; reprinted, San Francisco: Ignatius Press, 1993), Karol Wojtyla (Pope John Paul II) expressed matters this way: "A person is the kind of good which does not admit of use and cannot be treated as an object of use and as such the means to an end.... A person is a good towards which the only proper and adequate attitude is love."

2. Centuries ago St. Augustine rightly and wisely noted that one of the principal *goods* of marriage is the good of children, who are "to be received lovingly, nourished humanely, and educated religiously,": i.e., in the love and service of God and neighbor. See his *De genesi ad literam*, 9.7 (*PL* 34.397).

3. It is worth noting here that the principal reason St. Thomas gave to show that fornication is intrinsically evil is that acts of fornication may cause (and are known to cause) the conception of new human life, that the life thus generated would be deprived of the home to which it has a right, and that, therefore, by fornicating one was unjustly exposing children who could be generated by fornication to this deprivation. He observed that one might try to prevent their conception by contraceptive acts, but he judged contraception to be even more gravely immoral insofar as it constitutes an attack on the survival of the human species. See his *Summa contra gentiles,* 3.122.

4. I realize that many women valiantly struggle to care for children whom they have conceived out of wedlock. Their caring for these children is *good,* and I praise them for it. Despite this, it is *not* good for them to conceive children in this way nor for their children to be

deprived of the home that only loving spouses can provide — as these valiant women themselves realize. Nor is it good for the males who impregnate women outside of marriage to place themselves in a position where they cannot properly carry out their obligations to the women they have made pregnant nor to the children they have fathered.

5. As the German theologian Helmut Thielicke put the matter: "Not uniqueness establishes the marriage, but marriage establishes the uniqueness." *The Ethics of Sex* (New York: Harper, 1964), p. 95.

6. Here see John Paul II's perceptive observations in his commentary on Genesis 2: "The unity of which Genesis 2:24 speaks ('they become one flesh') is undoubtedly what is expressed and realized in the conjugal act. The biblical formulation, extremely concise and simple, indicates sex, femininity and masculinity, as that characteristic of man — male and female — which permits them, when they become one flesh, *to submit at the same time their whole humanity to the blessing of fertility"* (emphasis added). See John Paul II, "Marriage Is One and Indissoluble in the First Chapters of Genesis," General Audience of November 21, 1979, in *Original Unity of Man and Woman: Catechesis on the Book of Genesis* (Boston: St. Paul Editions, 1981), pp. 79-80. All of John Paul II's Wednesday conferences on the "theology of the body," originally published in English in four volumes (in addition to *Original Unity* these were: *Blessed Are the Pure of Heart, Theology of Marriage and Celibacy,* and *Reflections on Humanae Vitae*) have now been reprinted in a one-volume edition entitled *The Theology of the Body: Human Love in the Divine Plan* (Boston: Pauline Books & Media, 1997). This volume will henceforth be referred to as TB. The passage in question appears in TB, p. 49.

7. On this see Pope Paul VI, Encyclical *Humanae vitae,* no. 12; Pope John Paul II, Apostolic Exhortation on the Role of the Christian Family in the Modern World (*Familiaris consortio*), no. 32; *The Catechism of the Catholic Church*, no. 2369.

8. On this see John Paul II, "Analysis of Knowledge and Procreation," General Audience of March 5, 1980, *Original Unity of Man and Woman,* nos. 4-5, pp. 149-150 (TB, pp. 77-80). Here the Pope notes that in the marital act, whereby they come to "know" each other, husband and wife "reveal themselves to each other, with that specific depth of their own human 'self,' which, precisely, is revealed also by means of their sex, their masculinity and femininity …. [T]he

reality of the conjugal union ... contains a new and, in a way, a definitive discovery of the meaning of the human body in its masculinity and femininity."

9. On this see John F. Kippley, *Sex and the Marriage Covenant: A Basis for Morality* (Cincinnati: Couple to Couple League, 1991), pp. 7-12, 76-86.

10. The ideas briefly set forth here are developed by me at more length in *Marriage: The Rock on Which the Family Is Built* (San Francisco: Ignatius, 1995), chap. 2, "Marriage and the Complementarity of Male and Female." See also Robert Joyce, *Human Sexual Ecology: A Philosophy of Man and Woman* (Washington, D.C.: University Press of America, 1980), pp. 35-50.

11. On this see Robert P. George and Gerard V. Bradley, "Marriage and the Liberal Imagination," *The Georgetown Law Review* 84 (1995) 301-320; Germain Grisez, "The Christian Family as Fulfillment of Sacramental Marriage," a paper delivered to the Society of Christian Ethics Annual Conference, September 9, 1995 (unpublished manuscript, on file with *The Georgetown Law Review*).

12. Pope Pius XII, Address to the Italian Union of Midwives, October 21, 1951, text in *The Catholic Mind* 50 (1951) 61.

13. Pope Paul VI, Encyclical *Humanae vitae*, no. 12. My translation.

14. Ibid., no. 12.

15. Classic sources for the distinction between *transitive* and *immanent* action, between making and doing, and the significance of this distinction are: Aristotle, *Metaphysics,* Bk. 9, chap. 8, 1050a23-1051b1; St. Thomas Aquinas, *In IX Metaphysicorum,* Lect. 8, no. 1865.

16. Catholic Bishops' [of England] Committee on Bioethical Issues, *In Vitro Fertilization: Morality and Public Policy* (London: Catholic Information Services, 1983), no. 23.

17. Four of his addresses take up this issue: (1) Allocution to the Fourth International Conference of Catholic Doctors, September 29, 1949; text in *Papal Teachings on Matrimony,* ed. The Benedictine Monks of Solemnes, trans. Michael J. Byrnes (Boston: St. Paul Editions, 1963), pp. 381-385; (2) Allocution to Italian Catholic Midwives, October 29, 1951; in ibid., pp. 405-434; (3) Allocution to the Second World Congress on Fertility and Human Sterility, May 19, 1956; in ibid., pp. 482-492; and (4) Allocution to the Seventh Hematological Congress, September 12, 1958; in ibid., pp. 513-525. He discussed artificial insemination in all four of these addresses, and in no. 3 explicitly took up *in vitro* fertilization.

18. Allocution to the Second World Congress on Fertility and Human Sterility, ibid., p. 485.
19. Allocution to Italian Catholic Midwives, ibid., pp. 427-428.
20. Allocution to the Second World Congress on Fertility and Human Sterility, ibid., p. 470.
21. Allocution to the Fourth International Congress of Catholic Doctors, ibid., p. 559.
22. Pontifical Academy for Life, *Reflections on Cloning* (Vatican City: Libreria Editrice Vaticana, 1997), pp. 10, 14.
23. It is instructive to note that in his article on artificial insemination in the widely used and influential *Encyclopedia of Bioethics*, Luigi Mastroianni included under "homologous" fertilization procedures "utilizing the semen of the husband *or designated partner"* (emphasis added) ("Reproductive Technologies, Introduction," in *Encyclopedia of Bioethics,* ed. Warren T. Reich [2nd rev. ed.: New York: McGraw Hill, 1995] 2207). Inasmuch as this edition of the *Encyclopedia* now includes an essay entitled "Marriage and *Other Domestic Partnerships"* (emphasis added) by Barbara Hilkert Anderson (pp. 1397-1402) Mastroianni's apparent equation of husbands with "designated partners" is not too surprising.
24. See Mastroianni, "Reproductive Technologies, Introduction," 2207.
25. On this see David S. McLaughlin, M.D., "A Scientific Introduction to Reproductive Technologies," in *Reproductive Technologies, Marriage, and the Church*, ed. Donald G. McCarthy (Braintree, MA: The Pope John Center, 1988), pp. 55-56.
26. Walter Wadlington, "Reproductive Technologies, Artificial Insemination," *Encyclopedia of Bioethics,* 2220.
27. George J. Annas, "Artificial Insemination: Beyond the Best Interests of the Donor," *Hastings Center Report* 9.4 (August 1979) 14-15, 43.
28. Wadlington, "Reproductive Technologies, Artificial Insemination," 2217.
29. See McLaughlin, "A Scientific Introduction to Reproductive Technologies," p. 57.
30. On this see Mastroianni, "Reproductive Technologies, Introduction," 2209-2210; Andrea L. Bonnicksen, "Reproductive Technologies, In Vitro Fertilization and Embryo Transfer," *Encyclopedia of Bioethics,* 2221-2224; and McLaughlin, "A Scientific Introduction to Reproductive Technologies," pp. 58-59.
31. Mastroianni, "Reproductive Technologies, Introduction," 2211.

32. See Bonnicksen, "Reproductive Technologies, In Vitro Fertilization and Embryo Transfer," 2222.
33. On these and other technologies see McLaughlin, "A Scientific Introduction to Reproductive Technologies," 60-62.
34. Ibid.
35. Ibid. See also Mastroianni, "Reproductive Technologies, Introduction," 2211-2212.
36. "Somatic cell nuclear transfer" is the expression used to describe mammalian cloning by the National Bioethics Advisory Commission in its document, released in June, 1997: "Cloning Human Beings: The Report and Recommendations of the National Bioethics Advisory Commission." A summary of this report is printed in *Hastings Center Report* (September-October, 1997) 7-9.
37. Pontifical Academy for Life, *Reflections on Cloning,* pp. 10-11.
38. Catholic Bishops' (of England) Committee on Bioethical Issues, *In Vitro Fertilization: Morality and Public Policy,* no. 24.
38. Richard McCormick, *The Critical Calling: Reflections on Moral Dilemmas Since Vatican II* (Washington, D.C.: Georgetown University Press, 1989), p. 337. The internal citation is from William Daniel, S.J., *"In Vitro* Fertilization: Two Problem Areas," *Australasian Catholic Record* 63 (1986) 27.
40. Ibid.
41. See Thomas A. Shannon and Lisa Sowle Cahill, *Religion and Artificial Reproduction: An Inquiry Into the Vatican "Instruction on Respect for Human Life"* (New York: Crossroads, 1988), p. 138; Jean Porter, "Human Need and Natural Law," in *Infertility: A Crossroad of Faith, Medicine, and Technology,* ed. Kevin Wm. Wildes, S.J. (Dordrecht/Boston/London: Kluwer Academic Publishers, 1997), pp. 103-105. It should be noted that Shannon and Cahill, using an argument proportionalistic in nature — that is, that it can be morally permissible to intend a so-called nonmoral evil (e.g., heterologous generation of human life) should a sufficiently greater nonmoral good be possible (e.g., providing an otherwise childless couple with a child of their own), insinuate that, if the spouses consent, recourse to third parties for gametes and even to surrogate mothers might not truly violate spousal dignity or unity. See *Artificial Reproduction...,* p. 115.
42. See Pope John Paul II, Encyclical *Veritatis splendor,* nos. 71-83. An excellent collection of essays on this Encyclical is *Veritatis Splendor and the Renewal of Moral Theology*, eds. J. A. DiNoia, O.P. and Romanus Cessario, O.P. (Chicago: Midwest Theological Forum, 1999).

43. For critiques of proportionalism see my *An Introduction to Moral Theology* (rev. ed.: Huntington, IN: Our Sunday Visitor, 1994); Germain Grisez, *The Way of the Lord Jesus,* Vol. 1, *Christian Moral Principles* (Chicago: Franciscan Herald Press, 1983), chap. Six; Martin Rhonheimer, "Intrinsically Evil Acts and the Moral Viewpoint: Clarifying a Central Teaching of *Veritatis splendor,*" in *Veritatis Splendor and the Renewal of Moral Theology,* pp. 161-194.

44. Benedict Ashley, "The Chill Factor in Moral Theology," *Linacre Quarterly* 57.4 (1990) 71.

45. Ibid., 72.

46. The argument just advanced was set forth originally in an earlier essay I wrote on this issue: "*Donum Vitae:* Catholic Teaching on Homologous *In Vitro* Fertilization," in *Infertility: A Crossroad of Faith, Medicine, and Technology,* pp. 73-92, especially pp. 81-87, making use of material developed by Germain Grisez, Joseph Boyle, John Finnis, and me in our essay " 'Every Marital Act Ought To Be Open to New Life': Toward a Clearer Understanding," *The Thomist* 52 (1988) 365-426.

47. McCormick, "Notes on Moral Theology," *Theological Studies* 45 (1984) 102.

48. Here I must note that in her essay, "Human Needs and Natural Law" (see endnote 41), Jean Porter claims that my argument supporting *Donum vitae* is based on a "Kantian" sexual ethics that "gives pride of place to autonomy" (pp. 100-101). She even claims that I "dissent" from Catholic teaching in my analysis of the marital act because of my emphasis on the role of intention in determining the moral significance of human actions. Porter's criticisms are ludicrous and can only be attributed to a woeful ignorance of Thomistic moral theory and the teaching of John Paul II in *Veritatis splendor.* I may dissent from a "Suarezian" understanding of natural law, which Porter perhaps employs along with her own proportionalism, but I am by no means Kantian. As far as the role of intention in determining morality is concerned, has Porter read St. Thomas, *Summa theologiae,* II-II, 64, 7 (for instance), where he clearly says that "moral actions are specified according to what is intended and not by what lies outside the scope of one's intentionality" (the Latin text reads: "*morales autem actus recipiunt speciem secundum id quod intenditur, non autem ab eo quod est praeter intentionem*")?

49. It is important to stress here that Christian faith proclaims that the Word Incarnate, although not a human *person,* is still a *human be-*

ing, a man.. Christian faith rejects docetism, the doctrine that the Uncreated Word only seemed to become human and ceased so appearing after the resurrection.

50. Pope John Paul II, "To my brother bishops from North and Central America and the Caribbean assembled in Dallas, Texas," in *Reproductive Technologies, Marriage and the Church,* p. xv.

51. *Donum vitae,* II, B, 4, 7.

52. Rev. John Doerfler, *Assisting or Replacing the Conjugal Act: Criteria for a Moral Evaluation of Reproductive Techniques,* unpublished 1999 S.T.L. dissertation on file at the John Paul II Institute for Studies on Marriage and Family, Washington, D.C. A substantive summary of his study will appear in *Anthropotes: Rivista di Studi sulla Persona e Famiglia.* He has briefly summarized his work in "Technology and Human Reproduction," *Ethics & Medics* 24.8 (August, 1999) 3-4.

53. Josef Seifert, "Substitution of the Conjugal Act or Assistance to It? IVF, GIFT and Some Other Medical Interventions. Philosophical Reflections on the Vatican Declaration 'Donum Vitae,' " *Anthropotes: Rivista di Studi sulla Persona e Famiglia* 4 (1988) 273-286.

54. See Doerfler, *Assisting or Replacing the Conjugal Act,* pp. 89-90.

55. See, for example, Thomas J. O'Donnell, S.J., *Medicine and Christian Morality* (2nd rev. ed.: New York: Alba House, 1991), p. 238.

56. See, for instance, the following: Donald T. DeMarco, "Catholic Moral Teaching and TOT/GIFT," in *Reproductive Technologies, Marriage and the Church,* pp. 122-139; Nicholas Tonti-Filippini, " 'Donum Vitae' and Gamete Intra-Fallopian Tube Transfer," *Linacre Quarterly* 57.2. (May, 1989) 68-79; Benedict Ashley, O.P., and Kevin O'Rourke, O.P. , *Health Care Ethics: A Theological Analysis* (4th ed.: Washington, D.C.: Georgetown University Press, 1997), pp. 242-247; Germain Grisez, *Difficult Moral Questions,* Vol. 3 of *The Way of the Lord Jesus* (Quincy, IL: Franciscan Press, 1997), pp. 244-249.

57. See Grisez, *Difficult Moral Questions,* p. 248; Orville N. Griese, *Catholic Identity in Health Care: Principles and Practice* (Braintree, MA: The Pope John XXIII Medical Moral Center, 1987), pp. 443-44; John W. Carlson, "Interventions Upon Gametes in Assisting the Conjugal Act Toward Fertilization," in *Infertility: A Crossroad of Faith, Medicine, and Technology,* pp. 110-111; Tonti-Filippini, " 'Donum Vitae' and Gamete Intra-Fallopian Tube Transfer," 70.

58. This seems to me to be the position of Grisez, Griese, and Carlson (see preceding endnote for bibliographical details).

59. On this see Doerflert, *Assisting or Replacing the Conjugal Act,* pp. 89ff.
60. Two Catholic theologians explicitly accepting this procedure are: O'Donnell, *Medicine and Christian Morality,* p. 238; Griese, *Catholic Moral Identity in Health Care,* p. 46.
61. Good critiques of this procedure are provided by Grisez, *Difficult Moral Questions,* pp. 247-249; Tonti-Filippini, "*Donum Vitae* and Gamete Intrafallopian Tube Transfer."
62. The most extensive and initially plausible defense of GIFT is given by Peter J. Cataldo. His most detailed effort to justify it is found in his essay, "The Newest Reproductive Technologies: Applying Catholic Teaching," in *The Gospel of Life and the Vision of Health Care,* ed. Russell Smith (Braintree, MA: The Pope John XXIII Medical Moral Center, 1996), pp. 61-94. A briefer presentation of his argument is given in "Reproductive Technologies," *Ethics & Medics* 21.1 (January, 1996) 1-3. See also Donald McCarthy, "Infertility Bypass," *Ethics & Medics* 8.10 (October, 1983) 1-2; McCarthy, "Catholic Moral Teaching and TOT/GIFT: A Response to Donald T. DeMarco, in *Reproductive Technologies, Marriage, and the Church,* pp. 140-145; Griese, *Catholic Identity in Health Care,* pp. 47-49.
63. For Doerfler, in addition to the study referred to in endnote 52, see his "Is GIFT Compatible with the Teaching of *Donum Vitae?*" *Linacre Quarterly* 64.1 (February 1997) 41-47. See also Grisez, *Difficult Moral Questions,* pp. 246-248; Tonti-Filippini, " 'Donum Vitae' and Gamete Intrafallopian Tube Transfer," 68-89; DeMarco, "Catholic Moral Teaching and TOT/GIFT," in *Reproductive Technologies, Marriage, and the Church,* pp. 122-140; Ashley/O'Rourke, *Health Care Ethics,* pp. 246-247; Seifert, "Substitution of the Conjugal Act or Assistance to It ... ?"
64. Personal letter from Thomas W. Hilgers, M.D., June 9, 1999. He has developed the *Creighton Model Fertility/Care System* for helping married couples experiencing difficulties in conceiving.
65. In preparing this Part I have been helped greatly by the work of two of my graduate students at the John Paul II Institute for Studies on Marriage and Family, Geoffrey Surtees and Rev. Francis M. De Rosa. Surtees graduated with a master's degree in theology in 1996 and in what follows I will refer to an article he published on this issue in the *Homiletic and Pastoral Review* (the article was originally written as a research paper for a course I taught in bioethics). Father De Rosa, who is completing work on his licentiate in sacred theology at the

Institute, prepared another research paper in late 1999 (as yet unpublished) containing valuable material on this matter.

66. Jerome Lejeune, *The Concentration Can* (San Francisco: Ignatius Press, 1992).

67. One highly immoral way of handling frozen embryos has already occurred to entrepreneurs in the US, namely, the formation of business enterprises eager to locate and distribute abandoned frozen embryos to couples anxious to have a child. One such entity, called "Creating Families, Inc.," is located in Denver, CO. Although this company is careful to claim that it does not accept "fees" for its work in "creating families," it nonetheless solicits "donations" for its services, and it is somewhat naïve to think that the profit motive is not operative (see the website of Creating Families, Inc.: http://www.creatfam.com/embryodononor.html). Similarly, the Columbia Presbyterian Medical Center in New York can provide an already frozen embryo for $2,750 as opposed to the $16,000 needed to cover the entire IVF-ET procedure (on this, see Brian Caulfield, "Souls on Ice: With Frozen Embryo Technology, Life's Sanctity is Lost," *National Catholic Register,* 74.1 [January 4-10, 1998] 15).

68. Msgr. William B. Smith, "Rescue the Frozen?" *Homiletic and Pastoral Review* 96.1 (October, 1995), 72-74.

69. *Donum vitae*, I, 5 (emphasis added), cited by Smith, ibid., 72.

70. Ibid.

71. Ibid.

72. *Donum vitae,* II, 4, cited by Smith, ibid., 74.

73. Ibid. I believe that I have accurately summarized Smith's point here; nonetheless, this particular section of his essay does not seem to be clearly articulated.

74. Mary Geach, "Are there any circumstances in which it would be morally admirable for a woman to seek to have an orphan embryo implanted in her womb?" in *Issues for a Catholic Bioethic: Proceedings of the International Conference to Celebrate the Twentieth Anniversary of the foundation of The Linacre Centre 28-31 July 1997,* ed. Luke Gormally (London: The Linacre Centre, 1999), pp. 341-346.

75. Ibid., p. 343.

76. Ibid., p. 345. Although this passage occurs later in her essay, the point communicated in it is central to the reasoning developed on p. 344, as Geach herself indicates.

77. Ibid., p. 344.

78. Ibid., p. 345.
79. Germain Grisez, *The Way of the Lord Jesus,* Vol. 3, *Difficult Moral Questions* (Quincy, IL: Franciscan Press, 1997) p. 242, footnote 188. See also Geoffrey Surtees, "Adoption of a Frozen Embryo," *Homiletic and Pastoral Review* 96 (August-September 1996) 8-9.
80. Grisez, *Difficult Moral Questions,* p. 241, footnote 186.
81. Surtees, "Adoption of a Frozen Embryo," 11.
82. Helen Watt: "Are there any circumstances in which it would be morally admirable for a woman to seek to have an orphan embryo implanted in her womb?" in *Issues for a Catholic Bioethic,* pp. 349-350.
83. Dr. Geach communicated this information to me via e-mail on February 17, 2000. After I had revised this section of this chapter to take into account this information, I sent Dr. Geach another draft, and in an e-mail of February 20, 2000 she brought up additional objections to my way of presenting her position.
84. Geach, e-mail to William E. May of February 20, 2000.
85. The proposal that couples "volunteer" to rescue frozen embryos by adopting them prenatally was made by several persons active in the pro-life movement in 1996, when some 3,300 frozen embryos in England, who had been preserved in "concentration cans" for over five years and who had been "abandoned" by those who had had them produced and frozen, were to be thawed out and allowed to perish (on this see *The London Tablet*, Vol. 250, issues of July 27, 1996 and August 10, 1996). The Italian theologian, Maurizio P. Faggioni reported on this proposal in an important article in *L'Osservatore Romano* (Eng. ed.) no. 34 (August 21, 1996), 4. He wrote: "This would be a case of 'prenatal' adoption to be distinguished from surrogate motherhood and heterologous fertilization with a donor oocyte. In this case there would be no offense to matrimonial unity, nor to the equilibrium of familial relationships, because the embryo would have, from the genetic standpoint, the same relationship to both adoptive parents…. [S]uch a solution would highlight the significance of adoption as an expression of the fecundity of marital love and as fruit of a genuine openness to life which leads spouses to welcome into their families children whose parents have died or who have been abandoned." Although Faggioni himself does not clearly endorse this proposal, he does not seem to regard it as clearly immoral but he does think that it could have very bad consequences, paving the way for busi-

ness enterprises — like "Creating Families, Inc." [see footnote 67 above] — to seize an opportunity to encourage the production of embryos *in vitro* for "adoption" by infertile couples. Expressing the same fear that "rescuing" frozen embryos by "adopting" them prenatally *could* lead to very bad consequences, Bishop Elio Sgreccia, the vice president of the Pontifical Academy for Life, was quoted as saying: "The idea of a systematic organization of prenatal adoption of the frozen embryos would, in fact, end up by legitimising the practice which is substantially at the root of the whole problem" (as cited in *The London Tablet*, August 10, 1996.

86. At the conclusion of his brief essay, Smith said: "I would not be surprised if all do not agree and would welcome reasons why the above is not correct" (Smith, "Rescue the Frozen?" 74).

87. Surtees, "Adoption of a Frozen Embryo," note 2, pp. 8, 13-14.

88. Ibid., 11.

89. Ibid., 12-13.

90. Ibid.

91. Thus in ibid., note 23, pp. 13, 16, Surtees writes: "It has to be acknowledged that to be implanted in the womb of a woman who subsequently gives it up for adoption after birth is a much better solution for the child than remaining in a state of frozen captivity; but, as we have noted, to be adopted permanently into a family is a still better situation for the child's well-being and stability. But … this is a question of prudence, not an argument for or against the liceity of the action *per se."*

92. Smith, "Response [to Surtees]," *Homiletic and Pastoral Review* 96 (August-September, 1996) 16-17.

93. Grisez, *Difficult Moral Questions,* p. 242, footnote 187.

94. Ibid., p. 241.

95. Ibid., pp. 241-242.

96. Ibid., p. 243.

97. Watt: "Are there any circumstances in which it would be morally admirable for a woman to seek to have an orphan embryo implanted in her womb?," p. 351.

98. Ibid., p. 350.

99. In writing the final section of this chapter, on rescuing frozen embryos, I was helped greatly by Rev. Paul deLadurantaye, who showed me how to clarify my position. I am most grateful to him.

Chapter Four

CONTRACEPTION AND RESPECT FOR HUMAN LIFE

Introduction

Contraception is usually considered an issue in sexual ethics rather than one proper to bioethics. But, as I hope to show here, contraception is very much relevant to respect for human life inasmuch as it is not, of itself, a *sexual* act but rather an *anti-life* kind of act. It is indeed the "gateway to abortion"; widespread social acceptance of contraception has led to the "culture of death" described by John Paul II in his Encyclical *Evangelium vitae.*

The suggestion that contraception is "anti-life" and has led to the "culture of death" will offend many people, both Catholic and non-Catholic, who do not regard contraception as an anti-life kind of act and who can see no connection whatsoever between contraception and the "culture of death." For most people in our society, Catholic and non-Catholic as well, contraception by married persons is regarded as "natural." It is the obvious thing to do if there are good reasons for avoiding a pregnancy; and the suggestion that there is a link between contraception and the "culture of death" is considered outrageous, in particular, by married couples who are "pro-life" but nonetheless believe that there is nothing wrong with contraception.

This is illustrated by some of the contributors to the December 1998 symposium on contraception in the journal *First Things.* Gilbert Meilaender, a Lutheran theologian known widely for his opposition to abortion, and Philip Turner, an Anglican theologian also "on the side of life," in their joint contribution expressed the view that "contraceptive intercourse may sometimes be a fitting means by which husband and wife aim to nourish simultaneously the procreative and unitive purposes of their marriage."[1] Similarly, the editor of *First Things*, James Nuechterlein, reflecting on the symposium in a subsequent number of the journal, began by observing that he and his wife did not want children immediately because of their circumstances, although, had she become pregnant, "we would not for a moment have considered abortion. But," he continued,

> neither for a moment did we morally hesitate to practice contraception. We no more debated whether we would use contraception than we debated whether we would, in the fullness of time, have children. Of course we would someday, God willing, have children; in the meantime we would practice (non-abortifacient) contraception. This was not, for us, a matter of presuming on God's providence. It seemed rather a right use of reason in fulfilling the various goods of our marriage. We intended both the unitive and the procreative goods of marriage, but not necessarily both in every act of love.[2]

Concluding, Nuechterlein said: "The point of this self-revelation is to suggest how utterly typical that view was and is. There is nothing singular in our experience. I believe it is, mutatis mutandis, the experience of most Protestant couples of our generation and after."[3]

Note that Nuechterlein refers to the common experience of contemporary *Protestants* (and this, seemingly, was also in the mind of Meilaender and Turner). However, it is no doubt true that a great majority of Catholic couples agree with these writers. On reading their essays, in fact, I was reminded of the views set forth in the celebrated "Majority Papers" of the Papal Commission on Population, the Family, and Natality.[4] Two passages from these papers — to which I will return later for closer examination — seem in particular to express the view articulated by these contributors to *First Things*.

In one passage the Majority justify contraception by married couples as an intelligent use of reason to control biological nature:

> The true opposition is not to be sought between some material conformity to the physiological processes of nature and some artificial intervention. For it is natural for man to use his skill in order to put under human control what is given by

physical nature. The opposition is to be sought really between one way of acting which is contraceptive [in the sense of selfishly excluding children from marriage] and opposed to a prudent and generous fruitfulness, and another way which is in an ordered relationship to responsible fruitfulness and which has a concern for education and all the essential human and Christian values.[5]

In another passage they justify the use of contraception by married couples by distinguishing between individual acts of sexual union within marriage and the totality of the marriage. According to them,

When man interferes with the procreative purpose of individual acts by contracepting, he does this with the intention of regulating and not excluding fertility. Then he unites the material finality toward fecundity which exists in intercourse with the formal finality of the person and renders the entire process human. Conjugal acts which by intention are infertile or which are rendered infertile are ordered to the expression of the union of love; that love, however, reaches its culmination in fertility responsibly accepted. For that reason other acts of union are in a certain sense incomplete, and they receive their full moral quality with ordination toward the fertile act. Infertile conjugal acts constitute a totality with fertile acts and have a single moral specification.[6]

The "single moral specification" of such acts, as the Majority makes clear, is "the fostering of love responsibly toward a generous fecundity."

In this view, what married couples who use contraception as a way of spacing children *in* their marriage and not of excluding them *from* their marriage are doing is simply using appropriate means for nourishing both the procreative and unitive purposes of marriage. This is their "intention" — as Meilaender/Turner and Nuechterlein indicate in the passages previously cited — and surely this intention is not immoral.

This way of viewing the use of contraception by married couples who have serious reasons to avoid having children, at least for a time, is quite common in our society. Many, Catholic and non-Catholic alike, who hold it regard abortion with horror, and they also unambiguously judge sex outside of marriage to be immoral. But they can see nothing wrong with the "responsible" use of contraception within marriage, nor do they believe that there is some inexorable link between contraception and the "culture of death."

This widely held view, however, is mistaken. For centuries Christian writers regarded contraception an "anti-life" kind of act. In fact, one of the contributors to the *First Things* symposium, Alicia Mosier, an editorial assistant of the journal, forcefully expressed this view. She began by emphasizing that the issue does not center on the "artificiality" of the means used to prevent conception but with the nature of contraception itself. As she said, "what is wrong is contraception itself: the deliberate will, the choice, to subvert the life-giving order and meaning of the conjugal act."[7] Commenting on Pope Paul's description of contraception as "every action ... which proposes ... to render procreation impossible,"[8] she wrote:

> Proposing to render procreation impossible means, simply put, willing directly against the order of intercourse and consequently against life.... Couples who contracept introduce a countermeasure ... whose sole purpose is to make it impossible for a new life to come to be. Contraception is an act that can only express the will that *any* baby that might result from *this* sexual encounter not be conceived....it manifests a will aimed directly against new life.[9]

Mosier's way of expressing this view echoes the argument against contraception mounted by Germain Grisez, Joseph Boyle, John Finnis, and me in 1988.[10] But, as noted already, she articulates a position that was traditional in the Church, both East and West, both Catholic and Protestant, from the early days of Christianity to the mid-twentieth century. It is found in such Church Fathers as John Chrysostom, Ambrose, and Jerome, in medieval theologians such as Thomas Aquinas, in the canon law operative in the Roman Catholic Church from the mid-thirteenth century until 1917, in the thought of reformers such as John Calvin and in the teaching of the *Roman Catechism*, popularly known as the *Catechism of the Council of Trent*. There is no need here to recapitulate this tradition. In the accompanying note I cite representative witnesses.[11] There is thus a long and respected Christian tradition that judges contraception to be anti-life, expressing a will that is indeed at the heart of the "culture of death."

Here I will show why contraception is intimately related to the culture of death and, indeed, is the gateway to this culture. I will begin by considering Pope John Paul II's thought regarding the roots of the culture of death and his way of relating contraception to that culture. I will then take up his claim that the difference, anthropological and moral, between contraception and recourse to the rhythm of the cycle is enormous and involves ultimately "irreconcilable concepts of the human person and of human sexuality." This section will show that the acceptance of contraception is based on a dualistic anthropology of the human person and a consequentialist/proportionalist understanding of the morality of human acts: an anthropology and moral perspective central to the "culture of death." This section will likewise show how confusing and misleading talk about "intentions" can be. I will follow this with an analysis of the human act of contraception to show that it is and cannot not be anti-life, and that this is *the* reason why contraception is indeed the gateway to the "culture of death." In conclusion, I will consider contraception as an act both anti-love and anti-life, utterly incompatible with the "culture of life" and the "civilization of love." In an appendix I will briefly consider the morality of seeking to prevent conception if a woman is in danger of being raped or has already suffered this violence to herself.

1. POPE JOHN PAUL II ON THE ROOTS OF THE CULTURE OF DEATH AND CONTRACEPTION'S RELATIONSHIP TO IT

In the first chapter of his Encyclical *Evangelium vitae* Pope John Paul II identifies two roots of the "culture of death." This culture, he says, is rooted first of all in the "mentality which *carries the concept of subjectivity to an extreme* and even distorts it, and recognizes as a subject of rights only the person who enjoys full or at least incipient autonomy and who emerges from a state of total dependence on others" (no. 19). It is rooted, secondly, in a *"notion of freedom* which exalts the isolated individual in an absolute way" (no. 19).

Of these two roots the first is most relevant for showing the relationship of contraception to the culture of death. At its heart is the idea that only those members of the human species who enjoy at least "incipient autonomy," i.e., individuals with exercisable capacities of reasoning and will, are *truly* persons with rights that ought to be recognized by society. This mentality, John Paul II points out, "tends to *equate personal dignity with the capacity for verbal and explicit,* or at least perceptible, *communication"* (no. 19). On this view a "person" is preeminently a subject aware of itself as a self and capable of relating to other selves; and not all members of the human species are persons in this understanding of "person." This idea, as will be seen later, fits in well with the anthropology underlying the acceptance of contraception.

In the first chapter of *Evangelium vitae* John Paul II also discusses the relationship between contraception and abortion, whose justification and legalization is, of course, a hallmark of the "culture of death." To the common claim that contraception, "if made safe and available to all, is the most effective remedy against abortion," John Paul II replied:

> When looked at carefully, this objection is clearly un-founded. It may be that many people use contraception with a view to excluding the subsequent temptation of abortion. But the negative values inherent in the "contraceptive men-tality" — which is very different from responsible parent-hood, lived in respect for the full truth of the conjugal act — are such that they in fact strengthen this temptation when an unwanted life is conceived…. Certainly, from the moral point of view contraception and abortion are *specifically different* evils: the former contradicts the full truth of the sexual act as the proper expression of conjugal love, whereas the latter destroys the life of a human being; the former is opposed to the virtue of chastity in marriage, the latter is opposed to the virtue of justice and directly violates the divine command-ment "You shall not kill" (no.13).

It is important to emphasize that here John Paul II does *not,* as did the long Christian tradition noted above, identify contraception as an "anti-life" kind of act, akin to murder. He rather characterizes it as an "anti-love" kind of act, one that, as he says elsewhere, "falsifies" the meaning of the conjugal act as one in which the spouses give themselves unre-servedly to one another.[12] But he nonetheless insists that despite their differences "contraception and abortion are often closely connected, as fruits of the same tree," and he points out that the close link between the two "is being demonstrated in an alarming way by the development of chemical products, intrauterine devices and vaccines which, distributed with the same ease as contraceptives, really act as abortifacients in the very early stages of the development of the life of a new human being" (no.13).

John Paul II obviously sees a real and substantive link between con-traception and abortion and — through it — the "culture of death." But he does not here *directly* relate contraception to the culture of death. For him, contraception directly violates marital chastity and not the good of human life.

2. CONTRACEPTION VS. "RECOURSE TO THE RHYTHM OF THE CYCLE": THEIR ANTHROPOLOGICAL AND MORAL DIFFERENCES, ONE ULTIMATELY ENTAILING "IRRECONCILABLE CONCEPTS OF THE HUMAN PERSON AND OF HUMAN SEXUALITY"

In his apostolic exhortation on the *Role of the Christian Family in the Modern World (Familiaris consortio)* Pope John Paul II made the following bold claim:

> In the light of the experience of many couples and the data provided by the different human sciences, theological reflection is able to perceive and is called to study further *the difference, both anthropological and moral,* between contraception and recourse to the rhythm of the cycle: it is a difference which is much wider and deeper than is usually thought, one which involves in the final analysis *two irreconcilable concepts of the human person and of human sexuality* (no. 32).[13]

Perhaps many people who *practice* contraception — and many who *practice* periodic abstinence — are not consciously aware of the difference between these two ways of exercising responsible parenthood, but the difference is profound. I will show this by examining the rationale used to defend the legitimacy of contraception in order to disclose its underlying anthropology and moral methodology. I will then contrast this by presenting the anthropology and moral methodology on which the practice of natural family planning or periodic abstinence or what John Paul II calls here "recourse to the rhythm of the cycle" is based.

A. Contraception: Its Underlying Anthropology and Moral Methodology

A dualistic understanding of the human person and of human sexuality is at the heart of the defense of contraception. This anthropology regards the body as an instrument of the person, a good for the person insofar as it is a necessary condition for goods and values intrinsic to the person; the latter, so-called personalistic goods and values, are those whose existence depends on their being consciously experienced. This anthropology underlies several key arguments given to support contraception, in particular, that defending contraception as the exercise of intelligent human dominion over nature and that justifying it on the basis that it is in harmony with the nature of *human* sexuality.

Several passages from the Majority documents of the Papal Commission illustrate the first line of reasoning, based on humankind's dominion over the world of nature. I cited one of these at the beginning of this chapter, in which the authors stressed that "it is natural for man to use his skill in order to put under human control what is given by physical nature."[14] In another passage they declare that, "in the matter at hand," namely, contraception,

> [T]here is a certain change in the mind of contemporary man. He feels that he is more conformed to his rational nature, created by God with liberty and responsibility, when he uses his skill to intervene in the biological processes of nature so that he can achieve the institution of matrimony in the conditions of actual life, than if he would abandon himself to chance.[15]

In yet another passage the majority emphasized that "it is proper to man, created in the image of God, to use what is given in physical nature in a way that he may develop it to its full significance with a view to the good of the whole person."[16]

These passages make it clear that those defending contraception consider the biological fertility of human persons and the biological processes involved in the generation of new human life as physical or biological "givens." Human fertility, in other words, is part of the world of subhuman or subpersonal nature over which persons have been given dominion. The majority theologians of the Papal Commission, in fact, assert that "biological fertility ... ought to be assumed into the human sphere and be regulated within it."[17] Obviously, if the biological fecundity of human persons is intrinsically human, it does not need to be "assumed into the human sphere." Nothing assumes what it already is or has of itself. This passage is a clear assertion of dualism.

In other words, in this view human fertility is in and of itself a biological given belonging to the physical, not human, world over which the person has been given dominion. Biological givens, such as fertility, confront the person who is to control and regulate them by "assuming" them into the human and personal sphere, i.e., by making use of them when they serve "personalist" goods and by suppressing or impeding them when their continued flourishing inhibits participation in these goods, whose existence, as noted already, depends on their being consciously experienced.

The notion that human biological fertility is, of itself, subhuman and subpersonal is closely related to the understanding of human sexuality central to the defense of contraception. One of the major reason for changing Church teaching on the matter, the majority theologians argued, is the "changed estimation of the value and meaning of human sexuality," one leading to a "better, deeper, and more correct understanding of conjugal life and the conjugal act."[18] According to this understanding, *human* sexuality, as distinct from *animal* sexuality, is above all relational or unitive in character. As one theologian put it, "the most profound meaning of human sexuality is that it is a relational reality, having a special significance for the person in his relationships."[19] Human sexuality, as some other theological defenders of contraception contend, "is preeminently ... the mode whereby an isolated subjectivity [=person] reaches out to communion with another subject. Embodied subjectivity reaches out to another body-subject in order to banish loneliness and to experience the fullness of being-with-another in the human project."[20]

Proponents of this understanding of human sexuality acknowledge that human sexual union can be procreative — or, to use the term that the more secularistic of them prefer, "reproductive." Yet in addition to these "biological" needs, sexual union serves other, more personal values, those, namely, whose existence depends on their being consciously experienced. The fact that such union, at times, results in the conception of a new human being has, in the past and even today, frequently inhibited the realization of these more personal purposes. But today — and this is *the* important consideration — it is possible through efficient methods of contraception to sever the connection between the procreative and unitive or relational dimensions of human sexuality.

The more radical, secularistic proponents of contraception sever this connection totally. As George Gilder so perceptively observed over a quarter of a century ago,

> The members of the sex coalition go well beyond a mere search for better contraceptives. They are not satisfied merely to control the biological tie between intercourse and childbirth. They also want to eliminate the psychological and symbolic connections.... By far the most frequent and durably

important long-term use of sex, they would say, is the fulfillment of the physical and psychological need for orgasmic
pleasure and the communication of affection. For these purposes, sex is most adaptable if it is not connected with procreation, if it is regarded as a completely separate mode of
activity.[21]

It cannot be denied that many people in the Western (and increasingly
the non-Western) world regard the emergence of contraceptive technologies as a truly liberating event. They believe that the effective use of
contraceptives enables human persons to liberate the *personal* and *human* purposes of sexuality and of genital intercourse from the tyranny of
biology. Many today would agree with the claim of the well-known British writer, Ashley Montagu, that

> The pill provides a dependable means of controlling con-
> ception…. [T]he pill makes it possible to render every indi-
> vidual of reproductive age completely responsible for both
> his sexual and his reproductive behavior. *It is necessary to
> be unequivocally clear concerning the distinction between
> sexual behavior and reproductive behavior.* Sexual behavior
> may have no purpose other than pleasure … without the
> slightest intent of reproducing, or it may be indulged in for
> both pleasure and reproduction.[22]

The majority theologians of the Papal Commission and Protestant
authors such as Meilaender, Turner, and Nuechterlein, would not go so
far as Montagu and other secular supporters of contraception and sever
completely the bond between the unitive and procreative meanings of
human sexuality. Nonetheless, they deem the relational or unitive meaning its *personal*, as distinct from its procreative or *biological,* significance, the latter needing to be assumed into consciousness in order to
become human and personal. Coupling this understanding of human
sexuality with the dominion that human persons have over their biological fertility, they contend that if the continued flourishing of biological
fecundity inhibits the expression of the relational or unitive meaning of
sexuality, it is then licit to suppress this "biological given" so that the
personal, relational good of sexuality can be realized. They do not want
to sever the bond between the unitive (personal) and procreative (biological) meaning of our sexuality for the *whole* of the marriage, but they

think it proper intentionally to separate them in *individual acts* if doing so is thought necessary for serving the procreative-unitive meaning of marriage as a whole. Biological fertility is, for them, a lesser good — a good *for* the person (something like a coat), not a good *of* the person. For them goods *of* the person are goods whose existence depends on being consciously experienced. Since fertility does not so depend, it is not this kind of a good. On the other hand, they consider the union made possible by sexual coition — the unitive or relational aspect of our sexuality — to be a good *of* the person because its existence and flourishing depends on being consciously experienced.

The foregoing has clearly shown the dualistic anthropology and understanding of the human person and of human sexuality crucial to major arguments used to justify contraception. This anthropology distinguishes the person, i.e., the conscious subject of experiences (or, as John Paul II noted in *Evangelium vitae*, no. 19, the subject having "the capacity for verbal and explicit, or at least perceptible, communication"), from the *body* that this person uses, now for this purpose, now for that. If the person is really not his or her own body, then the person's sexuality can be "liberated" from regulation by biological laws and used for "interpersonal communication" or the "fostering of conjugal love."

This anthropology or understanding of the human person is central to the "culture of death." For, if the person is not his or her own body, then, as Germain Grisez has noted, "the destruction of the life of the body is not directly and in itself an attack on a value intrinsic to the human person." Continuing, he said:

> The lives of the unborn, the lives of those not fully in possession of themselves — the hopelessly insane and the "vegetating" senile — and the lives of those who no longer can engage in praxis or problem solving, become lives no longer meaningful, no longer valuable, no longer inviolable.[23]

The dualistic anthropology that has led to the justification of abortion on the grounds that the life thus taken, while "biologically" human, is not "meaningfully" human or the life of a "person," and to the justification of euthanasia on the grounds that it serves the needs of the "person" when biological life becomes a burden is thus definitely operative in the ideology behind contraception, even if this is not acknowledged by many.

I turn now to consider the *moral methodology* employed in the justification of contraception, in particular, contraception by married couples.

This methodology is clearly evident in the argument based on the distinction between individual or "isolated" marital acts and marriage as a whole or totality. This argument acknowledges (as Montagu and the most secular advocates of contraception do not) that procreation is indeed a good of marriage, and that marriage and children go together. But, this argument claims, the procreative good of marriage is properly respected and honored even when individual acts of marriage are deliberately made infertile, as long as those acts are ordered to the expression of love and to a generous fecundity within the marriage as a whole.

It will be useful here to review this very illuminating passage. It reads:

> When man interferes with the procreative purpose of individual acts by contracepting, he does this with the intention of regulating and not excluding fertility. Then he unites the material finality toward fecundity which exists in intercourse with the formal finality of the person and renders the entire process human.... Conjugal acts which by intention are infertile or which are rendered infertile are ordered to the expression of the union of love; that love, however, reaches its culmination in fertility responsibly accepted. For that reason other acts of union are in a certain sense incomplete, and they receive their full moral quality with ordination toward the fertile act.... Infertile conjugal acts constitute a totality with fertile acts and have a single moral specification.[24]

The "single moral specification" or moral object of this totality is the fostering of love responsibly toward a generous fecundity.

Note that this passage considers "recourse to the rhythm of the cycle" or periodic abstinence as simply another way of contracepting; it equates "acts which by intention are infertile," that is, marital acts chosen while the wife is not fertile, and acts "which are rendered infertile." The authors, in other words, see absolutely no *moral* difference between contraception and "recourse to the cycle." The latter is simply another way of contracepting.[25] They do so because they consider the moral "intentions" to be the same in both cases. Their "intention" is to avoid a pregnancy, perhaps for very serious and good reasons. I will return to this issue below.

The central claim of this passage is that the moral object specifying what couples who "responsibly" contracept individual acts of marital congress are doing is "fostering love responsibly toward a generous fecundity." Their aim, their "intention," as Meilaender and Turner later put it in their *First Things* essay, is to "nourish simultaneously the procreative and unitive purposes of their marriage."

This claim is rooted in the idea that we can identify the moral object specifying a human act *only* by considering the act in its "totality." According to this method of making moral decisions, it is not possible to determine the moral species of an action — its "moral object" — without taking into account the "intention" or end for whose sake the choice is made along with the foreseeable consequences for the persons concerned. If one does this, so the argument goes, one can conclude that, if the choice to contracept individual acts is directed to the end of nourishing conjugal love so that the good of procreation can also be served, then one can rightly say that *what* the spouses are doing — the *moral object* of their choice — is to foster conjugal love toward a generous fecundity, obviously something good, not bad.

But this reasoning is specious. It is so because it *re-describes* the contraceptive act, in fact, a whole series of contraceptive acts, in terms of hoped-for benefits. The *remote* or *further* end for whose sake the couple contracepts individual acts of sexual union may indeed be to nourish simultaneously the unitive and procreative goods of marriage. This end is indeed "intended." And this end, this "intention," is good. But "intended" also is the *choice* to contracept — and the couple cannot *not choose*, cannot *not intend,* to contracept. But this specious moral reasoning conceals this "moral object." This reasoning, moreover, relies on a faulty understanding of the marital *act*. According to this reasoning, which re-describes the spouses' behavior in terms of hoped-for benefits, the marital act is intended to foster love between spouses, to unite them. But it is not, as such, intended to be open to the gift of life; rather the marriage *as a whole* in which particular acts occur is so intended. Its proponents would surely hold that spouses ought not, in choosing to unite genitally, freely intend to set aside its unitive dimension. Why, then, do they hold that they can freely intend, in uniting genitally, to set aside its procreative dimension? They can do so only because, as we have seen, they regard this dimension as merely "biological," a "lesser" good than the "personal" good of being sexually united.

The moral methodology used, in other words, is consequentialistic. It fails to recognize that the morality of human acts, as we saw in Chapter Two and as John Paul II has so correctly said, "depends primarily and fundamentally on the 'object' rationally chosen by the deliberate will."[26] With respect to contraception that object is *not* "to foster love responsibly toward a generous fecundity" or to nourish simultaneously the unitive and procreative goods of marriage. Precisely what this object is will be taken up below. My point here, however, is that the consequentialist moral reasoning used in this central argument to justify contraception is plausible only because it re-describes the object of choice — contraception — in terms of the hoped-for benefits of contracepting individual acts of sexual union.

We have now seen the anthropology and moral methodology underlying the defense of contraception. The anthropology, a dualistic one, regards the person primarily as a subject of enduring experiences who uses his or her body now for this purpose, now for that. It likewise locates the *human* and *personal* meaning of human sexuality in its *relational* significance, i.e., its ability to allow two subjects of enduring experiences to enter into deep interpersonal union, while regarding the *procreative* meaning of human sexuality as of itself subpersonal, part of the subhuman world of nature over which the person has been given dominion. This anthropology, as has been shown, is central to the "culture of death."

The moral methodology employed is a form of consequentialism or proportionalism, one that re-describes chosen deeds in terms of their hoped-for benefits and by doing so conceals their true nature. This moral methodology is also central to the specious rationalizations used to justify the killings characteristic of the "culture of death." Thus abortion is not recognized as the intentional killing of an unborn child but is rather re-described as an act protecting the mother's health or the family's stability or something of this kind; rather than being called killing, euthanasia is re-described as helping persons to die with dignity, etc.

B. Recourse to the Rhythm of the Cycle: Its Underlying Anthropology and Moral Methodology

The anthropology supporting the practice of periodic continence as the way to harmonize the requirements of conjugal love with respect for the good of procreation is holistic; i.e., it regards the human person as a unity of body and soul. The person is, in the unity of body and soul, the subject of moral actions.[27] On this anthropology, the body and bodily life are integral to the person, goods *of* the person, not merely *for* the person.

Human persons are, in other words, body persons. When God created Man, he did not, as some dualistic-minded defenders of contraception claim, create "an isolated subjectivity ... who experiences existence in

Set

Ashely + O'Rourke

Compendium

c 23b 586 a ad
1 64 22 ebd
560fd 8b
1e 372 53

q d
GR $ ẽ 4 JV v 4

[either] a female body-structure ... [or] a male body-structure."[28] Quite to the contrary, God, in creating *human* persons, created bodily, sexual persons: "male and female he created them" (Gen 1:27). The human body expresses the human person; and since the human body is inescapably either male or female, it expresses a man-person or a woman-person. Precisely because of their sexual differences, manifest in their bodies, the man-person and the woman-person can give themselves to one another bodily. Moreover, since the body, male or female, is the expression of a human person, a man and a woman, in giving their bodies to one another, give their *persons* to one another. The bodily gift of a man and a woman to each other is the outward sign, the sacrament, of the *communion of persons* existing between them. The body is, therefore, the means and the sign of the gift of the male-person to the female-person. Pope John Paul II calls this capacity of the body to express the communion of persons the *nuptial meaning* of the body.[29]

In addition, human fertility or fecundity is *not* some subhuman, subpersonal aspect of human sexuality. As Vatican Council II clearly affirms, "Man's sexuality and the faculty of generating life wondrously surpass the lower forms of life" (Pastoral Constitution on the Church in the Modern World *Gaudium et spes,* no. 51). Pope John Paul II pointedly observes that human fertility "is directed to the generation of a human being, and so by its nature it surpasses the purely biological order and involves a whole series of personal values" (Apostolic exhortation *Familiaris consortio,* no. 11). The procreative meaning of human sexuality, in this non-dualistic anthropology, is *not* subhuman or subpersonal, in need of "being assumed" into the human. It is human and personal to begin with.

The rationale supporting recourse to the rhythm of the cycle does not judge the morality of human acts in terms of hoped-for results or of the anticipated overall proportion of good and evil that will come about. It holds, rather, that the morality of human actions depends on both the *end intended* and the *object chosen* and, because chosen, also *intended.* It distinguishes between the ulterior or remote end for whose sake one chooses to do *this,* and the proximate or immediate end, which is precisely the freely chosen object. Both end intended and object chosen must be morally good, i.e., in conformity with right reason; if either is not in accord with the truth, then the entire action is vitiated. But the primary source of the morality of the act is, as noted above, the "object" freely and rationally chosen by the acting subject. This is precisely *what one chooses to do.* The moral methodology underlying the practice of contraception ignores this object, the immediate end of one's choice to do *this* here and now, and focuses on the remote end or further intention of the act, i.e., the reason why one chooses to do this here and now. As we have seen, this consequentialist methodology conceals and keeps hidden from view the precise object of one's freely chosen act and *re-describes* it in terms of its hoped-for benefits, the remote end intended by the acting person, the object of one's "further" intention.

The non-consequentialist way of making moral judgments on which recourse to the rhythm of the cycle is based recognizes, as Pope John Paul II emphasizes, "that there are objects of the human act which are by their nature 'incapable of being ordered' to God, because they radically contradict the good of the person made in his image." Continuing, the pope says:

> These are the acts which, in the Church's moral tradition, have been termed "intrinsically evil"(*intrinsece malum*); they are such *always and per se,* in other words, on account of their very object, and apart from the ulterior intentions of the one acting and the circumstances (*Veritatis splendor,* no. 80).

We need now to examine the moral object specifying the act of contraception in order to show that it is indeed an anti-life kind of act.

3. CONTRACEPTION: AN ANTI-LIFE ACT

In order to pass moral judgment on contraception, it is first necessary to know precisely what we are speaking of. It is essential to provide an accurate description of the kind of human act an act of contraception is and then to judge whether it is a human act in accordance with right reason, with the truth, or not, and, if not, why not.

We have seen already that human acts are specified primarily by the "object" freely and rationally chosen by the deliberate will. But what is the "object" freely chosen in contraception? Pope Paul VI offers a good description when he says that the Church's teaching on the immorality of contraception excludes "every action, whether in anticipation of the conjugal act, or in its accomplishment, or in the development of its natural consequences, proposes [the Latin text reads *intendat*], either as end or as means, to impede procreation [here the Latin text reads: *ut procreatio impediatur*]" (*Humanae vitae,* no. 14). Paul here refers to the conjugal act, since his encyclical was concerned with contraception by married couples. But, if "conjugal act" is changed to "genital act," Paul's description accurately identifies the "object" morally specifying an act as contraceptive, whether within marriage or not.

As this description shows, the object freely chosen and willed by someone who engages in an act of contraception is precisely to impede the beginning of a new human life or to impede procreation. It is reasonable to think that a certain kind of behavior — genital behavior — is the kind of behavior in and through which new human life can come to be. If one does not want that life to come to be, perhaps for very good reasons (e.g., the woman's health, inability properly to care for a new baby, etc.), one therefore chooses to do something to impede the beginning of the new human life that one believes that genital behavior might initiate. If one did not reasonably think that this kind of behavior — genital behavior — could result in the beginning of a new human life, one would have no reason to contracept. If one wanted that life to come to be, obviously one would not contracept in order to impede its beginning. Contraception makes sense, i.e., is an *intelligible* human act, only because one does not want new human life to come into existence as a result of another kind of human activity, namely genital activity. As Mosier so well put it in the essay cited early in this work, "contraception is an act that can only express the will that *any* baby that might result from *this* sexual encounter not be conceived.... it [thus] manifests a will aimed directly against new life."[30]

This analysis of the object specifying an act as one of contraception makes it clear that contraception, although related to genital/sexual acts, is not itself a sexual or genital act. Fornication, adultery, masturbation, and marital coition are sexual/genital acts. But if a fornicating couple, an adulterous couple, or a married couple contracept, they choose to do something distinct from the genital act they likewise choose to engage in. In other words, they choose (a) to engage in genital coition and (b) to do something prior to, during, or subsequent to their freely chosen genital coition precisely to impede procreation, i.e., to impede the beginning of the new human life that they reasonably believe could begin in and through the freely chosen genital coition. The act specified by the second choice, (b), is the act of contraception. It is not even necessary for the person who contracepts to engage in genital coition. For instance, suppose a father provides a home for his newly married daughter and her husband. His daughter and her husband abhor contraception, deeming it a grave moral evil. They would never contracept, although perhaps they plan to practice periodic continence until they can move into their own quarters. But the girl's father, in order to make sure that she does not conceive while living in his house, regularly puts contraceptive pills into his daughter's cereal in the morning. He is the one who is choosing to contracept, not his daughter.[31]

Since the contraceptive act is distinct from any sexual act to which it is related, it cannot be considered a part or element of a sexual act and justified on the alleged grounds that it is merely a part of a larger whole, for instance, the marital or conjugal act. This, in essence, is what the specious argument considered above seeks to do, namely, to justify contraception as simply an aspect of a totality of marital acts that nourish both the unitive and procreative goods of marriage. But, as has now been made clear, contraception is not a part or aspect of any marital act or series thereof; it is a distinct kind of human act, specified by the choice to impede the beginning of new human life, either as an end or as a means to some further end, one perhaps good in itself.

Since contraception is specified precisely by the choice to impede the beginning of new human life, it is an anti-life kind of act, one expressing a contra-life will. It is precisely because contraception is specified by a contra-life will that it was, as we saw earlier, regarded for centuries as analogous to homicide by Christian writers. This analogy, a contemporary author rightly says, "no longer surprises us if we look not exclusively at the material nature of the behaviour in the two cases [contraception and homicide], but rather at the intention or movement of the will that has recourse to contraception. Ultimately, in fact, the decision is rationalized and motivated by the judgment: 'It is not good that a new human person should exist.' "[32] Contraception is always seriously wrong because it is always gravely immoral to adopt by choice the proposal to damage, destroy, or impede the good of human life.

If the contraception fails and a child is conceived despite the steps taken deliberately to prevent its life from beginning, the child comes to be as an "unwanted" child. This does not mean that those who sought to prevent his or her conception will now resort to abortion — for they may resolutely have set their hearts and minds against abortion, as did Nuechterlein and his wife, as we have seen. But one can hardly say that a child conceived despite efforts to prevent its conception is a "wanted child." Its initial status is that of an unwanted child and is so because its parents have intentionally done something to "unwant" it, namely, to contracept, to impede the beginning of its life.

This is not true of couples who have "recourse to the rhythm of the cycle" or to periodic abstinence and who avoid irresponsibly causing a pregnancy by abstaining from the marital act at times when they believe that the wife is fertile and hence could conceive.[33] It is true that, like a contracepting couple, they do not "want" to have a child in the sense that they do not, for good reasons, want to cause a pregnancy. But not wanting to have a child in this sense is quite different from not wanting to have the child one could have as a result of *this freely chosen act of sexual union* and then freely choosing to do something to *impede that prospective child's coming into being.* Couples who contracept do not "want" a child in this second sense, and hence if it does come to be despite their contraceptive efforts to prevent it from coming to be, it comes to be as an "unwanted" child. But a child conceived by a couple having recourse to the rhythm of the cycle does not come to be as an "unwanted" child because they have done nothing to "unwant" this particular child. He or she may be a "surprise" baby, but not an "unwanted" baby.[34]

4. CONTRACEPTION: BOTH ANTI-LOVE AND ANTI-LIFE

As we have seen, the principal argument proposed by John Paul II as pope against contraception is that it violates marital love and falsifies the language of the body: the natural dynamism of the conjugal act, which is ordered to the procreation and education of children and the mutual love of the spouses, is overlaid with an objectively contradictory language: a refusal to give oneself fully to the other (see Pope John Paul II, Apostolic exhortation *Familiaris consortio,* no. 32).[35] For John Paul II contraception directly violates marital love and marital chastity and only indirectly is opposed to the good of human life.

This argument, which has featured prominently in John Paul II's teaching on marriage and on the malice of contraception, was well expressed by Paul Quay, S.J., in the early 1960s and has been developed by Dietrich von Hildebrand, Mary Joyce, and others.[36] I believe it true that, by contracepting, a married couple fail to give themselves to each other fully and unreservedly. Yet the "not-giving" entailed is *not* the object specifying the choice to contracept, and most married couples who do contracept would vehemently deny that they are refusing to give themselves to one another. Nuechterlein, in his *First Things* article, illustrates this. He says that "if someone had told us [his wife and himself] that we were 'withholding our fertility' from one another' [or 'not giving themselves to one another'] he would have met with blank incomprehension."[37] The "not-giving" is *praeter intentionem* or outside the scope of the intentions of the married couples who are contracepting. It is, I believe, an *effect* or *consequence* of their contracepting their sexual union, but for the most part they do not consciously recognize this. It is surely *not* "the proximate end of a deliberate decision which determines the act of willing on the part of the acting person," as John Paul II himself describes the object morally specifying a human act in *Veritatis splendor*, no. 78. Indeed, contracepting married couples commonly attempt to justify their choice to contracept by claiming that contraception *is necessary* in order for them to express their love for one another. I will return to this issue later.

Although the argument summarized here is the principal one used by John Paul II to show that it is wrong for married couples to contracept, in some of his writings he has focused attention on the anti-life character of contraception. Thus, in a homily during a Mass for youth in Nairobi, Kenya, he pointed out that the fullest sign of spousal self-giving occurs when couples willingly accept children. Citing *Gaudium et spes*, no. 50, he said: "That is why *anti-life* actions such as contraception and abortion are wrong and are unworthy of good husbands and wives."[38] Moreover, writing as the philosopher Karol Wojtyla, Pope John Paul II had earlier written that the ultimate end served by the sexual urge in human persons, men and women "is the very existence of the [human] species. It follows therefore that that urge, on account of its very own nature, aims at the transmission of life, because on that depends the good of the human species."[39]

In addition, the human sexual urge aims at transmitting *personal* life, and the love of husband and wife, the philosopher Wojtyla argued, is shaped by this good. Indeed, as he says:

> Looked at more closely and concretely, these two persons, the man and the woman, facilitate the existence of another concrete person, their own child, blood of their blood, and flesh of their flesh. This person is at once an affirmation and a continuation of their own lives. The natural order of human existence is not in conflict with love between persons but in strict harmony with it.[40]

Thus John Paul II clearly recognizes the anti-life nature of contraception. It is both *anti-love* and *anti-life*. In his papal writings on marriage and the family, John Paul has obviously concluded that he can best persuade married couples to reject contraception by stressing its character as an act incompatible with conjugal love. And, if we think clearly about things, this is true, even if the precise "object" of contraception is to impede the beginning of new human life and *not* the "not-giving of spouses to one another."

Spouses cannot contracept merely by taking thought. They do so by choosing to do something to their body-persons, and different contraceptives work in different ways to "impede procreation." I here omit discussion of devices allegedly "contraceptive" that are either definitively abortifacient (e.g., morning-after pills, Norplant) or may "work" by preventing implantation in the event that conception occurs (e.g., the pills in use today and, for the most part, IUDs). I hence limit consideration to the so-called "barrier" (condoms, diaphragms, etc.) and "chemical" (spermicidal jellies and the like) methods.

Now consider this. A person does not put on gloves to touch a beloved one tenderly, unless one thinks that some disease may be communicated. But is pregnancy a disease? And is not the use of condoms, diaphragms, spermicidal jellies, and the like similar to putting on gloves? Do husband and wife really become "one flesh" if they must arm themselves with protective gear before "giving" themselves to one another genitally? The answers to these questions are obvious, and they help us see why the argument that contraception is anti-love and a falsification of the "language of the body" is true. Spouses who must "protect" themselves from one another in such ways are "not giving" themselves unreservedly to one another as bodily, sexual beings, even if this "not giving" is "outside the scope of their intention."

Contraception is thus anti-love as well as anti-life. It is utterly incompatible with the "culture of life" and the "civilization of love." It is rather the gateway to the "culture of death." This is implicit in the slogan frequently on the lips of those who defend our contraceptive culture by saying that "No unwanted child ought ever to be born." This banal slogan typifies the "culture of death," which seeks to avert the tragedy of an "unwanted child" by preventing its coming into being through contraception, and, should this fail, by abortion. It is utterly opposed to the truth that "no person, i.e., no human being, whether born or unborn, male or female, young or old, genius or demented, ought ever to be unwanted, i.e., unloved." And the only way to build a civilization in which every human person is indeed wanted is to respect both the love-giving (unitive) and life-giving meanings of human sexuality and marriage.

Appendix: Preventing Conception
When in Danger of Rape or After Rape

As we have seen, contraception is an intrinsically evil act and can never be morally justified. Contraception, as a human, moral act is specified by the object freely chosen, and this object is precisely *to impede the beginning of new human life that one reasonably foresees may come into existence through freely chosen genital acts.* Moreover, the *object specifying* a human act, as we have seen and as St. Thomas and Pope John Paul II make clear, is *not* merely some physical performance or outward behavior but is rather shaped by the present *intention* of the acting person: it is precisely what the acting person is freely choosing to do;[41] in contracepting, one is choosing to impede the beginning of a new human life that one believes might begin through a freely chosen genital act.

If a woman is in serious danger of being raped (for instance, if she is in an area where invading soldiers have already raped the women they have encountered), she has a right to protect herself from the rapist's sperm and the further violation to her bodily and personal integrity that his sperm could cause. Were she to use some device that would prevent the rapist's sperm from penetrating her ovum (e.g., a diaphragm or spermicidal jellies), the *object* specifying her act would *not* be *to impede the beginning of a new life that could begin through her freely chosen genital act*, but rather *to protect herself from further bodily and personal violation by a rapist,* and a human act, specified by this object, is *not* an act of contraception nor does it violate any moral norm. The woman has absolutely no obligation to permit the rapist's sperm to penetrate and fertilize her ovum because she has not consented to a genital act but has rather refused such consent and has been sexually violated by the rapist. In a fine passage Germain Grisez has put the matter this way:

> Rape is the imposition of intimate, bodily union upon some-one without her or his consent, and anyone who is raped rightly resists so far as possible. Moreover, the victim (or potential victim) is right to resist not only insofar as he or she is subjected to unjust force, but insofar as that force imposes the special wrong of uniquely intimate bodily contact. It can scarcely be doubted that someone who cannot prevent the initiation of this intimacy is morally justified in resisting its continuation; for example, if a woman who awakes and

finds herself being penetrated by a rapist need not permit her attacker to ejaculate in her vagina if she can make him withdraw. On the same basis, if they cannot prevent the wrongful intimacy itself, women who are victims (or potential victims) of rape and those trying to help them are morally justified in trying to prevent conception insofar as it is the fullness of sexual union.

The measures taken in this case are a defense of the woman's ovum (insofar as it is a part of her person) against the rapist's sperms (insofar as they are parts of his person). By contrast, if the intimate, bodily union of intercourse is not imposed on the woman but sought willingly or willingly permitted, neither she nor anyone who permits the union can intend at the same time that it not occur. Hence, rape apart, contraceptive measures are chosen to prevent conception not insofar as it is the ultimate completion of intimate bodily union but insofar as it is the beginning of a new and unwanted person.[42]

In other words, the moral object specifying the rape victim's (or potential rape victim's) human act is *not* to prevent the conception of a new human person but rather to prevent ultimate completion of an unjust act of sexual violence.

Similarly, a woman who has suffered the horrible violence of being raped, but who has not, prior to being raped, sought to protect herself from further violence from the rapist's sperm, can legitimately protect herself from the further violation that would be done to herself were the rapist's sperm to penetrate her ovum. Thus Directive 36 of the *Ethical and Religious Directives for Catholic Health Care Facilities*, promulgated by the National Conference of Catholic Bishops of the United States in 1994, reads as follows:

A female who has been raped should be able to defend herself against a potential conception from the sexual assault. If, after appropriate testing, there is no evidence that conception has occurred already, she may be treated with medications that would prevent ovulation, sperm capacitation, or fertilization. It is not permissible, however, to initiate or to recommend treatments that have as their purpose or direct effect the removal, destruction, or interference with the implantation of a fertilized ovum.[43]

In other words, human acts can legitimately be taken to protect the woman who has been raped from being made pregnant by the rapist's sperm. Such acts are *not acts of contraception,* which is intrinsically evil and can *never* be morally justified. Such acts are not acts of contraception because the *object* freely chosen and morally specifying them is *not* the impeding of a new human life that could begin through a freely chosen genital act (=definition of contraception) but is rather the *protecting of the raped woman from further violence by the rapist.*[44]

ENDNOTES

1. Gilbert Meilaender and Philip Turner, "Contraception: A Symposium," *First Things*, No. 88 (December, 1998) 24.
2. James Nuechterlein, "Catholics, Protestants, and Contraception," *First Things,* No. 92 (April, 1999) 10.
3. Ibid.
4. Pope John XIII established this Commission, whose function was exclusively to offer advice to the pope, in 1963. After Pope John's death Pope Paul VI ordered that it continue its work. The Commission's original charge was to determine whether the newly discovered "anovulant" pill was indeed a contraceptive (as Pope Pius XII had judged in an address given to a Congress of Hematologists on September 12, 1958, less than a month before he died), but it soon began to open up the entire issue of contraception. The Commission soon divided into a "minority," which held that the Church's teaching on the immorality of contraception is true and cannot change, and a "majority," which held that contraception by married couples can be justified. The Commission completed its work in 1966. Although its findings were supposed to have been given *only* to the Holy Father, the Commission's papers were leaked to the press in July 1967 and published in the United States in the *National Catholic Reporter.* The Commission issued four documents; all can be found in *The Birth-Control Debate: Interim History from the Pages of the National Catholic Reporter,* ed. Robert Hoyt (Kansas City: National Catholic Reporter, 1969). One, expressing the minority view, was entitled in Latin *"Status Quaestionis: Doctrina Ecclesiae Eiusque Auctoritatis,"* and is given the title "The State of the Question: A Conservative View" in the Hoyt volume. Three documents set forth

the majority position: (1) a rebuttal of the minority view ("*Documentum Syntheticum de Moralitate Nativitatum*" in Latin; entitled "The Question Is Not Closed: The Liberals Reply" in Hoyt); (2) the final theological report of the majority ("*Schema Documenti de Responsabili Paternitate*" in Latin and called "On Responsible Parenthood: The Final Report" in Hoyt); and (3) a pastoral paper, written in French under the title "*Indications Pastorales*" ("Pastoral Approaches" in Hoyt).

An interesting account of the Commission and its work, written by one fully in agreement with the "majority" position, is given by Robert McClory, *Turning Point: The Inside Story of the Papal Birth Control Commission, and How Humanae Vitae Changed the Life of Patty Crowley and the Future of the Church* (New York: Crossroad, 1995).

5. "On Responsible Parenthood," in Hoyt, p. 88.
6. "The Question Is Not Closed," in ibid., p. 72.
7. Alicia Mosier, "Contraception: A Symposium," *First Things* 88 (December, 1998) 26.
8. A better translation of the Latin text of *Humanae vitae* to which Mosier refers is "to impede procreation" insofar as the Latin reads "*ut procreatio impediatur.*"
9. Alicia Mosier, "Contraception: A Symposium," *First Things*, No. 88 (December, 1998), 26-27.
10. See Germain Grisez, Joseph Boyle, John Finnis, and William E. May, " 'Every Marital Act Ought To Be Open to New Life': Toward a Clearer Understanding," *The Thomist* 52 (1988) 365-426; reprinted in *The Teaching of Humanae Vitae: A Defense* (San Francisco: Ignatius Press, 1988), pp. 33-116.
11. See, for instance, the following:

(1) St. John Chrysostom, *Homily 24 on the Epistle to the Romans, PG* 60.626-627: "Why do you sow where the field is eager to destroy the fruit? Where there are medicines of sterility? Where there is murder before birth? You do not even let a harlot remain only a harlot, but you make her a murderess as well. Do you see that from drunkenness comes fornication, from fornication adultery, from adultery murder? Indeed, it is something worse than murder and I do not know what to call it; for she does not kill what is formed but prevents its formation. What then? Do you contemn the gift of God, and fight with his law? What is a curse, do you seek as though it were a blessing? Do you make the anteroom of birth the anteroom of slaugh-

ter? Do you teach the woman who is given to you for the procreation of offspring to perpetuate killing?" Cited by John T. Noonan, Jr., in his *Contraception: A History of Its Treatment by Catholic Theologians and Canonists* (Cambridge, MA: The Belknap Press of Harvard University, 1965), p. 98. On pp. 91-94 of this work Noonan shows that contraception, along with abortion, was considered equivalent to murder in such early Christian writings as *The Didache* and *The Epistle to Barnabas.* As Noonan shows in later sections of his work, e.g., pp. 146, 232-237, this tradition perdured in the Church for centuries.

(2) St. Thomas Aquinas, *Summa contra gentiles,* Bk. 3, chap. 122: "Nor, in fact, should it be deemed a slight sin for a man to arrange for the emission of semen apart from the proper purpose of generating and bringing up children ... the inordinate emission of semen is incompatible with the natural good of preserving the species. Hence, after the sin of homicide whereby a human nature already in existence is destroyed, this type of sin appears to take next place, for by it the generation of human nature is impeded."

(3) The *"Si aliquis"* canon, which was integrated into the canon law of the Church in the *Decretum Greg. IX,* lib. V, tit., 12, cap. V and was part of the Church's canon law from the mid-thirteenth century until 1917, clearly likened contraception to murder. It declared: "If anyone for the sake of fulfilling sexual desire or with premeditated hatred does something to a man or a woman, or gives something to drink, so that he cannot generate or she cannot conceive or offspring be born, let him be held as a murderer." Text in *Corpus iuris canonici,* ed. A. L. Richter and A. Friedberg (Leipzig: Tauchnitz, 1881), 2.794.

(4) In its treatment of marriage, the *Roman Catechism* declared: "Whoever in marriage artificially prevents conception, or procures an abortion, commits a most serious sin: the sin of premeditated murder" (Part II, chap. 7, no. 13). It should be noted that Pope Paul VI explicitly refers to this text in a footnote to no. 14 of *Humanae vitae* (footnote no. 16), precisely where Paul defines contraception as every act prior to intercourse, during it, or in the course of its natural effect that proposes (the Latin text reads *intendat*), either as end or as means, to impede procreation (*ut procreatio impediatur*).

(5) John Calvin, in his commentary on the sin of Onan in Genesis 38, had this to say: "Onan not only defrauded his brother of the right due him, but also preferred his semen to putrefy on the ground....The

voluntary spilling of semen outside of intercourse between man and woman is a monstrous thing. Deliberately to withdraw from coitus in order that semen may fall on the ground is doubly monstrous. For this is to extinguish the hope of the race and to kill before is born the hoped-for offspring.... . If any woman ejects a foetus from her womb by drugs, it is reckoned a crime incapable of expiation, and deservedly Onan incurred upon himself the same kind of punishment, infecting the earth by his semen in order that Tamar might not conceive a future human being as an inhabitant of the earth." *Commentaries on the First Book of Moses Called Genesis*, ch. 38:9,10; quoted in Charles D. Provan, *The Bible and Birth Control* (Monongahela, PA: Zimmer Printing, 1989), p. 15. Provan points out that the editor of the *unabridged* series of Calvin's Commentaries, published by Baker Book House, has omitted the commentary on these two verses of Genesis.

12. See, for instance, his apostolic exhortation *Familiaris consortio (The Role of the Christian Family in the Modern World)*, no. 32.
13. On this see Paul F. deLadurantaye, " 'Irreconcilable Concepts of the Human Person' and the Moral Issue of Contraception: An Examination of the Personalism of Louis Janssens and of Pope John Paul II," *Anthropotes: Rivista di Studi sulla Persona e la Famiglia* 13.2 (1997) 433-456. This essay is a summary of deLadurantaye's 1997 S.T.D. dissertation under the same title at the John Paul II Institute for Studies on Marriage and Family, Washington, D.C.
14. See endnote 5, above.
15. "The Question Is Not Closed," in Hoyt, p. 69.
16. "On Responsible Parenthood," in Hoyt, p. 87.
17. "The Question Is Not Closed," in Hoyt, p. 71.
18. "On Responsible Parenthood," in Hoyt, p. 89.
19. Louis Janssens, "Considerations on *Humanae Vitae*," *Louvain Studies* 2 (1969) 249.
20. Anthony Kosnik, et al., *Human Sexuality: New Directions in American Catholic Thought* (New York: Paulist, 1977), p. 83.
21. George Gilder, *Sexual Suicide* (New York: Quadrangle Books, 1973), p. 34.
22. Ashley Montagu, *Sex, Man, and Society* (New York: G. P. Putnam's, 1969), pp. 13-14; emphasis in the original.
23. Germain Grisez, "Dualism and the New Morality," *Atti del congresso internazionale Tommaso d'Aquino nel suo settimo centenario,* vol. 5, *L'agire morale* (Naples: Edizioni Domenicane Italiane, 1977), p. 325.

24. "The Question Is Not Closed," in Hoyt, p. 72.
25. In fact, some Catholic advocates of contraception, for instance, Rosemary Ruether and Louis Janssens, claim that with barrier methods of contraception one puts a "spatial" barrier between ovum and sperm, whereas with the use of periodic abstinence one puts a "temporal" barrier between ovum and sperm. Thus Ruether writes: "...sexual acts which are calculated to function only during the times of sterility are sterilizing the act just as much as any other means of rendering the act infertile. *It is difficult to see why there should be such an absolute moral difference between creating a spatial barrier to procreation and creating a temporal barrier to procreation"* ("Birth Control and Sexuality," in *Contraception and Holiness: The Catholic Predicament,* Introduced by Thomas D. Roberts, S.J. [New York: Herder and Herder, 1964], p. 74; emphasis added).
26. Pope John Paul II, Encyclical *Veritatis splendor ("The Splendor of Truth"),* no. 78.
27. See ibid., no. 48. In this section of his Encyclical Pope John Paul II explicitly refers to defined Catholic teaching on the unity of the human person as a unity of body and soul, namely the Council of Vienne, Constitution *Fides Catholica, DS* 902; Fifth Lateran Council, Bull *Apostolici Regiminis, DS* 1440; and Vatican Council II, Pastoral Consitution on the Church in the Modern World *Gaudium et spes,* no. 14. See footnotes 66 and 67 to no. 48 of *Gaudium et spes.*
28. Anthony Kosnik, et al., *Human Sexuality: New Directions in American Catholic Thought,* pp. 83-84.
29. The "nuptial meaning" of the body is developed in many of the addresses of Pope John Paul II on the "theology of the body." See in particular, "The Nuptial Meaning of the Body" (General Audience of January 9, 1980) in John Paul II, *The Theology of the Body: Human Love in the Divine Plan* (Boston: Pauline Books and Media, 1997), pp. 60-63; "The Man-Person Becomes a Gift in the Freedom of Love" (General Audience of January 16, 1980), in ibid., pp. 63-66; "Mystery of Man's Original Innocence" (General Audience of January 30, 1980), in ibid., pp. 66-69. On this issue see my essay, "Marriage and the Complementarity of Male and Female," chap. 2 of my *Marriage: The Rock on Which the Family Is Built* (San Francisco: Ignatius, 1995), pp. 39-66.
30. Mosier, "Contraception: A Symposium," p. 27.
31. In criticizing an earlier version of the argument given here (see endnote 10, above for bibliographical details of the Grisez et al. ar-

gument), Janet Smith accused the authors of "subjectivism" and of failing to recognize that "what one intends to do is defined as good or bad *independently of any act of the will*" (Janet Smith, *Humanae Vitae: A Generation Later* [Washington, D.C.: The Catholic University of America Press, 1991], p. 355). This criticism overlooks the fact that Paul VI, in order to reject every sort of contraception, had to define it in terms of the intention to impede procreation. Smith's critique in fact completely misunderstands the Grisez et al. argument; nowhere in her critique does she even report on the *arguments* given by Grisez et al. to show why it is always wrong to have an anti-life will. For a response to her criticisms, see William E. May, "A Review of Janet Smith's *Humanae Vitae: A Generation Later*," *The Thomist* 57 (1993) 155-161.

32. Carlo Caffarra, "*Humanae Vitae* Venti Anni Dopo," in "*Humanae Vitae: 20 Anni Dopo: Atti del II Congresso Internazionale di Teologia Morale* (Milan: Edizioni Ares, 1989), p. 192; English translation in *Why Humanae Vitae Was Right: A Reader,* ed. Janet Smith (San Francisco: Ignatius, 1993), p. 267.

33. I acknowledge that some individuals *can* abuse "recourse to the rhythm of the cycle," regarding it merely as another way of impeding new human life. Such individuals have, in fact, a "contraceptive mentality," and may decide to impede new life by this means rather than by barrier or chemical means for aesthetic or hygienic reasons. St. Augustine, who used a primitive form of "fertility awareness" (refraining from having sex with his mistress during certain periods), testifies to this, for in his *Confessions* he acknowledges that his son Adeotatus "was conceived against our wills," but that, once born, he forced Augustine and his mistress to love him (see Book 4, chap. 2). Such individuals are, in effect, putting a "temporal barrier between sperm and ovum" (as Rosemary Ruether claims) precisely in order to impede procreation. But those who have "recourse to the rhythm of the cycle," choosing to abstain, not as a means of impeding procreation but of not causing a pregnancy when it would not be prudent to do so, do not have this anti-life will. If told that they "are putting a temporal barrier between sperm and ovum," they would rightly find the charge incomprehensible. Augustine would not find it so because he apparently thought that this was precisely what he was doing, for he was contracepting.

34. The argument briefly set forth in this section is developed at much greater length by Grisez et al. in the essay referred to in endnote 10

above. It is masterfully presented in by Grisez in Vol. 2 of his *The Way of the Lord Jesus, Living a Christian Life* (Quincy, IL: Franciscan Press, 1993), pp. 506-519.

35. Pope John Paul II develops this argument in many of his papal writings. Janet Smith provides an excellent synthesis of his thought on this matter in her *Humanae Vitae: A Generation Later,* pp. 98-129. See also Paul deLadurantaye, work cited in note 13, above.

36. See Paul Quay, S.J., "Contraception and Conjugal Love," *Theological Studies* 22 (1961) 18-40. See also Mary Joyce, *The Meaning of Contraception* (Collegeville, MN: The Liturgical Press, 1969), Dietrich von Hildebrand, *The Encyclical Humanae Vitae: A Sign of Contradiction* (Chicago: Franciscan Herald Press, 1969), and John Kippley, *Sex and the Marriage Covenant: A Basis for Morality* (Cincinnati: Couple-to-Couple League, 1991), pp. 50-76. In *Contraception and the Natural Law* (Milwaukee: Bruce, 1964), pp. 33-35, Germain Grisez offers an appreciative critique of this argument as expressed by Paul Quay.

37. Nuechterlein, "Catholics, Protestants, and Contracepton," 10.

38. Pope John Paul II, "Homily at Mass for Youth, Nairobi, Kenya," *L'Osservatore Romano*, English ed., August 26, 1985, 8, p. 5; emphasis added. In saying this John Paul II was in some ways also reaffirming the thought of Pope Paul VI who referred to *Humanae vitae* as a defense of life "at the very source of human existence," and, citing the teaching of *Gaudium et spes*, no. 51, on abortion and infanticide, added: "We did no more than accept this charge when, ten years ago, we published the Encyclical *Humanae vitae*. This document drew its inspiration from the inviolable teachings of the Bible and the Gospel, which confirms the norms of the natural law and the unsuppressible dictates of conscience on respect for human life, the transmission of which is entrusted to responsible fatherhood and motherhood" (Paul VI, "Homily on the Feast of Sts. Peter and Paul," *L'Osservatore Romano*, English ed., July 6, 1978, 2, p. 3).

39. Karol Wojtyla, "Instynkt, milosc, malzenstwo," *Tygodnik Powszechny* 8 (1952) 39. Quoted in John M. Grondelski, *Fruitfulness as an Essential Dimension in Acts of Conjugal Love: An Interpretative Study of the Pre-Pontifical Thought of John Paul II* (New York: Fordham University Press, 1986), p. 49. I am indebted to Paul deLadurantaye for calling this text to my attention. This entire section of this chapter owes much to the final portion of deLadurantaye's unpublished S.T.D. dissertation, *"Irreconciliable Concepts of the Human Person"*

and the Moral Issue of Contraception: An Examination of the Personalism of Louis Janssens and Pope John Paul II, especially pp. 259-280. As noted in endnote 13 above, a summary of this excellent study is provided in the journal *Anthropotes.*

40. Karol Wojtyla, *Love and Responsibility,* trans. H. Willetts (New York: Farrar, Strauss, Giroux, 1981), pp. 53-54. See *Evangelium vitae,* no. 81: "The meaning of life is found in giving and receiving love, and in this light human sexuality and procreation reach their true and full significance."

41. For St. Thomas see, for example, *Summa theologiae, 2-2, 64, 7:* "moral acts are specified by what is intended, not by what falls outside the scope of one's intentionality" (*actus autem morales recipiunt speciem secundum id quod intenditur, non autem ab eo quod est praeter intentionem*). For Pope John Paul II, see Encyclical *Veritatis splendor,* no. 78.

42. Germain Grisez, *The Way of the Lord Jesus,* Vol. 2, *Living a Christian Life* (Quincy, IL: Franciscan Press, 1993), p. 512.

43. National Conference of Catholic Bishops, *Ethical and Religious Directives for Catholic Health Care Facilities* (Washington, D.C.: United States Catholic Conference, 1995), Directive 36.

44. A sound protocol for caring for women who have been raped has been developed by Eugene F. Diamond, M.D., who clearly identifies both legitimate, non-abortifacient measures that can rightly be taken to prevent conception after rape and abortifacient measures that can in no way be morally employed. See Eugene F. Diamond, M.D., "Rape Protocol," *The Linacre Quarterly* 60.3 (August 1993) 8-19; see also Diamond, "Ovral in Rape Protocols," *Ethics and Medics* 21.10 (October 1996) 2. Diamond shows definitively that ovral cannot be licitly used because it operates to prevent implantation of life already conceived.

Chapter Five

ABORTION AND HUMAN LIFE

Introduction: Structure of This Chapter

Although Chapter One set forth in some detail the Church's teaching on abortion, I begin this chapter with a résumé of that teaching, particularly in order to clarify that teaching on the "definition" of abortion, the question of "ensoulment," and the distinction between "direct" and "indirect" abortion.

I then defend the proposition that it is reasonable to believe that most people begin at fertilization* and unreasonable to deny this (in defending this proposition I criticize opposing views). I do so because the great majority of the arguments advanced to justify abortion, either throughout the entire pregnancy or at least during its early stages, contend that the being killed by abortion is not a human person. Next I consider the special gravity of abortion and the fallacies characterizing the major arguments used to justify it as a woman's right even if one grants that it kills a human person. I then focus on the distinction made by some thinkers today between abortion as "killing" and abortion as "removal" and the argument that the latter can, under certain conditions, be morally justified. Debates among Catholic theologians on the proper moral management of ectopic pregnancies are then considered.

---

*As we will see in this chapter, the only persons who do not begin at fertilization are some monozygotic twins or triplets, etc., of whom *one* may come into existence after fertilization whereas another, so it will be argued, was in being from fertilization onward.

The chapter, therefore, is divided as follows: (1) Résumé and Clarification of Church Teaching; (2) Most People Begin at Fertilization; (3) Abortion's Special Gravity, The "Right" of Women To Abort, The Difference Between a "Right" and a "Liberty"; (4) Abortion as "Killing" vs. Abortion as "Removal"; and (5) The Management of Ectopic Pregnancies. The issue of experimenting on unborn human life is taken up in Chapter Six.

1. RÉSUMÉ AND CLARIFICATION OF CHURCH TEACHING

The *Catechism of the Catholic Church* succinctly summarizes the teaching of the Church — reviewed extensively in Chapter One — on the inviolability of human life from its beginning and on the grave moral evil of abortion. Here it will be useful to cite two passages from the *Catechism*, along with their internal citations from Scripture, from the second-century document called the *Didache* (also known as *The Teaching of the Twelve Apostles*), and from Vatican Council II.

> Human life must be respected and protected absolutely from the moment of conception. From the first moment of his existence, a human being must be recognized as having the rights of a person — among which is the inviolable right of every innocent being to life. "Before I formed you in the womb I knew you, and before you were born I consecrated you" (Jer 1.5)). "My frame was not hidden from you, when I was being made in secret, intricately wrought in the depths of the earth" (Ps 139.15) (CCC no. 2270).

> Since the first century the Church has affirmed the moral evil of every procured abortion. This teaching has not changed and remains unchangeable. Direct abortion, that is to say, abortion willed either as an end or a means, is gravely contrary to the moral law. "You shall not kill the embryo by abortion and shall not cause the newborn to perish" (*Didache*, 2.2). "God, the Lord of life, has entrusted to men the noble mission of safeguarding life, and men must carry it out in a manner worthy of themselves. Life must be protected with the utmost care from the moment of conception: abortion and infanticide are abominable crimes" (*Gaudium et spes*, no. 51) (CCC no. 2271).

Moreover, as we saw in Chapter One, Pope John Paul II clearly affirmed that the teaching of the Church on the grave immorality of procured or direct abortion has been infallibly proposed by the ordinary and universal Magisterium of the Church. Mincing no words, he spoke as follows:

> ... by the authority which Christ conferred upon Peter and his Successors, in communion with the Bishops — who on various occasions have condemned abortion and who ..., albeit dispersed throughout the world, have shown unanimous agreement concerning this doctrine — *I declare that direct abortion, that is, abortion willed as an end or as a means, always constitutes a grave moral disorder,* since it is the deliberate killing of an innocent human being. This doctrine is based upon the natural law and upon the written Word of God, is transmitted by the Church's Tradition and taught by the ordinary and universal Magisterium (*Evangelium vitae,* no. 62; emphasis in original).

A. The Definition of Abortion

Shortly before making this powerful declaration John Paul II had defined direct or procured abortion as *"the deliberate and direct killing, by whatever means it is carried out, of a human being in the initial phase of his or her existence, extending from conception to birth"* (no. 58; emphasis in original). Note that here the Pope defines abortion as an act of "killing" and not as the "expelling" from the mother's womb of a living but not yet viable fetus. Some older manuals of Catholic moral theology had defined abortion in this way and used other terms, e.g., "craniotomy," "embryotomy," "feticide," to describe interventions which deliberately caused the death of the unborn child but did not do so by "expelling" it from the womb.[1] I bring this matter up here because of its relevance to the distinction made today by some scholars between abortion as "killing" and abortion as "removal," a matter to be consider later.

B. "Ensoulment" or Infusion of the Immortal Soul

We saw also in Chapter One that the Magisterium of the Church has not expressly committed itself to the position that individual human personal life begins at conception. As John Paul II declared in *Evangelium vitae,* when commenting on the views of those who seek to justify abortion by claiming that the result of conception, at least for a time, cannot be considered personal human life, "what is at stake is so important that, from the standpoint of moral obligation, the mere probability that a human person is involved would suffice to justify an absolutely clear prohibition of any intervention aimed at killing a human embryo." He concluded by saying: "Precisely for this reason, over and above all scientific debates and those philosophical affirmations [concerning the precise moment when a spiritual soul is infused] to which the Magisterium has not yet expressly committed itself, the Church has always taught and continues to teach that the result of human procreation, from the first moment of its existence, must be guaranteed that unconditional respect which is morally due to the human being in his or her totality and unity as body and spirit" (no. 60).[2]

In speaking in this way, Pope John Paul II voices the age-old tradition of the Church. No matter what their own personal views regarding the moment when the spiritual soul was infused into the body, the apostolic fathers, the early Christian apologists, the fathers and doctors of the Church both East and West — indeed, the entire tradition — unanimously condemned procured or direct abortion of any kind as utterly immoral.[3] Thus, for example, the Greek Church Father St. Basil the Great declared that whoever purposely destroys a fetus is a murderer, and it makes no difference whatsoever whether it is formed (animated by a spiritual soul) or unformed (not yet so animated).[4]

I believe that the individual personal human life of most people begins at conception/fertilization and that empirical evidence supports this belief. Later in this chapter this issue will be explored in depth. But it is very important to emphasize here that the Church's teaching on the grave immorality of procured or direct abortion deliberately leaves the question open for discussion. As we saw in Chapter Four, a long tradition in the Church regarded contraception as a gravely immoral *anti-life* kind of act, analogous to murder. It is thus obvious that during the centuries when all Christians judged contraception and abortion as gravely immoral, theoretical differences regarding the precise moment of "ensoulment" or infusion of an immortal soul to "form" the fetus made little or no difference in the practical judgment that every attempt to terminate pregnancy was absolutely immoral, no matter when this attempt was made.[5]

C. "Direct" vs. "Indirect" Abortion

In *Evangelium vitae* Pope John Paul II, like his predecessors in the chair of St. Peter and along with the *Catechism of the Catholic Church*, condemned as intrinsically evil and gravely immoral every act of "procured" or "direct" abortion. Moreover, he clearly defined the meaning of "direct" or "procured" abortion. Explicitly referring to and citing from the teaching of Pope Pius XII,[6] John Paul II said that "direct" abortion includes every act tending to destroy human life in the womb "whether such destruction is intended as an *end* or only as a *means* to an end" (no. 62). By direct or procured abortion, then, one means a human act specified morally as an act of *killing the unborn*. It is so specified because its "object" as a human act is precisely the destruction of unborn human life. This "object" is either the *end* for the sake of which the act is done, or, more frequently, the *means chosen* in order to bring about some *further* end. In any event, this "object" is the *proximate end* willed by the agent; it is the *proximate end* specifying a freely chosen human act, which may also be willed as a *means* to some "further" or "ulterior" end that may have motivated the act (e.g., to avoid the embarrassment of out-of-wedlock pregnancy, to prevent the birth of a child probably suffering from some genetically-induced malady, etc.). And this "object" is precisely the aborting or killing of unborn human life. That life's abortion (killing) cannot *not* be willed by the acting person.[7]

In so-called "indirect" abortion, the killing of the unborn child or its abortion is *not* the object of the act, neither as end nor as means. It is rather, as the passage from Pope Pius XII cited in endnote no. 6 makes clear, the foreseen but "unintended" consequence or result of a medical procedure that itself is specified as an act of healing a sick woman or protecting her life. Neither the end intended nor the means chosen to attain the end in question is the abortion or killing of the unborn. This is foreseen as an inevitable and unavoidable result of the deed chosen to protect or heal or safeguard the mother's life, but it is *not willed by the acting person*. It is "outside the scope of his or her intentions," and can be justified if there is urgent need to protect a great good, such as the life of the mother, and no other alternatives can be used to do so. Thus, for instance, it is morally permissible for a woman suffering from cancer of the uterus to have a hysterectomy or undergo radiation therapy to cure the cancer or protect her from dying of it even if she is pregnant and realizes that the unborn child will die as a result of the hysterectomy or radiation therapy, provided that no alternative therapies exist and those that do exist cannot be postponed until after the baby's safe delivery. The "abortion" in such conditions is no more "directly" willed than is one's baldness, which one foresees will occur as a result of undergoing chemotherapy for a life-threatening cancerous condition. The "baldness" is surely "outside the scope of the agent's intention" and is definitely *not* willed in any way. Similarly, in cases of so-called "indirect" abortion, the abortion or death of the unborn child is also "outside the scope of the agent's intention" and is definitely *not* willed in any way, even "indirectly." The abortion, understood as the death of the unborn child, is in no way willed by the acting person, neither as end nor as means. It is precisely an *unintended* side effect of an action good in itself because the "object" specifying it is precisely the saving or protecting of the mother's life. The unborn child's death is thus not "intended" in any way.

2. IT IS REASONABLE TO BELIEVE THAT MOST PEOPLE BEGIN AT FERTILIZATION AND UNREASONABLE TO DENY THIS

Here I will defend the position that the individual personal human life of most people begins at conception/fertilization. This position, of course, is denied by many. It is denied first of all by those who claim that the being killed by abortion is not even a *human being*, let alone a person. It is denied also by many who grant that the being killed by abortion is a *human being* or *member of the human species*, but who contend that it simply cannot be regarded as a *person* with rights. Still others adopt one or another variant of the "gradualist" view, which holds that at some point during gestation the entity that was conceived *becomes* human and personal in nature. There are many variants to this view, with some holding that a human person is in existence early on in the process, for instance, at implantation, while others claim it does not become a person until some later stage, say, the formation of the neocortex of the brain, the presence of all organ systems, viability, etc. This view, which has wide rhetorical appeal, regards early abortions (those done prior to the event that marks the beginning of personal as opposed to merely biological life, whatever that event might be) as morally permissible, while abortions done later are questionable, and the later an abortion the closer it is to being wrong or more seriously wrong. One of the finest presentations and critiques of these different views is provided by Patrick Lee in *Abortion and Unborn Human Life*, and I urge readers to consult his rigorously argued work.[8] Many others besides Lee have examined this matter in depth, and my obvious debt to them will be noted throughout.

I will first briefly consider some opinions, unfortunately common in our society, that are utterly incompatible with what we *know* about human procreation. I will then take up positions that at least seem more plausible. The falsification of the even more plausible views will help corroborate the claim that it is reasonable to hold that the human personal life of most people begins at conception/fertilization and that it is unreasonable to deny this.

There is no need to waste time with the utterly rhetorical and/or euphemistic assertions identifying the being brought into existence at fertilization as "protoplasmic rubbish" or a "gobbet of meat"[9] or a "blueprint"[10] or "gametic materials" or the "product of conception,"[11] or only a "part of the mother's body."[12] Such views, which rely on rhetoric and the abuse of language, are patently either false or totally inadequate in light of what we actually *know* about the process of human generation. They simply cannot be and ought not to be taken seriously.

Another common set of claims, slightly more credible, that deny the humanity and *a fortiori* the personhood of the human zygote and early embryo appeal to the fact that these organisms do not "appear" to be human or persons. Pictures and drawings of human beings at these stages of development *seem* to support claims of this kind. "How," they ask, "can you say that an organism with no face or hands or feet or organs can possibly be a human being, much less a person?" Or, "How can an organism no larger than the period at the end of a sentence possibly be regarded as a human being, a person?" Germain Grisez points out that arguments of this kind are plausible "because they use imagery and directly affect feelings. Usually, in judging whether or not to apply a predicate [such as *human being* or *person*] to an experienced entity, one does not examine it to see whether it meets a set of intelligible criteria; instead, one judges by appearances, using as guide past experience of individuals of that kind." However, he continues, such claims can be falsified by pointing out "that, while the particular difference [between a human zygote or early embryo and embryos and fetuses at a later stage of development] is striking because of the normal limits of human experience, (nevertheless) entities that are different in that way certainly are living human beings."[13] Stephen Schwarz, whom Grisez commends, has identified the element common to these denials of humanity and/or personhood to the zygote and early embryo and has responded to it decisively. He points out that all these objections are "based on the expectation that what is a person must be like us. It must be the right size (a size like ours); it must have a level of development comparable to ours; it must look like us; it must, like us, be conscious."[14]

But, he continues, "these are not true criteria for being a person [nor for being a human being]." They are rather "simply expressions of our expectations, of what we are used to, of what appears familiar to us. It is not that the zygote fails to be a person [or human being] because it fails these tests; rather, it is we who fail by using these criteria to measure what a person [or human being] is."[15]

It is unreasonable to expect that a human being in the first stages of his or her development will look like a familiar human being, or like a newborn baby or a four-year-old or a teenager, or a mature adult or a wheelchair-bound elderly man or woman. The way these persons "appear" during the early stages of their development says nothing of the status of their *nature* or *being*. Each of us develops and unfolds his or her personality every day of our lives, and we were developing and unfolding them before we were born just as we do so afterwards because we were alive then. This ought not to cause anyone surprise. "Horton," one of Dr. Seuss's lovable characters, hits the nail on the head in *Horton Hears a Who* when he says, "a person's a person, no matter how small."

Another claim denying personhood to the unborn, or at least to many unborn human beings, is widely held today, but it too is readily falsifiable. It is the claim that personhood is a status conferred on entities by others, and it is, surprisingly, held by many in our society. Proponents of this view contend that personhood is a *social status* conferred on an entity by others and that an entity is a *person* only when recognized by others as a person. They believe that this view is supported by the truth that persons exist only with other persons — personhood is *relational* in character.

One advocate of this view, Marjorie Reiley Maguire, proposes that the personhood of the unborn "begins when the bearer of life, the mother, makes a covenant of love with the developing life within her to birth.... The moment which begins personhood ... is the moment when the mother accepts the pregnancy." And, if she does not accept it and decides to abort the "developing life within her," that life must be regarded as not a person, for personhood has not been bestowed on it.[16]

This position, of course, leads to the absurdity that the same being can be simultaneously both a person and not a person; it is a "person," for instance, if at least one person, say its father, recognizes and esteems it as a person; but it is not a "person" if another person, say its mother, refuses to consider it a person. This claim presupposes that human meaning-giving *constitutes* persons; the truth is that human meaning-giving and human societies *presuppose* human persons.[17]

I will now consider and rebut more plausible views that deny personhood to the unborn. These have been well identified by Grisez, who offers excellent critiques of them.[18] In what follows I will use somewhat different categories than the ones he uses, but mine are essentially the same. The principal positions of this kind are the following: (A) personhood requires exercisable cognitive abilities; (B) personhood is dependent on sense organs and a brain (=the "delayed hominization" position); (C) individual persons, as phenomena such as twinning and the "wastage" of embryos prior to implantation indicate, are formed only two weeks after fertilization.

A. Personhood Requires Exercisable Cognitive Abilities

This view, widely held today, contends that for a human being to be regarded as a person, he or she must have developed at least incipiently exercisable capacities or abilities for understanding, choice, and rational communication. Many who hold it — and among its more influential proponents are Michael Tooley, Peter Singer, and Daniel Callahan[19] — are willing to grant that a human being, in the sense of a living biological member of the human species, is in existence from conception/fertilization or at any rate very early afterwards. But they contend that membership in the human species is not a sufficient criterion for personhood because only some members of the human species acquire the property or set of properties necessary if an entity is to be regarded as a "person." In fact, some who hold this position assert that those who believe that membership in the human species is of great moral significance are guilty of a form of discrimination, *speciesism,* a prejudice similar to such immoral prejudices as *racism*. Prominent among those who make this claim is Peter Singer, the champion of "animal rights," who contends that it is far more immoral to torture a kitten than it is to kill an unborn child or a young infant with a debilitating condition such as Down Syndrome.[20] In this view, not only are unborn children nonpersons but so too are newborns and, apparently, adult humans who no longer possess exercisable faculties of knowledge, recognition, consciousness, etc.

The reasoning behind this claim is fallacious. It fails to distinguish between a *radical* capacity or ability and a *developed* capacity or ability. A radical capacity can also be called an *active,* as distinct from a merely *passive,* potentiality. An unborn baby or a newborn child, precisely by reason of its membership in the human species, has the *radical capacity or active potentiality* to discriminate between true and false propositions, to make choices, and to communicate rationally. But in order for the child — unborn or newborn — to *exercise* this capacity or set of capacities, his radical capacity or active potentialilty for engaging in these activities — predictable kinds of behavior for members of the human species — must be allowed to develop. But it could never be developed if it were not there to begin with. Similarly, adult members of the human species may, because of accidents, no longer be capable of actually exercising their capacity or ability to engage in these activities. But this does not mean that they do not have the natural or radical capacity, rooted in their being the kind of beings they are, for such activities. They are simply inhibited by disease or accidents from exercising this capacity. Similarly, members of the species "bald eagle" have the *radical* capacity or *active* potentiality, rooted in their being the kind of beings they are, to soar loftily in the air; eaglets who have not as yet *developed* this capacity and adult eagles whose wings have been broken, are not able to *exercise* this capacity, but the fact that this capacity is not presently exercisable does not mean that it is not a radical capacity or active potentiality rooted in the nature of all members of the species "bald eagle" and not merely potential in a passive sense.

A human embryo has the *active* potentiality or *radical* capacity to develop *from within its own resources* all it needs to exercise the property or set of properties characteristic of adult members of the species. One can say that the human embryo is a human person *with potential*; he or she is *not* merely a *potential person*. Those, like Tooley and Singer, who require that an entity have *exercisable* cognitive abilities, recognize that the unborn have the *potentiality* to engage in cognitive activities. But they regard this as a merely *passive* potentiality and fail to recognize the crucially significant difference between an *active* potentiality and a merely *passive* one. In his excellent development of the significance of this difference, Patrick Lee makes two very important points. The first concerns the *moral* significance of the difference between an *active* and a merely *passive* potentiality. An active potentiality means "that the same entity which possesses it is the same entity as will later exercise that active potentiality. With a passive potentiality, that is not so; that is, the actualization of a passive potentiality often produces a completely different thing or substance [e.g., oxygen has the passive potentiality to become water when appropriately combined with hydrogen]." Lee's second key point answers the question "why should higher mental functions or the capacity or active potentiality for such functions be a trait conferring value on those who have it?" The proper answer is that such functions and the capacity for them are "of ethical significance not because [these functions] are the only intrinsically valuable entities but because entities which have such potentialities are intrinsically valuable. And, *if the entity itself is intrinsically valuable, then it must be intrinsically valuable from the moment that it exists.*"[21]

The claim that not all human beings are persons but that only those who possess exercisable cognitive abilities are to be so regarded, moreover, is marked by debates among its advocates over precisely *which* ability or abilities must be exercisable if an entity is to be classified as a "person." This claim thus inevitably leads to arbitrary and unjust criteria for "personhood." A group of Catholic thinkers in England gives a devastating critique of this arbitrariness, and it is worthwhile to cite it at some length because it so ably pinpoints the arbitrariness involved:

> The rational abilities necessary to these [cognitive] abilities are various, and come in varying degrees in human beings. If actual possession of such abilities is a necessary condition of the claim to be treated justly, questions will have to be faced precisely *which* abilities must be possessed, and how developed they must be before one enjoys this claim to be treated justly. And these questions can be answered only by *choosing* which to count as the relevant abilities and precisely how developed they must be to count. But any such line-drawing exercise is necessarily arbitrary…. Arbitrary choices may be reasonable and unavoidable in determining some entitlements…. But if one's understanding of human worth and dignity commits one to being arbitrary about who are to be treated justly (i.e., about who are the very *subjects* of justice), it is clear that one lacks what is recognisable as a framework of justice. For it is incompatible with our fundamental intuitions about justice that we should determine who are the subjects of justice by arbitrary choice. The need for a non-arbitrary understanding of who are the subjects of justice requires us to assume that *just treatment is owing to all human beings in virtue of their humanity.* This indispensable assumption is also intrinsically reasonable. It is true that the distinctive dignity and value of human life are *manifested* in those specific exercises of developed rational abilities in which we achieve some share in such human goods as truth, beauty, justice, friendship, and integrity. But the necessary rational abilities are acquired in virtue of an underlying or radical capacity, *given with our nature as human beings,* for developing precisely those abilities.[22]

The "only-those-with-exercisable-cognitive-abilities-are-persons" claim is also dualistic because it sharply distinguishes between the "person," the subject with exercisable cognitive abilities, and the living human body which the person, as it were, possesses. It is, of course, true that human persons can do things — think, make free choices, etc. — which show that they are *more* than their bodies and that they are also (or can be) consciously experiencing subjects with cognitive abilities. But, as Grisez notes, "persons can be more than their bodies without being realities other than their bodies, since a whole can be more than one of its parts without being a reality other than that part."[23] There is not one being who breathes, eats, sleeps, feels bodily pain, etc., and another being who thinks, chooses, and is aware of his rights, etc. The same subject, the same *human being*, *is* the living human body and the subject of cognitive activities. The dualistic view of man underlying the claim denying personhood to human beings who lack *exercisable cognitive abilities* is, therefore, a false understanding of man, male and female.[24]

A final comment on this position is that, as Grisez has said, it simply misses "what *person* means in ordinary language," where the word refers to a living, human individual.[25] The legitimate application of this term to non-adult human beings is rooted in its use in referring to adult human beings, who regularly think of their personhood not as a trait that they have acquired at some time in their lives but as an aspect of their very being. If one asks a person when he or she was born, he or she will spontaneously say that he or she was born on his or her day of birth, clearly implying that the person so responding considers himself or herself to be identical in being with the one born on that day. And were one to ask a person, "when were *you* conceived?" the person addressed would spontaneously reply "approximately nine months before I was born," thereby implying that he or she regards himself or herself as the very same being, i.e., person, conceived and born.[26]

B. Personhood Depends on Sense Organs and a Brain: The "Delayed Hominization" Theory

Unlike the claim just considered, this position repudiates a dualistic understanding of the human person; nonetheless, its advocates contend that the early human embryo cannot be considered a person because it lacks sense organs and a brain, material organs necessary for exercising human cognitive and volitional powers.

Among its proponents are several Roman Catholic philosophers and theologians, the more influential of whom are Joseph Donceel, S.J., Thomas A. Shannon, and Allan Wolter, OFM.[27] These writers seek to rehabilitate the "delayed hominization" theory of St. Thomas Aquinas. According to this view, the human embryo undergoes a substantial change from a subhuman entity to a human, personal entity, and does so when its body becomes sufficiently organized to be fit matter for the infusion of a spiritual soul. Donceel proposes that the body formed at conception is capable only of biological, not rational actions. It is capable of the latter only when the neural integration of the entire organism has been established, and this occurs only around the twentieth week of gestation when the cerebral cortex is present, and Shannon and Wolter hold a similar view. Their central claim is that what specifically distinguishes human and personal nature as superior to that of other animals is reason, and that the necessary condition for reasoning is the operation of the cerebral cortex. Thus it is only after formation of the cerebral cortex that a *personal* as distinct from a merely *animal* body, fit for reception of a spiritual soul, is in being. It is at this point that the entity in question undergoes a substantial change; i.e., it changes from being a nonpersonal entity into a person. They realize that it is absurd to suggest that babies undergo a substantial change after birth, even though they cannot actually engage in thought until some time later in their development. They thus hold that the developed brain itself is not the bodily basis for intellectual activities but only its precursor, but they hold that this is all that the hylomorphic theory of St. Thomas requires.

The attempt by Donceel, Shannon/Wolters and others to rehabilitate the "delayed hominization" theory in order to justify early abortions fails on several counts. First of all, these modern authors, in contrast to St Thomas, assume that abortion of a pre-personal entity might be justified. But, as we saw earlier, various opinions during patristic and medieval times on the infusion of the spiritual soul in no way changed their judgment that procured abortion was always gravely immoral. All Christian writers, including St. Thomas, absolutely condemned all deliberate abortion, no matter whether the embryo/fetus was "formed" or not.

Secondly, the attempted rehabilitation of the "delayed hominization" theory is philosophically untenable, and untenable on *Thomistic* grounds in light of what we *know* about the process of human generation. Many writers, among them Grisez, Lee, Benedict Ashley, Albert Moraczewski, Jean Siebenthal, Mark Johnson, and others have shown this very clearly.[28] Here I will summarize the critiques given by Grisez and Siebenthal.

Grisez first points out that even after birth babies cannot think and make choices, the rational actions characteristic of human persons and capacity for which distinguishes human, personal nature from subhuman, subpersonal nature. Thus, as the advocates of the delayed hominization theory themselves admit, the beginning of the brain's development during the gestation period cannot be the bodily basis required for specifically personal acts but only its precursor. Since this precursor satisfies the requirements of St. Thomas's theory, why cannot precursors at earlier stages of development satisfy them? Moreover, modern biology demonstrates that every human embryo has from the very beginning a specific developmental tendency, including the epigenetic primordia or sources for the development of *all* its organs, including the brain. The fact that a spiritual soul can exist only in matter able to receive it does not entail the conclusion that a human zygote cannot receive it since it has within itself the active potency to develop all its organs. Grisez then concludes that the assumption on which this theory rests, namely, that the human embryo is at first a pre-personal entity and only later becomes personal, "posits two entities where only one is necessary to account for the observed facts. But entities," he continues, "are not to be multiplied without necessity. Consequently, the view that the embryo becomes a person when the brain begins to develop should be rejected, and the personal soul should be considered to be present from conception."[29]

Siebenthal's refutation of this view is most interesting because he roots it in a careful analysis of the thought of St. Thomas himself — to whom Donceel, Shannon and others appeal for support. Siebenthal first stresses that for St. Thomas the origin of the *human body* coincides with the infusion of a spiritual or intellectual soul. For St. Thomas *human flesh gets its being* — its *esse* — from the human intellectual soul.[30] Since St. Thomas himself mistakenly thought, because he relied on the inadequate biological knowledge of his day, that in human generation the male seed was alone the active element, he concluded that the body first formed from the maternal blood by this seed was only vegetative in nature; later, a substantial change occurred and a new body, this time animated by an animal soul, was formed; finally, another substantial change occurred and a new body, human in nature and animated by an intellectual soul, came into being. But note that for St. Thomas the *bodies* first generated were *not human* in nature. He thus concluded that there was a radical discontinuity between the bodies formed during gestation. Siebenthal's point is that St. Thomas, were he alive today and cognizant of the biological evidence known today, would not hesitate in concluding that the *body* that comes to be when fertilization is completed is indubitably a *human* body and hence that its organizing and vivifying principle can only be a *human soul*, an intellectual or spiritual soul.[31]

Today, in addition to those advocating the "delayed hominization" theory, several thinkers believe that authentically human and personal life begins only once the brain has developed in the unborn. They do so because they think that a functioning brain is an essential property of a human being. Scholars taking this position draw an analogy between the end and the beginning of human life. They note that today a widely accepted criterion to show that death has occurred and that a living human person no longer exists is the irreversible cessation of the functioning of *the entire brain, including the brain stem.* Since we can say that a person is dead, i.e., no longer alive and among us, when his or her brain in its entirety has irreversibly ceased to function, then why can we not say that human, personal life begins when the fetus acquires a functioning brain?[32]

Even if it is granted that irreversible cessation of all the functions of the entire brain, including the brain stem, is an acceptable criterion that death has occurred, the analogy invoked is not accurate, as Lee, in particular, clearly shows. While it is true that what we say about the end of human life should be consistent with what we say about its beginning, advocates of this view locate the analogy in the wrong place, i.e., in a *functioning brain,* and not in the *unity of the organism.* Irreversible cessation of all functions of the entire brain may indeed show that death has occurred because in a mature human being the brain is the organ that integrates the functioning of all the systems of that mature human being. Hence, when the brain ceases to function (totally and irreparably) in a mature human being, all other tissues and organs cease to form a unified organism. A human being is essentially an organism, albeit a specific type, and so if the tissues and organs cease to constitute an organism, then the human being has ceased to be. But, since being an organism expresses in a very general way what a human being is, it is impossible for an organism to come to be at one time and, remaining the *same* organism, become human at a later time. Hence, "if an organism at one time is the same organism as a human organism at a later time, then the organism at the earlier time is a human organism also, the same human organism as the one which exists at a later time."[33] Proponents of this view must acknowledge that, before the formation of the brain in the developing biological organism, there is something in that organism during its zygotic and early embryonic stages that definitely integrates all its living activities — the essential function carried out by the brain in that same organism at later states of its existence. It is impossible to declare the organism dead or deny that it is identifiably biologically as a member of the human species as distinct from other animal species. The organism is alive, human in nature, and has within itself the active potential to develop its own brain. One cannot say this of the nonliving corpse of a person declared dead because there is certainty that there is irreversible cessation of all the functions of the entire brain, which serves, in the mature human, as the integrating, organizing factor.[34]

C. Individual Personhood Cannot Be Established Before Implantation

Another challenge to the thesis defended here, namely, that most persons begin at fertilization, is raised by those who contend, on the basis of certain facts (or alleged facts), that the thesis in question is unreasonable and that it is simply not possible for *individual human persons to come to be prior to implantation.*

The two major facts appealed to in support of this claim are the following: (1) the enormous "wastage" of life prior to implantation, and (2) the phenomenon of monozygotic twins (triplets, etc.) and the possibility of "fusion" or recombination of two or more zygotic individuals into a different individual prior to implantation. As I will now show, the first of these alleged "facts" is highly questionable. The second raises some difficulties but definitely does *not*, as those who appeal to it claim, "rebut" the idea that human personal life begins at conception.

(1)The question of "wastage": Some people, mainly Catholic theologians, contend that the loss or wastage of "fertilized eggs," "zygotes," "blastocysts" and other clusters of human genetic cells prior to implantation is so vast that it is highly unreasonable to call these entities "persons."[35] In fact, Shannon and Wolter say that "to ascribe such bungling of the [reproductive] process [as this "wastage" implies] to an all-wise creator would seem almost sacrilegious."[36]

The argument, in brief, is this: *Major:* An all-wise and providential God would not create new human persons made in his own image and likeness and then let them die even before they can be implanted in the wombs of their mothers. *Minor:* But enormous numbers of the beings resulting from human fertilization die before they can be implanted in the womb. *Conclusion:* Therefore, it is unreasonable and even sacrilegious to call these entities persons made in the image and likeness of God.

What can be said in response? First of all, the minor can be seriously challenged. Those who pose this problem cite studies claiming that from 40 to 60 percent of all "fertilized eggs" and their progeny are "wasted" prior to implantation. But if one carefully examines the studies in question—as several scholars have done, in particular, W. Jerome Bracken, C.P.[37]— one soon discovers that most such losses are the result of such severe chromosomal defects that the individual in all likelihood lacks the proper complement of genetic material for formation of a *human* body animated by a *spiritual* soul. In other words, the "fertilized eggs" that are "wasted" were not, in a great number of cases, individual human beings to begin with because of severe abnormalities in the process of fertilization.

How about the major? We are not God, and do not know his mind. We need to remember that, for most of human history, infant mortality was very high. Would those who invoke the "fact" of "fetal wastage" to support their claim that it is unreasonable and even sacrilegious to say that individual personal life begins at conception want to deny that the millions of babies who have died in infancy were not persons and that an all-wise God would allow such "bungling" of the infancy period?

(2) The question of monozygotic "twinning" and possible "fusion" or "recombination" of zygotes: The fact that two or more human individuals, with the same genetic composition (monozygotic twins — i.e., twins, or perhaps triplets or quadruplets etc., deriving from *one* original zygote) and the possibility that some human individuals may result from the "fusion" or "recombination" of two or more original zygotes — the name given to the organism resulting from the human fertilization process — has led some to conclude that it is not possible for an *individual human person* to be in existence from fertilization, and that it is impossible for individual human persons to exist prior to implantation (a process that takes place approximately two weeks *after* fertilization and after which twinning is not possible).

Many today champion this position. It has been perhaps most extensively presented by an Australian Catholic priest, Norman Ford, S.D.B., in his highly influential book *When Did I Begin? Conception of the Human Individual in History, Philosophy, and Science,*[38] and by many others, for instance, Michael Coughlan.[39]

According to Ford, Coughlan, and others who hold this position, the zygote and the very early or "pre-implantation" embryo (or, as they prefer to call it, the "pre-embryo," a term that ought not be employed, as Angelo Serra and Roberto Columbo emphasize in an important study[40]) is *genetically and biologically human* and distinct from its parents; but it is not as yet an *ontologically distinct human individual* until after "gastration," the formation of the "primitive streak," and implantation, events after which twinning and recombination cannot take place. What exists during this time of gestation, they insist, is not an ontologically distinct human individual but rather a colony of cells held together in an artificial way, each with the active potentiality and "totipotential" to become more than one human individual.

This is the basic claim made by proponents of this view. Shannon and Wolter, who adopt this view, attempt to strengthen it by appealing to the work of the biologists C. A. Bedate and R. C. Cefalo[41] who contend that the early embryo or "pre-embryo" must receive information from the mother before a distinct human individual can begin to exist.

Before offering a definitive rebuttal to the claims made by Ford and others on the basis of the phenomenon of twinning and the possibility of recombination, I will first comment on Shannon and Wolter's assertion that the pre-implantation embryo lacks the genetic information necessary for being a distinct human individual but must receive it from its mother. This contention has been devastatingly rebutted by the embryologist Antoine Suarez, who shows that contemporary research into early embryonic development definitively proves that "during pregnancy the embryo does *not* receive any messages or information from the mother able to control the mechanisms of development or to produce the type of cellular differentiation necessary for building the tissues of the new human adult." To the contrary, recent empirical research supports the conclusion that *"the pre-implantation embryo is the same individual of the human species (the same animal) as the adult into whom the pre-implantation embryo can in principle develop."*[42]

The claims made by Ford and others based on the phenomenon of twinning have been subjected to devastating criticism by many, including philosophers, theologians, and embryologists. Among the more incisive critiques are those given by Grisez, Lee, Ashley/Moraczewski, Nicholas Tonti-Filippini, Anthony Fisher, and Angelo Serra/Roberto Columbo.[43] Here I will summarize the principal reasons given by these authors to show that the Ford-et-al. hypothesis is untenable.

The Ford-et-al. view claims that in the early embryo (or "pre-embryo") prior to implantation, formation of the "primitive streak," etc. the various cells within the *zona pellucida* (the membrane surrounding the zygote and early embryo) are all "totipotential," i.e., each *can* become distinct individual human persons (monozygotic twins, triplets, etc.), all with the same genetic endowment. Their thesis, as we have seen, is that whle this entity is *biologically and genetically human* and distinct from its parents, it is not yet an *ontologically distinct* human individual person. It is rather a *colony* of individual cells, each capable of developing into a distinct human person.

However, as embryologists such as R. Yanagimachi and Antoine Suarez note in summarizing what is scientifically known about mammalian fertilization, "fertilization in mammals normally represents the beginning of life for an individual."[44] In light of all the evidence, the claim that cell division in the early embryo actually gives rise to a colony of really distinct individuals "until a small army of them form the true human individual" is not at all plausible.[45] Ford and those who agree with him think that the individual cells within the early embryo have the *active* potentiality to become individual human beings — and if so, then they would so develop unless some accident prevented such development. But they do not have such "active" potentiality; their "totipotentiality" is not "active" but hypothetical. It is hypothetical because for it to be actualized some extrinsic cause must separate the individual cells within the pre-implantation embryo. We can grant that during the early stages of its development (i.e., prior to implantation) the individual cells of the embryo are as yet relatively unspecialized and therefore *can* become whole human organisms *IF* they are divided and have an appropriate environment after division. But, as Patrick Lee points out, "this does not in the least indicate that prior to such an extrinsic division the embryo is an aggregate rather than a single, multicellular organism," and one identifiably of the human species, distinct from other members of the species.[46]

The crucial question raised by such phenomena as monozygotic twinning and possible recombination is this: Do they, *of themselves*, demonstrate that the "ontological" human individual comes into being only after implantation? The attempts to demonstrate this by Ford and others are very implausible and rest on the presupposition, not credible, that the individual cells within the *zona pellucida* surrounding the early embryo have the *active* potentiality to become individual human persons. But if they did have an *active* potency of this kind, then they would *all* become individual persons, and this is absurd. Thus, as Grisez says, "contrary to what Ford asserts (without argument), in those zygotes which develop continuously as individuals the facts do not evidence an *active* potentiality to develop otherwise. Rather, at most the facts show that all early embryos could *passively* undergo division or recombination."[47]

In short, the argument that individual human persons *cannot* begin at fertilization because of such phenomena as identical twinning is based on appearances and alleged common sense, but it fails to prove what it claims to prove. It is far more likely, as Ashley/Moraczewski and others argue, that identical twinning is a developmental accident and that the coming into being of identical twins can be explained reasonably as a mode of asexual reproduction (cloning).[48]

Twinning and similar facts in no way compel us to conclude that individual human persons do not begin to be at conception/fertilization. It is possible that *some* human individuals begin to be between fertilization and implantation, but *most* human individuals do come to be at fertilization/conception; it is reasonable to hold that they do and unreasonable to claim that they do not. I believe that this section of this chapter has provided evidence and arguments to support the truth of this proposition.

3. THE SPECIAL MORAL GRAVITY OF ABORTION, A WOMAN'S "RIGHT" TO ABORTION, THE DIFFERENCE BETWEEN A "RIGHT" AND A "LIBERTY"

Here I will first reflect on the unique moral gravity of abortion. I will then comment on some of the principal arguments, passionately advanced, by those who claim that a woman has a "right" to abortion, and conclude by considering the crucial difference between a "right" and a "liberty" and the relevance of this distinction to the issue of abortion.

A. The Unique Moral Gravity of Abortion

Abortion, as we have seen, is the intentional killing of an innocent human person. As we saw in Chapter Two, the intentional killing of *any* innocent human person is an intrinsically evil act insofar as it is utterly opposed to *love* of the person made in the image and likeness of God. But the intentional killing of unborn human children and of infants has a unique kind of gravity. Human life, the life of human persons, is a magnificent gift from God, a truth that John Paul II develops eloquently in Chapter Two of his Encyclical *Evangelium vitae*. Although we saw this in detail in Chapter Two, it is useful here to summarize what he had to say there and elsewhere.

Human life, the Pope reminds us, is surpassingly good because "the life which God gives man is quite different from the life of all other living creatures, inasmuch as man, although formed from the dust of the earth (cf. Gn 2:7; 3:19; Jb 34:15; Ps 103:14; Ps 104:29), *is a manifesta-*

tion of God in the world, a sign of his presence, a trace of his glory (cf. Gn 1:26-27; Ps 8:6)" (*Evangelium vitae,* no. 34). Human life indeed is the " 'place' where God manifests himself, where we meet him and enter into communion with him" (no. 38). This great truth is immeasurably deepened and enriched by the incarnation of God's only-begotten Son, his uncreated Word who for love of us became, like us, God's "created word." And his Son, Jesus, has made known to us not only who we are — God's created "words," his living images — but also who we are meant to be! As John Paul II reminds us, 'Eternal life ... is the life of God himself," and at the same time "is *the life of the children of God* (cf. 1 Jn 3:1-2).... *Here the Christian truth about [human] life becomes most sublime.* The dignity of this life is linked not only to its beginning, to the fact that it comes from God, but also to its final end, to its destiny of fellowship with God in knowledge and love of him" (no. 38).

God so loves us and wills that we share in his creative work that he entrusts to us in a special way the gift of new human life. This life, as the Pope reminds us, is entrusted "to each and every other human being." "But," he continues, it "is entrusted in a special way ... to woman, precisely because the woman, in virtue of her special experience of motherhood, is seen to have a *specific sensitivity* towards the human person and all that constitutes the individual's true welfare, beginning with the fundamental value of life."[49] New human life comes to be in and through the intimate union of man and woman (a union honored, as we saw in Chapter Three, only when *marital*). In its beginnings, this life is particularly vulnerable and dependent on others for its well-being. It is a gift to be welcomed and received with love, as each one of us knows. How grateful we must be if the man and the woman who gave us life welcomed our coming! And how sad it must be should one come to know that they did not, even if they did not kill one in the womb.Yes, the intentional killing of children, and in particular unborn children — and each one of us was, when we came into existence, an unborn child — has a particular gravity, a betrayal, as it were, of a sacred trust committed to our care. We must remember that God's eternal Word, his only-begotten Son, became man — became truly one of us — as a helpless and utterly dependent unborn child in womb of his mother. He is one with unborn children in the wombs of their mothers.[50]

Unfortunately, many today, because of the contraceptive/abortifacient culture in which we live, fail to realize this truth or to take it into account. But it *is* a truth, one we must have the courage to face, even as we seek to care compassionately for women who experience pregnancies "unwanted" for one reason or another.

B. A Woman's "Right" to an Abortion

In our society many claim today that a woman has a "right" to an abortion. It will be, I think, worthwhile to consider some of the major arguments given to support this claim, and then to show why they are not good arguments. In the final section of this part I will show that the alleged "right" to an abortion is not a right at all but rather a supposed "liberty," one that cannot be genuine insofar as it is nonexistent in view of the unborn child's authentic "right" to life.

As Sidney Callahan remarks in an interesting essay,[51] the most highly developed feminist arguments for the morality and legality of abortion can be found in Beverly Wildung Harrison's *Our Right to Choose* (Boston: Beacon Press, 1983) and Rosalind Pollack Petchesky's *Abortion and Woman's Choice* (New York: Longmans, 1984). Callahan identifies four major strands of argumentation. Of these, the one dependent on the claim that the unborn child cannot be regarded a person has already been sufficiently rebutted. Another, claiming that abortion is necessary if women are to be considered socially equal to men, simply avoids facing the basic questions. The other two lines of argument, however, are very popular, somewhat more plausible, and appeal to many people today. They should therefore be confronted, the truth they inadequately express acknowledged, and their specious character identified.

The two arguments in question are: (1) the woman's moral right to control her own body, and (2) the moral necessity of autonomy and choice in personal integrity. The first claims that in choosing an abortion a woman is simply exercising a basic right of bodily integrity. If she does not choose to be pregnant she should not be compelled to be so against her will. It is *her* body that is involved, and intimately so. If no one can be compelled to donate an organ to another or to submit to other invasive procedures on his or her own body for however noble a cause, why should women be so compelled just because they happen to become pregnant? This would seem especially the case, as another feminist author, Judith Jarvis Thomson, claimed in a celebrated essay originally published in 1970,[52] if the woman has taken precautions not to become pregnant by using an effective contraceptive. The alternatives, on this argument, are these: either *compulsory pregnancy* or the right to terminate a pregnancy, i.e., have an abortion. Of these two alternatives, this argument contends, the second is obviously the right moral one, for it alone recognizes the woman's right to bodily integrity.

The second argument holds that in order for a woman to be a full adult in the moral sense, not only does she have a right to *bodily* integrity but also to make and keep commitments and determine her own lifestyle. In order to do this she must have control over reproduction, because if she does not she is not capable of keeping prior and present commitments, and/or of making future ones, particularly in the areas of family, work, and education. A right to abortion is integral to a woman's adult, mature responsibility and autonomy.[53]

With respect to the first argument, it simply refuses to take into consideration the truth that abortion affects the body and bodily integrity of the unborn child, whose life is destroyed by it, far more than it does the body and bodily integrity of his or her mother. As Callahan so well says in her critique of this argument, during pregnancy "one's own body no longer exists as a single unit but is engendering another organism's life. This dynamic passage from conception to birth is genetically ordered and universally found in the human species. Pregnancy is not like the growth of a cancer or infestation by a biological parasite; it is the way every human being comes into the world. Strained philosophical analogies fail to apply: having a baby is not like rescuing a drowning person, being hooked up to a famous violinist's artificial life-support system,[54] donating organs for transplant — or anything else."[55]

Proponents of this argument are correct in saying that civil law protects, and rightly so, one's own bodily integrity and considers as a crime against the person any invasions of that person's body without free and personal consent. This is the kernel of truth in the argument that gives it some plausibility. But the same civil law clearly and rightly holds that it is wrong and criminal intentionally to harm the bodies, bodily integrity, and lives of *other persons*, of other *bodies*. Although the protection that civil law thus affords has been unjustly removed from the unborn, it clearly recognizes the difference between invasive procedures affecting one's own body and attacks on the body of another. Thus the argument is specious.

The second major argument advanced by feminists is rooted in the individualistic understanding of human autonomy so prevalent in our culture, an understanding that refuses to recognize that human persons can exist only within a community of persons, and that our freedom to choose is not independent of the truth and is not the same as the autonomy to determine what is right and what is wrong (cf. Chapters One and Two). The truth it contains, making it somewhat plausible, is that we must make commitments in our lives and be faithful to them. But these commitments, which are particular choices affecting broad areas of our lives, must themselves be morally good and in accord with the truth, and we may have to set some aside, once made, in the light of moral responsibilities which we have either freely taken upon ourselves or which have been placed on us (e.g., caring for an injured person when we are the only ones able to do so, even if this means sacrificing something worthwhile in itself).

C. The Difference Between a "Right" and a "Liberty"

There is a great deal of talk in our society today about "rights." As we have seen, many claim that a woman has a "right" to an abortion; pro-lifers, on the other hand, claim that the unborn child has a "right" to life. How is it possible to distinguish between authentic rights and alleged rights? I believe that the distinction between a right in the strict sense or a "claim right" and a "liberty" or a "liberty right" is most helpful here. In what follows I will paraphrase and to some extent simplify the brilliant discussion of this matter presented by John Finnis in chapter 8 of his *Natural Law and Natural Rights*.[56]

Very frequently, particular in popular discussions (as on TV talk shows, etc.), people talk about rights as two-term relations between persons and one subject-matter or *thing* (e.g., a woman's right to an abortion, an innocent person's right to life, a worker's right to a just wage, a smoker's right to smoke, etc.). In order to distinguish a right in the strict sense, or what can be called "claim right" from a liberty or a "liberty right," it is necessary to speak of a three-term relationship between two persons (or groups of persons) and an act of a specific type. If we do so, we can speak of a claim-right as follows:

> *A* (=a person or group of persons, or all persons if we are speaking of basic human and inalienable rights of human persons) has a *right* (a "claim right") that *B* (=another person group of persons or all persons) should *x* (=some specifiable act), if and only if *B* has a *duty* to *A* to *x*.

To illustrate: Innocent human persons (=A) have a *right* in the sense of a claim right to life if and only if innocent human persons (=A) have a right that all other persons (=B) have a duty to innocent human persons (=A) to forbear from intentionally killing them (=x). In other words, the right of innocent human persons to life, if genuine, means that all other persons have an obligation or duty *not to kill them* intentionally. Applying this to unborn children, we can say: Unborn children have a strict right or claim right to life if, and only if, unborn children (=A) have a right that their mothers and other persons (=B) have a duty to unborn children *to forbear from aborting them, i.e., intentionally killing them* (=x). And, as we have seen already, this right is genuine because all persons, including mothers, have a strict obligation or duty to forbear from intentionally killing innocent human persons, and abortion is the intentional killing of an innocent human person.

Note that with respect to a right in the strict sense, a claim right, the action in question is required, not of the right-holder, but of other persons. With reference to the right to life, the action required is first and foremost an act of forbearance (of refusal to kill intentionally) required of all who must respect this right. With respect to abortion, the action in question is not an action of the unborn, but an action of others (mothers, etc.) and is again an act of forbearance, of refusing intentionally to kill the unborn by aborting them.

What about the alleged "right" of a woman to an abortion? If we express this, not as a two-term relationship between a person (a woman) and a thing (an abortion), but in a three-term relationship between two persons and a specifiable action, we see that the alleged right is really a "liberty" claimed by women. It can be put generally as follows:

> B (=a person, group of persons, etc.) has a *liberty* relative to A (=a person, a group of persons, etc.) to x (=some specifiable act), if and only if A has no claim right that B should not x.

Translating this talk about the woman's alleged "right" to an abortion into this language we have the following: A woman (=B) has a liberty relative to the unborn baby (=A) intentionally to abort it (=x) if and only if the unborn baby (=A) has no claim right that the woman (=B) should not abort it (=x). But, as we have seen, the unborn has the claim right that his or her mother (and others) forbear from aborting it. Consequently, the liberty (and not right) claimed by women to abort is spurious.

There are, of course, many genuine liberties or "liberty rights," e.g., the right to worship God, the right of persons of the opposite sex to marry and have children, etc.

4. ABORTION AS "REMOVAL" VS. ABORTION AS "KILLING"

Patrick Lee puts the title of the fourth chapter of his excellent book on abortion in the form of a question, "Is abortion justified as nonintentional killing?" In it he examines the view that abortions, or at least many of them, can be justified because they are not intentional killings of innocent human persons but are rather to be regarded as "indirect" abortions, or abortions that are not intended. As we have seen, the Magisterium condemns procured or "direct" abortion, i.e., acts in which the abortion is intended either as end or as means, but recognizes that under certain conditions one can rightly engage in an act which has abortion as a foreseen, even inevitable, yet unintended effect. In such instances the abortion is unintended or nonintended.

If abortion is *defined* as the "removal" or "expulsion" of a living but not yet viable unborn child from the womb of his or her mother, then the question posed by Lee as the title of his chapter is intelligible, for it is at least conceivable that some "removals" or "expulsions" of a living but not yet viable unborn child from his or her mother's womb might not have as its moral object, either as end or as means, the killing or death of the unborn child. Assume, for the sake of argument, that the unborn child in the womb of a woman diagnosed with cancer of the uterus could be removed from her womb and placed in an artificial womb for the three months necessary for it to become viable. The woman is in danger of dying from the cancer, and traditionally Roman Catholic moralists (and the Magisterium) would justify the woman's having a hysterectomy or undergoing chemotherapy to protect her from dying of cancer even though it was foreseen that the unborn child would die as a result of the hysterectomy or chemotherapy. The reasoning was that the "removal" of the child from the mother's womb — the abortion itself — and consequent death were not "directly intended" but only foreseen as unavoidable but not intended effects of the hysterectomy or chemotherapy. It seems obvious that it would be far better, if it were possible, to save the life of the unborn child in such instances by "removing" him or her from the mother's womb to an artificial womb than to "allow" him or her to die as a foreseen but nonintended result of the chemotherapy or hysterectomy. But one would, in this instance, definitely *intend* the "removal" of the unborn child from the mother's womb; one could not *not* intend this. Thus, if abortion is defined as "removal," then it seems that in at least some instances (like the hypothetical one I just gave) a "direct abortion" would be morally justifiable. This is the kind of issue with which Lee is concerned, and I will reflect on his treatment of this issue below.

But before doing so, it seems only obvious to note that if we *define* abortion as the *intentional killing of an innocent unborn child*, then it is not possible to distinguish between abortion as "removal" and abortion as "killing." If abortion is *defined* as the *intentional **killing** of an unborn child*, then directly intended *removals* of the unborn from their mothers' wombs cannot be considered *abortions*, **if** the *killing or death of the unborn* is intended neither as end nor as means, i.e., is not intended at all. But, as we have seen and as I emphasized in the first section of this chapter, Pope John Paul II in *Evangelium vitae* defines abortion as the *intentional killing of the unborn*. I will return to the relevance of this. I will begin, however, by summarizing and reflecting on Patrick Lee's analysis.

A. Lee's Analysis and Position

The question Lee poses is whether direct abortions, or at least many abortions (understood as removing or expelling nonviable unborn children from their mother's wombs) can be justified because they are nonintentional killings of innocent human persons.

He notes that this line of justifying abortions (or most abortions) was developed by Judith Jarvis Thomson in her celebrated "In Defense of Abortion" article,[57] and Lee's first concern is to reject her claim that the great majority of abortions can be justified as nonintentional killings. She argued that even if we grant that the unborn baby is a human person with a right to life, this does not mean that it has a right to everything it needs to support its life, particularly the use of a woman's body. According to Thomson, no woman has the right to *kill* the fetus, but no woman has the obligation to let it use her body for life-support *unless* she has voluntarily assumed this duty; and, particularly if she has tried to avoid conception by using contraceptives, very frequently she has not assumed that duty. Therefore, Thomson concludes, she can expel the unborn child from her body even if she knows that it will die as a result.

In short, she argues that there is a real difference between intentional killing or securing someone's death and causing death as a side effect. Many abortions are not intentional killings because the objective of the women having them is not the securing of the death of the child they are carrying; they are rather cases of causing death as a side effect of "removing" the unborn child from the womb, justifiable when one has no obligation to allow the unborn child use of one's womb and one simply wants its removal. Consequently, many abortions are morally right even if we grant that the unborn child or fetus is a person.[58]

Lee grants that the distinction between intentional killing and causing death as a side effect is valid (and I agree, as can be seen from what
was said above). But he argues, and rightly so, that the great majority of
abortions are intentional killings because those who procure them want
to get rid of the unborn. However, he continues, even if some abortions
(="direct" abortions understood as intentional "removals" of living but
not yet viable unborn children from their mothers' wombs) are not intentional killings, they are not, for the most part, morally justified. He
then distinguishes two types of abortion cases which are not (or at least
need not be) intentional killings and in which the mother's life is not
significantly in danger. In one type of case, the man and the woman
freely choose to have sex, realizing that by doing so the woman can
conceive (even if they use contraceptives). In such a case, even if one
grants that the "object" of the abortion is not the securing of the child's
death but its "removal" so that the woman could, for instance, maintain
her figure, "removing" it and thereby "causing its death" as a foreseen
side effect is gravely immoral because, Lee writes, "(a) they have a specific duty to the child because they placed him or her in that dependent
relationship, and (b) the harm caused to the child is immensely worse
than the harm that the woman (and others involved) is avoiding by having the abortion." In a second type of case, abortion is performed because of rape or incest. Here (a) does not apply, but because of (b) and
other factors, such as the unborn child's innocence and the moral significance of the mother's biological relationship to it, abortion is not
morally justified here either, even if it is not an instance of intentional
killing but rather of intentional removal. It is not morally justified because it is grossly unjust and unfair and thus violates the moral principle
of fairness or the Golden Rule in a serious way.[59]

Lee thus concludes that in the great majority of cases, one cannot
justify direct abortion as "removal" rather than as "killing' because the
death of the unborn child can and ought to be prevented; there are grave
moral reasons why "allowing" its death would be seriously immoral.[60]
But Lee then goes on to argue that in cases in which the mother's life is
significantly in danger, then permitting the death of the unborn child as
a foreseen but not intended side effect of its removal could be morally
justifiable. It is so, he says, "if the choice to save the mother rather than
the child is fair" — for example, if both cannot be saved — because in
such cases "it seems that it would be causing the child's death as a side
effect and with a grave reason to do so." Lee says that he has no *philosophical* objections against (direct) abortion, understood as "removal"

and not as "killing," in such cases, but in a footnote he advises his readers to follow the teaching of the Church if the act is against Catholic teaching.[61]

B. Critique

It is thus evident that Lee thinks that some abortions, clearly *intended* and hence "direct," can be justified in very special cases when necessary to save the mother's life as "removals" causing the death of the unborn child as a foreseen but *not intended* effect of its removal and an effect that one can rightly "permit." His position was set forth originally by Grisez (whom Lee follows on this matter) in his 1970 massive study, *Abortion: The Myths, the Realities, and the Arguments*. Grisez applied St. Thomas Aquinas's analysis of killing in self-defense,[62] the classic source for the principle of double effect, to some sorts of procedures, for instance craniotomies and salpingo(s)tomies, that Catholic moral theologians — who, as we have seen at the beginning of this chapter, *defined* abortion as the "expulsion" of a living but not yet viable unborn child from the womb — considered "direct" abortions and therefore intrinsically immoral. Grisez argued (as does Lee in his book) that under certain conditions when such procedures are used, the death of the unborn child need be neither the end intended nor the means chosen and that, therefore, it is possible to regard the evil done by these procedures, namely, the death of the unborn child, as not intended and therefore justifiable.[63] As did Lee later, Grisez maintained that this was a position he had reached as a philosopher, but that, should Catholic teaching judge otherwise, Catholics like himself were not at liberty to set that teaching aside and act on the basis of his analysis.[64]

As indicated at the very beginning of this section, when I considered the possibility of "removing" an unborn child from the womb of a mother about to undergo a hysterectomy or chemotherapy to save her life from cancer to an artificial womb, I think that the distinction between abortion as "killing" and abortion as "removal" is a valid distinction, and is relevant to the issue of abortion when it is *defined* as the removal or expulsion of a nonviable fetus from the mother's body, and that if abortion is defined is this way, then some "direct" abortions are, at least in principle, justifiable. It is obvious, however, that if "direct" abortion, i.e., abortion intended either as end or as chosen means, is *defined* — as it is by Pope John Paul II — as the "killing" of an innocent unborn person, then all "direct" abortions are gravely immoral and in no way justifiable.

My major problem with the Grisez-Lee analysis, however, is with its application and the perhaps euphemistic use of the term "removal." For example, Grisez and his colleague Joseph Boyle have explicitly justified craniotomy or embryotomy and other procedures as non-killing kinds of acts if necessary to save the mother's life and hence justifiable "removals" of the unborn. Craniotomies, for instance, were recommended in the past when the woman was in labor but could not deliver the baby because the child could not pass through her pelvic cavity. If the labor did not end, the mother would die, and the *only way* to end labor was to remove the unborn child by a craniotomy or embryotomy. But this requires the perforation of the baby's skull, the emptying out of its brain, and the collapsing of the skull. I think it not unreasonable to say that most of us would conclude that "removing" the unborn child in this way necessarily includes the willingness, however reluctant, to "kill" it. Although its death is not the end aimed at, it is a means chosen to bring about the good effect.

But Grisez and Boyle claim that this is not so. Boyle, for instance, argues (and Grisez agrees) that in this sort of case "the death of the fetus in no way contributes to the continuance of labor and thus to saving the mother's life, and thus the bringing about of this effect just as such is not a means to these ends.... it is not the *killing* which removes the threat; the means here appears to be the craniotomy itself insofar as it *alters the dimensions of the skull* [my emphasis] *in order* [Boyle's emphasis] to allow labor to proceed. It is the dimensions of the baby's skull being altered and not its being dead which saves the mother's life."[65]

I think this analysis is quite wrong and that it *redescribes* the action from "killing" or at least fatally wounding the unborn to "altering the dimensions of its skull," or, as it is sometimes said, to a "cranium-narrowing" operation. It seems to me that the "altering" of the measurements of its skull is the end, ordered to the further end of allowing the child's removal and the saving of the mother's life. But the "altering" of the measurements is *not* what one freely chooses to do in this instance: one is freely choosing *to crush the baby's skull and empty it of its contents*, and one cannot *not* intend to do this. One thus intends and cannot *not* intend to attack fatally the body-person of the unborn child.[66]

Moreover, Kevin Flannery, S.J., has developed a very good argument against some of the *applications* that Grisez and others make of the distinction between abortion as "killing" and abortion as "removal." Flannery contrasts the logical structure of a craniotomy with that of a hysterectomy required when a pregnant woman is dying of cancer of the uterus.

In a hysterectomy, first of all, the operation is performed on the *woman* whereas the craniotomy is performed on the *unborn child*. Secondly, in the hysterectomy, no "redescribing" of the act is needed in order to show that the death of the unborn child is not within the scope of one's intention. But in the craniotomy it is necessary to "redescribe" the act by calling it a "cranium-narrowing" operation or "altering of the measurements of the skull" operation. After noting these significant differences between a hysterectomy and a craniotomy, Flannery argues that the difference in the logical structure between the two cases is morally relevant precisely because it "involves the good (or ill) done to the subject who is operated upon. The practice of medicine has as its sole legitimate object ... the health of the individuals it turns its attention to. But in the craniotomy case this is not its object: the fetus, who is clearly the object of the operation, is killed. In this instance, medicine has not been practiced in a reputable manner. This is morally relevant."[67]

In other words, so long as the operation is performed on the body-person of the pregnant woman, for the good of her life, it is not necessary to redescribe the act in order to hide the fact that the unborn child is fatally attacked and to justify the claim that harm done it is not intended. But if the act undertaken for the good of the mother's life is an act performed on the unborn child, and *not* for its benefit but, on the contrary, is an act that fatally harms the unborn child, then redescriptions or euphemisms are necessary, resulting in a failure to describe the act properly.

I thus conclude that there is a vast moral difference between an action in which the *killing* of an unborn child is and cannot not be intended, either as means or as end, and an action in which its *removal* from the mother's womb may be directly *intended* but in which its *killing* or *death* is not intended. The former type of action is always gravely immoral and intrinsically evil; the latter is not intrinsically evil and can be justified if certain conditions are fulfilled. This, at least, is true in principle, and I have suggested one sort of case in which it would surely be verified. But some attempts to justify the second type of procedure are flawed because they require one to redescribe the action in question, concealing its character as an intended fatal attack on the body-person of the unborn child. When the second type of procedure is justifiable, it must either be performed (a) on the body-person of the woman in order to protect her life or (b) on the body-person of the unborn child in order to protect its life. But if it is performed on the body-person of the unborn child for the benefit of the *mother's* life and to the *harm* of the unborn child's life, it is *not* morally justifiable.

Summary: I believe that the distinction between abortion as "killing" and abortion as "removal" is valid. But there is problem with the term "removal." If the unborn child can be "removed" by a means that does not kill the child in the process of its removal, then the distinction is valid. But if the means used to "remove" the unborn child are in truth death-dealing or fatal attacks on his or her body person — as is true in the case of craniotomy — then it is misleading to speak of his or her "removal." This is a euphemism to disguise the truth that the unborn child is being killed by the means chosen to remove it and *not* merely as a consequence, not intended, of its removal.

5. THE MANAGEMENT OF ECTOPIC PREGNANCIES

Currently there is a debate among non-dissenting Catholic theologians regarding the legitimacy of different methods of managing ectopic pregnancies, specifically tubal pregnancies. Before taking up this debate I will briefly describe ectopic pregnancies, their frequency, and current medical procedures available for their management. I will also summarize relevant material from the *Ethical and Religious Directives for Catholic Health Care Services* promulgated by the Bishops of the United States in November 1994.

A. Ectopic Pregnancies and Their Frequency

An ectopic ("out of place," from the Greek *ek,* out of, and *topos,* place) pregnancy occurs when a developing new human person does not implant in the uterus, where it belongs, but elsewhere in the mother's body, usually in the fallopian tube or, more rarely, in the ovary, the cornua, the abdomen, or the cervix. Such pregnancies pose serious risks to the mother's life because of the danger of hemorrhage. During the last thirty years there has been an alarming increase in the number of ectopic, and particularly tubal, pregnancies. The principal factors responsible for this increase include the alarmingly growing number of sexually transmitted diseases, especially pelvic inflammatory disease, tubal sterilization, the use of intrauterine devices or progesterone contraceptive pills, and *in vitro* fertilization.[68]

B. Medically Available Procedures for Coping with Ectopic Pregnancies

Medical authorities recognize four major treatment procedures for managing ectopic pregnancies: (1) "expectant" therapy; (2) drug therapy; (3) conservative surgical treatment; and (4) radical surgical treatment.[69]

(1) "Expectant" therapy simply means that nothing is done and one simply waits for the tubal pregnancy to resolve itself by spontaneous abortion or miscarriage. This may occur in as many as 64 percent of the cases. (2) Drug therapy involves the uses of methotrexate (MTX). MTX interferes with the synthesis of DNA and resolves tubal pregnancies by attacking the trophoblast, i.e., the outer layer of cells produced by the developing baby, connecting it to its mother. According to the scientific literature, actively proliferating trophoblastic tissue "is exquisitely sensitive to this effect [interference with the synthesis of DNA], which forms the rationale for its use in the treatment of ectopic pregnancies."[70] Under (3), "conservative surgical treatment," are included (a) partial salpingectomy or removal of the portion of the fallopian tube *affected* by the tubal pregnancy, i.e., that portion of the tube containing the tubal pregnancy, with subsequent resectioning of the fallopian tube and (b) salpingostomy, procedures in which an incision is made in the affected part of the fallopian tube and the developing embryo is extracted by the use of forceps or other instruments along with portions of the fallopian tube itself. [71] (4) "Radical surgical treatment" is necessary if the fallopian tube has ruptured and consists in a total salpingectomy or the removal of the entire affected fallopian tube and, with it, the unborn child.[72]

C. The *Ethical and Religious Directives*

In the 1971 set of *Ethical and Religious Directives for Catholic Health Care Facilities* the Bishops of the United States included the following directive, no. 16:

> In extrauterine pregnancy the affected part of the mother (e.g., cervix, ovary, or fallopian tube) may be removed, even though fetal death is foreseen, provided that (a) the affected part is presumed already to be so damaged and dangerously affected as to warrant its removal, and that (b) the operation is not just a separation of the embryo or fetus from its site within the part (which would be a direct abortion from a uterine appendage) and that (c) the operation cannot be postponed without notably increasing the danger to the mother.[73]

This directive clearly authorizes as morally licit the use of partial salpingectomy or total salpingectomy in order to safeguard the mother's life when there is grave danger of hemmorhaging from the fallopian-tube pregnancy. But it also clearly excludes use of a salpingostomy. At the time this directive was written, the management of tubal pregnancies by methotrexate was not known.

Yet the relevant directive in the 1994 *Ethical and Religious Directives for Catholic Health Care Services* is markedly different. It says simply: "In case of extrauterine pregnancy, no intervention is morally licit which constitutes a direct abortion" (no. 48).[74] But, theologians now ask, what constitutes a "direct abortion" in the management of tubal pregnancies?

D. Current Theological Debate Over Management of Tubal Pregnancies

In considering abortion as "killing" vs. abortion as "removal," above, we saw that Grisez and Boyle sought to justify craniotomy and salpingostomy as morally justified "removals" of the unborn, removals in which their death was not intended. It would seem that they, like Lee, would also justify the use of methotrexate in managing ectopic pregnancies on the grounds that these procedures are not direct killings but rather "removals" of the unborn from its site within the mother. I have already criticized the euphemistic use of the term "removal" and have argued that craniotomy is surely abortion as "killing" and not simply abortion as "removal," inasmuch as the procedure is performed on the *body person* of the unborn child and not on that of the mother; that the procedure is indeed death-dealing, and cannot in any way be justified in analogy to the nonintended killing of an assailant in self-defense.

I similarly hold that managing ectopic pregnancies by the use of salpingostomy and methotrexate constitutes direct abortion, i.e., abortion as killing, inasmuch as these procedures are lethal and are performed on the body person of the unborn child; they are performed on it, not for its good, but for the good of the mother; moreover, they are *not necessary* to save her life if this is jeopardized by the tubal pregnancy inasmuch as her life can be preserved by a salpingectomy, whether partial or complete, a procedure performed on the body of the mother, not the child, and one that is not itself a lethal invasion of the unborn child's body. A salpingostomy, on the other hand, is performed on the *child's body person*, securing its death in the very act of removing it. Methotrexate operates in a similar way. Methotrexate, as we saw above, attacks the DNA in the trophoblastic tissue, and this tissue is a vital organ of the developing child even though it is later discarded. This drug is used precisely because it has this destructive, lethal effect on the trophoblastic tissue of the unborn child. As a result of this destructive effect, the unborn child is no longer attached to the tube and is flushed out. Therefore, in my judgment, a salpingostomy and the use of methotrexate "manage" the tubal pregnancy by lethally invading the unborn child's body and effecting its "removal."[75]

Some Catholic theologians, however, defend the use of methotrexate and salpingostomy in managing ectopic pregnancies. The leading proponent of the legitimacy of these methods is Albert Moraczewski, O.P., whose position has been accepted by Kevin O'Rourke, O.P., Patrick Norris, O.P., and Jean deBlois, C.S.J., and defended perhaps most ably by Peter A. Clark, S.J.[76]

Moraczewski argues that in a salpingostomy the moral object is not the abortion but rather the "removal of the damaged *tubal tissue* and damaging trophoblastic tissue, not the destruction or death of the embryo,"[77] and that in using methotrexate the object is to stop the "destructive action of the trophoblastic cells," it is not to *kill* or bring about the death of the unborn child.[78]

I believe that Moraczewski's analysis is mistaken; in particular, he refuses to recognize that the trophoblastic tissue is a vital organ of the unborn child, considering it not part of the baby, whereas in fact it is.[79] In addition, Charles E. Cavagnaro III, M.D., has faulted Moraczewski's efforts to justify salpingostomy and the use of methotrexate. With other doctors,[80] Cavagnaro considers salpingostomy to be a direct and lethal attack on the body of the unborn child. Cavagnaro thinks that it is conceivable that a salpingostomy could be performed in which the embryo can be removed with its trophoblastic tissue intact — and this might be considered its removal and not death. But he maintains that this is not the way it is actually performed and that it cannot now be done without destroying the tissues and organs on which the life of the unborn child depends. With respect to the use of methotrexate, he notes that, first of all, it is administered even before the embryo is implanted in the tube to such a degree that the mother's life is threatened. It is given precisely to prevent the embryo from so implanting; "embryonic death," he writes, "is going to occur before the threat is serious and is exactly the means by which the serious threat has been avoided. Dead embryos do not continue to implant.... Because MTX benefits only the mother and exerts its pertinent actions on the child, it seems fair to conclude that in this case we have chosen to hurt the child with a lethal force *for the sake of the mother*."[81]

I thus conclude that the proper morally legitimate ways of managing ectopic pregnancies are "expectant therapy," i.e., make no interventions and allow the problem to be resolved naturally, with no harm to the mother, and by the use of a partial salpingectomy or if necessary a total salpingectomy. I judge the use of the drug methrotrexate and the surgical procedure of salpingostomy to be acts of abortion understood as the intentional killing of the innocent unborn.[82]

Conclusion

This lengthy chapter has examined in detail the issue of abortion and respect for human life and its dignity. Human life is truly a gift, and a surpassing one at that, from God himself.. It is indeed the "place" where we encounter God in our everyday lives. It is a *good of the person,* not a mere good *for* the person. If we are to love God, we must love our neighbor; and if we are to love our neighbor, we must respect the good of his or her life; and our neighbor includes the unborn child hidden in his or her mother's body (or, perhaps, in petri dishes), no matter how small he or she may be. We ought never adopt by choice the proposal to take his or her life, to kill him or her. Intentionally to kill any innocent person is always gravely immoral; intentionally to kill the innocent unborn is particularly heinous because of their utter dependence on others for the continuance of their existence. Their inviolable right to life makes no sense if adult members of the human species do not have the absolute obligation to forbear from intentionally killing them. But, as I have argued, all adult members of the human species have this obligation. In a certain way, the innocent unborn symbolize their adult brothers and sisters, for the latter must admit that, at one time, they too were "innocent unborn" human persons.

ENDNOTES

1. On this see the helpful essay by Angel Rodriguez Luño, "La valutazione teologico-morale dell'aborto," in *Commento Interdisciplinare alla "Evangelium Vitae,"* under the direction and coordination of Ramon Lucas Lucas, Italian edition by Elio Sgreccia and Ramon Lucas Lucas (Vatican City: Libreria Editrice Vaticana, 1997), p. 419. As examples of older moral manuals defining abortion as the expelling of a living but not yet viable fetus from the mother's womb, Luño refers to those by D. M. Pruemmer and H. Noldin.

    In his *Manuale Theologiae Morale* (Friburgi Brisg./Rome: Herder, 1961), vol. 2, no. 137, Pruemmer defined abortion as "*eiectio immaturi foetus viventis ex utero matris*" (expelling of an immature living fetus from the mother's womb). In his *Summa Theologiae Moralis* (Oeniponte-Lipsiae: P. Rauch, 1941), vol. 2, no. 342, Noldin offered a similar definition, *"foetus abortus est eiectio immaturi ex utero matris"* (abortion is the expelling of an immature fetus from its mother's womb).

2. See Chapter One, above, pp. 27-28.

3. On this see, for example, Germain Grisez, *Abortion: The Myths, the Realities, and the Arguments* (New York/Cleveland: Corpus Instrumentorum, 1970), pp. 137-156.

4. St. Basil the Great, *Epistles* 188, 2. *PG* 32.671. Indeed, he condemned as quibbling unworthy of Christians debates over the precise moment when the soul is infused, and in saying this he simply voiced the view of *all* the early fathers.

5. On the Magisterium's teaching on this matter see the excellent essay by Ignacio Carrasco de Paula, "The Respect Due to the Human Embryo: A Historical and Doctrinal Perspective," in *Identity and Statute (sic) of the Human Embryo: Proceedings of the Third Assembly of the Pontifical Academy for Life* (Vatican City, February 14-16, 1997), ed. Juan de Dios Vial Correa and Elio Sgreccia (Vatican City: Libreria Editrice Vaticana, 1998), pp. 48-74, esp. pp. 66-73. The title of the book should have "Status" where "Statute" is printed. An obvious error was made in the English version.

6. Pope Pius XII, "Address to the Biomedical Association of St. Luke," November 12, 1944, in *Discorsi e Radiomessagi di Sua Santità Pio XII* (Vatican City: Libreria Editrice Vaticana, 1945) 6 (1944-1945), p. 191; "Address to the Italian Catholic Union of Midwives," October 29, 1951), no. 2, in *Acta Apostolicae Sedis* 43 (1951) 838. In his "Address to the Biomedical Association of St.Luke" Pius had said: "We have on purpose always used the expression *'direct* attack on the life of the innocent,' *'direct* killing.' For if, for instance, the safety of the life of the mother-to-be, independently of her pregnant condition, should urgently require a surgical operation or other therapeutic treatment, which would have as a side effect, in no way willed or intended yet inevitable, the death of the fetus, then such an act could not any longer be called a *direct* attack on innocent life. With these conditions, the operation, like other similar medical interventions, can be allowed, always assuming that a good of great worth, such as life, is at stake, and that it is not possible to delay until after the baby is born or to make use of some other effective remedy."

7. On this, see Chapter Two above, pp. 50-52. See also Pope John Paul

II, Encyclical *Veritatis splendor,* no. 78: *"The morality of the human act depends primarily and fundamentally on the 'object' rationally chosen by the deliberate will....*The object of the act of willing is in fact a freely chosen kind of behavior.... By the object of a given moral act ... one cannot mean a process or an event of the merely physical order, to be assessed on the basis of its ability to bring about a given state of affairs in the outside world. Rather, that object is the proximate end of a deliberate decision which determines the act of willing on the part of the acting person."

8. Patrick Lee, *Abortion and Unborn Human Life* (Washington, D.C.: The Catholic University of America Press, 1997). In the first two chapters Lee examines and rebuts claims that the fetus killed by abortion is not a person; in the third he does this with respect to claims that what is killed by abortion is not even a human being. In his fourth chapter he considers the view that even if abortion involves the killing of an innocent person, it is not "intentional" killing — a view that will be examined at more length later in this chapter. In the final chapter of his book Lee rebuts the contention that even if one grants that abortion is the intentional killing of an innocent person, nonetheless it is sometimes right to kill the innocent in order to achieve a greater good or avoid gravely bad consequences. I am much indebted to Lee for material in the chapter.

9. Philip Wylie, *The Magic Animal* (Garden City, NY: Doubleday, 1968), p. 272. These characterizations are found in a particularly vitriolic passage, filled with invective against the notion of the sanctity of human life.

10. A claim made by the biologist Garrett Hardin, "Abortion — or Compulsory Pregnancy?" *Journal of Marriage and Family* (May, 1968) 250. An obvious and insuperable difficulty with this way of describing the being in question is that it is alive and developing, whereas a blueprint is not.

11. A typical representative of this view is the late and widely influential ethicist Joseph Fletcher. See his essay, "New Beginnings of Life," in *The New Genetics and the Future of Man*, ed. Michael Hamilton (Grand Rapids: Eerdmans, 1972), p. 76. Such descriptions conceal rather than reveal the nature of the being in question.

12. This claim, made early in the twentieth century by the sexologist Havelock Ellis in his *Studies in the Psychology of Sex* (New York: 1924) 6.607, is quite common today and seems in fact to be a tenet of some leading feminists. It is obviously false in view of the fact

that every cell of the being that comes into existence at fertilization is identifiably quite different in nature from every cell of the mother.

13. Germain Grisez, *The Way of the Lord Jesus,* Vol. 2, *Living a Christian Life* (Quincy, IL: Franciscan Press, 1993), pp. 494-495.

14. Stephen Schwarz, *The Moral Question of Abortion* (Chicago: Loyola University Press, 1990), p. 73.

15. Ibid.

16. Marjorie Reiley Maguire, "Personhood, Covenant, and Abortion," in *Abortion and Catholicism: The American Debate*, ed. Patricia Beattie Jung and Thomas A. Shannon (New York: Crossroad, 1988), p. 109. Maguire's essay was originally published, it should be noted, in the 1983 volume of *The Annual of the Society of Christian Ethics* (Knoxville, TN: Society of Christian Ethics, 1983). Her essay, delivered at the annual convention of the Society, was among those judged worthy of publication in the Society's *Annual*. Others who hold this position include Pierre de Locht, former professor of moral theology at the Catholic University of Louvain, "Discussion," in *L'Avortement: Actes du Xieme colloque international de sexologie* (Louvain: Centre International Cardinal Suenens, 1968) 2.155; Louis Beinaert, S.J., "L'avortement est-il un infanticide?" *Etudes* 333 (1970) 520-523; Mary Warnock, "Do Human Cells Have Rights?" *Bioethics* 1 (1987) 2.

17. On this see Grisez, "When Do People Begin?," *Proceedings of the American Catholic Philosophical Association* 63 (1989) 29; *Living a Christian Life,* p. 489.

18. See, in particular, Grisez, "When Do People Begin?" 27-47.

19. See Michael Tooley, *Abortion and Infanticide* (New York: Oxford University Press, 1983); Daniel Callahan, *Abortion: Law, Choice, and Morality* (New York: Macmillan, 1970), pp. 383-389, 497-498; Peter Singer, *Rethinking Life and Death: The Collapse of Our Traditional Ethics* (New York: St. Martin's Press, 1994).

20. See Singer, *Rethinking Life and Death*. Singer notes that the expression "speciesism," which "was coined by the Oxford psychologist Richard Ryder in 1970, has now entered the *Oxford English Dictionary,* where it is defined as 'discrimination against or exploitation of certain animal species by human beings, based on an assumption of mankind's superiority.' As the term suggests, there is a parallel between our attitudes to nonhuman animals, and the attitudes of racists to those they regard as belonging to an inferior race. In both cases there is an inner group that justifies its exploitation of an outer

group by reference to a distinction that *lacks real moral significance"* (p. 173; emphasis added). See also pp. 202-206, where Singer elaborates on his "fifth new commandment: *'Do not discriminate on the basis of species.'"*

21. Lee, *Abortion and Unborn Human Life,* pp. 26-27, emphasis added.
22. This passage is found in a book dealing with the question of euthanasia, where debates over "personhood" similar to those over this issue in considering abortion are common. The book, authored by the members of a "Working Party" of the Linacre Centre of London, is entitled *Euthanasia, Clinical Practice and the Law*, ed. Luke Gormally (London: The Linacre Centre for Health Care Ethics, 1994), pp. 123-124. Among the members of the "Working Party," in addition to Gormally, were John Finnis and Elizabeth Anscombe.
23. Grisez, *Living a Christian Life,* p. 491; see "When Do People Begin?" 31-32. For another excellent defense of the proposition that membership in the human species is a sufficient criterion for personhood, see Lee, *Abortion and Unborn Human Life,* pp. 58-62.
24. For an excellent critique of the dualism underlying this position see Lee, *Abortion and Unborn Human Life,* pp. 32-37. See also Lee's essay, "Human Beings Are Animals," in *Natural Law and Moral Inquiry: Ethics, Metaphysics, and Politics in the Work of Germain Grisez,* ed. Robert P. George (Washington, D.C.: Georgetown University Press, 1998), pp. 135-151.
25. Grisez, *Living a Christian Life*, p. 490. In a footnote (no. 54) Grisez observes that both *Webster's New International Dictionary* and the *Oxford English Dictionary* say that a standard use of the term *person* is to refer to a living, human individual.
26. Grisez, *Living a Christian Life*, pp. 490-491; "When Do People Begin?" 30-31. See also *Euthanasia, Clinical Practice and the Law,* p. 41.
27. See the following: Joseph Donceel, S.J. "Immediate Animation and Delayed Hominization," *Theological Studies* 31 (1970) 76-105; Donceel, "A Liberal Catholic's View," in *Abortion and Catholicism: The American Debate*, pp. 48-53; Thomas A. Shannon and Allan B. Wolter, OFM, "Reflections on the Moral Status of the Pre-Embryo," *Theological Studies* 51 (1990) 603-636. Shannon and Wolter, in their efforts to rehabilitate the "delayed hominization" view, appeal to additional supposed facts made known by contemporary science.
28. For Grisez, see "When Do People Begin?" 33-34; *Living a Christian Life,* pp. 492-493. For Lee, see *Abortion and Unborn Human Life,*

pp. 79-90. See also the following: Benedict Ashley, O.P., "A Critique of the Theory of Delayed Hominization," in *An Ethical Evaluation of Fetal Experimentation: An Interdisciplinary Study*, ed. Donald McCarthy (St. Louis: Pope John XXIII Medical-Moral Research Center, 1976), pp. 113-133; Benedict Ashley, O.P. and Albert Moraczewski, O.P., "Is the Biological Subject of Human Rights Present from Conception?" in *The Fetal Tissue Issue*, ed. Peter Cataldo and Albert Moraczewski, O.P. (Braintree, MA: Pope John XXIII Medical-Moral Research and Education Center, 1994) , pp. 33-60; Jean Siebenthal, "L'animation selon Thomas d'Aquin," in *L'Embryon: Un Homme. Actes du Congrès de Lausanne 1986* (Premier Congrès de la Societé Suisse de Bioetique 8 et 9 novembre 1986) (Lausanne: Centre de documentation civique, 1987), pp. 91-98; Mark Jordan, "Delayed Hominization: Reflections on Some Recent Catholic Claims for Delayed Hominization," *Theological Studies* 56 (1995) 743-763; Stephen J. Heaney, "Aquinas and the Presence of the Human Rational Soul in the Early Embryo," in *Abortion: A New Generation of Catholic Responses,* ed. Stephen J. Heaney (Braintree, MA: Pope John XXIII Medical-Moral Research and Education Center, 1992), pp. 43-72; Augustine Reagan, C.Ss.R., "The Human Conceptus and Personhood," *Studia Moralia* 30 (1992) 97-127.

29. Grisez, *Living a Christian Life,* pp. 492-493.
30. Siebenthal refers to the following Thomistic texts to show this: *Summa theologiae,* I, q. 118, a. 3; q. 76, a. 4 and a. 6, ad 1; III, q. 6, a. 4, ad 1; q. 2, a. 5.
31. Siebenthal, "L'animation selon Thomas d'Aquin," 96-97.
32. Among scholars who accept this view are the following: Baruch Brody, *Abortion and the Sanctity of Human Life: A Philosophical View* (Boston: Massachusetts Institute of Technology Press, 1975); Robert M. Veatch, " Definitions of Life and Death: Should There Be a Consistency?" in *Defining Human Life: Medical, Legal, and Ethical Implications,* ed. Margery W. Shaw and A. Edward Dondera (Ann Arbor, MI: AUPHA Press, 1983), pp. 99-113.
33. Lee, *Abortion and Unborn Human Life,* pp. 76-77.
34. See Grisez, "When Do People Begin?" 34; *Living a Christian Life,* pp. 493-494.
35. For this claim see the following: Karl Rahner,, S.J., "The Problem of Genetic Manipulation," in *Theological Investigations,* Vol. 9, *Writings of 1965-67: I,* tr. Graham Harrison (New York: Herder & Herder, 1972), p. 226; Lisa S. Cahill, "The Embryo and the Fetus: New Moral

Contexts," *Theological Studies* 54 (1993) 124; Richard A. McCormick, S.J., "Who or What Is the Pre-embryo?" *Kennedy Institute of Bioethics Journal* 1 (1991) 3; Shannon and Wolter, "Reflections on the Moral Status of the Pre-Embryo," 618-619.

36. Shannon and Wolter, "Reflections on the Moral Status of the Pre-Embryo," 618, no. 60.

37. W. Jerome Bracken, C.P. "Is the Early Embryo a Person?" in *Life and Learning VIII: Proceedings of the Eighth University Faculty for Life Conference,* June 1998, ed. Joseph W. Koterski, S.J. (Washington, D.C.: University Faculty for Life, 1999), 443-467, where he cites a recent scientific study by D. Wilcox et al., "Incidence of Loss in Early Pregnancy," *The New England Journal of Medicine* 319/4 (July 28, 1988) 189-194 and others to challenge the claims frequently made.

38. Norman Ford, S.D.B., *When Did I Begin?: Conception of the Human Individual in History, Philosophy, and Science* (Cambridge/New York: Cambridge University Press, 1988).

39. Michael Coughlan, *The Vatican, the Embryo, and the Law* (Iowa City: University of Iowa Press, 1990).

40. In their superlative study, "Identity and Status of the Human Embryo: The Contributions of Biology," in *Identity and Statute (sic) of the Human Embryo* (cf. endnote no. 5 for bibliographic details), in which they show the fatal flaws in the theory of Ford and others, Angelo Serra and Roberto Columbo note that the term "pre-embryo" was introduced into the literature in 1986 by A. McLaren. She and others (like Shannon and Wolter) who use this term claim that until approximately the fourteenth day after fertilization all that occurs is the preparation of the protective and nutritional systems required for the future needs of the embryo, and that only at the fifteenth day after fertilization, when the "primitive streak" appears, does the embryo in the strict sense appear (see A. McLaren, "Prelude to Embryogenesis," in *Human Embryo Research: Yes or No?*, the Ciba Foundation [New York: Tavistok, 1986], p. 12). Serra and Columbo, along with others, point out that the embryonic disk, which appears on the fifteenth day and to which McClaren gives such significance, is a structure "which derives from a further differentiation *of the embryoblast, which is already present* when the embryo *as a whole* provides, under genetic control, for a *faster differentiation of the trophoblastic derivatives*, which are extremely necessary for a correct and smooth progress of the body-building process. As a matter of fact," they continue, "the

trophoblast and the embryoblast, both deriving from the zygote, *simultaneously* make their own way as a *whole,* according to a finely orchestrated program" (p. 167). Serra and Columbo thus conclude (with the majority of human embryologists), that it is not correct to distinguish between the so-called "pre-embryo" and the "embryo" proper. It is more scientifically accurate to speak of the "pre-implantation" embryo than of the "pre-embryo" when referring to the living human organism at the pre-implantation stage of development. It is here important to note that Ronan O'Rahilly, internationally regarded as one of the most outstanding human embryologists of our day, regards the term "pre-embryo" as scientifically inaccurate and erroneous and refuses to use the term. See Ronan O'Rahilly and Fabiola Muller, *Human Embryology and Teratology* (New York: John Wiley & Sons, 1994), p. 55.

41. Shannon and Wolter, "Reflections on the Moral Status of the Pre-Embryo," refer to the work of C. A. Bedate and R. C. Cefalo, "The Zygote: To Be or Not to Be a Person," *Journal of Medicine and Philosophy* 14 (1989) 641-645).

42. Antoine Suarez, "Hydatidiform Moles and Teratomas Confirm the Human Identity of the Preimplantation Embryo," *Journal of Medicine and Philosophy* 15 (1990) 627. The same number of this journal carried an essay by Thomas J. Bole, III, "Zygotes, Souls, Substances, and Persons," ibid., 637-652. Bole criticized Suarez's essay on the grounds that normal zygotes have developed into partial hydatidiform moles (whereas Suarez argues that they cannot). Bole's claim, however, is contradicted by competent embryologists, for instance, Stanley J. Robboy, Marie A. Duggan, and Robert J. Kurnam, "The Female Reproductive System," *Pathology,* ed. Emmanuel Rubin and John L. Farber (2nd ed. Philadelphia: J. B. Lippincott, 1994) 967. On this see Bracken, "Is the Early Embryo a Person?," p. 448.

43. See the following: Grisez, "When Do People Begin?" 35-40; *Living a Christian Life,* pp. 495-497; Lee, *Abortion and Unborn Human Life,* pp. 90-102; Ashley and Moraczewski, "Is the Biological Subject of Human Rights Present at Conception?," 33-60; Nicholas Tonti-Filippini, "A Critical Note," *The Linacre Quarterly* 56.3 (August 1989) 36-50; Anthony Fisher, O.P., "Individuogenesis and a Recent Book by Fr. Norman Ford," *Anthropotes: Rivista di studi sulla persona e la famiglia* 7 (1991) 199-244; Serra and Colombo, "Identity and Status of the Human Embryo: The Contribution of Biology," especially pp. 166-176.

44. R. Yanagimachi, "Mammalian Fertilization," in *The Physiology of Reproduction,* ed. E. Knobil, J. Neill et al. (New York: Raven Press, 1988), p. 135; cited by Grisez, "When Do People Begin?" 45, n. 49; *Living a Christian Life,* p. 495, n. 66. For Suarez, see his "Hydatidiform Moles…." (note 42).

45. Grisez, "When Do People Begin?" 37.

46. On this see Lee, *Abortion and Unborn Human Life,* pp. 92-93.

47. Grisez, "When Do People Begin?" 38.

48. Ashley/Moraczewski, "Is the Biological Subject of Human Rights Present from Conception?" pp. 50-53.

49. Pope John Paul II, Apostolic exhortation *Christifideles laici¸* no. 51. See also his Apostolic letter *Mulieris dignitatem,* no. 30: "The moral and spiritual strength of a woman is joined to her awareness that *God entrusts the human being to her in a special way.* Of course, God entrusts every human being to each and every other human being. But this entrusting concerns women in a special way — precisely because of their femininity — and this in a particular way determines their vocation."

50. On this see John Saward, *Redeemer in the Womb: Jesus Living in Mary* (San Francisco: Ignatius Press, 1993), in particular, pp. 165-168.

51. Sidney Callahan, "Abortion and the Sexual Agenda: A Case for Prolife Feminism," in *Abortion and Catholicism: The American Debate*, pp. 128-145, at 128-129.

52. Judith Jarvis Thomson, "In Defense of Abortion," *Philosophy and Public Affairs* (1970).

53. Here I have paraphrased Callahan's summary of these two arguments in "Abortion and the Sexual Agenda…," pp. 128-129.

54. This was the analogy used by Thomson in her celebrated "defense" of abortion (cf. endnote 52).

55. Callahan, "Abortion and the Sexual Agenda…," p. 131.

56. John Finnis, *Natural Law and Natural Rights* (Oxford/New York: Oxford University Press, at the Clarendon Press, 1980). Finnis's book is a volume in the Oxford Law Series. See pp. 199-205, "An Analysis of Rights Talk."

57. See endnote 52 above.

58. Here I follow Lee's summary, pp. 107-108, of Thomson's argument.

59. Ibid., pp. 113-116.

60. According to the principle of "double effect" it is permissible to "allow" or permit an evil to result from an act that is not intrinsically

evil provided that this effect is not intended either as end or as means *and* that there is a "proportionate reason" for "permitting" or "allowing" the evil effect. Lee's argument is that, even if the abortions in question can legitimately be regarded as "removals" rather than "killings"— that is, the evil effect, the unborn child's death, is not intended either as end or as means — there is no "proportionate reason" for "permitting" or "allowing" the evil effect. On the contrary, there are serious moral reasons, based on justice, that require one *not* to "permit" this evil.

61. Lee, *Abortion and Unborn Human Life*, p. 116.
62. St. Thomas Aquinas, *Summa theologiae*, II-II, 64, 7.
63. Grisez, *Abortion: The Myths, the Realities, and the Arguments* (New York and Cleveland: Corpus Instrumentorum, 1970), pp. 340-346.
64. Ibid., pp. 345-346. Here Grisez writes: "Roman Catholic readers may notice that my conclusions about abortion diverge from common theological teachings, and also diverge from the official teaching of the Church as it was laid down by the Holy Office in the nineteenth century. I am aware of the divergence, but would point out that my theory is consonant with the more important and more formally definite teaching that direct killing of the unborn is wrong. I reach conclusions that are not traditional by broadening the meaning of 'unintended' in a revision of the principle of double effect, not by accepting the rightness of direct killing or the violability of unborn life because of any ulterior purpose or indication." He then continues: "Most important, I cannot as a philosopher limit my conclusions by theological principles. However, I can as a Catholic propose my philosophic conclusions as suggestions for consideration in the light of faith, while not proposing anything contrary to the Church's teaching as a practical norm of conduct for my fellow believers. *Those who really believe that there exists on this earth a community whose leaders are appointed and continuously assisted by God to guide those who accept their authority safely through time to eternity, would be foolish to direct their lives by some frail fabrication of mere reason instead of by conforming to a guidance system designed and maintained by divine wisdom"* (emphasis added).
65. Joseph M. Boyle, Jr., "Double Effect and a Certain Kind of Embryotomy," *Irish Theological Quarterly* 44 (1977) 309.
66. I think that Grisez, Boyle, and those who agree with them here are misled by comparing the situation to killing in self-defense. For in-

stance, in a legitimate act of self-defense one might aim a gun at the asssailant's head, pull the trigger and as a result a bullet enters his skull and empties it of its contents and at the same time stops the attack. Precisely because the assailant *is* unjustly attacking one's life, one can rightly regard the act in question as aimed at *stopping the attack* by the only means possible and not as an act aimed at perforating the assailant's skull and emptying it of its contents. But in the craniotomy case the unborn child is most definitely not an *unjust assailant* doing something that threatens the mother's life that must be stopped.

67. Kevin Flannery, S.J., "What Is Included in a Means to an End?" *Gregorianum* 74 (1993) 511-512.

68. John A. Rock, M.D., "Ectopic Pregnancy," in *TeLinde's Operative Gynecology* (Philadelphia: J. B. Lippincott, 1992), pp. 412-414. In 1970 approximately 17,800 ectopic pregnancies were reported in women aged 15 to 44; by 1980 the figure had risen to 52,000 women in this age group; today it is estimated that 1 pregnancy in every 60 is ectopic, with the rate increasing. It is ironic that among the causes of tubal pregnancies are *in vitro* fertilization (frequently resorted to as a way of providing children to women with blocked fallopian tubes) and the use of contraceptives.

69. Ibid., 421-427.

70. J. Cannon and H. Jesionowska, "Methotrexate Treatment of Tubal Pregnancy," *Fertility and Sterility* 55 (June, 1991) 1034.

71. Rock, "Ectopic Pregnancy," 427. See also Charles E. Cavagnaro III, "Treating Ectopic Pregnancy: A Moral Analysis," *The NaProEthics Forum* 3.6 (November, 1998) 4.

72. Rock, 427; Cavagnaro, 4.

73. National Conference of Catholic Bishops, *Ethical and Religious Directives for Catholic Health Care Facilities* (Washington, D.C.: NCCB, 1971), no. 16.

74. National Conference of Catholic Bishops, *Ethical and Religious Directives for Catholic Health Care Services* (Washington, D.C.: NCCB, 1994), no. 48.

75. See William E. May, "The Management of Ectopic Pregnancies: A Moral Analysis," in *The Fetal Tissue Issue: Medical and Ethical Aspects*, ed. Peter J. Cataldo and Albert S. Moraczewski, O.P. (Braintree, MA: Pope John XXIII Medical-Moral Research and Education Center, 1994), pp. 121-148, esp. pp. 133-145. I believe that I was the first moral theologian to consider the use of methotrexate in the management of ectopic pregnancies.

76. Albert Moraczewski, O.P., "Managing Tubal Pregnancies, Part I," *Ethics & Medics*, 21.6 (June, 1996) 3-4; "Managing Tubal Pregnancies, Part II," *Ethics & Medics*, 21.9 (August 1996) 3-4; Jean deBlois, C.S.J., Patrick Norris, O.P., and Kevin O'Rourke, O.P., *A Primer for Heath Care Ethics* (Washington, D.C.: Georgetown University Press, 1994), pp. 208-210. See in particular, Patrick A. Clark, S.J., "Methotrexate and Tubal Pregnancies: Direct or Indirect Abortion?" *The Linacre Quarterly* 67.1 (February 2000) 7-24. Clark, in a very informative and clearly written essay, argues that the trophoblast is not, as I hold, a vital organ of the unborn child, but part of the placenta (Moraczewski holds this too). He claims that the intent in administering methotrexate is not to kill or even injure the embryo or unborn child but rather to inhibit the synthesis of DNA in the trophoblastic tissue whose growth imperils the health and life of the mother.

77. Moraczewski, "Managing Tubal Pregnancies, Part I, " 4.

78. Moraczewski, "Managing Tubal Pregnancies, Part II," 4.

79. See William E. May, "Methotrexate and Ectopic Pregnancy," *Ethics & Medics* 23.3 (March 1998) 1-3. See Moraczewski's reply, "Ectopic Pregnancy Revisited," in ibid., 3-4.

80. I have discussed this matter with three eminent doctors — Thomas W. Hilgers, John Bruchalski, and Bernard Nathanson — and all three have informed me that in their judgment salpingostomy and the use of methotrexate are not morally licit insofar as they indeed constitute direct abortions. Before their own change of heart, both Bruchalski and Nathanson had performed salpingostomies and clearly considered that in peforming them they were securing the death of the infant.

81. Charles Cavagnaro III, M.D., "Treating Ectopic Pregnancy: A Moral Analysis (Part II)," in *The NaProEthics Forum* 4.2 (March 1999) 5. For his analysis of salpingostomy as abortive, see "Treating Ectopic Pregnancy: A Moral Analysis (Part I)," in *The NaProEthics Forum* 3.6 (November 1998) 4-5.

82. This is also the position defended by Msgr. William B. Smith, "Questions Answered: Management of Ectopic Pregnancy," *Homiletic and Pastoral Review* 99.10 (July 1999) 66-68.

Chapter Six

EXPERIMENTATION ON HUMAN SUBJECTS

This chapter will take up the morality of experimentation on human subjects. I will first (1) introduce the topic and articulate and explain the cardinal principle governing human experimentation, namely, the principle of free and informed consent. I will then (2) examine the meaning and limits of proxy consent, in particular, proxy consent for nontherapeutic experiments to be carried out on incompetent human persons or those whom the late Paul Ramsey called "voiceless patients," and follow the analysis of this issue with a consideration of (3) research on the unborn, in particular embryo stem-cell research, (4) gene therapy, (5) prenatal and pre-implantation genetic screening, (6) genetic counseling, and (7) the human genome project.

1. INTRODUCTION: THE CARDINAL PRINCIPLE OF FREE AND INFORMED CONSENT[1]

One of the most unforgettable television newscasts I ever witnessed was a May 1973 CBS Special Report, "The Ultimate Experimental Animal: Man." It included a scene that struck me as especially illuminating, which well serves to introduce the question of experimenting on human beings. A black woman, who had been a prisoner in a Detroit jail, had participated in a program testing a new type of birth-control pill. This particular pill was known to the researchers to carry a high risk of causing cancer, but this fact was deliberately withheld from the women who had "volunteered" to participate in the program testing its effectiveness. When the woman learned, after her release from prison, that the pill she and other women had been taking posed a serious risk of causing cancer, she was outraged at having been "used," declaring to the CBS correspondent that she had been "treated like an animal."

Her reaction is very instructive. In saying that she had been treated like an animal and in being outraged at having been so treated, she voiced the conviction that human beings ought not to be treated like animals. She was not necessarily denying that she — with other human beings as well — is an animal (for, after all, we are); rather, she was affirming that a human being is an *animal with a difference*, an entity of moral worth, a subject of rights that demand respect and protection from the society in which one lives. She was saying, in a simple and unsophisticated way, what the philosopher Roger Wertheimer has called a "standard belief" among human beings. This is the belief that "being human has moral cachet; a human being has human status in virtue of being a human being";[2] that being a member of the human species has *moral* significance and has so because every member of the human species is a *person,* not a thing or mere animal.[3]

She was also affirming that any experiment performed on the "human animal" must, if it is to be rightly carried out, respect the truth that human beings are persons, beings of moral worth, subjects of rights rooted in their being and not conferred on them by others. She was affirming, at least implicitly, that no human being can be regarded simply a part subordinated to a larger whole, the society at large, but must be considered as a whole that cannot rightly be subordinated to the interests of others. Expressed in more philosophical terms, this woman was articulating what Karol Wojtyla called the "personalistic norm," which, "in its negative aspect, states that the person is the kind of good which does not admit of use and cannot be treated as an object of use and as such the means to an end," and which, "in its positive form ... confirms this: the person is a good towards which the only adequate attitude is love."[4]

This is the cardinal point to be kept in mind as we consider the ethics of experimenting on human subjects. The moral worth of every human being from conception/fertilization until death is *the* crucial truth in considering this important topic in all its ramifications. That every human being *is* indeed a being of moral worth, a person of irreplaceable and priceless value, is a truth central to the Gospel and is eloquently proclaimed by the Church, as we have seen in our review of relevant magisterial documents in Chapter One. It is this truth alone that renders intelligible the cardinal principle in human experimentation, namely, the principle of free and informed consent, that "canon of loyalty," as Paul

Ramsey terms it,[5] which is operative in all situations wherein one human person is the experimenter and another is his "co-adventurer" in the experiment.

A. Basic Types of Experimentation

Before we look into this principle and its meaning, however, it will be useful to distinguish different types of experimental situations. There are many types of such situations, but from the perspective of moral analysis the two most basic kinds are *therapeutic* and *nontherapeutic* or purely *research* experiments. Among the first can be included experiments whose purpose is to (1) diagnose an illness or condition afflicting a person, (2) alleviate or cure a malady from which the subject is suffering, and (3) prevent a person from becoming afflicted with a specifiable malady. Therapeutic experiments, in short, can be diagnostic, curative or alleviating, or preventive. Despite the differences in these kinds of experiments, all are therapeutic in that they are aimed at being of medical benefit to the subject experimented on. Some therapeutic experiments are *research* experiments in the sense that they study the effects of using diagnostic, prophylactic/therapeutic, or preventive methods that depart from ordinary medical practice, but nonetheless offer reasonable hope of success. Such research experiments are thus truly therapeutic insofar as they are designed not only to acquire knowledge but also *to be of benefit* for the subject.[6]

Nontherapeutic or purely research experiments are not, of themselves, designed to be of medical benefit to the subject. They are rather intended to further biomedical and behavioral research, to advance the frontiers of knowledge, and thus enable us eventually to develop new techniques for coping with the diverse maladies that plague humankind and thereby to enhance the common good. It is true that at times the subjects of such nontherapeutic experiments may be benefited in spiritual and psychological ways, but such benefits to the subject are incidental to the experiment (and experimenter!) as such, inasmuch as the experiment (and the experimenter) *intend* or *aim at* acquiring knowledge that *may* be beneficial to human beings in the future, whereas the therapeutic experiment is aimed at benefiting the subject of the experiment.

B. The Key Principle or "Canon of Loyalty": The Principle of Free and Informed Consent

The canon of loyalty that must be observed in experimental situations, whether therapeutic or nontherapeutic, is the principle of free and informed consent. This principle is at the heart of medical ethics and bioethics. It was eloquently expressed in the articles of the Nuremberg Code (1946-1949), and it is salutary today, a half-century later, to recall that this code was formulated when the memories of the atrocities carried out on human subjects by the Third Reich in the name of scientific research was fresh in the minds of men. According to the first article of the Nuremberg Code,

> The voluntary consent of the human subject is absolutely essential. This means that the person involved should have legal capacity to give consent; should be so situated as to be able to exercise free power of choice, without the intervention of any element of force, fraud, deceit, duress, overreaching, or other ulterior form of constraint or coercion; and should have sufficient knowledge and comprehension of the elements of the subject matter involved as to enable him to make an understanding and enlightened decision. This latter element requires that before the acceptance of an affirmative decision by the experimental subject there should be made known to him the nature, duration, and purpose of the experiment; the method and means by which it is to be conducted; all the inconveniences and hazards reasonably to be expected; and the effects upon his health or person which may probably come from his participation in the experiment.[7]

The moral demand that a human person who is to be the subject of an experiment give free and informed consent is also embodied in the code of ethics adopted by the World Health Organization in the *Declaration of Helsinki* in 1964 and by the American Medical Association.[8] This principle is at the heart of traditional Jewish and Christian medical ethics, and has been reaffirmed time and time again by the Magisterium of the Church.

The Principle of Free and Informed Consent and Relevant Teaching of the Magisterium

The *Charter for Health Care Workers*, promulgated by the Pontifical Council for Pastoral Assistance to Health Care Workers in 1994, provides a valuable summary of magisterial teaching on the need to secure the patient's informed consent in number 72, citing liberally from and referring to relevant magisterial documents. Thus it will be useful here to present the text of this number and in the endnotes refer to the magisterial documents either cited in the text of this number or referred to in the footnotes contained in it.

> To intervene medically, the health care worker should have the express or tacit consent of the patient. In fact [as Pope Pius XII affirmed], "he does not have a separate and independent right in relation to the patient. In general, he can act only if the patient explicitly or implicitly (directly or indirectly) authorizes him."[9] Without such authorization he gives himself an arbitrary power.[10] Besides the medical relationship there is a human one: dialogic, non-objective. The patient [as Pope John Paul II insists] "is not an anonymous individual" on whom medical expertise is practiced, but "a responsible person, who should be given the opportunity of personally choosing, and not be made to submit to the decisions and choices of others."[11] So that the choice may be made with full awareness and freedom, the patient should be given a precise idea of his illness and the therapeutic possibilities, with the risks, the problems and the consequences that they entail.[12] This means that the patient should be asked for an *informed consent.*[13]

Interpreting This Principle

It is frequently difficult, if not impossible, as many authorities have pointed out,[14] to secure *fully* informed consent. They have noted that frequently it is not possible to explain to the person about to undergo an experiment all of the complications involved. At times, some hazards may not be known; at other times the persons to be subjected to the experiment may not be capable of understanding all the pertinent and known factors; at other times full details of all possible hazards and complications might so terrify a person that he or she may become paralyzed in thought and unwilling to consent to a procedure that is really not hazardous and that offers solid hope of being beneficial.

This means that this cardinal principle or canon of loyalty, demanding the subject's free and informed consent, is to be understood as requiring "reasonably" free and "adequately" informed consent, and the reasonableness and adequacy are to be determined in accord with the "Golden Rule" of doing unto others as you would have them do unto you and not do unto them what you would not have them do to you.

Ramsey puts matters this way: "A choice may be free and responsible despite the fact that it began in an emotional bias one way or another, and consent can be informed without being encyclopedic."[15] In their *Ethical and Religious Directives for Catholic Health Care Services* (1994), the bishops of the United States expressed the requirement of free and informed consent as follows: "Free and informed consent requires that the person or the person's surrogate [the issue of "proxy consent" will be explored below] receive all reasonable information about the essential nature of the proposed treatment and its benefits; its risks, side-effects, consequences, and cost; and any reasonable and morally legitimate alternatives, including no treatment at all."[16]

Basically, what is at stake here is *trust* between the subject and the doctor/researcher: trust that the doctor/researcher will *not* propose any experiment without communicating to the subject sufficient information for him or her to make an informed decision, for after all, it affects that person's life and health. Unfortunately today, this trust between patients and doctors/researchers has been to a great extent eroded for a wide variety of reasons, and it is imperative that such trust be restored. It can only be restored if doctors and researchers are willing, in informing subjects of proposed experiments, to shape their choices and actions in accord with the Golden Rule or basic principle of justice and fairness.[17]

This requirement, the canon of loyalty demanding reasonably free and informed consent, is imperative in *all* types of experimentation on human persons (who come to be at conception/fertilization and remain in being so long as they are living human bodies). The reason is rooted in the inviolability of the human person as a being of moral worth, as an entity surpassing in value the entire material created world, the bearer of inalienable rights that must be recognized and respected by society and by all persons. As we have seen before, human beings are ends, not means, and all human beings are equal in their dignity as persons.[18] Ramsey has put the matter beautifully by saying, "No man is good enough to experiment upon another without his consent."[19] To experiment on a human subject without securing his consent is to treat him as a being who is no longer a person, no longer a being of moral worth, to make of him a means, not an end, to subordinate him to others, to deny his humanity.

With respect to medical treatments there is one clear exception from the requirement of expressed consent, an exception which in no way weakens the normative demand governing medical practice by consent alone. This is the kind of case in which consent is reasonably presumed or implied when a person is in extreme danger and cannot explicitly give consent. As the *Charter for Health Care Workers* says, in extreme situations of this kind, "if there is a temporary loss of knowing and willing, the health care worker can act in virtue of *the principle of therapeutic trust....* Should there be a permanent loss of knowing and willing, the health care worker can act in virtue of *the principle of responsibility for health care,* which obliges the health care worker to assume responsibility for the patient's health."[20] As Ramsey has said, "Indeed, we might say that if a doctor stops on the road to Jericho, instead of passing by on his way to read a research paper before a scientific gathering or to visit his regular, paying customers, he is self-selected as good enough to practice medicine without the needy man's expressed consent."[21]

2. PROXY CONSENT: ITS MEANING, JUSTIFICATION, AND LIMITS

There are many instances when it is impossible to secure adequately informed and free consent from the person who is to be the subject of the experimentation. It is obviously impossible to obtain such consent from incompetent human persons, the unborn, infants and children, the demented, etc., those whom Ramsey has called "voiceless patients."

A. Proxy Consent in the Therapeutic Situation

There is no serious debate among authorities — legal, medical, or moral — that proxy consent, i.e., consent given by another acting as a surrogate for the person on whom the experiment is to be performed, is justifiable when the experiment in question is therapeutic, that is, when it is designed to secure some benefit for the subject.

Frequently, the responsibilities of those who give proxy consent for therapeutic procedures on behalf of voiceless patients are described as making choices in accord with the incompetent individual's own preferences, if these are known, or else making these choices in accord with the "best interests" of the individual concerned if he or she had never expressed personal preferences, for instance, if one is acting as a proxy for an infant or for an adult who has never been able to exercise moral responsibility because of some anomaly. Thus the bishops of the United States declare that decisions made on behalf of an individual by a designated surrogate (or responsible family member) should "be faithful to Catholic moral principles and to the person's intentions and values [so long as these are compatible with Catholic moral principles], or if the person's intentions are unknown, to the person's best interests."[22]

I believe that the basic moral principle justifying "proxy" consent in the therapeutic situation is in fact the Golden Rule. We are to do unto others as we would have them do unto us and not do unto them what we would not have them do to us. If the health or life of a fellow human person for whom we have responsibility (as parents do for their children) is in danger and there are means that can be taken to protect and/or enhance that person's health and life and/or ameliorate his or her condition *without imposing grave burdens upon that person*, then we are morally obligated to authorize use of those means for protecting/preserving/ enhancing/ameliorating the life and health of the person for whom we have responsibility. The *Charter for Health Care Workers,* I believe, expressed this requirement, rooted in the principle of the Golden Rule, in what it termed the *"principle of responsibility for health care."*[23]

In other words, I think that "proxy consent," when made on behalf of those who have never been able to articulate their own preferences with respect to the kind of therapeutic care they are willing to accept, is not so much "proxy consent," i.e., consent made in the name of another person (as godparents act as proxies for infants in consenting to baptism) as it is the *personal consent* of the one morally responsible for the care of the incompetent individual. In giving consent to *therapeutic* experiments, that is, those reasonably expected to *benefit* the subject, to protect his *goods,* on such incompetent persons, those giving it are not so much speaking in the name of those voiceless patients but are rather exercising their own proper moral responsibility.

If consent is given on behalf of a now incompetent person who, while competent, had expressed his or her preferences for the kind of therapeutic treatment he or she is willing to accept, then we are indeed speaking of "proxy consent," and the U. S. bishops are quite correct in saying that the choice made (the free consent given) ought to be faithful to person's intentions and values, *as long as such a choice is faithful to Catholic moral principles.* This issue will be taken up in greater depth in the following chapter where we set forth the criteria to be observed in making moral choices regarding the kind of therapeutic medical treatment proposed to persons.

B. Proxy Consent in the Nontherapeutic Situation

But can proxy consent be justified in the nontherapeutic situation, i.e., in cases when the proposed experiment is *not aimed* at benefiting the subject of the experiment, but is rather aimed at securing knowledge that may, in the future, be of great benefit to others? Such experiments, which the *Charter for Health Care Workers* calls "clinical experimentation," can be practiced on a healthy person "who *voluntarily* offers himself 'to contribute by his initiative to the progress of medicine and, in that way, to the good of the community.' In this case, 'once his own substantial integrity is safeguarded, the patient can legitimately accept a certain degree of risk.' "[24] *Personal* consent to such clinical (nontherapeutic) experimentation is justified, the *Charter* continues, "by the human and Christian solidarity which motivates the gesture: 'To give of oneself, within the limits marked out by the moral law, can be a witness of highly meritorious charity and a means of such significant spiritual growth that it can compensate for the risk of any insubstantial physical impairment.' "[25]

Thus *personal* consent to nontherapeutic or clinical experiments, i.e., those not designed to benefit the subject of the experiment but rather designed to acquire knowledge that may be beneficial to others, is fully justified under certain conditions. But can *proxy consent* to such experiments be justified? Is it, for instance, morally licit for parents to consent to nontherapeutic experiments on their infants (born or unborn) and young children?

There is a lively debate today over this issue. The two principal positions, as we shall see, are: (1) proxy consent on behalf of incompetent, voiceless persons to nontherapeutic experiments is *never* justifiable; and (2) proxy consent on behalf of such persons to nontherapeutic experiments is justifiable *if* the experiment in question promises great benefits, cannot be carried out on other human subjects, and entails no "significant" risk to the well-being of the subject. Before examining these positions more closely, I want first to examine some teachings of the Magisterium relevant to this issue. And here, as we will see, there are grounds for perplexity with reference to nontherapeutic experiments on incompetent persons after birth.

Magisterial Teaching

The universal Magisterium of the Church clearly and unambiguously rejects as absolutely immoral proxy consent to nontherapeutic experiments on *unborn human persons*. Thus *Donum vitae (Vatican Instruction on Respect for Human Life in Its Origin and on the Dignity of Procreation)* firmly teaches:

> No finality, even if in itself noble, such as the foreseeing of a usefulness for science, for other human beings or for society, can in any way justify experimentation on live hu-

man embryos and fetuses, whether viable or not, in the maternal womb or outside of it. The informed consent, normally required for clinical experimentation on an adult, cannot be given by the parents, who may not dispose either of the physical integrity or the life of the expected child. On the other hand, experimentation on embryos or fetuses has the risk, indeed in most cases the certain foreknowledge, of damaging their physical integrity or even causing their death. To use a human embryo or the fetus as an object or instrument of experimentation is a crime against their dignity as human beings.[26]

Pope John Paul II has, moreover, condemned "in a most explicit and formal way experimental manipulation of the human embryo, because it is a human being; from the moment of its conception until death it can never be instrumentalized for any reason whatsoever."[27]

This teaching of Pope John Paul II and of the Congregation for the Doctrine of the Faith repudiating *all* nontherapeutic experimentation on the unborn (and hence rejecting "proxy consent" to such experimentation) has been explicitly reaffirmed by the Pontifical Council for Pastoral Assistance to Health Care Workers in its *Charter for Health Care Workers* (no. 82) and by the bishops of the United States in their *Ethical and Religious Directives for Catholic Health Care Facilities* (no. 51).[28]

It is thus very clear that the Magisterium of the Church absolutely excludes as immoral proxy consent to *nontherapeutic* experiments on unborn human persons. But does the Magisterium absolutely exclude such experimentation on incompetent or voiceless persons after birth? I believe that this conclusion can be legitimately inferred from the magisterial teaching we have reviewed here, and I hope to show why. But first, it seems to me, it is necessary to call attention to a specific directive in the U.S. Bishops *Ethical and Religious Directives* which *authorizes* proxy consent to nontherapeutic experiments on incompetent patients. The directive in question is number 31, which reads in part: "No one should be the subject of medical or genetic experimentation, even if it is therapeutic, unless the person or surrogate first has given free and informed consent. *In instances of nontherapeutic experimentation, the surrogate can give this consent **only if the experiment entails no significant risk to the person's well-being**"* (emphasis added). Note that no *reasons* are given to justify such proxy consent to nontherapeutic experiments on the incompetent; it is simply asserted that such consent can be given on condition that the experiment entails no significant risk to the well-being of the incompetent or voiceless person. But it seems to me difficult to reconcile this directive, permitting such proxy consent under certain conditions, with directive no. 51 which, as we have seen, explicitly prohibits proxy consent to nontherapeutic experiments on the unborn (living embryos and fetuses). Why the double standard?

Although the universal Magisterium, so far as I can determine, has not *explicitly* addressed the question of proxy consent to nontherapeutic experiments on voiceless persons who have been born, it seems to me that the *reason* advanced by the Magisterium to exclude totally such consent when the subjects in question are unborn human beings applies as well to those persons who are born and are incapable of giving personal consent to such experiments. For the *reason* given to exclude such consent is simply that human embryos and fetuses are *human beings* and that it is contrary to the dignity of human beings to be used as subjects of nontherapeutic experiments without their personal consent. Thus, as we saw above (see text cited at endnote no. 27) Pope John Paul II condemned in most formal and explicit terms experimental manipulation of the human embryo *"because it is a human being; from the moment of its conception until death it can never be instrumentalized for any reason whatsoever."* Moreover, in the *Charter on the Rights of the Family* issued by the Holy See in 1983, it was affirmed that all kinds of experimental manipulation or exploitation of the embryo are excluded because *"respect for the human being"* so demands.[29] This is, moreover, the reason why the Congregation for the Doctrine of the Faith in *Donum vitae* excluded, as we saw above (cf. text and endnote 26), all nontherapeutic experimentation on the unborn. I therefore believe that one can legitimately infer that magisterial teaching firmly repudiates proxy consent to nontherapeutic experiments on voiceless human persons, on the incompetent, whether they be born or unborn.

Moral Arguments Pro and Con Proxy Consent to Nontherapeutic Experiments on the Voiceless

During the 1970s, as Robert J. Levin has said, "the debate between Paul Ramsey and Richard McCormick over the legitimacy of proxy consent to authorize the participation of an incompetent person in research is one of the classics in the brief history of bioethics."[30] Ramsey firmly opposed the legitimacy of such consent, whereas McCormick authorized such consent in situations where the experiment promised great good and posed no risk or minimal risk to the voiceless or incompetent subject. I was myself a party to this debate, supporting Ramsey and, in my critique of McCormick, developing reasons that Ramsey subsequently adopted in replying to McCormick's position. Here I will summarize the debate.

Ramsey first addressed the issue in his 1970 classic *The Patient as Person.* Speaking of the use of children in purely experimental situations, i.e., when the proposed experimentation is in no way related to their own good, Ramsey declared: "To experiment on children in ways that are not related to them as patients is already a sanitized form of barbarism; it already removes them from view and pays no attention to the faithfulness-claims which a child, simply by being a normal or sick or dying child, places upon us and upon medical care. We should expect no morally significant exceptions to this canon of faithfulness to the child. To expect future justifiable exceptions is, in some sense, already to have forgotten the child."[31] Continuing, he affirms,

> to attempt to consent for a child to be made an experimental subject is to treat the child as not a child…. If the grounds for this are alleged to be the presumptive or implied consent of the child, this must simply be characterized as a violent and false presumption. Nontherapeutic, nondiagnostic experimentation involving human subjects must be based on true consent if it is to proceed as a human enterprise. No child or incompetent adult can choose to become a participating member of medical undertakings, and no one else on earth should decide to subject those people to investigations having no relation to their own treatment. That is a canon of loyalty to them. This they claim simply by being a human child or incompetent.[32]

In his essay "Proxy Consent in the Experimental Situation," originally published in *Perspectives in Biology and Medicine* 18 (1974) and reprinted as Chapter Four of *How Brave a New World? Dilemmas in Bioethics* (1981), the late Jesuit moral theologian Richard McCormick sought to justify proxy consent to nontherapeutic experiments on incompetent or voiceless subjects. His basic argument was based on an analogy. He argued that proxy consent for children and other incompetent subjects in the *therapeutic* situation is justified precisely because parents (and other surrogates) can presume that the subjects themselves *would*, if they could, consent because they *ought* to consent because of their obligation to protect their own life and health. Similarly, he argued that in those nontherapeutic experiments where no risk or minimal risk is entailed and great good is promised, proxy consent for children and other incompetents is justifiable inasmuch as one can reasonably assume that the incompetent subjects themselves *would*, if they could, consent because they would realize that they *ought* to consent to such experiments because of their social nature and their obligation to promote the common good of the society when they can do so with little effort and no danger or minimal danger to themselves.[33] This is McCormick's basic rationale for justifying proxy consent to nontherapeutic experiments on voiceless persons.

I criticized McCormick in an article published in *The Linacre Quarterly* in 1974 and subsequently revised and included in part of Chapter One of *Human Existence, Medicine and Ethics*.[34] I argued that McCormick did not, first of all, give the right reason why proxy consent in the therapeutic situation was morally justifiable. There is no need to presume, as McCormick did, that children would consent to such experiments because they would realize that they ought to do so. There is no need to infer that children and other incompetents have any moral obligations, that they *ought* to do something. They are not moral agents, although they are beings of moral worth. Proxy consent in the therapeutic situation is justified and indeed demanded because *parents* and *other adult care-givers* have duty to meet *their own moral obligations*. They are obliged to care for the life and health of children and other incompetent persons entrusted to them, and this requires them to use the ordinary, obligatory means for protecting and preserving the life and health of these persons. They need infer no moral obligations incumbent upon children and other voiceless persons. Ramsey thought my critique of McCormick sound, and he made it his own in a reply to McCormick's position which he published in 1976.[35]

In a reply to this criticism, McCormick accused Ramsey (and, implicitly, me) of having an individualistic understanding of human existence. His central defense of his original position was that it was not, after all (as I had said and as Ramsey had argued), an attempt to treat children not as the children they are but as moral agents with moral responsibilities. Rather, he now claimed, his argument was rooted in the *social nature* of human persons, and he claimed, without argument, that Ramsey (and I) simply ignore or deny the social dimension of human existence by treating children as individualistic bearers of rights. In essence this was his reply to our criticism.[36]

But his reply completely misses the mark. Both Ramsey and I fully affirm the social nature of our existence. We (and here I speak in the name of Ramsey, whose thought on this matter was crystal-clear) would prefer to speak of the *covenantal* character of human existence. But there is a vast difference in the way this dimension is expressed in an adult and in a child (born or pre-born). An adult, who is a moral agent, is consciously aware of the social, corporate, covenantal character of his existence. He is acutely conscious (or *ought* to be conscious) of the obligations he has to others, of the demand that he recognize them for who they are — persons like himself and equal in personal dignity to himself. By definition, an adult is a morally responsible agent, aware of his social nature and of his obligation to contribute to the common good. But a child is not yet aware of his social obligations. His sociability consists in his need for and right to the protection and care of others, who are, among other things, required to help educate the child so that he can arrive at an understanding of himself as a social being with responsibilities to others. But until he arrives at this understanding he is incapable of contributing to the common good by *freely chosen actions* because he is not capable of such actions. As a child, he contributes to the common good simply by *being*, and the adults in the community have the obligation to respect him as a person equal in dignity to themselves. And they violate this dignity if they "volunteer" him for actions, such as participation in nontherapeutic experiments, that require free, personal consent if they are to be truly human.

I conclude, therefore, that to authorize that a child or other voiceless patient be made to participate in an experiment that is in no way related to his well-being and in which his participation is required simply because his participation is either most useful or indispensable to the success of the venture is an act that ruptures the covenantal, social bonds meant to exist among human persons, for it is to regard this particular human person, this being of irreplaceable and non-substitutable value, either as an impersonal "it" or as the bearer of social responsibilities, neither of which a child or voiceless patient is. To do so is also to erode the very fabric of human social existence, for it is a betrayal of the *trust* confided to moral agents to care, and only care, for those members of the human species who cannot care for themselves. I believe that this conclusion, moreover, is fully in accord with magisterial teaching on human experimentation and its limits. The Dominican moral theologians and bioethicists Ashley and O'Rourke agree with the position developed and defended by Ramsey and me.[37]

McCormick's position seemingly provided the basis for the National Commission for the Protection of Human Subjects of Biomedical and Behavioral Research. McCormick was one of the members of this Commission, which was established, ironically, in the wake of *Roe v. Wade's* conferring of the abortion "liberty," precisely because abortions now made available a new group of "human subjects" on whom experiments could be carried out, namely the unborn about to aborted, and guidance was sought as to what kind of nontherapeutic experimentation might be done on such (and other) "human subjects." The Commission in 1975 essentially adopted the view that such experimentation was morally permissible if it promised great good and posed no significant risk to the incompetent subjects.[38] McCormick's view is evidently the one accepted by the U.S. Bishops in no. 31 of their 1994 *Ethical and Religious Directives for Catholic Health Care Services*, which I cited earlier in this section. I obviously regard this specific directive as erroneous and incompatible with the teaching of the universal Magisterium and, indeed, incompatible with directive no. 51, as noted above.

3. RESEARCH ON THE UNBORN, IN PARTICULAR, EMBRYONIC STEM-CELL RESEARCH

The basic norm, clearly developed by *Donum vitae (Vatican Instruction on Respect for Human Life in Its Origin and on the Dignity of Procreation)*, as we saw in the previous section and also in Chapter One, rightly condemns as utterly immoral any nontherapeutic experimentation or research on human embryos. Any form of experimentation or research on a human embryo performed on it not for its own benefit but for that of others is unethical and gravely immoral, particularly if the experimentation is such as to gravely harm the unborn child. Any procedure whereby new human life is generated *in vitro* in order either to use it for implantation and gestation later on or to freeze it or to use it for experimental purposes is radically immoral and unjust, however good the motivation for doing so.

Experimenting on human embryos and using them as subjects of scientific research is today common in our society. Doing this is "justified" by appeals to the great good that can be accomplished by using tissues, organs, etc., from these early human beings in order to cure or at least ameliorate dread diseases such as Parkinson's disease.

A. What Are Human Embryonic Stem Cells and Why Are They Used for Research?

In the final years of the twentieth century, embryo stem-cell research, in particular, became a matter of great interest. Stem cells are cells that develop very early in the human embryo after fertilization. They form the "inner cell mass" of the early embryo during the blastocyst stage, when the embryo is about to implant in the womb (the "outer cells mass" of the blastocyst are called the trophoblast and form the placenta and other supporting and vital organs needed for the development of the unborn child within the mother). These cells go on to form the body of the developing human person and are thus called the embryonic stem cells. Although they are not "totipotential," as are the cells organized into a unitary whole in the pre-implantation embryo, they are "pluripotential" since they have the capacity to develop into any of the 200 and more different kinds of cells that make up the adult human body. In theory, if these cells are extracted early enough during embryonic life, they can be cultured and manipulated to become the cells needed for specific therapeutic purposes. The cells thus produced can be transferred into an organ (e.g., the brain), where they can proliferate and replace or repair cells that are injured or dying because of some disease. With modern technology, there is reason to think that they can be designed to repair or replace muscle or brain cells, transplanted into human hearts or brains in order to treat such maladies as Parkinson's disease, Alzheimer's disease, and various heart maladies, and in this way restore health to many people.[39]

Three principal methods, all of them intrinsically immoral, are currently being proposed for retrieving embryonic stem cells. The first is to induce the abortion of early embryos and retrieve their stem cells. The second is to produce embryos *in vitro* solely for the purpose of research, including stem-cell research. The third — favored by the presidentially-appointed National Bioethics Advisory Commission — is to use the so-called "spare" embryos produced *in vitro* for infertility treatment and cryopreserved. According to the proposal favored by the Commission — although its final report, as of this writing (February 2000), has not yet been issued — such frozen embryos would be thawed and allowed to develop to the blastocyst stage, when the stem cells would be extracted from the inner cell mass. All three of these methods require the *intentional* killing of unborn human children and are hence intrinsically evil. Even those who advocate such experimentation and research acknowledge that a living thing must be destroyed for the potential gain for others that its destruction can serve.[40]

As a position paper prepared by Senator Sam Brownback of Kansas and released on July 1, 1999, rightly says, "The prospect of government-sponsored experiments to manipulate and destroy human embryos should make us all lie awake at night. That some individuals would be destroyed in the name of medical science constitutes a threat to us all."[41] Such experimentation and research is barbaric, disguised, and hidden by utilitarian rhetoric and visions of the great good promised by being willing to close one's mind to the human dignity of the early unborn child, seeing in its place only "tissues" and "cells" with no inherent value.

B. Legitimate Sources of Stem Cells for Research

Ironically, there are procedures available for obtaining human stem cells that do not require the destruction of human embryos. As Edmund D. Pellegrino, M.D., among others, has pointed out, "Creditable laboratories have identified a wide variety of sources for pluripotential cells with the capability of embryonic stem cells. For example, stem cells from the bone marrow, placenta, or umbilical cord of live births are already in use in treating leukemia. Work currently in progress indicates that such cells can be altered to develop into cartilege and bone tissue and used in replacing diseased bone tissue. Recently (1998) neural stem cells were successfully isolated from living nerve tissue … and show promise for possible use in treating Parkinson's disease or brain injuries."[42] Moreover, in 1999 Dr. Jonas Frisen and colleagues at the Karolinska Institute in Stockholm, Sweden, isolated adult brain stem cells that divided. He is convinced that it will be possible, for instance, to retrieve adult brain stem cells from patients suffering from Parkinson's disease and to treat them with their own stem cells. This procedure would avoid not only grave ethical problems but immunological problems as well.[43]

Efforts to use human embryos, whether generated in the body of their mothers or *in vitro*, as subjects of nontherapeutic research and experimentation are utterly immoral, indeed barbaric and inhuman. As *Donum vitae* put matters, "no objective, even though noble in itself, such as a foreseeable advantage to science, to other human beings, or to society, can in any way justify experimentation on living human embryos or fetuses, whether viable or not, either inside or outside the mother's body."

4. GENETIC THERAPY

A. Gene Therapy: Its Definition and Types

"Gene therapy," as the Working Party of the [UK's] Catholic Bishops' Joint Committee on Bioethical Issues has said, "is the intentional alteration of genes in cells or tissues in such a way as to treat or prevent an inherited disorder, or to make another pathological condition more amenable to treatment." Continuing, the Working Party describes two of the basic types of such therapy: "Such intervention is termed *somatic* gene therapy if the alteration affects only the individual on whom it is carried out. If the intervention takes place on the germ-line cells — that is, sperm, ova, or their precursors — it is termed *germ-line* gene therapy, and will affect not only a particular individual but also his or her descendants."[44]

The goal of gene therapy is to treat human diseases by correcting the genetic defects underlying genetic maladies or by adding new genes to the patient in order to provide or enhance a given therapeutic operation.

In addition to these forms of gene *therapy* there exists also the possibility of genetic *enhancement,* i.e., efforts to improve or enhance, by genetic engineering, characteristics such as size, skin color, intelligence, etc. Speaking of this possibility W. French Anderson, one of the leading world authorities on gene therapy, had this to say: "To the extent that defects in these traits constitute truly damaging errors or disease, they ought to, and will, be treated with all the tools at our command [and efforts to treat these defects would then come under gene *therapy*]. But to the extent that they are not errors but rather normal human variations, the pursuit of forms of enhancement modification is fraught with risks for society." Anderson then goes on to enumerate some of these serious risks.[45] I will not here consider enhancement genetic engineering. At present, there are no good ethical reasons for attempting such engineering and many good moral reasons for not doing so; the medical hazards are as yet not even known: who decides and on what criteria, which genes to select for "enhancement," how one could avoid unjust discrimination in selecting those who would presumably benefit from such enhancement, etc.

Thus in what follows attention focuses on gene *therapy,* and, in particular — for reasons to be given later — on *somatic gene therapy.*

B. How Gene Therapy "Works"

Today it is possible to treat or prevent a genetically based malady because of the breakthroughs that have occurred with ever-increasing frequency in molecular biology and DNA research over the past half-century. Each human cell, except for the mature red blood cell, has a nucleus containing *chromosomes.* Each chromosome is made up of DNA (deoxyribonucleic acid), which takes the form of a double-stranded helix, and attached to each strand of the helix is a series of alternating nucleotides called *bases*. DNA is the "genetic alphabet" and its bases are the "letters" of this alphabet. There are four, and only four, such bases or letters, namely, adenine (A), cytosine (C), guanine (G, and thymine (T), and the "words" of the genetic language or DNA are constructed of these "letters" or bases. The sequence of bases on either strand of the DNA constitutes a gene, the basic unit of heredity whereby traits are passed on from one generation to another.

Scientists now know a good deal about this genetic language. They realize that the substitution of even one "letter" for another can cause a cell to produce or not produce a given enzyme or protein essential for the normal functioning of the organism. If the organism is not functioning properly because of an error in the language of its DNA, it is possible, in light of new breakthroughs in molecular biology and recombinant DNA, to put the "right" letter into the pertinent genetic "word," to replace one that is "incorrect," etc., and in this way to correct a given genetically-induced defect. In theory, such genetic therapeutic intervention can be done either to the body or somatic cells of the person afflicted with the malady — *somatic cell* therapy as described above — or to the germ cells of the persons transmitting the genetic traits to their offspring through generation of human life — *germ-line* therapy as described above.[46]

The major problem, once the "correct gene" has been designed or produced, is to get it into appropriate body cells of the person receiving the therapy.

C. Strategies for Gene Therapy

According to Anderson, there are three basic approaches to the genetic correction of diseases, namely (1) *ex vivo*, (2) *in situ*, and (3) *in vivo*. The first requires the removal of cells from the patient, "correcting" them outside his body by inserting the normal gene, and then returning the corrected cells to the patient. The second introduces the new, correct gene, directly into the site of the disease within the body of the patient either in the form of a "virus vector" (on this, see below) or naked DNA. The third approach, not yet developed sufficiently for practical use, requires developing " vectors" that can be injected directly into the bloodstream and carry the therapeutic gene to the proper cell tissue safely and efficiently.[47]

In addition, Anderson notes that all current (c. 1995-2000) clinical protocols for gene therapy are based on the idea of adding a normal gene rather than replacing or correcting the malfunctioning gene present in the patient's body. This approach assumes that the newly added gene will be introduced into a site in the genome different from that of the defective gene and that the new gene's expression will override the effects of the defective gene.[48]

D. Delivering Therapeutic Genes

The English Bishops' Working Group pointed out that effective gene therapy requires not only the recognition and isolation of the appropriate gene for effecting therapy but also an efficient delivery system. The latter — the delivery system — is called a *vector*.[49] Although the desired genes to be delivered into the cells of the patient needing therapy can be delivered by physical techniques (e.g., ingestion of an organic salt called calcium phosphate containing the appropriate DNA and the placing of DNA into fatty bubbles or liquid vesicles that can be fused with human body cells), such techniques have not as yet proved very effective. At present the most effective way to deliver therapeutic genes is through the use of *viruses* and *viral vectors*.

Viruses have a natural tendency to enter human cells and insert their genetic information into the genome of the cells that they enter. Thus therapeutic gene cells, developed through recombinant DNA, can be inserted into various kinds of viruses capable of introducing their genetic information into target cells and allow those genes to become a permanent and functional part of the host-cell genome. The newly introduced gene is a new cellular gene of the patient. However, the viruses themselves can often have bad effects on the cells of the person into whom they are introduced. But, again as a result of the advances made in molecular cellular biology, it is now possible to inactivate or remove deleterious viral genes, replacing them with the desired therapeutic genetic material.[50]

This type of genetic *somatic cell* therapy has proved beneficial and successful in the treatment of several genetically-based diseases, e.g., cystic fibrosis, adenosine deaminase deficiency (ADA) — a genetic disorder caused by the lack of the gene product adenosine deaminase and leading to abnormality of bone marrow cells and thus giving rise to serious infections — and there is hope that as time goes on more and more genetically based diseases can be treated by somatic cell therapy.

E. The Morality of Somatic Cell Gene Therapy

Somatic gene therapy raises problems similar to those posed by other forms of treatment. Such therapy is morally warranted as long as the risks posed by this new type of therapy are not significant when compared with the reasonable expectation that employment of such therapy will indeed bring great benefit *to the patient*. Somatic cell gene therapy is today, of course, *experimental* in nature and does not constitute "standard" treatment. As with other experimental procedures (e.g., as kidney transplants were when they were first initiated), there is reason for reserving such therapy for serious diseases for which there is no satisfactory alternative treatment.[51] There is urgent need that, wherever possible, attempts at somatic therapy on human persons be preceded by studies on animals.

There is the possibility that somatic gene therapy may have side-effects, possibly deleterious, affecting the germ-line or gametic cells. Such risk is not limited to gene therapy, as other medical treatments can risk harming the children conceived while their mothers, in particular, are undergoing treatment. To reduce the risk of unintentionally harming progeny, some have recommended, as Helen Watt has observed, that female patients participating in trials of somatic cell therapy be required to use contraceptives.[52] As Watt goes on to note, correctly, "Those who recognize the use of contraception as incompatible with sexual integrity will wish to recommend, instead, the use of natural family planning — always assuming there really is no appreciable risk of transmitting an effect to the germ line."[53]

In the next section of this chapter, devoted to prenatal and pre-implantation screening, I will consider the morality of somatic gene therapy on the pre-implantation embryo.

F. Germ-line "Therapy"

At present such "therapy" seems unrealizable and the risks entailed, particularly if human subjects (and their progeny — for such "therapy" affects not only particular individuals but all their descendants) are involved, are far too great, and even unknown, to warrant its use. Much more research must be done on animals before one can even begin to think of morally licit applications of such "therapy." The problems and risks raised by germ-line therapy are such as to provide serious grounds for thinking that it should never be carried out. Watt describes these serious risks — to the immediate subject, to future generations, to the human embryos that would no doubt be used for purely research purposes, etc. — in great detail in her excellent article, and I refer readers interested in pursuing the matter to it.[54] Such therapy is *not* to be regarded in any way as intrinsically evil. It is simply that at present, with other pressing health needs and in view of the serious and unresolved problems and unknown risks raised by this line of therapy, it would be better to leave it alone. But it might perhaps be morally licit in the future, once sufficient studies have been done on animals and there is reasonable hope that the terrible risks such therapy raises both for the individuals immediately affected and for their descendants can be avoided or minimized.

5. PRENATAL AND PRE-IMPLANTATION SCREENING

A. Prenatal Diagnosis and Screening

As Thomas Hilgers, M.D., has said, "Prenatal diagnosis is as old as obstetrics and having babies."[55] Its original purpose was to help protect the health and life of both the unborn child and its mother. It had as its major emphasis the diagnosis or assessment of conditions to assist the physician help the unborn child to a more normal and healthy life.

With the development of sonography, which allowed one to see into the uterus and to observe the development of the embryo/fetus, and an explosion of technological tools helpful in diagnosing such as amniocentesis or chorionic villus sampling (CVS), it is now possible to identify and evaluate at least 20 different chomosome anomalies and 700 to 1,000 different biochemical or molecular conditions with a genetic base.[56]

(1) Moral Misuse of Prenatal Screening

When the possibility of terminating a pregnancy became legal in the U.S. in 1973, the pressure for accurate diagnosis grew and the legal penalty imposed on obstetricians for failing to warn or diagnose fetal anomalies became a driving force in obstetric care. As a result of this pressure, the stated objective of prenatal diagnosis today is "to offer the widest range of informed choice to couples at risk of having children with an abnormality, and to allow such couples the opportunity to achieve a healthy family by avoiding the birth of affected children through selected abortion."[57] In fact, as Hilgers notes, in a recent review of the practice of fetal testing one leading advocate of such testing declared, in a statement which seems to summarize current attitudes of Western medicine, that "The advantages of ever-earlier prenatal testing seem obvious. The sooner a problem is detected, the sooner therapy or termination can be undertaken."[58] Commenting on this author's statement, Hilgers says: "While lip service is given to 'therapy,' it is clear that 'termination' or abortion is the overwhelming approach utilized as a result of these [screening] programs.... over the last 35 years, we have moved, in prenatal diagnosis, from making a diagnosis for the purposes of assisting the patient (in this case the fetus), to making a diagnosis so that the patient can be eliminated. This shift has already taken place and, to a great extent, has taken a strong hold in medical practice."[59]

This does not mean, however, that prenatal diagnosis as such is immoral. Diagnostic information is not of itself morally wrong. But a great many of the diagnostic procedures now available are used primarily to detect, as soon possible, whether an unborn child suffers from a malady such as Down Syndrome, Trisomy 18 or Trisomy 13, spina bifida, Tay-Sachs disease, etc. All women are now offered a blood test designed to detect neural tube defects (such as those that cause spina bifida), and physicians who fail to offer the tests in areas where proper follow-up is available (practically the entire U.S.) are liable to malpractice suits.[60] A set of tests is now available for detecting chromosomal defects such as Down Syndrome: amniocentesis, chorionic villus sampling, and sampling of maternal serum alpha-fetoprotein (MSAFP). Amniocentesis involves removal of a small amount of amniotic fluid, containing cells from the fetus, by the use of a hollow needed inserted into the amniotic sac. This procedure for the purpose of analyzing the chromosomes of the fetus is usually performed at about the sixteenth week of gestation, and it requires approximately three to four weeks to obtain results of the chromosomal testing. Chorionic villus sampling can be performed much earlier in pregnancy. MSAFP tests the maternal serum. If the alpha-fetoprotein in this serum is high, this indicates an increased risk of neural tube defects and requires further study. If the AFP is low, this indicates an increased risk of Down Syndrome or other chromosome disorders.

The MSAFP test has now been expanded to look for the presence of two other substances (estriol and HCG) making the test far more sensitive. This so-called triple test makes it much easier to detect Down Syndrome — better than 80 percent of such unborn children can be identified by this test, which also, incidentally, has a high false positive rate (i.e., the identifying of unborn children as being afflicted with Down Syndrome when in reality they are not). The usual outcome is recommendation that those unborn children identified as "abnormal" be terminated or aborted.[61]

(2) Morally Good Uses of Prenatal Testing

As noted already, prenatal diagnosis as such is useful and can be put to good use. Hilgers says that for the most part invasive procedures which jeopardize the embryo and fetus (e.g., amniocentesis) are medically unnecessary in medical practice in which neither the doctor nor the patient is willing to abort. He says that in some select kinds of cases, having adequate knowledge of the child's condition can be useful in guiding proper medically therapeutic treatment of the unborn child. Diagnostic ultrasound, he argues, is noninvasive and is probably not sufficiently employed to afford proper management of pregnancies.[62]

Prenatal diagnosis can be very valuable. For example, by detecting neural tube anomalies such as spina bifida it is frequently possible to engage in therapeutic actions on the developing embryo in the womb. For example, a shunt can be inserted into the child's brain and fluid causing pressure on the brain drained from it, thus providing great benefit to a child suffering from spina bifida. In fact, at a hearing at the U.S. Senate some years ago sponsored by pro-life Senator Gordon Humphrey, I witnessed testimony from a couple with their physician and their child — now born and resting on her mother's lap — in which they described the wonderful surgery that had been done on the child while still in womb, a therapeutic intervention indicated after prenatal diagnosis had shown that she suffered from a neural tube defect and that fluids were building up in her cranium, exerting pressure on her brain. This timely intervention was successful in minimizing the harm this child suffered.

(3) Conclusion

Magisterial teaching provides solid guidance regarding prenatal diagnosis. In *Donum vitae* (I, 2) the Congregation for the Doctrine of the Faith declared such diagnosis "permissible if the methods used, with the consent of the parents who have been adequately instructed, safeguard the life and integrity of the embryo and its mother and does not subject them to disproportionate risks. But this diagnosis is gravely opposed to the moral law when it is done with the thought of possibly inducing an abortion depending upon the results: a diagnosis which shows the existence of a malformation or a hereditary illness must not be the equivalent of a death-sentence." Similar teaching is found in other relevant magisterial documents, such as John Paul II's *Evangelium vitae,* the Pontifical Council for Pastoral Assistance to Health Care Workers' *Charter for Health Care Workers,* and U.S. Bishops' *Ethical and Religious Directives for Catholic Health Care Services.*[63]

Baumiller has observed that, because the contemporary attitude (described above so well by Hilgers) is to "terminate" the life of an unborn child identified by modern methods of prenatal diagnosis as suffering a serious anomaly, "most medical centers with a moral concern about the sacredness of all life have traditionally not offered prenatal diagnostic services. Patients are commonly sent to centers where a pro-life stance is not expected.... Thus Catholic hospitals and those who practice obstetrics have too frequently abandoned those people most in need of support. That support must be to affirm the sanctity of human life. Prenatal diagnosis offers information to a woman, a couple; such information is good because it delineates reality."[64] A true challenge is here presented to the Catholic health-care community.

B. Pre-Implantation Diagnosis and Screening

The treatment of this issue can be relatively brief. Pre-implantation diagnosis and screening of human embryos have grown out of the technology of *in vitro* fertilization and, as Hilgers has put it, "the challenge to clinicians and investigators to improve the 'take home baby rate.' "[65] Embryos subject to such screening/diagnosis come from two sources. The first and by far the largest source of embryos subject to pre-implantation diagnosis is *in vitro* fertilization, and the principal aim of such screening/diagnosis is to determine whether embryos in question are at risk of suffering from some serious (or perhaps not so serious) disease or anomaly and, if so identified, to "terminate" their lives by refusing to implant them in their mothers' wombs (or the wombs of "surrogates").. Diagnosis and screening for such purposes (along with the way in which these tiny humans have been "produced") is utterly immoral, as the *Vatican Instruction on Respect for Human Life in Its Origin and on the Dignity of Human Procreation* (*Donum vitae*) made crystal clear — and as we saw in reviewing this document in Chapter One.

Another source of embryos for pre-implantation diagnosis/screening are pre-implantation embryos flushed from the uterus by uterine lavage.[66] This procedure is usually done to seek out embryos at high risk and then "terminate them."

Pre-implantation diagnosis can, however, have truly *therapeutic ends* in view. For instance, it is possible to use gene therapy on a pre-implantation embryo to correct a possible serious malady. Thus on February 3, 2000, the *London Times* (I happened to be in London at the time) reported that doctors had helped a married couple who had already had one child who suffered from cystic fibrosis to have a child free of this disease, despite the fact that they stood at risk of having another child so afflicted. What they had done was to have the couple provide the ovum and sperm, fertilize these gametic cells *in vitro*, and then subject the developing pre-implantation embryo to a test to see whether or not it carried the genes responsible for cystic fibrosis. It did. But then the physicians introduced a viral vector carrying a gene to "correct" this problem, and they succeeded in doing so. The child was then implanted in the mother's womb and approximately nine months later (early February 2000) a baby girl was born, one totally free of cystic fibrosis.

Here the moral problem is that this child was not conceived in the mother's womb after a marital act but was rather "produced" in the laboratory in a petri dish and, had the gene therapy not been successful, the pre-implantation embryo would have been "discarded" and not implanted in the mother's womb.

But would it be immoral to remove an early, pre-implantation embryo from the womb by uterine lavage if there is serious reason to think that it suffers from a serious genetic malady that could be cured by the introduction of the "right" gene through gene somatic cell therapy?

The Magisterium has not addressed this issue. Although *Donum vitae* condemns *in vitro* fertilization and the freezing of embryos (cryopreservation), "even when carried out in order to preserve the life of an embryo" as an offense contrary to human dignity because this exposes the embryo to grave risks of harm (cf. *Donum vitae,* I, 6), it had previously acknowledged, as we have seen already in discussing *prenatal* diagnosis, that if such diagnosis respects the embryo's life and is directed toward its safeguarding, it can be morally licit (cf. ibid., I, 2). Thus might it not be in conformity with magisterial teaching to remove an early embryo from the womb by uterine lavage, if there is serious reason for believing it subject to a devastating genetic disease, and, if there are good reasons for thinking that gene somatic line therapy would be successful, deliver the "correct" genes to the embryo, and then re-introduce it into the mother's womb for implantation? It seems to me that this may be a valid moral option.[67]

6. GENETIC COUNSELING

In their *Ethical and Religious Directives for Catholic Health Care Services,* the U.S. Bishops state: "Genetic counseling may be provided in order to promote responsible parenthood and to prepare for the proper treatment and care of children with genetic defects, in accordance with Catholic moral teaching and the intrinsic rights and obligations of married couples regarding the transmission of life" (no. 54). Genetic counseling, therefore, is morally legitimate in itself.

The need for such counseling is growing, as today we know that many, many diseases and anomalies affecting human persons are genetically based. In fact, a genetic component has been identified for over 4,000 diseases, disorders, and traits,[68] and as the Human Genome Project (see below) advances, and after virtual completion, more and more such diseases may be identified. As a result today many persons, particularly married couples, are legitimately concerned to know whether or not there is likelihood that any children they may generate may be afflicted by some serious genetically induced malady. The moral issue concerns the *kind* of counseling to be given.

Today, in our secular society, many think that if genetic testing shows that a couple is at high risk of conceiving a child afflicted by a serious genetically based malady, that couple ought to take effective steps to prevent either the conception or birth of such a child. By effective steps for preventing conception, moreover, they mean various contraceptive procedures, in particular tubal ligation, and by effective steps for preventing birth should tests *in utero* show that the child is, or may well be, afflicted by such a malady, they mean abortion. They may also recommend artificial insemination by a donor, *in vitro* fertilization (followed by pre-implantation diagnosis with "termination" of embryos identified as afflicted by a genetic malady), and other immoral methods of coping with the dangers that genetic testing may indicate. Obviously, a morally upright person cannot offer such "counseling."

Germain Grisez has provided very practical guidance for morally upright counselors, in particular, physicians who might be asked by their patients for advice on these matters. Obviously, a Catholic physician/counselor or any morally upright counselor should tell potential patients that he or she is committed to the good of human life and will never advise anyone to even consider contraception, sterilization, abortion, *in vitro* fertilization, etc. Because of the current climate in our society, physicians and others who refuse to provide such counseling may be vulnerable to legal malpractice suits. They ought therefore to seek competent legal advice. Grisez also makes the following practical suggestion:

> You may be able to minimize your vulnerability arising from your nonconformity [to secular standards] by not only telling those who come to you where you stand but having them read, and perhaps even sign, a carefully drafted summary of your position on matters where your standards of good practice will diverge from those the courts would be likely to use. Without anticipating the legal advice you will receive, I think such a summary probably should include a

clear statement that, as a matter of principle, you will not prescribe contraceptives, do sterilizations, or perform abortions; you will give no medical advice regarding these matters and no information about their availability; and in respect to these matters you will not refer patients to others from whom they might obtain any service, advice, or information that, as matter of principle, you would not provide personally.[69]

This seems eminently good, practical advice for counselors.

If a couple seeking counsel is not married, the results of a genetic test would either remove reasons for concern or disclose a reason, not necessarily conclusive but surely worth considering, for either abstaining from marriage or continuing one's search for a spouse. If the couple is married, negative results of genetic testing would of course allay any fears they might have. But if the tests disclosed that there were indeed risks of conceiving a child who would be afflicted by a genetic malady, the couple would then need helpful counseling. Above, a morally wrong kind of counseling was excluded.

The choice whether to accept the risk and seek to generate life through the conjugal act or to avoid doing so by the practice of periodic continence is, of course, the responsibility of the couple. The Magisterium of the Church clearly recognizes that the likelihood of generating a child who might suffer from a serious genetic illness provides a *serious* reason for deciding not to have a child for either a certain or indefinite period of time.[70] The couple might legitimately reach the conclusion (and their counselor might well concur and indeed recommend) that running the risk would either be unfair to others or that they either could not fulfill or would be seriously tempted to omit fulfilling the responsibilities they would incur in caring for a child afflicted by the malady. Such a conclusion and/or recommendation would not be immoral.

However the couple might conclude (and their counselor might well agree and recommend) that they courageously agree to accept the risk and by doing so firmly commit themselves to carry out the responsibilities that they would incur should their child indeed be afflicted by the malady in question. Although some people, particularly in our secular culture, might argue that if a couple deliberately risks having a child who might suffer from a serious malady such as cystic fibrosis, they are being unjust, either to the child exposed to such a risk, or to the larger society (which will have to help in providing suitable health care), or to both. I believe that those who argue this way are mistaken. If the child is generated, a new and precious human person has come into existence, and his or her life is of surpassing value and contributes to the common good. Frequently the burdens such a child might himself suffer and present for others are highly exaggerated while the possible benefits of the child's life, to itself, its parents, and to society as a whole, are ignored or minimized. Thus, as Grisez correctly says, "one cannot rule out the possibility that a couple could rightly decide that they need not abstain from possibly fertile intercourse, despite the probability that a child will be afflicted with a severe disease, genetic or other. Moreover, in the case of genetic diseases, a couple accept not only more or less risk; avoiding parenthood on this basis means also forgoing children who would themselves be healthy, though perhaps carriers of the genetic defect."[71]

7. THE HUMAN GENOME PROJECT

The genome is the sum of the genetic material that defines a biological species. The Human Genome Project (HGP) is an international research program whose goal is to map in detail the positions of genes on their respective chromosomes, to determine the complete nucleotide sequence of human DNA, and to localize the estimated 50,000-100,000 genes on each of the 46 human chromosomes within the human genome.[72] By late June 2000 this vast project was completed.

Human genome studies of genetically related disorders and diseases are of tremendous importance not only to scientists and physicians but to everyone. The major *moral* question is how this knowledge will be used. It can obviously be used to develop new kinds of genetic therapy, and it may perhaps become feasible to attempt some kinds of germ-line therapy that would not raise grave moral objections.

The greatest (and legitimate) fear people have is that, if genetic testing made possible by HGP showed them susceptible to or carriers of serious genetic maladies, they would experience prejudicial and indeed unjust treatment from those who learn of their genetic defects or dispositions. Such unjust treatment could be extended by parents to children whose genetic propensities become known to them, by employers and potential employers, by health care providers and insurance companies, and by the government. The possibility exists that some individuals would not be allowed to marry or to have children, that efforts to make sterilization and abortion compulsory would be made, etc.

But these potential problems are not *per se* the result of the Human

Genome Project, which in itself is essentially a research project intended to enrich the human community by expanding its knowledge. The problems lie in the human heart and will, not in the HGP.

ENDNOTES

1. In the introduction and first two parts of this chapter I have adapted, with substantive additions and developments, some material from my earlier book, *Human Existence, Medicine, and Ethics: Reflections on Human Life* (Chicago: Franciscan Herald Press, 1977), Chapter One, Experimenting on Human Subjects. The matter presented here, however, is in essence a complete reworking of the issue.

2. Roger Wertheimer, "Philosophy on Humanity," in *Abortion: Pro and Con,* ed. Robert L. Perkins (Cambridge, MA: Schenkmann, 1975), pp. 107-108.

3. Today, of course, many influential authors explicitly claim that membership in the human species has absolutely *no* moral significance and that those who claim that it does are guilty of "speciesism." Among the more prominent and better-known advocates of this view are Michael Tooley (see his *Abortion and Infanticide* [Oxford and New York: Oxford, at the Clarendon Press, 1983], esp. pp. 61-76), Peter Singer (see his *Rethinking Life and Death: The Collapse of Our Traditional Ethics* [New York: St. Martin's Press, 1994], esp. pp. 202-206, and Joseph Fletcher, "Indicators of Humanhood," *Hastings Center Report* 2 (November 1972) 1-4. This denigration of the moral worth of human beings, a cornerstone of the "culture of death," was criticized above in Chapter Five. One of the finest philosophical rebuttals of this position is given by Patrick Lee, *Abortion and Unborn Human Life* (Washington, D.C.: The Catholic University of America Press, 1997), Chapter One.

4. Karol Wojtyla, *Love and Responsibility*, trans. H. Willetts (New York: Farrar, Straus, Giroux, 1981), p. 41.

5. Paul Ramsey, *The Patient as Person: Explorations in Medical Ethics* (New Haven and London: Yale University Press, 1970), Chapter One, "Consent as a Canon of Loyalty with Special Reference to Children in Medical Investigation," pp. 1-58. This chapter is *must* reading on this subject.

6. See, for example, Benedict Ashley, O.P., and Kevin O'Rourke, O.P., *Health Care Ethics: A Theological Analysis* (4th ed.: Washington, D.C.: Georgetown University Press, 1997), pp. 345-346.

7. Articles of the Nuremberg Tribunal, article 1; cited by Ramsey, *The Patient as Person,* p. 1.
8. The text of the *Declaration of Helsinki* can be found in Henry K. Beecher, *Research and the Individual* (Boston: Little, Brown, and Co., 1970), p. 227.
9. Here the *Charter* refers to Pius XII, "To the Doctors of the G. Mendel Institute," Nov. 24, 1957, in *AAS* 49 (1957) 1031.[Pius XII spoke about this topic many times. A useful collection of his addresses on this subject can be found in *The Pope Speaks* 1.3 and 4 (1954). Among his principal addresses are those to the First International Congress on the Histopathology of the Nervous System (September 14, 1952), the Sixteenth International Congress of Military Medicine (October 19, 1953), and the Eighth Congress of the World Medical Association (September 30, 1954).]
10. In a footnote at this point, the *Charter* quotes from the following passage from the Pontifical Council *Cor Unum's* "Some Ethical Questions Relating to the Gravely Ill and the Dying" (July 27, 1981): "The patient cannot be the object of decisions which he will not make, or, if he is not able to do so, which he could not approve. The 'person,' primarily responsible for his own life, should be the center of any assisting intervention: others are there to help him, not to replace him." The full text of this document is found in *Enchiridion Vaticanum 7, Documenti ufficiali della Santa Sede 1980-1981* (Bologna: EDB, 1985) 1137, no. 2.1,2.
11. The *Charter* cites this text from Pope John Paul II's Address to the World Congress of Catholic Doctors, October 3, 1982, published in *Insegnamenti di Giovanni Paolo II* 5.3 (Vatican City: Libreria Editrice Vaticana, 1983) p. 673, no. 4.
12. Here the *Charter* refers to Pope John Paul II's Address to the Participants at Two Congresses on Medicine and Surgery, October 27, 1980, published in *Insegnamenti di Giovanni Paolo II* 3.2 (Vatican City: Libreria Editrice Vaticana, 1981) pp. 1008-1009, no. 5.
13. The text of no. 72 of the *Charter* can be found in Pontifical Council for Pastoral Assistance to Health Care Workers, *Charter for Health Care Workers* (Boston: Pauline Books and Media, 1995), pp. 70-71.
14. For instance, Henry K. Beecher, *Research and the Individual,* pp. 18-19, 121ff.
15. Ramsey, *The Patient as Person,* p. 3.
16. National Conference of Catholic Bishops, *Ethical and Religious Di-*

rectives for Catholic Health Care Facilities (Washington, D.C.: United States Catholic Conference, 1995), no. 27.

17. In *The Patient as Person*, p. 8, footnote 6, Ramsey notes that "Sir Harold Himsworth said (1953) that the Hippocratic Oath can be given in a single sentence: *Act always so as to increase trust* (quoted by Ross G. Mitchell, 'The Child and Experimental Medicine,' *British Medical Journal* 4, no. 1 [March 21, 1964]: 726). This might better read: *Act always so as not to abuse trust; act always so as to exhibit faithfulness,* to deserve and inspire trust."

18. On this I have already referred to the "personalistic norm" articulated by Karol Wojtyla in *Love and Responsibility.* Other excellent and eloquent defenses of the inviolable dignity of all human beings, all human persons, are set forth by Jacques Maritain, *The Person and the Common Good* (New York: Charles Scribner's Sons, 1947), Chapter 3; Mortimer Adler, *The Difference of Man and the Difference It Makes* (New York: Meridian, 1968).

19. Ramsey, *The Patient as Person,* p. 7.

20. Pontifical Council for Pastoral Assistance to Health Care Workers, *Charter for Health Care Workers,* p. 72, no. 73.

21. Ramsey, *The Patient as Person,* pp. 7-8.

22. National Conference of Catholic Bishops, *Ethical and Religious Directives for Catholic Health Care Facilities,* no. 25.

23. Pontifical Council for Pastoral Assistance to Health Care, *Charter for Health Care Workers,* p.72, no. 73.

24. Ibid., p. 77, no. 81. The internal citation in this passage is taken from Pope John Paul II, Address to the Participants at Two Congresses on Medicine and Surgery, October 27, 1980, in *Insegnamenti di Giovanni Paolo II* 3.2 (Vatican City: Libreria Editrice Vaticana, 1981) p. 1009, no. 5.

25 Ibid., p. 77, no. 81. Here the internal citation is from the same address of Pope John Paul II, ibid.

26. Congregation for the Doctrine of the Faith, *Donum vitae,* in *AAS* 80 (1988) 81-83.

27. Pope John Paul II, Address to Participants at a Meeting of the Pontifical Academy of Sciences, October 25, 1982, in *AAS* 75 (1983) 37.

28. The text of this directive reads as follows: "Nontherapeutic experiments on a living embryo or fetus are not permitted, even with the consent of the parents."

29. *Charter on the Rights of the Family,* 4/b, in *L'Osservatore Romano,* Italian ed., October 25, 1983.

30. Robert J. Levin, "Informed Consent. III. Consent Issues in Human Research," *Encyclopedia of Bioethics,* ed. Warren T. Reich (2nd rev. ed.: New York: McGraw-Hill, 1995) 1246.

31. Ramsey, *The Patient as Person*, pp. 12-13.

32. Ibid., p. 14.

33. Richard A. McCormick, S.J., *How Brave a New World? Dilemmas in Bioethics* (Garden City, NY: Doubleday, 1981), Chapter Four, "Proxy Consent in the Experimental Situation," pp. 61-62.

34. See William E. May, "Experimenting on Human Subjects," *The Linacre Quarterly* 41.3 (November, 1974) 238-252; see also my *Human Existence, Medicine, and Ethics,* pp. 21-28.

35. Ramsey, "A Reply to Richard McCormick: The Enforcement of Morals: Nontherapeutic Research on Children," *Hastings Center Report* 6.4 (May, 1976) 21-30. It is in this essay that Ramsey used the expression "voiceless patients" to refer to children and non-competent adults.

36. McCormick presented his reply in his essay, "A Reply to Paul Ramsey: Experimentation in Children: Sharing in Sociality." This essay was originally published in *Hastings Center Report* 6.6 (October, 1976) 41-46, and was reprinted under the title "Sharing in Sociality: Children and Experimentation" as Chapter Six of *How Brave a New World?*, pp. 87-98. In some other essays, for instance, "Notes on Moral Theology," *Theological Studies* 36 (March, 1975) 127-128 McCormick offered other objections to my criticism of his position. I responded to these objections in *Human Existence, Medicine, and Ethics,* pp. 28-32, and I refer interested readers to these pages of my earlier book for further details.

37. Ashley and O'Rourke, *Health Care Ethics* (4th ed.), p. 351. I must, however, note that these authors do not accurately present the *reason* why Ramsey and I reach our conclusion. According to them "the justification for this position is that a proxy should make a decision in accord with the best interests of the subject. In nontherapeutic experimentation the interests of the subject are not clearly evident, however, and since the subject does not have the capacity to make a free choice about the matter, the proxy (guardian) has no right to presume or say anything on behalf of the ward" (p. 350). It should be evident, from what has been said in the text, how woefully inaccurate Ashley and O'Rourke are here.

38. On this issue see the essays by McCormick, LeRoy Walters, Peter

Steinfels, and Stephen Toulmin published in the *Hastings Center Report* 5 (June 1975), an issue largely devoted to a discussion of the Commission's work.

39. A good presentation of this matter is given by Edmund D. Pellegrino, M.D., "Human Embryos and the Stem Cell Controversy," *The NaProEthics Forum* 4.6 (November 1999), 2-3. See also Edward J. Furton and Micheline M. Mathews-Roth, M.D., "Stem Cell Research and the Human Embryo, Part One," *Ethics & Medics* 24.8 (August, 1999) 1-2.

40. See, for example, Nicholas Wade, "Embryo Cell Research: A Clash of Values," *New York Times,* Friday, July 2, 1999, A21.

41. Cited in ibid.

42. Pellegrino, "Human Embryos and the Stem Cell Controversy," 3. Pellegrino cites the following scientific sources to support his affirmations: P. Rubinstein et al., "Outcomes Among 526 Recipients of Placental-Blood Transplants from Unrelated Donors," *New England Journal of Medicine* 399 (November 26, 1998) 1565-1577; R. Lewis, "Human Mesenchyma Stem Cells Differentiate in the Lab," *The Scientist* 13 (April 12, 1999) 1 ff; Claire Lowry, "Adult Human Brain Stem Cells Reproduce In Vitro," *UniSci Science and Research News* April 28, 1999.

43. On this see Ellen G. Pearson, "Agency Seen Trying to Rewrite Rules on Embryos," *National Catholic Register*, June 27-July 3, 1999. See also Robert J. White, M.D., "Do Human Embryos Have Rights?" *America* 180.21 (June 19, 1999) 7-9.

44. *Genetic Intervention on Human Subjects: The Report of a Working Party of the Catholic Bishops' Joint Committee on Bioethical Issues* (London: The Catholic Bishops' Joint Committee on Bioethical Issues, 1996), p. 6. Members of the Working Party were Dr. A. P. Cole (Chairman), Rev. John Henry, John Duddington, Dr. Ian Jessiman, Dr. John McLean, Agneta Sutton, Dr. Helen Watt.

45. W. French Anderson, "Gene Therapy. I. Strategies for Gene Therapy," *Encyclopedia of Bioethics,* 911.

46. On all this see *Genetic Intervention on Human Subjects,* pp. 6-15; Anderson, "Genetic Therapy," in *The New Genetics and the Future of Man*, ed. Michael Hamilton (Grand Rapids, MI: Eerdmans, 1972) pp. 109-117.

47. Anderson, "Gene Therapy. I. Strategies for Gene Therapy," 908.

48. Ibid.

49. Ibid., 909f; *Genetic Intervention on Human Subjects,* p. 12.

50. Anderson, "Gene Therapy I. Strategies for Gene Therapy," 909f.
51. See L. Archer, "Genetic Testing and Gene Therapy," in *Man-Made Man: Ethical and Legal Issues in Genetics*, eds. P. Doherty and A. Sutton (Dublin: Open Air, 1997), p. 38.
52. This is recommended, for instance, by the British Gene Therapy Advisory Committee in its *First Annual Report November 1993-December 1994* (London: Health Departments of the United Kingdom, 1995), pp. 5-6. Helen Watt calls attention to this in her very helpful essay, "Human Gene Therapy: Ethical Aspects," in *Human Genome, Human Person, and the Society of the Future: Proceedings of the Fourth Assembly of the Pontifical Academy for Life* (Vatican City, February 23-25, 1998), eds. Juan de Dios Vial Correa and Elio Sgreccia (Vatican City: Libreria Editrice Vaticana, 1999), p. 256, footnote 6.
53. Watt, "Human Gene Therapy: Ethical Aspects," p. 256.
54. Ibid., pp. 256-268.
55. Thomas W. Hilgers, M.D., "Prenatal and Pre-Implantation Genetic Diagnosis: Duty or Eugenic Prelude?" in *Human Genome, Human Person, and the Society of the Future*, p. 172.
56. Ibid. Hilgers provides a detailed description of various methods of prenatal testing, accurately assessing their moral value, on pp. 175-185.
57. R. Penkenth, "The Scope of Preimplantation Diagnosis," in *Preconception and Preimplantation Diagnosis of Human Genetic Disease*, ed. R. G. Edwards (Cambridge: Cambridge University Press, 1993), p. 82. Cited by Hilgers, "Prenatal and Pre-Implantation Screening," p. 174, note 1.
58. E. Jauniaux, "Fetal Testing in the First Trimester of Pregnancy," *The Female Patient* 22 (1997) 51-52, cited by Hilgers, "Prenatal and Pre-Implantation Screening," p. 186.
59. Hilgers, "Prenatal and Pre-Implantation Screening," p. 186.
60. On this see Robert C. Baumiller, S.J., "Prenatal Diagnosis," *Ethics & Medics* 20.11 (November, 1995) 3. Baumiller also provides a brief synoptic description of major kinds of prenatal diagnosis.
61. Ibid., 3; see Hilgers, "Prenatal and Pre-Implantation Screening," pp. 178-179.
62. Ibid., pp. 186-187.
63. Thus in *Evangelium vitae*, no. 14, Pope John Paul II says: "Prenatal diagnosis, which presents no moral objections if carried out in order to identify the medical treatment which may be needed by the child

in the womb, all too often becomes an opportunity for proposing and procuring an abortion…." See *Charter for Health Care Workers,* nos. 59-61 and *Ethical and Religious Directives for Catholic Health Care Services,* no. 50.

64. Baumiller, "Prenatal Diagnosis," 4.

65. Hilgers, "Prenatal and Pre-Implantation Genetic Diagnosis," p. 184.

66. Hilgers notes this possibility on p. 184. The procedure is described more fully by Dr. Alan Handyside. See June Berlfein, "The Earliest Warning," *Discover* (February, 1992) 14.

67. On this see Albert Moraczewski, "Genes and Pandora's Box," *Ethics & Medics* 18.3 (March 1993) 2.

68. See John Haas, "Human Genetics," *Ethics & Medics* 21.2 (February 1996) 1-2.

69. Germain Grisez, *The Way of the Lord Jesus,* Vol. 3, *Difficult Moral Questions* (Quincy, IL: Franciscan Press, 1997, p. 300.

70. See, for example, Pope Paul VI, Encyclical *Humanae vitae,* no. 10.

71. Grisez, *Difficult Moral Questions,* p. 302.

72. On this see Albert Moraczewski, "Genes and Ethics," *Ethics & Medics* 16.5 (May 1991) 2; see also National Institutes of Health web site: http://www.nhgri.nih.gov/HGP/, "The Human Genome Project," 2/16/2000.

Chapter Seven

EUTHANASIA, ASSISTED SUICIDE, AND CARE OF THE DYING

The Contemporary Movement for Euthanasia and Assisted Suicide

In 1935 the first Voluntary Euthanasia Society was founded in London, and a Euthanasia Society was established in the United States in 1938, but by the early 1970s neither had had much success in gaining support. At the beginning of 1975 the U.S. Euthanasia Society was reactivated as the Society for the Right to Die, and by the beginning of the 1990s support for euthanasia and physician-assisted suicide in the English-speaking world had grown enormously. Public opinion polls in the U.S. and Britain during the last decade have shown increasing willingness to sanction euthanasia and assisted suicide both morally and legally, and those agitating for change are no longer, as Daniel Callahan, president of the Hastings Center (an influential think tank on bioethical issues), has noted, "a small minority, the usual reformist suspects, but a larger, more influential group of academics, physicians, legislators, judges, and well-placed and well-organized lay people."[1]

To account for this "sea change" in public opinion, Callahan points to:

> A growing fear of a long, lingering death, the consequence of changes in the way people die occasioned by more chronic illness and more death in old age; the publicity given to a number of cases where seemingly conservative resistance

kept people alive longer than most people found tolerable; ... the AIDS epidemic, with its well publicized cases of young people dying miserable deaths from a particularly noxious and degrading disease ...; the potent Anglo-American movement toward greater self-determination and autonomy — fostered most explicitly on the political left but implicitly abetted ... by the libertarian strains so prominently espoused by conservatives for free market solutions to social problems, and perhaps a diminished willingness on the part of many to accept the pain and suffering of dying as an acceptable fact of life.[2]

The reasons Callahan cites have undoubtedly contributed to the growing success the movement is enjoying.[3] Note, in particular, that he singles out the emphasis on autonomy in contemporary society and an unwillingness to accept pain and suffering. In his Encyclical *Evangelium vitae*, Pope John Paul II points to an exaggerated and false understanding of individual autonomy and to hedonism as critical factors contributing to the "culture of death" (cf. *Evangelium vitae,* nos. 20, 23). I believe that another major factor helping to win acceptance of euthanasia and assisted suicide is the idea that *personal* life, as distinct from "merely" biological life, requires exercisable cognitive abilities. This dualistic understanding leads many to conclude that once an individual no longer has such exercisable abilities or when there is danger that they will be lost because of disease or illness, then that individual's biological life is of no value to him or her and that he or she is better off dead than alive; one's life is no longer worth living. Another contributing factor, I believe, is the acceptance of abortion. It is frequently justified on the grounds that the life destroyed is merely "biologically human" and not "personal," and it is at times resorted to as a kind of "mercy killing" or euthanasia of unborn children diagnosed as suffering from maladies that will, so it is alleged, make their lives burdensome and miserable.

Pope John Paul II offers insights into the reasons accounting for the appeal euthanasia has for many today. Thus he writes in *Evangelium vitae:*

> In the sick person the sense of anguish, of severe discomfort, and even of desperation brought on by intense and prolonged suffering can be a decisive factor. Such a situation can threaten the already fragile equilibrium of an individual's

personal and family life, with the result that, on the one hand, the sick person, despite the help of increasingly effective medical and social assistance, risks feeling overwhelmed by his or her own frailty; and on the other hand, those close to the sick person can be moved by an understandable even if misguided compassion. All this is aggravated by a cultural climate which fails to perceive any meaning or value in suffering, but rather considers suffering the epitome of evil, to be eliminated at all costs ... [and assumes] a certain Promethean attitude which leads people to think that they can control life and death by taking the decisions about them into their own hands.... As well as for reasons of a misguided pity at the sight of the patient's suffering, euthanasia is sometimes justified by the utilitarian motive of avoiding costs which bring no return and weigh heavily on society. Thus it is proposed to eliminate malformed babies, the severely handicapped, the disabled, the elderly, especially when they are not self-sufficient, and the terminally ill (no. 15).

Although euthanasia and physician-assisted suicide are becoming more and more accepted as morally right and legally necessary, these forms of intentional killing of the innocent remain intrinsically immoral. The *Catechism of the Catholic Church,* referring to the *Vatican Declaration on Euthanasia,* ably summarizes what Catholic faith holds. It recognizes that "whatever its motives and means, direct euthanasia consists in putting an end to the lives of handicapped, sick, or dying persons," and is therefore "morally unacceptable" (no. 2277). Continuing, it declares: "Thus any act or omission which, of itself or by intention, causes death in order to eliminate suffering constitutes a murder gravely contrary to the dignity of the human person and to the respect due to the living God, his Creator. The error of judgment into which one can fall in good faith does not change the nature of this murderous act, which must always be forbidden and excluded" (ibid.).

In this chapter I will proceed as follows. (1) First, I will clarify the terminology used in debates over euthanasia. (2) Second, I will set forth the major arguments given to support what I call the "ethics of euthanasia," including the argument to gain legal approval of voluntary active euthanasia. (3) Third, I will offer a critique of the "ethics of euthanasia" and show why a willingness intentionally to kill a human person is absolutely incompatible with respect for his dignity as a person. (4) I will develop what I will call the "ethics of benemortasia" or of caring, and only caring, for the dying. In developing this alternative to the "ethics of euthanasia" I will identify criteria that help us to distinguish between "ordinary" or "proportionate" medical treatments and "extraordinary" or "disproportionate" treatments. The former are morally required, whereas the latter can, and at times ought, rightly be refused. (5) I will then take up the care to be given persons who are judged to be permanently unconscious or in the so-called "persistent vegetative state." I will conclude (6) with a discussion of living wills and advance directives.

1. CLARIFYING THE TERMINOLOGY

The *Vatican Declaration on Euthanasia* (1981) defines euthanasia as "an action or an omission which of itself or by intention causes death, in order that all suffering may in this way be eliminated. Euthanasia's terms of reference, then, are to be found in the intention of the will and of the methods used" (Part II). This is a very clear and precise definition, explicitly and rightly noting that one can kill another "in order that all suffering may in this way be eliminated" by acts of *omission* as well as by acts of *commission*. This is most important to recognize, because advocates of euthanasia seek to win support by claiming that so-called "passive euthanasia," which for them encompasses "allowing" a person to die of some underlying pathology by withholding or withdrawing medical treatments, is already regarded as morally and legally permissible and that, therefore, "active" euthanasia ought also to be recognized as morally and legally permissible.[4] This is completely false.

The term "euthanasia" is derived from the combination of two Greek words, *eu* (good or well) and *thanasia* (death), and originally meant a good or happy death. But today, as the *Vatican Declaration on Euthanasia* makes clear, it has acquired the meaning of "mercy killing." In fact the revised edition of *The Random House College Dictionary* gives the following as the first meaning of "euthanasia": "1. Also called **mercy killing,** the act of putting to death painlessly a person suffering from an incurable and painful disease or condition."[5]

Euthanasia takes the following forms: 1. *Active euthanasia* (at times called "direct" or "positive" euthanasia), in which someone intentionally chooses to kill a person by an act of commission. Active euthanasia can be either (A) *voluntary active euthanasia,* when it is performed on persons who give free and informed consent to being killed mercifully; (B) *nonvoluntary active euthanasia,* when performed on individuals who are not capable of giving free and informed consent to being killed mercifully; (C) *involuntary active euthanasia,* when done to individuals who refuse to give free and informed consent to being killed mercifully but who nonetheless are so killed. 2. *Passive euthanasia* (at times called "indirect" or "negative" euthanasia), in which someone brings about the death of a person for merciful reasons by an act of omission, i.e., by withholding or withdrawing medical treatments that could preserve that person's life precisely in order to bring death about. Like active euthanasia, passive euthanasia can also be (a) *voluntary,* when the person killed gives free and informed consent to the withholding or withdrawing of treatments precisely as a way of bringing about his or her own death, (b) *nonvoluntary,* when the person so killed is incompetent and incapable of giving consent, and (c) *involuntary,* when the person so killed refuses to consent to the withholding or withdrawing of life-preserving treatments.[6]

Today the euthanasia movement is principally concerned with establishing the moral rightness and legal permissibility of *active voluntary euthanasia,* claiming erroneously that *passive euthanasia,* both voluntary and nonvoluntary, has already been recognized as morally and legally permissible. Many euthanasia advocates are also agitating for acceptance of *active nonvoluntary euthanasia,* and, as will be seen, they clearly hold it to be the morally right way of "treating" many incompetent patients.

Physician-assisted suicide is accurately defined by one of its champions, Dr. Timothy E. Quill, as "the act of making a means of suicide (such as a prescription for barbiturates) available to a patient who is otherwise physically capable of suicide, and who subsequently acts on his or her own. It is distinguished from voluntary euthanasia, where the physician not only makes the means available but is the actual agent of death upon the patient's request."[7] Thus the principal difference between euthanasia and assisted suicide is that in euthanasia a person other than the one killed is the principal cause of the killing whereas in assisted suicide the person killed is himself or herself the principal cause while the physician or other person (spouse, etc.) formally cooperates in the killing act and is, as it were, an instrumental cause. Since it is usually a physician who "assists" in the suicide, the expression "physician-assisted suicide" is most common in the literature. The most prominent practitioner and advocate of physician-assisted suicide, of course, is the notorious Dr. Jack Kevorkian,[8] popularly known as "Dr. Death," who was convicted of murder and sentenced to prison in 1999.

Since the moral and juridical issues regarding physician-assisted suicide are basically the same as those regarding euthanasia, in what follows I will speak only of euthanasia and the ethics of euthanasia. The rationale justifying physician-assisted suicide is the same as that underlying euthanasia. Those in favor of euthanasia support physician-assisted suicide, while those rejecting it as intrinsically immoral similarly repudiate physician-assisted suicide.

Note, above all, that active euthanasia, brought about by an act of commission, and passive euthanasia, achieved through an act of omission, are morally the same. Each is the *intentional killing* of an innocent human person for reasons of mercy. Such *intentional killing* of an innocent person for reasons of mercy is completely different from the choice (intention) to withhold or withdraw medical treatments from a person because the *treatments* in question are either useless or burdensome, realizing that the person will die without such treatments. In euthanasia, one chooses to kill either by an act of commission or of omission because one judges that the *life* of the person to be killed is either useless or excessively burdensome and that the person is better off dead than alive. In what I shall call "benemortasia," one refuses to kill a person because one respects his or her life as something incomparably good; one rather chooses to withhold or withdraw *treatments* that are either futile (useless) or impose unnecessary burdens upon the dying person. This is a key distinction, frequently ignored today, that will be developed further in this chapter.

2. THE "ETHICS OF EUTHANASIA"

The "ethics of euthanasia" has been developed by a great many persons. Although the euthanasia movement began in the 1930s,[9] it picked up momentum in the 1970s, particularly after the Supreme Court's *Roe v. Wade* abortion decision in 1973, and the 1970s witnessed a host of books and articles setting forth the rationale underlying euthanasia.[10] The arguments advanced in the 1990s (another decade of great agitation for the euthanasia movement) are rooted in the same ideology.[11] I will first consider the rationale underlying the drive for voluntary active euthanasia and then the rationale underlying the movement for nonvoluntary active euthanasia.

A. Voluntary Active Euthanasia
(1) The "Principle of Autonomy"
The argument justifying voluntary active euthanasia morally and also for sanctioning it by law is fundamentally the following: In voluntary

active euthanasia the patient, even if not terminally ill, gives free and informed consent to being killed mercifully. The patient wants to die. The patient's desire to die is, moreover, understandable because of the pain and/or suffering experienced. Pain relievers may not be wholly effective in eliminating pain and other discomforts, including embarrassment, humiliation arising from the illness, a desire to alleviate the burdens his or her care imposes on others, etc. The patient has reached a mature and settled judgment that he or she is better off dead than alive. Since the person to be killed mercifully gives free and informed consent to being killed, no injustice will be done. Respect for this person's integrity and autonomy require one to honor his or her request to die. In fact, not to do so is not only to fail to respect the person's autonomy and dignity, it is to compel him or her to live in a way he or she believes is a horrible mockery of all he or she holds dear and to force him or her to die a miserable, pain-ridden death. Thus the request of such persons to be killed ought to be honored; carrying it out is, in fact, an act of kindness or beneficence. Not only is voluntary active euthanasia morally right but it ought also to be protected by law. To continue its prohibition is cruel to those who are made to suffer needlessly and infringes on the liberty of those who would choose to be killed or to kill in order to prevent needless suffering.[12] Indeed, as several champions of voluntary active euthanasia put matters, "death control, like birth control, is a matter of human dignity. Without it persons become puppets."[13]

From this we can see that the major argument given to justify voluntary active euthanasia is rooted in the premise that human persons are autonomous, i.e., that their freedom of self-determination includes the freedom to choose to be killed when doing so is judged reasonable on the grounds that they are better off dead than alive, that their lives are no longer of any value to them and that others have the duty to respect their choice to be killed mercifully rather than bear the indignity of a life no longer worth living. Meaningful human dignity, in this understanding, consists in the ability to control one's own life and death and to determine the manner of one's demise.[14]

Voluntary active euthanasia, therefore, is justified on an alleged "principle of personal autonomy," or on the right of persons to be in control of their own life and death. As Singer puts it, linking the right to die to the right to life, "the most important aspect of having a right to life is that one can choose whether or not to invoke it. We value the protection given by the right to life only when we want to go on living. No-one can fear being killed at his or her own persistent, informed and autonomous request."[15]

(2) "Personal" Life vs. "Biological" Life

But voluntary active euthanasia also rests on the dualistic presupposition, implicit if not explicit, that physical, bodily life is radically distinct from "personal" life. The former is merely "biological" in nature; the latter, personal or meaningful life, consists in the exercisable ability to communicate, to make judgments, to reason. This dualistic presupposition is, as we will see, more central to the defense of nonvoluntary euthanasia, but it is likewise prominent in the defense of voluntary active euthanasia mounted by many of its more ardent advocates. Thus Fletcher, elaborating on the right of autonomous persons to exercise their dominion over physical nature, including bodily life and its processes, had this to say:

> Physical nature — the body and its members, our organs and their functions — all of these things are a part of "what is over against us," and if we live by the rules and conditions set in physiology or another *it* we are not *thou*.... Freedom, knowledge, choice, responsibility — all these things of personal or moral stature are in us, not *out there*. Physical nature is what is over against us, out there. It represents the world of *its*.[16]

Similarly, Maguire rails against the "physicalistic ethic that left moral man at the mercy of his biology" and condemned him to "await the good pleasure of biochemical and organic factors and allow these to determine the time and manner of his demise." Technological man, Maguire continues, now realizes that he has the moral right to intervene "creatively" and "to terminate his life through either positive action [active voluntary euthanasia] or calculated benign neglect [passive voluntary euthanasia] rather than await in awe the dispositions of organic tissues."[17] Similarly, Harris and Singer sharply distinguish mere biological life from personal life, claiming that persons have a right to choose death rather than become depersonalized through debilitating illnesses.[18]

B. Nonvoluntary Euthanasia

Although the contemporary legal battle is over voluntary active euthanasia, advocates of the "ethics of euthanasia" likewise maintain that nonvoluntary euthanasia is also the right moral choice to make on behalf of many incompetent patients and that this ought to be legally permissible. As noted earlier, "nonvoluntary" euthanasia is used to describe the mercy killing of patients who are *not capable* of giving or withholding consent to being killed mercifully, but whose lives are judged no longer of any value to them.

(1) Quality of Life Judgments Justifying Nonvoluntary Euthanasia

Two major arguments are given to justify nonvoluntary euthanasia or the mercy killing of incompetent individuals. The first is based on the "quality of life" and the judgment that an incompetent person's life is no longer of any value to him or to her and that killing such a person is a benefit rather than a harm. Arguments based on "quality of life" judgments have been advanced by many euthanasia supporters. Among the more ardent advocates of nonvoluntary euthanasia, in particular the "beneficent" mercy killing of handicapped newborns, are Glanville Williams, Marvin Kohl, H. Tristram Englehardt, Jr., Robert F. Weir, Anthony Shaw, Raymond S. Duff and A. G. M. Campbell.[19] Frequently nonvoluntary euthanasia, particularly in the case of newborns, is administered by withholding or withdrawing life-preserving measures (including feeding, even by mouth, e.g., some celebrated cases of Down Syndrome babies killed by "benign" neglect). The life-preserving measures are withheld or withdrawn precisely as a means of bringing about death, and the killing is justified on the grounds that the individuals killed are, because of their low quality of life, better off dead than alive. Different advocates of nonvoluntary euthanasia based on a poor quality of life differ greatly, however, in identifying "criteria" to determine whether one's quality of life is so bad that death is a benefit and not a harm. Although quite frequently nonvoluntary euthanasia is accomplished by an act of omission (so-called "passive" euthanasia), its advocates hold that active euthanasia is also morally justifiable, and preferable to passive euthanasia because the former is quicker than the lingering death frequently resulting from nontreatment.[20]

The basic argument is simply this: one can determine that an individual's quality of life is so poor that continued existence is for that person not a benefit but a burden. Thus, killing that person is an act of benevolence or kindness, for by killing that person, whose life has been judged to be no longer worth living, one is doing something good.

(2) Nonpersonhood and Nonvoluntary Euthanasia

The justification of nonvoluntary euthanasia based on "quality of life" judgments does not deny the personhood of those to be killed mercifully. Another argument to justify nonvoluntary euthanasia, whether by an act of commission (active) or by one of omission (passive), is that those killed are either not yet persons or are no longer persons. Thus their intentional killing can be likened to the killing of other animals for reasons of mercy.

Joseph Fletcher, Michael Tooley, and Peter Singer are among the most vociferous champions of this latter claim (these authors, and many others, likewise justify abortion, as we saw in a previous chapter, on the grounds that the unborn cannot be regarded as persons).[21] They argue that abortion is frequently justified because intrauterine examination has disclosed that the unborn entity suffers from some serious (or not too serious) malady (e.g., Down Syndrome, Tay-Sachs disease, cystic fibrosis, etc.) and that one ought to prevent its birth and subsequent experience of a life not worth living, what one could call euthanasia of the unborn. But at times, prenatal examination does not take place or fails to detect some serious (or not too serious) malady. Since both the unborn and the newborn are not, in their judgment, persons because they lack exercisable cognitive abilities, their parents ought to have the right to kill them to spare such infants a burdensome life.

Here it is worth noting that John Harris, a leading advocate of euthanasia, justified the withholding of nutrition and hydration by means of tubes to Tony Bland, an Englishman said to be in the so-called "persistent vegetative state," on the grounds that Bland could no longer be considered a "person" because he had no exercisable cognitive faculties and was hence "no longer capable of possessing any interests at all" — an ability which Harris deems necessary if an entity is to be regarded as a "person" — and that consequently "death was in his best interests." Harris held that the withdrawing of tubally provided food and hydration from Bland was done precisely in order to bring about his death — a clear case of nonvoluntary euthanasia.[22] In another section of this chapter I will discuss in more detail the care to be given persons in the so-called "persistent vegetative state," and we will see that some hold that withholding or withdrawing the provision of food and hydration from such persons is justified as the withholding or withdrawing of *useless* and/or *burdensome* treatment, with the subsequent death not intended, and not as an act of euthanasia by an act of omission. But Harris clearly sees such withholding or withdrawing of nutrition and hydration as the *intentional* killing of a human being who is no longer to be regarded as a person, as an act of nonvoluntary but justified euthanasia.

C. The Legal or Jurisprudential Issue

Although the champions of euthanasia approve of both voluntary and nonvoluntary euthanasia, whether active or passive, as morally good choices that ought to be legally permissible, the major goal of euthanasia supporters today is to win legal approval of voluntary active euthanasia. At present the law of homicide (at least in the U,S.) protects the lives of all innocent human persons who have survived birth by strictly prohibiting intentionally killing them. Thus the law now regards active euthanasia, even if voluntary, as criminal homicide. This accounts for the great contemporary agitation clamoring for a change in the legal status. Here I will merely summarize the basic argument advanced by apologists for euthanasia to effect a change in the law. It can be stated as follows:

> By definition, if euthanasia is voluntary, the person to be killed mercifully gives free and informed consent to being killed; hence killing him or her does no injustice. The person's desire to be killed mercifully is reasonable in view of the suffering and/or pain and/or humiliation he or she experiences; at times others too are suffering terribly, psychologically or economically or both. Killing this person, who after all, freely consents to being killed and may even be begging to be killed, is thus a reasonable way to end all this suffering. Although some people in our society regard such killing as immoral for various reasons, it would be cruel and unjust to impose their values on those who freely choose to be killed and on those who seek to compassionately execute their choice. Thus, voluntary active euthanasia ought to be legally permissible.

This argument would seem to find legal support in the understanding of the Fourteenth Amendment undergirding the 1992 Supreme Court decision in *Planned Parenthood v. Casey*. In that case, Justices Souter, Kennedy, and O'Connor gave as one of the major reasons for reaffirming the "central holding" of *Roe v. Wade* the meaning of "liberty" in the Fourteenth Amendment. According to them, matters "involving the most intimate and personal choices a person may make in a lifetime, choices central to personal dignity and autonomy, are central to the liberty protected by the Fourteenth Amendment. At the heart of liberty is the right to define one's own concept of existence, of meaning, of the universe, and of the mystery of human life."[23] Fortunately, the drive to legalize voluntary active euthanasia has not yet succeeded.

D. Summary and Conclusion: The "Ethics of Euthanasia"

Arthur Dyck, a Protestant theologian teaching at Harvard University, is a champion of innocent human life, both prior to birth and through the whole of life until death. In my opinion, Professor Dyck gives us one of the most accurate and succinct summaries of the major claims upon which the "ethics of euthanasia" is based — claims he subsequently countered with the truths underlying what he called the "ethics of benemortasia." According to Dyck the case for active voluntary euthanasia rests on the following presuppositions:

> (1) that the dignity that attaches to personhood by reason of the freedom to make moral choices demands also the freedom to take one's life or to have it taken when this freedom is absent or lost; (2) that there is such a thing as a life not worth living, a life that lacks dignity, whether by reason of distress, illness, physical or mental handicaps, or even sheer despair or whatever reason; (3) that what is sacred or supreme in value is the "human dignity" that resides in the rational capacity to choose to control life and death.[24]

The first and third of these presuppositions, taken together, constitute the so-called "principle of autonomy" invoked by so many today to provide a moral and jurisprudential justification of euthanasia. The second of these presuppositions is also at the heart of the alleged jusrification of nonvoluntary euthanasia, along with the claim that some of the noncompetent individuals who are to be killed mercifully are not persons because they lack exercisable cognitive abilities. This second presupposition implies a dualism, one that regards physical, bodily life as an instrumental good: a good *for* the person, not a good *of* the person, and thus different in kind from the truly *personal* goods that perfect the person and are thus goods *of* the person, goods such as knowledge, free choice, meaningful interpersonal relationships, etc., i.e., goods whose very being depends on consciousness.

3. CRITIQUE OF THE "ETHICS OF EUTHANASIA"

Here I will focus on the following: (A) the claim that voluntary euthanasia is justified by human autonomy, (B) the contention that nonvoluntary euthanasia is justified on the basis of "quality of life" judgments, (C) the dualism underlying the entire euthanasia movement, and (D) the reasons why voluntary active euthanasia ought not to be legalized.

A. Autonomy and Voluntary Euthanasia vs. the Sanctity of Life

As we have seen, the basic argument for voluntary euthanasia is this: the person to be killed mercifully gives free and informed consent to being killed in this way. He chooses death, regarding it as a benefit. In doing so he is simply exercising his autonomy. Respect for this autonomy should therefore lead others, including doctors, to confer the benefit of a merciful death on him.

But a doctor, even one not opposed in principle to euthanasia, would refuse to kill a patient, even if the patient begged to be killed, if he thought that the patient still had a worthwhile life to live. Thus, as the authors of a superb study prepared by a group of British Catholics rightly point out, *"it is precisely the judgement that a patient no longer has a worthwhile life which will seem to justify euthanasia,"* and, continuing, they affirm: ***"But precisely that contention is inconsistent with recognising the continuing worth and dignity of the patient's life."***[25] In a magnificent passage these authors then show why this is so:

> In any apparent conflict between, on the one hand, the re-
> quirement that we do not deny equal human dignity and re-
> spect for the sanctity of human life and, on the other, the
> putative claims of respect for autonomy, the principle of the
> sanctity of human life must always trump those claims. For
> recognition of equal human dignity is fundamental to recog-
> nition of all human beings as subjects of justice. There is no
> authentic conflict between rightly respecting the sanctity of
> human life and rightly respecting autonomy. The exercise of
> human autonomy in giving shape, direction, and character
> to a human life is not a source of value and dignity at *odds*
> with the fundamental source of human worth and dignity in
> human nature itself. For … what makes it reasonable to
> recognise human nature as the source of our basic worth and
> dignity as human beings is the fact that our nature in its de-
> velopment is intrinsically directed to human fulfilment and
> human good. And what best makes sense of the ideal of re-

spect for autonomy is the role played by free choice in the achievement of that fulfilment to which our nature is directed; for self-determining choice is integral to that achievment. But if the moral significance of autonomy is understood in that way, then the value of autonomy is derivative from, and reflective of, that which gives value to our humanity. So it should be clear that the claims of autonomy cannot properly extend to choices, which are inconsistent with recognising the basic worth and dignity of every human being.[26]

In other words, human autonomy (self-determination) is not unlimited. Its *rightful* exercise enables us to achieve our fulfillment, our perfection, but it is subservient to our *good as persons*. I have cited this passage at length not only because it is, in my opinion, so powerful, but also because much that is said in it fits in beautifully with Pope John Paul II's correct understanding of legitimate human autonomy and the role that a false notion of autonomy has played in the development of the "culture of death."

Legitimate human autonomy, or self-government, is rooted in our capacity to determine our lives in and through our self-determining acts of free choice. Pope John Paul II, as we saw in Chapter Two, emphasized the truth that "it is precisely through his acts that man attains perfection [=the "fulfillment" referred to in the above passage] as man, as one who is called to seek his Creator of his own accord and freely to arrive at full and blessed perfection by cleaving to him" (*Veritatis splendor,* no. 71). Our freely chosen deeds, as the Pope stresses, "do not produce a change merely in the state of affairs outside of man, but, to the extent that they are deliberate choices, they give moral definition to the very person who performs them, determining his *profound spiritual traits"* (no. 71). They are a *"decision about oneself* and a setting of one's own life for or against the Good, for or against the Truth, and ultimately, for or against God" (no. 65). In other words, as we saw in Chapter Two, we *give to ourselves our identity as moral beings in and through the actions we freely choose to do.*

Moreover, as John Paul II likewise rightly stressed, human freedom of choice, our legitimate autonomy, must be guided, if we are to exercise it rightly, by the *truth.* Human freedom and autonomy are not unlimited, creative of the moral order. Human freedom is exercised rightly and in a way conducive to human fulfillment or perfection only when guided by the *truth.* This truth is rooted ultimately in God's wise and loving plan for human existence, the eternal law, and God has so made us that we are capable of participating actively in this wise and loving plan through our knowledge of the practical truths necessary to guide our choices so that they can be lead us to our perfection, and our knowledge of these truths is what we know as natural law (*Veritatis splendor*, nos. 38-45; cf. Chapter Two, pp. 55-60). When human autonomy is conceived as the creator and arbiter of good and evil, of right and wrong, we are no longer able to guide our choices by the truth but only by subjective and changing human opinions (cf. ibid., nos. 35-37), and human autonomy, so conceived, gives birth to the "culture of death" (cf. *Evangelium vitae*, no. 19).

In short, human autonomy, human freedom of choice, is limited. It is valued precisely because we can exercise it with a view to our flourishing or fulfillment as persons living in communion with others. By exercising it in accord with the truth, we choose in such a way that we give to ourselves our identity as persons willing to respect the truth and to shape our lives in accord with it. If our choices seriously undermine in us our capacity to flourish as human persons, and if, *a fortiori,* they aim to damage aspects of this capacity in others, there is no reason to respect such choices. And the intentional killing of ourselves or others, no matter what the reason, is a choice that sets us against the inherent goodness of human life, of this great and incomparable good gift that God has given us. In choosing to *kill,* moreover, we give to ourselves the identity of *killers.* This is the reason, as Vatican II reminds us, why morally bad choices, such as the choice to *kill* innocent human life, not only poison society and dishonor the Creator, but "harm their perpetrators more than those who are harmed by them" (*Gaudium et spes,* no. 27).

B. "Quality of Life" Judgments and Justice

We have seen that two principal arguments are advanced to justify nonvoluntary euthanasia. One claims that the individuals to be killed mercifully, although certainly members of the human species, are no longer to be regarded as persons because they lack presently exercisable cognitive faculties, etc. Since this claim has been sufficiently refuted in the chapter on abortion, it is not necessary to discuss it here.

The second asserts that even if we grant that the individuals to be killed mercifully are indeed persons, their "quality of life" is so poor that life is no longer of any benefit to them and death can be regarded as a kindly release from a burdensome and/or useless existence demeaning to human persons. This claim is utterly incompatible with the justice due to human persons. "Quality of life" judgments are inescapably arbitrary and unjust. Different authors assign different qualities that one needs to possess "meaningful" life, and the same authors at times list different qualities in different apologias for their position. More significantly, the qualities alleged to make life worthwhile (intelligence, ability to respond to stimuli, awareness of others, etc.) all admit of enormous differences in degree. But some cutoff point has to be assigned, above which the quality of life is "meaningful," and below which it is not so that death can be mercifully administered. Such cutoff points are arbitrarily asserted, with different authors assigning different "weight" to different factors and different degrees of ability within the chosen criteria. It is evident that this way of determining who should live and who should die is utterly arbitrary and unjust.[27]

C. Dualism and Euthanasia

Advocates of euthanasia are in essence dualists. They regard human persons as consciously experiencing subjects, free to do as they choose, whose bodily life is merely an instrumental good, a good *for* persons, i.e., consciously experiencing subjects. When this life becomes burdensome it is, for them, no longer of value; it is rather a burden which the experiencing subject is free to set aside. As the authors of *Euthanasia, Clinical Practice and the Law* so perceptively say, "propaganda puts into the mouth of the potential, theoretical suicide [or advocate of euthanasia]: 'I belong to myself, and I can set conditions on which I will consent to go on living.' Life is regarded as a good or bad hotel, which must not be too bad to be worth staying in."[28] But our bodily life is integral to our lives as persons; it is not something foreign to it. Human persons are bodily persons, and bodily life is not merely, as we saw in a previous chapter, a useful or instrumental good *for* the person, but it is rather integral to the human person, an aspect of his or her *being*. One cannot respect a human person without respecting his or her bodily life.

The dualism underlying euthanasia is false. Human persons are bodily beings, whose bodies are integral to their being as persons. When God created human persons, "male and female he created them" (Gn 1:24), i.e., men and women of flesh and blood. He did not create conscious minds to which he then added a body as an afterthought. Moreover, when the Father's only-begotten Son, his uncreated Word, became man to show us how deeply God loves us, he did not become a conscious mind using a body as his instrument; rather, he became "living flesh" (*sarx egeneto,* as the Greek of John 1:14 reads). Although human persons are *more* than their bodies because their life-giving principle, the principle that makes their bodies to be *human* bodies, is a spiritual soul, they are nonetheless *bodies, living flesh*. If a person breaks his or her arm, he does not damage his property or break an "instrument," he or she hurts *himself* or *herself*.

The bodily life of a human person, however heavily burdened it may be, is still that person's life, his very being. To attack one's life is to attack one's person. One cannot kill a person's body without killing the person. Although the latter's soul is immortal, the soul is not the "I," the self,[29] for the self is a unit of body and soul. Christians believe that Christ has conquered death, so that death has lost its sting. But death itself is not good; it is the deprivation of life, and life is a good, and an incalculable good *of* the person. To judge that a person's life no longer has any value, that it is worthless, is to judge that a *person* no longer has any value, that a *person* is worthless.

Here it is worth recalling what Dr. Leo Alexander, who took part in the Nuremberg trials after World War II, had to say about "medical science under dictatorship." After a careful study of the "culture of death" characteristic of the Third Reich, he showed that it has its origins in the acceptance of mercy killing. He concluded: "Whatever proportion these crimes [of the Nazis] finally assumed, it became evident to all who investigated them that they had started from small beginnings.... It started with the acceptance of the attitude, basic in the euthanasia movement, *that there is such a thing as a life not worthy to be lived*."[30]

D. Voluntary Active Euthanasia and the Law

We have already seen the major argument advanced to secure the legalization of voluntary active euthanasia, namely, that it is not unjust because the person to be killed freely consents to being so killed and that its legal proscription violates their liberty and the liberty of those who want, compassionately, to honor their request to be killed mercifully.

The basic counterargument, advanced with great skill by Grisez and Boyle, can be summarized as follows. Legalizing euthanasia without stringent governmental regulation would inevitably be unjust because some persons who would not freely consent to being killed mercifully would surely be pressured or coerced into giving consent to such killing and these persons would unjustly be deprived of the protection that the current law of homicide extends to them. But to avoid this kind of injustice, strict governmental regulation would be indispensable. But government involvement, including the use of tax monies, for this purpose would infringe on the liberty of all those citizens who find such killing abhorrent and who do not wish their government to be involved in such killing, undertaken, moreover, not for the *common* good, but to serve the *private* interests of individuals. Legalizing euthanasia without government regulation would unjustly endanger the lives of those who might then be pressured into giving consent to being killed mercifully; legalizing it with strict governmental supervision would infringe the liberty of others; since voluntary active euthanasia cannot be legalized without causing injustice to those to be killed or unjustly infringing on the liberty of citizens who find government involvement in such killing for some individuals' private good repugnant, it cannot be legalized without doing injustice. Therefore, it ought not be legalized.[31]

4. THE "ETHICS OF BENEMORTASIA"

"Benemortasia" is a term meaning a "good" or "happy" "death" (from the Latin, *bene* [good] and *mortasia* [death]) coined by Arthur Dyck of Harvard University, who, as we have seen already, vigorously opposes the "ethics of euthanasia." A similar term, "agathansasia," from the Greek *agathos, agathe* (good) and *thanasia* (death) was coined by the late Paul Ramsey, for many years professor of Christian ethics at Princeton University and a champion of the culture of life vs. the culture of death.[32]

I believe that the "ethics of benemortasia" can be adequately set forth by reflecting on and developing the following truths: (1) It is always wrong, and utterly incompatible with love for God and neighbor, intentionally to kill innocent human life; (2) in caring for the dying, a proper love for life requires one to make use of "ordinary" or "proportionate" means of preserving life, but one is free to withhold or withdraw "extraordinary" or "disproportionate" means of doing so.

A. The Intrinsic Good of Human Life and the Evil of Intentional Killing

We believe, and rightly so, that human persons are radically different in kind from other animals and that, because they are, they are beings of moral worth, whose lives are precious. The ultimate reason why human life is precious is that it is a good and great gift of God, a created participation in his life. He has given it to us to guard and protect, to be its stewards. But "why," the authors of *Euthanasia, Clinical Practice and the Law,* inquire, "cannot we stewards of our life return it to its rightful owner when the indications are that it has served its purpose and that

God is recalling it to himself? Why cannot we then hasten death?" Their answer to this question is eloquent:

> The Christian response is that one's stewardship of one's life does not include the choice to terminate the stewardship itself. We did not ourselves participate in initiating the gift and task of that stewardship; we could not accept it on conditions chosen by us. Why God should have brought us (or anyone) into existence as "persons created for their own sake" is deeply mysterious. So we should not be particularly surprised if we also find it mysterious that God sees meaning and value in every part — even the most miserable and reduced—of the lifespan he allots us. But that God can and does is central to the faith of Israel and to Christian faith. His ways are not our ways, and the particular workings of his purposes are inscrutable to us. The conditions of our stewardship, then, are provided by God's commandments or "mandates." Men and women can come (though not without the risk of uncertainty and confusion) to a knowledge of those commandments by a conscientious exercise of "natural" reason, i.e., even without the benefit of God's self-disclosure.... In that self-disclosure there is revealed a commandment which, as explained through Scripture and the tradition of the Church, forbids us to intend to terminate our life. It has always been Christian belief that that expression of God's will holds good in all the circumstances and conditions of life.... We are all in the hands of a loving God who has given us each a life to be lived out in loving worship of him and in loving service of our neighbour, in preparation for a further life of perfect fulfillment with the God of all love and consolation.... The ultimate source of the dignity and inviolability of the human being is God's creative love and loving purpose, which are at the depth of the mystery of every human person, and uniquely for everyone.[33]

The life God has given us includes our bodily life, which is integral to our *being* as human persons. So true is this that "to regard the body as a prison, or as an instrument or detachable launching rocket of the *real* person, is incompatible with the faith in which incarnation and redemption are central.... The good of human life, protected by God, is the good of bodily life. One cannot justify an attack on that life, even in one's own person, by arguing that one's bodily life is useless or an encumbrance to one's *real* vocation as a person. Reverence for that bodily life is thus integral to one's earthly existence."[34]

As John Paul II reminds us in *Veritatis splendor*, love for our neighbor requires us to respect our neighbor's *good*, and we can do this only by respecting his *goods*, the goods perfective of him at the various levels of his existence, goods such as *life* itself (cf. nos. 12, 13). One cannot love one's neighbor if one judges the neighbor to be better off dead than alive, if one *wills* that he or she be dead.

B. Criteria for Distinguishing Between "Ordinary" ("Proportionate") and "Extraordinary" ("Disproportionate") Treatments
(1) Relevant Church Teaching and Its Interpretation

Two major documents of the Church's Magisterium clearly distinguish between "ordinary" or "proportionate" treatments — i.e., treatments that one is morally obliged to use in order to respect the dignity of human life and rightly to exercise one's stewardship of it — and "extraordinary" or "disproportionate" treatments, i.e., treatments that one is at liberty to withhold or withdraw in exercising stewardship over one's own or another's life. We reviewed the teaching in one of these documents, the *Vatican Declaration on Euthanasia* (1981) in Chapter One, and here we will note its relevance. The other document is a 1957 address of Pope Pius XII to a congress of anesthesiologists. In the course of his remarks, Pius had this to say:

> ... normally one is held to use only ordinary means [to prolong life] — according to the circumstances of persons, places, times, and culture — that is to say, means that do not involve any grave burden for oneself or another. A stricter obligation would be too burdensome for most men and would render the attainment of the higher, more important good too difficult. Life, health, all temporal activities are in fact subordinated to spiritual ends. On the other hand, one is not forbidden to take more than the strictly necessary steps to preserve life and health, so long as he does not fail in some more important duty.[35]

This statement of Pius XII is obviously relevant to the distinction between "ordinary" and "extraordinary" means of treatment and to the criteria for determining whether or not it is morally appropriate to with-hold or withdraw treatment. Here he indicates that "ordinary" medical treatment is that kind of treatment which offers reasonable hope of ben-efiting the subject without imposing unacceptable burdens on the sub-ject or others, whereas "extraordinary" medical treatment is treatment which imposes unacceptable burdens on the subject and/or others. The pope did not himself address the *specific* criteria for distinguishing be-tween treatments which are ordinary and those which are extraordinary. Rather, he outlined a general approach that seems clear enough, but one which obviously requires more specification.

(2) Interpreting Pius XII's Statement: Kevin O'Rourke's View Criticized

A crucial issue in interpreting this statement by Pius XII has to do with the proper understanding of what he meant when he said that life, i.e., physical, bodily life, is subordinated to "spiritual ends." Here I want to call attention to and criticize the way Kevin O'Rourke, O.P., inter-prets this passage of Pius XII (he applies this interpretation to the treat-ment to be given persons said to be in the "persistent vegetative state"). O'Rourke maintains that Pius XII's emphasis on the supremacy of the spiritual goal of human life

> specifies more clearly the terms "ordinary" and "extraor-dinary." A more adequate and complete explanation of "or-dinary" means to prolong life would be: those means which are obligatory because they *enable* a person to strive for the spiritual purpose of life. "Extraordinary" means would seem to be: those means which are optional because they are *inef-fective* or a grave burden in helping a person strive for the spiritual purpose of life.[36]

I would agree, for reasons to be set forth below, that a means is ex-traordinary if it *imposes* a "grave burden" on a person and prevents him or her from striving for the spiritual purpose of life. Thus if a proposed medical treatment has a high risk of rendering a person permanently unconscious, the person could rightly refuse the treatment, preferring to live out his or her life consciously. The burden this proposed treatment would impose on the person is truly excessive.

But O'Rourke errs seriously when he claims that a means is "ordi-nary" only if it *enables* a person to pursue this goal and that it is "extraordinary" and hence not obligatory if it is *ineffective* in helping a person strive for the spiritual goal of life. He errs seriously because there are many people, including some seriously mentally impaired infants and children and some elderly people who are "not with it," persons who are not actually able to make judgments and choices and thus incapable of pursuing the "spiritual goal of life" But these unfortunate human beings are still persons; their lives are still good and of value, and it is good for them to be alive. If they should fall sick or be in danger of death, they surely have a right to some kinds of medical treatments that would preserve their lives even if these treatments would be *ineffective* in helping them pursue the spiritual goal of life. Thus, for example, if elderly persons no longer mentally competent or infants suffering from trisomy 21 (a disorder entailing severe mental incapacity and leading to an early death) were to cut an artery, one could not simply allow them to bleed to death, or, if they should break their arm, one could not omit putting it into a cast so that it could be healed. But these "treatments" would not *enable* them to pursue the spiritual goal of life and they would be *ineffective* for that purpose, and on O'Rourke's analysis would thus be "extraordinary" and not obligatory. But this is surely false.

A proper interpretation of Pius's statement, as noted above, is that treatments which would *prevent* a person from pursuing the spiritual goal of life, *disabling* him or her, would be truly "extraordinary" because of the terrible burden it would impose upon them. But preventing a noncompetent patient from bleeding to death, repairing his or her broken limbs, giving him or her antibiotics to combat severe flu, etc., would surely be "ordinary" and mandatory treatments. In O'Rourke's exegesis of the text, they would not be. Thus I regard his interpretation as seriously defective and tending to the view that bodily life is merely an instrumental good *for* the person, not a good *of* the person.[37]

The other major magisterial document is the *Vatican Declaration on Euthanasia*. While unequivocally condemning suicide and all forms of euthanasia as absolutely immoral, this document reaffirmed traditional Catholic teaching that one is not obliged to use all possible means to preserve and prolong human life. It referred to the distinction between "ordinary" and "extraordinary" means of preserving life, noting that the imprecision of these terms is the cause of some ambiguity and that, therefore, some more recent writers have suggested that the term "proportionate" be used to designate means which are morally obligatory and that the term "disproportionate" be used to designate means which are not morally obligatory. It stated that no matter what terms are used, it will nonetheless be possible to make a correct judgment "by studying the type of treatment to be used, its degree of complexity or risk, its cost and the possibility of using it, and comparing these elements with the result that can be expected, taking into account the state of the sick person and his or her physical and moral resources" (sect. IV).*

Moreover, the same document maintained that "one cannot impose on anyone the obligation to have recourse to a technique which is already in use but which carries a risk or is burdensome. Such a refusal is not the equivalent of suicide; on the contrary, it should be considered as an acceptance of the human condition, or a wish to avoid the application of a medical procedure disproportionate to the results which can be expected, or a desire not to impose excessive expense on the family or community" (ibid.). In addition, it says that "when inevitable death is imminent in spite of the means used, it is permitted in conscience to take the decision to refuse forms of treatment which would only secure a precarious and burdensome prolongation of life, so long as the normal care due to a sick person in similar cases is not interrupted" (ibid.).

---

*Note well: The use of the terms "proportionate" and "disproportionate" in this document of the Congregation for the Doctrine of the Faith in no way is an endorsement of the moral methodology known as "proportionalism," which holds that one can intend so-called "premoral evil" for the sake of an alleged "proportionately" greater good — a moral methodology repudiated by John Paul II in *Veritatis splendor*. First of all, the *Declaration*, prior to introducing these terms, had previously affirmed in unambiguous language the truth that the intentional killing of innocent persons, for whatever reason, is always gravely immoral — a truth denied by proportionalism. Moreover, judgments of proportionality can be made *when there is some measure that can be used to compare measurable things.* Here the things to be measured are medical treatments of various kinds, each with its own risks, hazards, expense, pains, debilitating effects etc., and with their benefits. The judgment to be made in such cases is basically a technical one requiring help from health-care personnel who can advise one of specific benefits and burdens of proposed treatments for specific patients so that one can make a reasonable comparison of he different benefits and burdens. The best discussion of this issue is provided by John Finnis, *Fundamentals of Ethics* (Washington, D.C.: Georgetown University Press, 1985), pp. 106-107.

The precise interpretation of these statements will occupy us more fully below.

(3) Legitimate vs. Illegitimate "Quality of Life" Judgments

Note that the *Vatican Declaration* affirms that in assessing treatments it is proper to take "into account the state of the sick person and his or her physical and moral resources." Here the *Declaration* makes it clear that, although it is *always* gravely immoral to kill a person mercifully because one judges that the "quality" of his or her life is so wretched that he or she would be better off dead than alive, it is legitimate to consider the "quality" of his or her life *in relationship to specific kinds of treatments* for a person *in that condition*, i.e., with that "quality of life." What would not be too risky, painful, burdensome, etc., for an otherwise healthy teenager or adult might well be so for persons suffering from advanced stages of lethal diseases, etc. Thus, for instance, an amputation of a limb would not be "disproportionate" or "extraordinary" for an otherwise vigorous youth or mature adult but would be so for someone suffering from advanced pancreatic cancer or something similar. Such "quality of life" judgments, which bear on the uselessness or burdensomeness of specific kinds of *treatments* for persons in *specific kinds of conditions* are not the same as "quality of life" judgments asserting that those persons' *lives* are no longer of any value.[38] The late John R. Connery, S.J., summed this matter up well when he said that while the Catholic tradition has repudiated a quality of life ethic which would deny persons needed medical care simply on the basis of the poor quality of their lives, it nonetheless "allowed quality of life considerations in decisions about prolonging life *if they were related to the means themselves.*"[39]

(4) Richard McCormick's "Quality of Life" Position

In two exceptionally influential essays[40] Richard McCormick, S.J., insisted that it is not possible to judge which treatments are "extraordinary" and hence not morally obligatory without necessarily making "value of life" judgments. "There has been a tendency, " he wrote, "to shift the problem from the means to reverse the dying process to the quality of life sustained or preserved.... Granted that we can easily save the life, *what kind of life are we saving?*"[41] According to McCormick, bodily, physical life, while indeed "basic" and "precious," is a relative good, one "to be preserved precisely as the condition of these other values [interpersonal relationships]. It is these other values and possibilities which found the duty to preserve physical life and also dictate the

limits of this duty."[42] In his view the Judeo-Christian tradition holds that "the meaning, substance, and consummation of life are to be found in human *relationships* and the qualities of justice, respect, concern, compassion and support that surround them."[43] Because this is so, one can judge that bodily life is not a value to be preserved when the potential for these relationships has been lost or if it can never be attained. He maintains that "when in human judgment this potentiality [for human relationships] is totally absent or would be, because of the condition of the individual, totally subordinated to the mere effort for survival, that life can be said to have achieved its potential."[44] He claims that the reason for withholding or withdrawing a treatment is based on a judgment about the quality of life which the treatment will preserve. Thus he writes: "Often it is the kind of, the quality of, the life thus saved (painful, poverty-stricken, and deprived, away from home and friends, oppressive) that establishes the means as extraordinary. *That* type of life would be an excessive hardship for the individual."[45]

There are very serious problems with McCormick's proposal. The principal one is that there is a vast difference between concluding that a particular *treatment* is excessively burdensome and hence "extraordinary" and not morally required for this particular patient, taking into account his condition or "quality of life" relative to the treatment proposed, and concluding that someone's *life* is excessively burdensome. Pius XII and the *Vatican Declaration* direct our attention to the nature of the *treatments* to be used, taking into account the patient's physical and moral resources. McCormick *redirects* our attention to the quality of the person's *life* which the proposed treatments would preserve. McCormick then judges that person's *life* as the burden. The burden to be lifted is the person's life, not the proposed or presently used treatment. McCormick's proposal, consequently, is not compatible with the teaching of these magisterial documents. It seems clearly dualistic, regarding physical, bodily life as a useful good, a condition for the experiencing of truly personal goods, and not itself a *personal good*.

(5) Criteria for Determining Whether Treatments Are "Ordinary" ("Proportionate") or "Extraordinary" ("Disproportionate")

We will be helped to discover the criteria for withholding or withdrawing treatments (=criteria for distinguishing between "ordinary/proportionate" and "extraordinary/disproportionate" treatments) by first considering non-suicidal reasons for refusing treatment. As Grisez and Boyle have noted,

Individuals who are competent can refuse treatment upon themselves without the intent to end their own lives, which would be their motive if they appraised their future prospects and decided that they would be better off dead. Such refusal of treatment, including treatment without which life will be shortened, can be based upon *objectionable features of the treatment itself, its side effects, and its negative consequences.* An individual who has no desire to die can take such factors into account and decide that life without treatment, so long as life lasts, will be better than life with it. Such a decision is not a choice of death.[46]

A human person, in short, can refuse a treatment — choose that it be withheld or withdrawn — without adopting by choice a proposal to kill himself or herself. The treatment refusal is based on the judgment that the treatment itself, or its side-effects or deleterious consequences, are so burdensome that undergoing the treatment is not morally obligatory. The treatment in question is truly "extraordinary/disproportionate" since the burdens it imposes far exceed the benefits likely to result from its use.

What are some major reasons for refusing treatment on these grounds? Here too Grisez and Boyle offer helpful criteria that flesh out the general guidelines given by Pius XII and the *Vatican Declaration.* They write:

First, sometimes treatment is experimental or risky; ... second, some treatment is itself painful or brings about other experienced conditions which are undesirable;... third, in many cases, the requirements for the application of medical care would interfere with the activities and experiences which one desires during the time [of life] remaining;... fourth, many persons object to certain forms of care on the basis of some principle [for example, Jehovah's witnesses refuse blood transfusions because they believe that this is immoral, the equivalent of taking life, and others refuse organ transplants from the newly dead because they fear that the organs were taken while the "donor" was still alive];... fifth, there is a variety of reasons why persons find medical care psychologically repugnant;... sixth, in many cases medical care for one individual makes very severe demands upon others.[47]

To the reasons for making a given treatment unduly burdensome assigned by Grisez and Boyle in the above paragraph, we can add the cost of some medical treatments; one is not obligated to bankrupt his or her family in order to undergo a treatment. All these factors are *objectively discernible features in the treatment itself, its side-effects, and its negative consequences that impose undue burdens on the patient and/or others*. One can rightly reject such treatments and withhold them or withdraw them. The choice to do so is not suicidal, not rooted in the "ethics of euthanasia" but rather in the "ethics of benemortasia." We could say that *excessive burdensomeness* is the major criterion for determining whether a proposed treatment is "extraordinary/disproportionate." Excessive burdensomeness is, as it were, the genus, and species of such burdensomeness include the treatment's riskiness, its bad side-effects and bad consequences on the life of the person, the excessive pain of the treatment, treatments judged morally or psychologically repugnant, and excessive expense that would imperil the economic security of the patient, the patient's family, and/or the community. Withholding or withdrawing such treatments is not a choice to kill oneself or another for merciful reasons. It is *not* euthanasia. One does not judge a *life* excessively burdensome, one judges a *treatment* excessively burdensome. And, as we have seen already, in making this judgment the "physical and moral resources of the patient" — his or her "quality of life" in *that* sense — can rightly be taken into account.

In addition to the criterion of *burdensomeness* another criterion that enables us to judge whether a given treatment, for a given patient, is: "extraordinary/disproportionate" and hence not morally required is the criterion of *usefulness*. In the Catholic tradition a means has been judged useless in the strict sense if the benefits it promises are nil or useless in a wider sense if the benefits conferred are insignificant in comparison to the burdens it imposes.

The authors of *Euthanasia, Clinical Practice and the Law* provide a very detailed analysis of the reasons why a competent patient may rightly refuse treatment. In addition to excessive risk or financial cost, they identify four potentially acceptable reasons for rejecting treatment because it is "extraordinary/disproportionate." These are: "a) the burdens attendant on treatment impress one as more than one can cope with; b) the burdens attendant on treatment seem hardly warranted by the promised benefits; c) treatment is not worthwhile because a dying patient has reason to think that he no longer has an obligation to seek to prolong his life; d) treatment is straightforwardly futile, i.e., inappropriate to the biological nature of one's condition, as, for example, when putatively curative treatment is offered to someone in an irreversible state of dying."[48]

In summary, we can say that the two principal criteria for determining whether to withhold or withdraw a treatment because it is "extraordinary/disproportionate" are *burdensomeness* and *uselessness*. The former is the major criterion, insofar as the relative uselessness of many treatments is contingent upon the burdens they impose when compared with the benefits they bring. But what is most important is that these criteria draw attention to the *burdensomeness* and/or *uselessness* of the means used to preserve life. They do not lead one to conclude that treatments are to be withheld or withdrawn because of a judgment that the patient's *life* is either burdensome or useless — and this, as we have seen, is the judgment reached in the "ethics of euthanasia." Judgments of the burdensomeness and/or uselessness of treatments are compatible with a respect and love for the dignity of human life, which is *always* a precious good, a gift from God, no matter how heavily burdened it may be.

D. Summary: The Presuppositions of the "Ethics of Benemortasia"

A fitting conclusion for this section is provided, I believe, by Arthur Dyck, who, as we have seen, coined the term "benemortasia." Just as he ably set forth the presuppositions underlying the "ethics of euthanasia," so he also neatly expressed the presuppositions underlying the "ethics of benemortasia." These are:

> 1. A human being's life is not solely at the disposal of that person; every human life is part of a human community that is held together in part by respect for life and love for the lives of its members.

> 2. The dignity of the person, by reason of his freedom of choice, includes the freedom of dying persons to refuse noncurative, death-preventing interventions, but it does not include the freedom to choose death and to set one's will against life.

> 3. Every life has some worth. Life itself is a precious good; it is an intrinsic good, a good *of* the person, not merely a useful or instrumental good, a good *for* the person.

4. The supreme good is God himself, to whom the dying and those who care for the dying are responsible.[49]

5. CARING FOR THE PERMANENTLY UNCONSCIOUS AND PERSONS IN THE "PERSISENT VEGETATIVE STATE"

Directive no. 58 of the *Ethical and Religious Directives for Catholic Health Care Services* promulgated by the United States Conference of Bishops in November 1994 states: "There should be a presumption in favor of providing nutrition and hydration to all patients, including patients who require medically assisted nutrition and hydration, as long as this is of sufficient benefit to outweigh the burdens involved to the patient."

The relevant criteria for determining whether artificial feeding of patients is morally required are clear: such feeding is obligatory unless it is either useless (offering no reasonable hope of benefit) or excessively burdensome But applying these criteria to persons said to be in the "persistent vegetative state" (an expression that in my judgment is offensively dehumanizing since it suggests that individuals in such a condition no longer enjoy human personal life but merely exist at a vegetative level)[50] is a matter of serious controversy among both Catholic bishops and moral philosophers and theologians, with some contending that such feeding is futile and hence not obligatory and others maintaining that, unless the contrary can be clearly shown, such feeding is neither futile nor unduly burdensome and is therefore morally obligatory as an ordinary means of preserving life. I believe and hope to show that the latter position is the correct one.[51]

Here I will (A) provide an accurate description of this condition (hereafter abbreviated PVS), (B) note recommendations of some professional bodies and bioethics centers and comment on the question of consciousness and the experience of pain by PVS patients, (C) summarize major responses by bishops of the United States, following this with (D) a summary and critique of the view of theologians and philosophers who claim that such feeding is not obligatory, and (E) conclude with a summary of the argument given by theologians and philosophers who maintain that such feeding is morally obligatory unless it can be clearly shown to be futile.

A. Description of "Persistent Vegetative State"

Individuals in this condition are not comatose. A true coma is a state of "unarousable unresponsiveness" which may last as long as six months but will inevitably resolve itself into another state. The person may emerge into consciousness (of varying degrees) or sink into PVS, and it may take a long time, even months, before an accurate diagnosis of the person's true condition can be made.[52]

PVS itself is a form of deep unconsciousness. The upper part of the brain (the cerebral cortex) gives evidence of impaired or failed operation. Since it is this part of the brain which is neurologically involved in such activities as understanding, willing, and communicating, persons in this condition are not able to engage in these activities. But the brain stem, which controls involuntary functions such as breathing, blinking, circulating blood, cycles of waking and sleeping, etc., is still functioning. As a result, persons in this condition may open their eyes and sometimes follow movements with them or respond to loud or sudden noises (although such responses will not be long sustained nor are they apparently purposeful).[53] It is commonly held that persons in this condition have no consciousness experience and are incapable of experiencing pain, and that it is unlikely that persons in this condition will recover consciousness. However, their condition has stabilized, and they are not in immediate danger of death so long as they are given appropriate "food," and this can be provided them by various artificial means made possible by modern medical technology.

It is important to note that persons in this condition can, in fact, be fed orally in the beginning. However, those caring for them will usually prefer not to feed them orally because this is quite time-consuming, particularly if there are other persons for whom they must care. Thus feeding them by means of tubes is far more convenient. If not fed orally, the ability of persons in this condition to take food orally gradually atrophies.[54]

Since persons diagnosed as being in the PVS condition are by no means imminently in danger of death and since their lives can be protected, perhaps for several years, the moral question in caring for them is whether providing them with food and nourishment by tubes is morally obligatory or "ordinary" or whether withholding or withdrawing food so provided is "extraordinary."

B. Recommendations by Professional Bodies, etc.: PVS Patients, Consciousness, and Pain

During the 1980s and 1990s court cases involving termination of tubal feedings of PVS patients proliferated, eliciting responses from various professional organizations. In 1981 the Judicial Council of the American Medical Association declared it ethical to withdraw all means of life support, including such feeding, "where a terminally ill patient's coma is beyond doubt irreversible."[55] The President's Commission for the Study of Ethical Problems in Medicine and Biomedical and Behavioral Research addressed this issue in its 1983 monograph on forgoing life-sustaining treatments; it concluded that the decision to provide or forgo tube feeding of PVS patients was best made by the patient's surrogates and not by the courts; it likewise concluded that forgoing all treatment, including tubally administered food and hydration, was an ethically legitimate option.[56] Other organizations issuing guidelines favoring the withholding of tubal feeding from PVS patients the Hastings Center (1987), the American Academy of Neurology (1989), and the American Medical Association (1990).[57] It should be noted that a significant number of the individuals who drafted statements of this kind think that "personhood" is lost if an individual is no longer capable of exercising cognitive abilities.

More importantly, as D. Alan Shewmon, M.D., himself a leading neurologist and an expert particularly on the neurology of the brain, has noted, the unquestioned acceptance among medical authorities that patients with widespread cortical damage are ipso facto unconscious and incapable of experiencing pain and suffering is not based on verifiable evidence but is accepted "because official neurology says so." Shewmon, who had himself accepted this as doctrine, was forced to revise his views because of empirical evidence, namely, the lives of some hydrancephalic children (children whose brains lack the neocortex) who clearly manifest consciousness and cognitive abilities. Shewmon thus concluded that upon critical examination the "evidence" alleged to support the claim that patients with widespread cortical damage are by definition unconscious and incapable of feeling pain is "of an exclusively negative nature: patients with diffuse cortical destruction do not manifest clinical signs of awareness of self or environment. But there was no positive evidence that such patients are not inwardly conscious." Continuing, he observed that "no one seemed concerned that perhaps what is eliminated by cortical destruction might be the capacity for external manifestation of consciousness rather than consciousness itself; in other words, that what is called 'PVS' might in reality be merely a 'super-locked-in' state [a condition in which the person is indeed conscious but is utterly incapable of manifesting this externally]."[58] Shewmon then went on to say, in a passage of singular importance with respect to the question of pain experienced by PVS patients, the following:

The more I reconsidered the matter, the more I began to realize that the supposed lack of evidence for consciousness was not even complete. For example, all treatises on the neurophysiology of pain traced the anatomical pathway from the cutaneous nociceptors centrally, invariably ending not at the cortex but at the thalamus. Patients with strokes involving somatosensory cortex lose tactile discrimination and joint position sense, but not the capacity to perceive and to localize pain. Thalamic injury, however, can cause a distressing form of central pain. In the pain literature it is clear that the cortex's role in pain perception is merely modulatory and that the experience is mediated subcortically, but in the PVS literature these well known phenomena are systematically ignored. PVS patients often grimace to noxious stimuli and manifest primitive withdrawal responses. Advocates of the cortical theory write off such behaviors as mere brain-stem or spinal reflexes, but that dismissive attitude is based more on an a priori assumption than a scientific conclusion.[59]

C. Responses by U.S. Bishops

The universal Magisterium of the Church has not specifically addressed this question, but the bishops of the U.S. have given contradictory answers. We have already seen that Directive no. 58 of the *Ethical and Religious Directives for Catholic Health Care Services* (November 1994) holds that one ought to presume that nourishment so provided be given "as long as this is of sufficient benefit to outweigh the burdens involved to the patient." Despite this, however, some individual bishops and the Texas Conference of Catholic Bishops conclude that providing "food" through tubal means is futile and useless. The Texas bishops, who did not provide extensive argument to support their position, believed that someone in PVS was "stricken with a lethal pathology which, without artificial nutrition and hydration will lead to death." They held that withholding or withdrawing artificially provided food from such persons "is simply acknowledging the fact that the person has come to the end of his or her pilgrimage and should not be impeded [by artificially provided food] from taking the final step." In short, the Texas bishops judged such provision of food futile or useless and hence not obligatory.[60] Some individual bishops issued statements of a similar nature.[61]

On the other hand, on March 24, 1992, the Administrative Committee of the National Conference of Catholic Bishops authorized the publication of a substantive document prepared by the Committee for Pro-Life Activities of the NCCB. This document surveyed, somewhat extensively, relevant medical literature dealing with the issue and different positions taken by moral theologians. In their review of theological opinions, the authors of this document explicitly state that they do not find persuasive the rationale of some theologians that since persons in the PVS condition can no longer pursue the spiritual goal of life, feeding them artificially is futile and unduly burdensome. In the conclusion of their paper, the authors have this to say: "We hold for a presumption in favor of providing medically assisted nutrition and hydration to patients who need it, which presumption would yield in cases where such procedures have no medically reasonable hope of sustaining life or pose excessive risks or burdens."[62]

A somewhat similar document, also replete with references to pertinent medical literature, had been issued shortly before by the Pennsylvania bishops on January 14, 1992. This document concluded by declaring: "As a general conclusion, in almost every instance there is an obligation to continue supplying nutrition and hydration to the unconscious patient. There are situations in which this is not the case [e.g., when the patient can no longer assimilate the food and its provision is hence useless], but these are exceptions and should not be made into the rule." In their judgment artificially providing food to PVS patients is "clearly beneficial in terms of preservation of life," nor does it, in almost every case, add a "serious burden." Consequently, it is morally obligatory.[63]

Several individual bishops and other conferences of bishops issued statements reaching similar conclusions to that of the Pro-Life Committee and the Pennsylvania bishops.[64]

D. The Theological Position Claiming That Tubal Feeding of PVS Patients Is Futile and Unduly Burdensome

The leading proponent of this position is Kevin O'Rourke, O.P. As was noted above, in discussing the proper interpretation of Pope Pius XII's 1957 address to a congress of anesthesiologists, O'Rourke claims that treatments which are "ineffective … in helping a person strive for the spiritual purpose of life" are to be regarded as "extraordinary" and hence not obligatory. Applying this to persons said to be in the PVS condition, O'Rourke maintains that since these individuals are not capable of pursuing the spiritual goal of life and since feeding them tubally is ineffective in helping them do so, then such feeding is not required. He maintains, in addition, as do the Texas Bishops, that such individuals are suffering from a "fatal pathology." He likewise maintains that all one does by "feeding": such persons tubally is to preserve "mere physiological functioning." His associate Benedict Ashley, O.P., shares this position.[65] I have already criticized the basic rationale given by O'Rourke in the section discussing the proper interpretation of Pius XII's remarks. I believe, in addition, that his view at least tends toward dualism if it is not in essence dualistic, since he claims that all one preserves by providing food to such persons is mere physiological functioning. I think that what one preserves is the *life* of those persons, who are not, as he contends, suffering from a fatal pathology such as cancer or AIDS or congestive heart disease. It was apparently to this position, moreover, that the Pro-Life Committee of the National Conference of Catholic Bishops was referring in explicitly maintaining that this "rationale" for withholding or withdrawing artificially provided food to PVS patients was not persuasive.[66]

E. The Theological Position Holding That Artificially Providing Food to PVS Persons Is Obligatory

This view, like that of the Pennsylvania Bishops and the Pro-Life Committee of the National Conference of Catholic Bishops, holds that artificially providing food to permanently unconscious persons (those in the PVS state) is to be regarded ordinarily as morally obligatory insofar as it is neither useless nor unduly burdensome.

This was the position developed by me and my collaborators (Robert Barry, O.P., Orville Griese, Germain Grisez, Brian Johnstone, C.Ss.R., Thomas J. Marzen, Bishop James T. McHugh, Gilbert Meilaender, Mark Siegler, M.D., and William B. Smith) in the article noted in endnote 51. This essay was written after a series of discussions among most of the co-authors, during which several of the persons involved, including me, changed our position. I had previously thought such feeding either futile or unduly burdensome, believing that those in the PVS condition were in fact dying. But the evidence given to us by health-care personnel (doctors, nurses, etc.) showed clearly that these persons were not in fact dying of any fatal pathology. They are simply persons seriously impaired. Feeding them is not in itself expensive (many people spend more on pet food than it takes to provide these persons with food and water), it does not cause pain or suffering, etc.

We granted that the total cost of caring for PVS patients (providing them with a heated room, nursing care, etc.) could be quite great, but that in our affluent society, which provides similar care for other persons in severely compromised positions (e.g., those who must be institutionalized because of chronic but non-fatal illnesses, etc.), it would be unfair and unjust to deprive the permanently unconscious of their fair share. Moreover, we argued, if one were to seek to avoid the expense involved in caring for these persons by denying them food and water, the means chosen to avoid this expense would not be the withholding of food and water as such but the subsequent death of those persons, a point developed more fully by one of the co-authors, Germain Grisez, in a later essay.[67] Grisez likewise develops the truth, insufficiently referred to in the essay I co-authored, that another human good served by feeding PVS patients in this way is the good of human solidarity. In still another work Grisez expresses this idea as follows: "life-sustaining care for [persons] severely handicapped does have a human and Christian significance in addition to the one it would derive precisely from the inherent goodness of their lives. This additional significance is ... profoundly real, just as is the significance of [a husband's faithfulness to a permanently unconscious] wife, which continues to benefit not only the person being cared for but the one giving care."[68]

Some, for example O'Rourke, argue that the expense entailed in feeding PVS patients must realistically be regarded as terribly burdensome in our society. He posed a question in his "Open Letter to Bishop McHugh" (who had held that the expense of feeding such persons is not excessive) that merits response. He said that McHugh was "disingenuous" in saying that "assisted nutrition and hydration ... are not overly expensive" in view of the fact that "care in a hospital or long-term care facility costs anywhere from $600 to $1300 a day...."[69]

No one, we can presume, would want his family bankrupted in order to provide him with tubally assisted feeding. But does this mean that O'Rourke is correct? At present, the cost for taking care of PVS patients is usually covered in great part by insurance or other programs. But, as Grisez notes, one can legitimately avoid excessive expense (if this does become an issue) *without abandoning care for the person and without bringing his death about by starvation.* Persons put into the situation of caring for a loved one in the PVS state or other conditions are not obliged to have them cared for in highly expensive hospitals or nursing homes (if insurance and governmental help are inadequate). They can remove them from these costly institutions, take them home and do the best they can with the help of such services as hospice care, volunteers from the parish or neighborhood, etc. The high standards of care possible in expensive institutions might not be possible, but one can still maintain solidarity with the person doing what one can, including providing food and nourishment by tubal means (not too difficult to do once begun, even at home). One does not have to endure undue financial burdens.

This position is also that taken by the authors of *Euthanasia, Clinical Practice and the Law*,[70] and I believe it to be the right one.

6. ADVANCE DIRECTIVES

An advance directive is a document by which a person makes provision for health care decisions in the event that, in the future, he or she is no longer competent to make such decisions for himself or herself. Advance directives are of two main types: (1) the "living will" and (2) the "durable power of attorney for health care." A third type of advance directive (3) is a hybrid of these two.

A. The Living Will

This is a signed, witnessed or notarized document that allows a patient to direct that specified life-sustaining treatments be withheld or withdrawn if the patient is in a terminal condition and unable to make health-care decisions. Since an attending physician who may be unfamiliar with the signer's wishes and values has the authority to carry out the directives of the will, its terms may be interpreted in a way not envisioned by its signer. Moreover, the language used in such documents is often vague and general, and fails to distinguish clearly the difference between a suicidal intention (to forgo treatment precisely as a way of ending one's life) or the non-suicidal intention to forgo treatment because of the treatment's uselessness or burdensomeness. Frequently, models of a living will are promoted by supporters of euthanasia, using language that is easy to interpret in a way favorable to euthanasia. Because of these features of the so-called living will — a document prepared in advance of the time when one will be in a situation calling for careful judgment about the appropriateness or non-appropriateness of specific treatments — it seems to me (and to others who have examined this issue far more deeply than I) that it is not advisable to make use of a "living will" as an advance directive regarding one's health care.

B. The Durable Power of Attorney

This is a signed, witnessed or notarized document in which the signer designates an agent to make health-care decisions for himself or herself in the event that he or she becomes incompetent. The agent must, of course, be chosen with great care since the agent will have great power and authority to make decisions about whether health care is to be provided, withheld, or withdrawn. The signer of such a document has the obligation to discuss his or her values, wishes, and instructions with the agent before and at the time the document is signed, and the agent must be willing to respect and carry out the signer's wishes.

The major advantage of appointing a health-care-decisions agent is that it leaves decision-making in the hands of a person of one's own choosing. Obviously, a Catholic will choose only someone who respects and lives up to the Church's teaching on the dignity of human life. The Catholic Conference for the District of Columbia issued a pastoral letter containing a set of criteria for selecting a health-care agent with the power of attorney. These are most useful, in my opinion. Thus I here reproduce them:

Appoint someone who has the strength of character to make good judgments in painful circumstances.

Appoint someone who you know you can trust to make decisions on the basis of the Church's teaching. The prudent person will select an agent who will act as he or she would have acted in whatever circumstances evolve.

No one should agree to act as an agent for another person if that person would expect or require the agent to make decisions which disregard the teaching of the Church. It is not morally acceptable to carry out immoral decisions on behalf of someone else. No agent and no physician should ever feel obliged to act contrary to their well informed consciences, even on behalf of another person.

Appoint someone who is likely to be available to care for you in the distant future ... it may be advisable to name alternate agents, in the event that your first choice proves unable or unwilling to act for you when the need arises.

Discuss the specifics of your directive with the person whom you wish to choose as your agent....

Generally avoid: 1. Stating that you wish to reject certain treatments under all circumstances except in case of imminent death or when one's present medical condition makes it clear in advance that such treatments would be futile; 2. Stating without qualification that you want medical remedies restricted in the event that you become permanently unconscious or terminally ill. Such stipulation can amount to providing a premature self-diagnosis. You should allow your health care agent and physician latitude to offer you appropriate care based on your actual condition.

Include a provision regarding treatment at the time of imminent death. Recall that the Church allows a person on the verge of death to refuse a treatment which would result in only a burdensome prolongation of life. Your advance directive should authorize your agent to observe this norm.

Periodically review the provisions of your directive.... Make copies of your directive and distribute them to your agent and each of your health care providers and anyone else you deem appropriate.[71]

The International Anti-Euthanasia Task Force has developed a very worthwhile document called the "Protective Medical Decisions Document" (PMDD). This is a durable power of attorney for health- are documents specifically prohibiting suicide, assisted suicide, and euthanasia. It is a document fully compatible with Catholic teaching. Among its provisions are the following:

I wish to receive medical treatment appropriate to my condition which offers a reasonable hope of benefit. I direct that food and water be provided to me unless death is inevitable and truly imminent so that the effort to sustain my life is futile or unless I am unable to assimilate food or fluids. I ask that, even in the face of death, I be provided with ordinary nursing and medical care, including pain relief, appropriate to my condition. Nothing should be done which will directly and intentionally cause my death, nor should anything be omitted when such omissions would directly and intentionally cause my death. Euthanasia (an action or omission which of itself or by intent causes death), whether by commission or omission, is not permitted.[72]

In conclusion, I advise persons not to sign living wills, which are vigorously promoted by euthanasia advocates. Rather, appoint a person whom you trust to be your agent by giving him or her durable power of attorney. Consider making use of the Protective Medical Decisions Document available from the International Anti-Euthanasia Task Force.[73]

ENDNOTES

1. Daniel Callahan, "Foreword" to *Euthanasia Examined: Ethical, Clinical and Legal Perspectives*, ed. John Keown (Cambridge: Cambridge University Press, 1995), pp. xiii-xiv.
2. Ibid., p. xiv.
3. On factors contributing to acceptance of the euthanasia movement see also Patrick Nowell-Smith, "In Favour of Voluntary Euthanasia," in *Principles of Health Care Ethics,* ed. Raanan Gillon (New York: John Wiley & Sons, 1994), pp. 754-755.
4. See, for example, the following: Nowell-Smith, "In Favour of Voluntary Euthanasia," pp. 75-761; Joseph Fletcher, "Ethics and Euthanasia," *American Journal of Nursing* 73 (April, 1973) 675; reprinted in *To Live and To Die,* ed. Robert H. Williams (New York: Springer Verlag, 1973).
5. The *Random House College Dictionary* (rev. ed. New York: Random House, 1996), p. 456.
6. On this see Germain Grisez and Joseph Boyle, *Life and Death with Liberty and Justice: A Contribution to the Euthanasia Debate* (Notre Dame, IN: University of Notre Dame Press, 1979), pp. 86-87. This excellent work, now two decades old, remains one of the finest studies available to show that respect for the intrinsic goodness of human bodily life absolutely proscribes euthanasia of any kind. I am in great debt to the authors, whose work, unfortunately, has never received the attention it merits for both its moral and jurisprudential arguments against euthanasia.
7. Timothy E. Quill, "Death and Dignity," in *Last Rights: Assisted Suicide and Euthanasia Debated,* ed. Michael M. Ulhmann (Washington, D.C./Grand Rapids, MI: Ethics and Public Policy Center/William B. Eerdmans Publishing Co., 1998), pp. 327-328. Quill's essay originally appeared in his book *Death and Dignity: Making Choices and Taking Charge* (New York: Norton, 1993).

8. See Jack Kevorkian, "A Fail-safe Model for Justifiable Medically Assisted Suicide," in *Last Rights,* pp. 263-296; originally published in *American Journal of Forensic Psychiatry* 13.1 (1992).

9. Among the early advocates of euthanasia were Glanville Williams, an English lawyer, and Joseph Fletcher, at that time an Anglican clergyman. Glanville's most important work advocating euthanasia was his *Sanctity of Life and the Criminal Law* (New York: Alfred A. Knopf, 1957). Fletcher devoted a chapter defending euthanasia in his *Morals and Medicine* (Boston: Beacon Press, 1960), a work reprinted in the 1970s and 1980s. During the 1970s Fletcher wrote frequently in defense of euthanasia (see endnote 10).

10. Three authors in particular wrote extensively (and influentially) on the subject, namely, Joseph Fletcher (a professor at the Episcopal Theological School in Cambridge, Mass., and later at the University of Virginia), Daniel Maguire (a Catholic theologian teaching at Marquette University), and Marvin Kohl (a philosopher at the State University of New York in Buffalo). Among Fletcher's writings on the subject at this time were: "Ethics and Euthanasia" (see endnote 4); "The Patient's Right to Die," in *Euthanasia and the Right to Death,* ed. A. B. Downing (London: Peter Owen, 1969), pp. 66-69; and "The 'Right' to Life and the 'Right' to Die," in *Beneficent Euthanasia,* ed. Marvin Kohl (Buffalo: Prometheus Books, 1975). Maguire authored a book and several essays, among them *Death by Choice* (New York: Doubleday, 1974); "The Freedom to Die," in *New Theology # 10,* ed. Martin Marty and Dean Peerman (New York: Macmillan, 1974); and "A Catholic View of Mercy Killing," in *Beneficent Euthanasia.* Among Kohl's contributions to the literature was his essay "Voluntary Beneficent Euthanasia" in the volume he edited, *Beneficent Euthanasia.* That volume ended with "A Plea for Beneficent Euthanasia," pp. 233-236, written by Kohl and Paul Kurtz (editor of the *Humanist*) and signed by Fletcher, Maguire, several Nobel laureates, physicians, religious leaders, and academics.

11. More contemporary articulations of the "ethics of euthanasia" include the following: Patrick Nowell-Smith, "In Favour of Voluntary Euthanasia," in *Principles of Health Care Ethics* (see endnote 3 for details), pp. 751-762; John Harris, "Euthanasia and the Value of Life," in *Euthanasia Examined* (see endnote 1 for details), pp. 6-22; Jean Davis, "The Case for Legalising Voluntary Euthanasia," in ibid., pp. 83-95; Ronald Dworkin, *Life's Dominion: An Argument About Abortion, Euthanasia, and Individual Freedom* (New York: Harper, 1993);

Dworkin, "Do We Have a Right to Die?" in *Last Rights* (see endnote 7 for details), pp. 75-94; Peter Singer, *Rethinking Life and Death: The Collapse of Our Traditional Ethics* (New York: St. Martin's Press, 1995); Derek Humphrey and Ann Wickett, *The Right to Die: Understanding Euthanasia* (New York: Harper & Row, 1988).

12. This, in essence, is the argument advanced by a host of writers. See, for instance, Kohl, "Voluntary Beneficent Euthanasia," esp. pp. 131-133, where he emphasizes that voluntary euthanasia is rooted in a respect for the dignity of the person to control his or her own life; Fletcher, "Ethics and Euthanasia," "The 'Right' to Life and the 'Right' to Die"; Maguire, "The Freedom to Die." Dworkin believes it is tyrannical to oppose a person's well considered decision to ask to be killed mercifully: "making someone die in a way ... that he believes [is] a horrifying contradiction of his life, is a devastating, odious form of tyranny" (*Life's Dominion ...,* p. 217). See also Harris, "Euthanasia and the Value of Life," pp. 14-16.

13. Fletcher, "The Patient's Right to Die," p. 69. See also Maguire, "The Freedom to Die," pp. 188-189.

14. Thus Kohl, one of the leading proponents of "beneficent euthanasia," distinguishes sharply between the dignity human beings have by reason of their nature as members of the human species — he refers to this as dignity — and the dignity human persons have insofar as they are capable of controlling their own lives — dignity — and his contention is that it is dignity that is at stake in the issue of euthanasia and that this dignity justifies the "right to die" and to choose to be killed mercifully, a choice that others are obliged to respect. See his "Voluntary Beneficent Euthanasia," pp. 132-133.

15. Singer, *Rethinking Life and Death,* pp. 218-219.

16. Fletcher, *Morals and Medicine,* p. 211.

17. Maguire, "The Freedom to Die," pp. 188-189. It is instructive to note that both Fletcher and Maguire explicitly link the freedom to choose death (in euthanasia) to the freedom to control conception by contraceptive methods. This helps one see the link between acceptance of contraception and the "culture of death." See Chapter 4.

18. Harris, "Euthanasia and the Value of Life," pp. 8-9; Singer, *Rethinking Life and Death,* pp. 180-183, 202-206.

19. Marvin Kohl, *The Morality of Killing: Sanctity of Life, Abortion and Euthanasia* (Atlantic Highlands, NJ: Humanities Press, 1974), pp. 81-96; Glanville Williams, *Sanctity of Life,* p. 316; Williams, "Euthanasia," *Medico-Legal Journal* 41 (1973) 22; H. Tristram

Englehardt, Jr., "Ethical Issues in Aiding the Death of Young Children," in *Beneficent Euthanasia,* pp. 180-192; Robert F. Weir, *Selected Nontreatment of Handicapped Newborns* (New York: Oxford University Press, 1984), esp. pp. 188-223; Anthony Shaw, "Dilemmas of 'Informed Consent' in Children," in *Death, Dying, and Euthanasia,* ed. Dennis J. Horan and David Mall (Frederick, MD: University Publications of America, 1984), pp. 75-90; Raymond S. Duff and A. G. M. Campbell, "Moral and Ethical Dilemmas in the Special-Care Nursery," in *Death, Dying, and Euthanasia,* pp. 91-104.

20. See, for example, Weir, *Selective Nontreatment of Handicapped Newborns,* pp. 215-221.

21. Fletcher, "Indicators of Humanhood: A Tentative Profile of Man," *Hastings Center Report* 2 (November 1972) 1; "Four Indicators of Humanhood — The Enquiry Matures," *Hastings Center Report* 4 (December 1974) 5-7; Tooley, "Abortion and Infanticide," *Philosophy and Public Affairs* 2 (1972) 37-65, esp. 44-48; Singer, *Rethinking Life and Death,* pp. 202-206.

22. Harris, "Euthanasia and the Value of Life," pp. 7-8, 17-18.

23. Supreme Court of the United States, *Planned Parenthood of Southeastern Pennsylvania et al. v. Robert P. Casey*, June 29, 1992, p. 9. An excellent analysis and critique of this decision is Russell Hittinger, "Et Tu, Justice Kennedy?" *Crisis* 10.8 (September 1992) 16-22.

24. Arthur Dyck, "Beneficent Euthanasia and Benemortasia: Alternative Views of Mercy," in *Beneficent Euthanasia,* p. 127.

25. *Euthanasia, Clinical Practice and the Law,* ed. Luke Gormally (London: The Linacre Centre for Health Care Ethics, 1994), pp. 131, 132, emphasis, including bold face, in the original. The first part of this truly excellent volume upholding the sanctity of life and providing devastating criticism of the rationale to justify euthanasia contains a reprint of the important Linacre Centre Working Party Report, whereas the second part contains the submission made on behalf of The Linacre Centre to House of Lords' Select Committee on Medical Ethics. Among the members of the Working Party were Luke Gormally, John Mahoney, S.J., G. E. M. Anscombe, and John Finnis.

26. Ibid., p. 132.

27. The best treatment of the injustice of "quality of life" criteria for determining who should live and who should die is given by Grisez and Boyle in *Life and Death with Liberty and Justice,* chapter 6.

28. *Euthanasia, Clinical Practive and the Law,* p. 42.

29. As St. Thomas says, commenting on St. Paul's teaching on the resurrection of the body, *"anima mea non est ego"* ("my soul is not me"). *In 1 Cor. 10.*

30. Leo Alexander, "Medical Science Under Dictatorship," in *Death, Dying, and Euthanasia,* p. 584. Alexander's essay, which should be read by everyone who wants to understand the evil of euthanasia, originally appeared in the *New England Journal of Medicine* 241 (1949) 39-47.

31. See Grisez and Boyle, *Life and Death with Liberty and Justice* (Notre Dame, Ind.: University of Notre Dame Press, 1978), pp. 154-168.

32. Ramsey proposed the term "agathanasia" in his long essay, "On (Only) Caring for the Dying" in his *Patient as Person* (New Haven: Yale University Press, 1970), pp. 113-164. Dyck developed his analogous notion of "benemortasia" in two essays: "An Alternative to an Ethics of Euthanasia," in *To Live and To Die*, pp. 98-112, and in "Beneficent Euthanasia and Benemortasia: Alternative Views of Mercy," in *Beneficent Euthanasia,* pp. 117-129.

33. *Euthanasia, Clinical Practice and the Law,* pp. 53-54.

34. Ibid., p. 55.

35. Pope Pius XII, "The Prolongation of Life: An Address to an International Congress of Anesthesiologists," as reprinted in *Death, Dying, and Euthanasia,* p. 284.

36. Kevin O'Rourke, O.P., "Evolution of Church Teaching on the Prolongation of Life," *Health Progress* (January-February, 1988) 32; emphasis added. O'Rourke set forth the same understanding of Pope Pius's statement in the following essays: "The A.M.A. Statement on Tubal Feeding: An Ethical Analysis," *America* (November 22, 1988) 321-323, an essay that the Society for the Right to Die, an advocacy group for legalizing euthanasia subsequently saw fit to reprint in its newsletter; "Should Nutrition and Hydration Be Provided to Permanently Unconscious and Other Mentally Disabled Persons?" *Issues in Law and Medicine* 5 (1989) 181-196; "On the Care of 'Vegetative' Patients," *Ethics & Medics* 24.4 (April, 1999), 3-4; 24.5 (May, 1999) 1-2. The same position is also set forth by O'Rourke in the work he co-authored with Benedict Ashley, O.P., *Health Care Ethics* (4th ed. Washington, D.C.: Georgetown University Press, 1997), pp. 421-426.

37. My interpretation of O'Rourke's position (and it is important to note it is shared by Benedict Ashley, O.P., as endnote 36 clearly shows) is correct. It is precisely the interpretation given it by one who finds it

the correct way of understanding what Pius XII meant, namely, Thomas F. Schindler, S.S., director of ethics at Mercy Health Services in Farmington, Mich. Schindler, who considers O'Rourke's position "excellent," concludes that "we should no longer state the ethical obligation as one of 'prolonging life.' Rather, we should refer to the obligation of maintaining a life 'capable of reaching life's spiritual goals' or 'capable of realizing life's purposes.'" ("Implications of Prolonging Life," *Health Progress* [April, 1988] 12). This, it seems to me, is definitely a "quality of life" view subject to the kind of criticism given above in discussing the "ethics of euthanasia." A similar position is taken by Richard M. Gula, S.S. "Quality of Life: A Focus on the Patient's Total Good," *Health Progress* (July-August, 1988), 34-39, 84.

38. This matter is very clearly discussed in *Euthanasia, Clinical Practice and the Law*, pp. 43-45. See also Grisez and Boyle, *Life and Death With Liberty and Justice*, pp. 260-269.

39. John R. Connery, S.J., "Prolonging Life: Its Duty and Its Limits," in *Moral Responsibility in Prolonging Life Decisions*, ed. Donald McCarthy and Albert Moraczewski, O.P. (St. Louis: Pope John XXIII Medical-Moral Center, 1981), p. 133.

40. Richard McCormick, S.J., "To Save or Let Die: The Dilemma of Modern Medicine," published simultaneously in *Journal of the American Medical Association* 229 (1974) 171-176 and *America* 130 (July 7, 1974) 6-10, and reprinted in McCormick's *How Brave a New World? Dilemmas in Bioethics* (Garden City: Doubleday, 1981), pp. 339-351, and "The Quality of Life, the Sanctity of Life," *Hastings Center Report* 8.1 (1978) 30-36, reprinted in *How Brave a New World?*, pp. 383-401. References will be to these essays as found in *How Brave a New World?*

41. "To Save or Let Die," in *How Brave a New World?*, p. 345 (emphasis added).

42. Ibid.

43. Ibid., p. 346.

44. Ibid., p. 349.

45. Ibid., p. 347; emphasis in the original.

46. Grisez and Boyle, *Life and Death With Liberty and Justice*, p. 260.

47. Ibid., pp. 268-269.

48. *Euthanasia, Clinical Practice and the Law*, p. 66.

49. Dyck, "An Alternative to an Ethics of Euthanasia," in *To Live and To Die*, pp. 111-112; Dyck provides a similar list, omitting the fourth,

in "Beneficent Euthanasia and Benemortasia: Alternative View of Mercy;" in *Beneficent Euthanasia*, pp. 128-129. I have modified somewhat his way of articulating these presuppositions.

50. As we saw earlier, in reviewing the "ethics of euthansia," John Harris, in justifying the withholding and withdrawing of food and nourishment from Tony Bland, an individual said to be in this state, did so by claiming that Bland's personal life had been extinguished already and that the life thus terminated by withdrawing such nourishment was not that of a person. He clearly regarded the withdrawing of nourishment as a means to bring death about, to kill.

51. I am the author and co-author of several essays on this matter. See the following: William E. May et al., "Feeding and Hydrating the Permanently Unconscious and Other Vulnerable Persons," *Issues in Law and Medicine* 3 (1987) 203-217; "Caring for Persons in the 'Persistent Vegetative State,' " *Anthropotes: Rivista di Studi sulla persona e la famiglia* 13.2 (1997) 317-331; "Tube Feeding and the 'Vegetative' State," Part One, *Ethics & Medics* 23.12 (December 1998) 1-2; Part Two, ibid 24.1 (January 1999) 3-4.

52. See Council on Scientific Affairs and Council of Ethical and Judicial Affairs, "Persistent Vegetative State and the Decision to Withdraw or Withhold Life Support," *Journal of the American Medical Association* 263 (1990) 427: "Abrupt loss of consciousness usually consists of an acute sleeplike state of unarousability called *coma* that may be followed either by varying degrees of cognitive and physical recovery or by severe, chronic neurological impairment. The stage of coma itself, however, is invariably temporary and in progressive diseases is often absent altogether."

53. See R. Cranford, "The Persistent Vegetative State: The Medical Reality (Getting the Facts Straight)," *Hastings Center Report* 18 (1988) 27-32.

54. The common ways of providing these persons with "food" by artificial means are set forth in detail in such sources as *The Merck Manual of Diagnosis and Therapy*, ed. R.Berkow (15th ed.: Rahway, NJ: Merck Sharp and Dohme Laboratories, 1987) 904-911, and D. Major, "The Medical Procedures for Providing Food and Water: Indications and Effects," in *By No Extraordinary Means: The Choice to Forego* (sic) *Life-Sustaining Food and Water* (Bloomington, Ind.: University of Indiana Press, 1986), pp. 21-38. There are two basic ways of feeding such persons artificially: *enteral* and *perenteral*. *Enteral* (within the bowel) feeding means that the nourishment is placed directly into the

upper end of the small intestine by use of a nasogastric tube (through the nose and into the stomach), a nasoduodenal tube (through the nose and into the upper end of the small bowel), or jejunostomy (an opening into the upper part of the small bowel). Enteral methods ordinarily cause no complications, and even if some arise they are usually not serious. *Parenteral* (outside the bowel) feeding refers to the supplying of food intravenously by different methods. Such feeding risks more serious complications.

55. American Medical Association, Judicial Council, *Current Opinions of the Judicial Council of the American Medical Association. Including the Principles of Medical Ethics and Rules of the Judicial Council* (Chicago: American Medical Association, 1981), p. 9, par. 2.11.

56. President's Commission for the Study of Ethical Problems in Medicine and Biomedical and Behavioral Research, *Deciding to Forego [sic]Life-Sustaining Treatment: Ethical, Medical, and Legal Issues in Treatment Decisions* (Washington, D.C.: U. S. Government Printing Office, 1983), pp. 171-196.

57. Hastings Center, *Guidelines on the Termination of Life-Sustaining Treatment and the Care of the Dying* (Briarcliff Manor, NY: The Hastings Center, 1987); American Academy of Neurology, "Position of the American Academy of Neurology on certain aspects of the care and management of the persistent vegetative state patient," *Neurology* 39 (1989) 125-126; American Medical Association, Council on Scientific Affairs and Council on Ethical and Judicial Affairs, "Persistent Vegetative State and the Decision to Withdraw or Withhold Life Support," *Journal of the American Medical Association* 263 (1990) 426-430.

58. D. Alan Shewmon, M.D., "Recovery from 'Brain Death': A Neurologist's Apologia," *The Linacre Quarterly* 64.1 (February, 1997) 59-60.

59. Ibid., 60.

60. Texas Conference of Catholic Bishops, "On Withdrawing Artificial Nutrition and Hydration" (May 7, 1990), in *Origins: NC News Service* 20 (1990) 53-55. It should be noted that 2 of the 18 members of the Texas Conference of Catholic Bishops refused to sign this statement.

61. See, for example, The Most Reverend Louis Gelineau, Bishop of Providence, R. I., "On Removing Nutrition and Water from a Comatose Woman" (January 10, 1988), in *Origins: NC News Service* 17 (1988) 546-547.

62. Committee for Pro-Life Activities, National Conference of Catholic

Bishops, *Nutrition and Hydration: Moral and Pastoral Reflections* (Washington, D.C.: United States Catholic Conference, 1992), Publication No. 516-X, p. 7. The document was also printed in *Origins: NC News Service* 21 (1992) 705-711; the citation is found at 711.

63. Pennsylvania Conference of Catholic Bishops, "Nutrition and Hydration: Moral Considerations," in *Origins: NC News Service* 21 (1992) 542-553.

64. See, for example, the following: New Jersey State Catholic Conference, " 'Friend-of-the-Court Brief to the New Jersey Supreme Court': Providing Food and Fluids to Severely Brain Damaged Patients" (November 3, 1987), in *Origins: NC News Service* 16 (1987) 542-553; The Most Reverend James McHugh, Bishop of Camden, N. J., "Artificially Assisted Nutrition and Hydration" (September 21, 1989), in *Origins: NC News Service* 19 (1989) 314-316. The episcopal conferences of Missouri and Florida also issued statements on this matter, as did the Most Reverend John Myers of Peoria. One researcher, Thomas Shannon (who himself holds that providing food artificially to PVS patients is not obligatory) sent a questionnaire to the ordinaries of U.S. dioceses on the matter. 78 ordinaries responded, offering conflicting and contradictory directives, often prepared by diocesan bioethics committees or hospital committees within the diocese. Shannon summarizes his findings in an essay co-authored by James Walter, "The PVS Patient and the Forgoing/Withdrawing of Medical Nutrition and Hydration," *Theological Studies* 49 (1988) 623-647, reprinted in *Quality of Life: The New Medical Dilemma*, ed. James J. Walter and Thomas A. Shannon (New York: Paulist, 1990) 203-223; the summary of Shannon's survey is found on pp. 204-210.

65. For O'Rourke's position (shared by Ashley) see above, endnote 36. In his 1999 two-part essay in *Ethics & Medics* (details given in endnote 36) he offers a response to the position I set forth in the same journal. But his response, in my judgment, failed to address the principal criticism offered of his view, namely, that many treatments "ineffective" in helping a person pursue the spiritual goal of life are obviously morally required, e.g., stopping the bleeding of a trisomy 21 child.

66. A view somewhat analogous to O'Rourke's is taken by James J. Walter and Thomas Shannon. See their joint essay referred to above in endnote 64. See also Walter, "Food and Water: An Ethical Burden," *Commonweal* (1986) 616-619.

67. Grisez, "Should Nutrition and Hydration Be Provided to Permanently

Comatose and Other Mentally Disabled Persons?" *Linacre Quarterly* 57 (1990) 30-43.

68. Grisez, *Difficult Moral Questions* (Quincy, IL: Franciscan Press, 1997), p. 223.

69. O'Rourke, "Open Letter to Bishop McHugh: Father Kevin O'Rourke on Hydration and Nutrition," *Origins: NC News Service* 19 (1989) 351-352.

70. *Euthanasia, Clinical Practice and the Law,* pp. 140-143.

71. Roman Catholic Bishops of the District of Columbia (His Eminence James Cardinal Hickey, the Most Rev. Alvaro Corrada, the Most Rev. Leonard Olivier), *Care of the Sick and Dying: A Pastoral Letter* (Washington, D.C.: The District of Columbia Catholic Conference, 1994), pp. 26-28.

72. International Anti-Euthanasia Task Force, "Protective Medical Decisions Document," P.O. Box 760, Steubenville, Ohio 43952.

73. On this issue see also John Finnis, " 'Living Will' Legislation," in *Euthanasia, Clinical Practice and the Law*, pp. 167-176.

Chapter Eight

DEFINING DEATH AND ORGAN TRANSPLANTION

Introduction

An issue of crucial importance in bioethics today focuses on the definition of death and on criteria for determining that a person has died. This issue is critical because it is possible to save the lives of persons threatened by death because one or more of their vital organs — the heart, lungs, liver, etc. — no longer functions. Although paired vital organs such as kidneys can be provided for them by living donors— organ transplants from the living will be taken up in the concluding section of this chapter — living donors, obviously, cannot be the source of unpaired organs such as the heart. A possible source for such organs (and of paired vital organs as well) is the body of a person who has just died. But organ transplants from a cadaver *must* take place almost immediately after death. Were the transplantation delayed, the organs in question would quickly deteriorate and would no longer be of any help in preserving the lives of those in need of them.

In our legitimate desire to obtain a life-saving organ for a fellow human being whose life can be saved by transplant surgery, we must strenuously resist any temptation to diminish our care of a dying person because he or she happens to be a prospective donor. This is the reason why the World Medical Assembly, at a 1968 meeting in Sydney, Australia, accepted the principle that there be complete separation of authority and responsibility between the physician or group of physicians charged with caring for the dying person and the physician or group of physicians whose task is to care for the person in need of an organ. It is for this reason that one of the provisions of the Uniform Anatomical Gift Act is the following:

> The time of death shall be determined by a physician who attends the donor at his death, or, if none, the physician who certifies the death. This physician shall *not* participate in the procedures for removing or transplanting a part.[1]

Our rightful concern in the practical order to protect the dignity of the dying person is paralleled, or *ought* to be paralleled, in the intellectual order with a concern to separate the question of defining death and the use of organs for transplants. The late Paul Ramsey forcefully made this point when he said:

> If in the practical order we need to separate between the physician who is responsible for the care of a prospective donor, and the physician who is responsible for a prospective recipient, do we not need in the intellectual order to keep the question of the definition of death equally discrete from the use of organs in transplantations? If only the physician responsible for a dying man should make the determination that he has died, with no "help" from the medical team that has in its care a man who needs a borrowed organ, should not also the definition of death and the tests for it that he uses be ones that he thinks are sound or were agreed to by the profession without having transplantation in view? There would be too little protection of life attained in the practical order by entirely separating the authority and responsibility of the teams of physicians if the definition of death and the tests used for it have already been significantly invaded by the requirements of transplant therapy. If no person's death should *for this purpose* be hastened, then the definition of death should not *for this purpose* be updated, or the procedures for stating that a man has died be revised as a means of affording easier access to organs.[2]

I call attention to this passage because Ramsey eloquently emphasizes our absolute obligation to respect and care for our fellow human beings, especially those who are dying. Because of contemporary developments in medical technology, it is becoming more and more difficult to die and to determine whether the body before us is, in truth, a *living human body* (and therefore a living human person) or a cadaver (the mortal remains of a *once* living human body). The concern to redefine "death" and to establish criteria for determining that death has, in fact, occurred has in large measure been caused by this twofold difficulty.[3]

It would be foolish to ignore the fact that attempts to "update" death have not also been influenced, and greatly so, by the enormous strides in transplant surgery and the need to find suitable organs. Indeed, many influential persons today claim that a human person is "dead" when the functioning of the neocortex of the brain is irreversibly lost so that the individual can no longer engage in the cognitive/affective activities specific to human persons. In this view, an individual living human body capable of breathing, circulating blood, and assimilating nourishment on its own, without the aid of any technological instrumentation, can be regarded as a cadaver, a corpse, and hence potential source of vital organs for those in need of such. This way of viewing death, dualistic in nature and utilitarian in practice, is utterly inimical both to the Christian understanding of human life and to sound philosophy. It is, nonetheless, advocated by many people today.[4]

Procedure

I will begin (1) by reviewing briefly a remarkable address given by Pope John Paul II to the participants of a Working Group of the Pontifical Academy of Sciences at a meeting held in Rome December 10-14, 1989. The Working Group was assembled to consider the question of defining death and of determining the relationship between "brain death" and the death of a human person. In his address John Paul II not only clearly articulates the ethical importance of the subject matter being studied by the Working Group but also expresses the Christian understanding of death and the need for identifying properly criteria to determine that a person has died. The final conclusions of the Working Group will then (2) be summarized. As will be seen, the Working Group agreed that "brain death" can be truly regarded as human death. The rationale underlying this consensus on "brain death" will be the next topic taken up (3). I will (4) follow this by giving the reasons advanced more recently by one of the major participants at the meeting, D. Alan Shewmon, M. D., compelling him to abandon the view adopted by the working group regarding the relationship between "brain death" and human death. In this section I will also summarize his proposal for retrieving vital organs for transplantation from persons who have been declared dead because of the irreversible cessation of the functioning of the entire brain. In the section devoted to Shewmon's views I will also consider representative responses that his position has elicited. I will conclude this section with a summing up of organ transplants from those declared "brain dead." In conclusion (5) I will consider the morality of organ transplants *inter vivos,* among the living.

1. POPE JOHN PAUL II ON DEATH

In his address to the participants of the working group of the Pontifical Academy of Sciences, Pope John Paul II took up three matters of critical importance in bioethics and indeed in human existence, namely, (A) the value of human life, including bodily life; (B) the definition of death; and (C) the death of a human person and organ transplantation.

A. The Value of Human Life, Including Bodily Life

The pope first emphasized that the value of human life "springs from what is spiritual in man," and that the body "receives from the spiritual principle — which inhabits it and makes it what it is — a supreme dignity, a kind of reflection of the Absolute. The body is that of a person, a being which is open to superior values, a being capable of fulfillment in the knowledge and love of God (cf. *Gaudium et spes,* 12, 15). When we consider that every individual is a living expression of unity and that the human body is not just an instrument or item of property, but shares in the individual's value as a human being, then it follows that the body cannot under any circumstances be treated as something to be disposed of at will (cf. ibid., 14)."[5]

John Paul II thus clearly affirms the intrinsic goodness of the human body and human bodily life. He in effect says: "a living human body is a living human person." Precisely because of its inherent, personal value, the human body cannot be made a "mere object of experimentation." The pope observes that the refusal to treat the human body in this way "may seem unreasonable" when such refusal hinders a "feasible and promising experiment," particularly when "it is almost certain that other people, who feel less bound by ethical restraints, will in any case carry out the same research." He notes that the difficulty is even greater when the prohibition of using a human body merely as an object of experimentation — a prohibition made in the name of respect for life—"seems to conflict with other important values, not only the value of scientific knowledge, but also values connected with the concrete good of humanity, such as the improvement of living conditions, health, the relief or healing of illness and suffering, etc." Noting that this is the very problem facing the working group, he then asks:

> How does one reconcile respect for life — *which forbids any action likely to cause or hasten death* — with the potential good that results for humanity if the organs of a dead person are removed for transplanting to a sick person who needs them, keeping in mind that the success of such an intervention depends on the speed with which the organs are removed from the donor after his or her death?[6]

B. The Meaning of Death

The pope then reflects on the meaning of death, particularly for a Christian. After noting that "it is not easy to reach a definition of death which can be accepted by all," John Paul says that "it occurs when the spiritual principle which ensures the unity of the individual can no longer exercise its functions in and upon the organism, whose elements, left to themselves, disintegrate." From a theological perspective one can say that death occurs when there is a separation of soul from body; the body then is no longer a *living **human** body*, a person, but the mortal remains of a person. While "Christian faith — and it is not alone here — affirms the continuation of man's spiritual principle after death," nonetheless this "state of 'beyond' — for those who do not have faith — is without a clear face or form, and everyone feels anguish when confronted by a separation which so brutally contradicts our will to live, our wish to exist." The pope then goes on to say: "Unlike animals, man knows that he must die *and he perceives this as an affront to his dignity. Although in the flesh he is mortal, he also realizes that he **ought not to die,** because he carries within himself an openness, an aspiration towards the eternal.*"[7]

I have emphasized the final part of this remarkable citation, for it clearly shows that in John Paul II's mind (a very Christian mind) death is the ultimate indignity to the human person. It is the human person who dies, not merely his body, for the separated soul is not the full human person,[8] who is a body-person, not a spirit-person. Death as such is *not* a good; it is rather an evil, the deprivation of the good of life, and as such an affront to the dignity of the human person.[9] Christians believe that death has lost its sting because Jesus Christ, by suffering death, has conquered it and enabled us, because of our union with him, to rise to a new life in glorified human bodies.

C. Human Death and Organ Transplants

After reflecting on the Christian understanding of death in light of Christ's resurrection from the dead and his victory over death, the pope observes that hope in a resurrected life cannot "prevent death from being a painful separation." He then addresses the specific issue studied by the participants in the working group, i.e., identifying the signs enabling us to state with confidence that a human person has indeed died. "The problem of the moment of death," he said,

> has serious implications at the practical level, and this aspect is also of great interest to the Church. In practice, there seems to arise a tragic dilemma. On the one hand, there is the urgent need to find replacement organs for sick people who would otherwise die or at least would not recover.... It is conceivable that in order to escape certain and imminent death a patient may need to receive an organ which could be provided by another patient, who may be lying next to him in the hospital, but about whose death there still remains some doubt. Consequently, in the process there arises the danger of terminating a human life, of definitively disrupting the psychosomatic unity of a person. More precisely, there is a real possibility that the life whose continuation is made unsustainable by the removal of a vital organ may be that of a living person, whereas the respect due to human life absolutely prohibits the direct and positive sacrifice of that life, even though it may be for the benefit of another human being who might be felt to be entitled to preference.[10]

After identifying the problem in this way, John Paul II says that two tasks must be addressed. The first concerns scientists, analysts and scholars, who "must pursue their research and studies in order to determine as precisely as possible the exact moment and the indisputable sign of death. For once such a determination has been arrived at, then the apparent conflict, between the duty to respect the life of one person and the duty to effect a cure or even save the life of another, disappears. One would be able to know at what moment it would be perfectly permissible to do what had been definitely forbidden previously, namely, the removal of an organ for transplanting, with the best chances of a successful outcome."[11] A second task concerns moralists, philosophers, and theologians who must exercise the virtue of prudence in finding appropriate solutions to new problems and new aspects of age-old problems in light of new data.[12]

Note that John Paul II, like Pope Pius XII before him,[13] assigns responsibility for determining the signs that death has occurred to doctors and scientists, not to theologians and philosophers.

2. THE CONCLUSIONS OF THE "WORKING GROUP" OF THE PONTIFICAL ACADEMY OF SCIENCES

The major conclusions or "final considerations" of the scientific members of the Working Group centered on: (A) the clinical definition of death; (B) the clinical indications that death has occurred; and (C) the artificial prolongation of organ functions in the event of "brain death."

A. The Clinical Definition of Death

In their "final considerations" the scientific participants in the working group offered the following clinical definition of death: "a person is dead when there has been total and irreversible loss of all capacity for integrating and coordinating physical and mental functions of the body as a unit."[14] This definition, as its authors noted, is essentially the same as that given at the conclusion of a meeting held in Rome October 19-21, 1985, of another Working Group of the Pontifical Academy of Sciences. That body had declared: "a person is dead when he has suffered irreversible loss of all capacity for integrating and coordinating physical and mental functions of the body."[15]

I believe that the "clinical definition" of death offered by the Working Group of the Pontifical Academy of Sciences in both 1985 and in slightly different form in 1989 fits in well with the common-sense understanding of death and harmonizes well with the Judeo-Christian tradition. It is a biologically based definition focusing on the integrative unity of the body.

In several of his essays Shewmon, while not explicitly relating his considerations to this definition, supports the idea that the death of a human person necessarily entails loss of the integrative unity of the body, and it is worthwhile here to note some of his observations. He first of all relates this understanding of death to the Aristotelian-Thomistic tradition, according to which the principle of unity of any living thing is its "substantial form" or "soul," which in humans has a spiritual dimension.

This means that "the principle of personhood is one and the same with the principle of substantial unity of the body."[16] Shewmon likewise observes that this definition harmonizes with Pope John Paul II's comments on death in the address previously noted. As we have seen already, according to the Holy Father, "[Death] occurs when the spiritual principle [the soul] which ensures the unity of the individual can no longer exercise its functions in and upon the organism, whose elements, left to themselves, disintegrate."[17] Shewmon points out that the same concept of life-principle has been given secular expression, for example, in the following statement of a group of medical scientists: "We define death as the permanent cessation of functioning of the organism as a whole ... [that is] [T]he [cessation of] the spontaneous and innate activities carried out by the integration of all or most subsystems."[18]

B. Clinical Indications That Death Has Occurred

There was consensus among the scientific participants in the 1989 Working Group (as there had been among the scientific participants in the 1985 Group) that death, as defined above, has in fact occurred when

> a) spontaneous cardiac and respiratory functions have irreversibly ceased, which rapidly leads to a total and irreversible loss of all brain functions, or

> b) there has been an irreversible cessation of all brain functions, even if cardiac and respiratory functions which would have ceased have been maintained artificially.[19]

The scientific participants in the 1989 Working Group, like their counterparts in the 1985 meeting, thus concluded that "the establishment of total and irreversible loss of all brain function is the true medical criterion of death," and it is possible to show that this criterion has been met either (i) indirectly, by establishing the cessation of circulation and respiration or (ii) directly by showing the irreversible loss of all brain functions (brain death). They took care to note that these criteria do *not* apply to human life in the womb.[20]

C. Artificial Prolongation of Organ Functions

The position taken by the scientists on this issue is clearly expressed: "In the case of brain death, artificial respiration can prolong cardiac function for a limited time, thus permitting a short period of survival for organs for the possibility of transplantation. This is possible only in cases of complete irreversible loss of all brain functions (brain death)."[21]

Thus the scientific participants in the 1989 Working Group of the Pontifical Academy of Sciences, to whom was assigned the task of investigating the determination of brain death and its relationship to human death, agreed that a human person can be truly declared dead once it has been established that "there has been an irreversible cessation of all brain functions" and that it is morally proper, once a person has been declared dead by reason of "brain death," to use artificial means to prolong cardiac function (in other words, to keep the heart beating in the person declared dead) for a limited time in order to preserve vital organs for transplantation.

3. THE RATIONALE FOR IDENTIFYING "BRAIN DEATH" WITH HUMAN DEATH

A. Historical Background

The "clinical definition" of death advanced by the Working Group of the Pontifical Academy of Sciences, as we have seen, harmonizes well with the truth that a human person is a bodily being and that a living human body is a person. What makes the body *to be* human and alive is its vital principle, the soul. And although the soul is immaterial, the human person is not, for the human person is a body-person, a biological organism, a living whole. The human person is *more* than his body, because he is capable, by reason of his vital principle, of nonmaterial acts — knowing the truth and making free choices. But the human person is nonetheless inescapably and essentially a *body person,* not a *spirit person,* and when the body dies the person dies. As the Working Group's clinical definition, which, as we have seen, harmonizes well with what Pope John Paul II had to say about death, makes clear, a *living human body is a person,* and, conversely, *a dead human body is a dead person,* i.e., is no longer a person but rather the mortal remains of a person. We can truly say that death is the irreversible cessation of the integrated organic functioning that is characteristic of the living human body as a whole.

Before the middle of the twentieth century, there was no major dispute over the criteria for determining that a person had died because the integrated organic functioning characteristic of the body as a whole had irreversibly ceased. A person was judged to be dead when his heart stopped beating and his blood stopped circulating, when he stopped breathing, etc. However, beginning with the development of more effective artificial respirators in the middle of the last century and subsequent breakthroughs in medical technology and life-support systems, troubling and serious questions were raised about the traditional ways of declaring a person dead. As Ronald E. Cranford notes, "Prior to the widespread use of respirators, defibrillators, intensive-care units, and cardiopulmonary resuscitation, failure of cardiac, respiratory, and neurologic functions were closely linked. When one system failed, the other two inevitably failed as well. But respirators and other advanced life-support systems can now sustain cardiac, respiratory, and other autonomic functions for prolonged periods of time even after neurologic functions have ceased."[22]

B. The Consensus on "Brain Death": The Report of the President's Commission

Beginning in the 1960s, the medical community responded to the difficulties noted above by developing new criteria for determining that a person has in fact died. Despite differences among the proposals made, a consensus emerged (one accepted by the Working Group of the Pontifical Academy of Sciences in 1985 and again in 1989) that the total and irreversible absence of the function of the entire brain is as valid a criterion for determining that death has occurred as the traditionally accepted cardio-respiratory indications of death. In the United States this consensus was well articulated by the members of the U.S. President's Commission for the Study of Ethical Problems in Medicine and Biomedical and Behavioral Research in its 1981 report.

It should be noted that the members of this important Commission *explicitly* rejected efforts to define death in terms of the irreversible cessation of the function of the neocortex of the brain [on this view of death, persons said to be in the PVS condition could be declared dead!!!]. But they advocated statutory enactment of a Uniform Definition of Death Act (subsequently enacted in more than half of all U.S. jurisdictions). This Act, supported by the U.S. President's Commission, provides that an individual who has sustained either (1) irreversible cessation of circulatory and respiratory functions, or (2) irreversible cessation of all functions of the entire brain, including the brain stem, is dead.[23]

It is most important, I believe, to note that the "clinical indications that death has occurred" accepted by the Working Group of the Pontifical Academy of Sciences in its 1989 meeting are almost exactly those identified by the President's Commission in its proposed statutory definition.

C. The Presuppositions Underlying This Consensus

As several commentators have noted, the statute proposed by the President's Commission first of all presupposes that by "death" is understood the death of a human being or human person *as a whole, as a unified organism.* A common misunderstanding of " brain death" is to regard it designating the death of an organ and not of the whole organism. The truth is that organs can cease functioning. But what *dies* is the living organism whose organ or organs have ceased to function. Another central presupposition underlying this approach to understanding death is that we must be able to draw a line between those who are alive and those who are dead. Although *dying* is a process insofar as not all parts of the body "die" at the same time (fingernails and hair, for instance, continue to grow some time after the human person whose fingernails and hair they were is dead), death is not a process but the definite termination of the life of a living being.[24] The line drawn by the President's Commission and the Uniform Definition of Death Act is arbitrary in the sense that it is the choice, by competent authorities, of one proposal among others, but it is by no means arbitrary insofar as it is rooted in the reasonable belief that once either circulatory/respiratory functions *or* the functions of the *entire brain* have irreversibly ceased, one can be confident that a once living human person is dead.

A final presupposition on which this consensus depends is the belief that the *brain is the central integrating organ of the human body* in human beings who have advanced beyond the embryonic stage. Since the brain is the central integrator or critical organ of the whole human body, its destruction or irreversible nonfunctioning necessarily entails loss of somatic integrative unity, a thermodynamic "point of no return," a literal "dis-integration" of the organism as a whole.[25]

Confirmation of the belief that the brain is the central integrating organ of the whole human body is provided, defenders of the "brain death" criterion have emphasized, by the fact that the bodily functions and organs of those declared brain-dead simply cannot be kept alive, even by advanced mechanical means, for very long. Rather they inevitably and promptly collapse and deteriorate despite the most aggressive therapy and efforts to resuscitate. The following citations from authoritative sources suffice to illustrate this:.

> Even with extraordinary medical care, these [somatic] func-
> tions [e.g., circulation of blood] cannot be sustained indefi-
> nitely — typically, no longer than several days.[26]

> Despite all efforts to maintain the donor's circulation, irre-
> versible cardiac arrest usually occurs within 48 to 72 hours
> of brain death in adults, although it may take as long as 10
> days in children. Indeed, general acceptance of the concept
> of brain death depended on this close temporal association
> between brain death and cardiac arrest.[27]

> What was clearly established in the early 1980s was that
> no patient in apneic coma declared brain-dead ... had ever
> failed to develops asystole [absolute cessation of blood pres-
> sure, etc.] within a relatively short time. That fundamental
> insight remains as valid today [1996] as it was twenty years
> ago.[28]

It was in this way that the concept, rationale for, and consensus on brain death developed. As we have seen, the Pontifical Academy of Sciences is in basic agreement with this concept, rationale, and consensus.

4. ALAN SHEWMON'S CHALLENGE TO "BRAIN DEATH"

In a series of articles, D. Alan Shewmon, a pediatric neurologist acknowledged to be an authority on the function of the brain, has set forth the reasons, based on empirical evidence, leading him to abandon the concept of "brain death."[29] Shewmon, who himself had accepted this concept, is now certain that it cannot be sustained.

Shewmon accepts in essence the clinical definition of death articulated by the Working Group of the Pontifical Academy of Sciences. A person is dead when the integrative unity of the body has been irretrievably lost. He affirms that a living human body is a person and that, therefore, as the members of the Working Group of the Academy had affirmed, "a person is dead when there has been total and irreversible loss of all capacity for integrating and coordinating physical and mental functions of the body as a unit." Thus Shewmon does not attempt to redefine death.

But he now challenges the criterion, accepted by the Working Group of the Academy, by the U.S. President's Commission, and by numerous medical societies, that death has occurred when it can be established that there has been irreversible cessation of the functions of the entire brain, including the brain stem. He likewise challenges the fundamental assumptions on which this criterion is based, namely, (A) that the brain is the central integrating organ of the entire human body and (B) that the body even has one localized central integrating organ.

A. Evidence Challenging the Claim That the Brain Is the Central Integrating Organ of the Whole Human Body

As we saw above, a fundamental assumption underlying the acceptance of "brain death" as signifying the death of the whole human person is that the brain is the central integrating organ of the entire body. We likewise saw that a major line of evidence advanced to support the claim that a "brain dead" body cannot maintain stable cardiovascular and respiratory function in the absence of a functioning brain is the fact (alleged) that even with the most aggressive mechanical support, the organs and organic systems of the body collapse within a very short time, leading one to conclude that such a body is no longer a living whole, a living human body, but merely an unorganized collection of disparate, disunited organs and parts.[30] In several of his essays Shewmon calls attention to this alleged evidence. In addition to the sources listed in endnotes 26, 27, and 28, Shewmon cites an exceptionally clear and eloquent expression of this view by the British author David Lamb, who wrote as follows:

> When evidence is cited that, despite the most aggressive support, the adult heart stops within a week of brainstem death[31] and that of a child within two weeks, one is not marshalling empirical support for a *prediction* of death. What is being said is that a point has been reached where the various subsystems lack neurological integration and their continued (artificial) functioning only mimics integrated life. That structural disintegration follows brain death is not a contingent matter; it is a necessary consequence of the death of the critical system. The death of the brain is the point beyond which other systems cannot survive with, or without, mechanical support.[32]

Shewmon says that recent literature and collective personal experiences cast grave doubts on this longstanding doctrine underlying the acceptance of brain death. I will now summarize the evidence that he has marshaled.

Shewmon compiled all known cases of brain-death survival of individuals declared brain-dead who were placed on mechanical ventilators for a week or longer. His search showed that there were approximately 175 who survived brain death for at least a week. Of these, approximately 80 survived 2 weeks, approximately 44 at least 4 weeks, approximately 20 at least 2 months, 7 at least 6 months, and 4 longer than a year, with the record being 15 years (in 1998) and still, as of this writing, in the year 2000, surviving!! Of the total of 175 cases, there was sufficient information about fifty-six of them for statistical meta-analysis, allowing Shewmon (and others) to identify factors influencing survival capacity. Of these the most important was age; the longest survivors (all those over two years) were all young children when declared brain-dead, whereas those who survived less than two and a half months were all over thirty years old.[33]

Summarizing, Shewmon says that these data

> teach us several lessons: (1) "Brain death" does *not* necessarily lead to imminent cardiac arrest despite all treatment [the "evidence" repeatedly advanced to support acceptance of "brain death"]. (2) The heterogeneity of survival duration is largely explainable by non-brain factors. Moreover, the process of brain damage leading up to "brain death" frequently induces secondary damage to heart and lungs. Therefore, the tendency to early cardiac arrest in the majority of patients is attributable more to *somatic* factors than to mere absence of brain activity *per se*. (3) The first few weeks are especially precarious. But those who make it through tend to stabilize, no longer requiring sophisticated technological support. Some have even been discharged home on a ventilator. Although some personhood-consciousness reductionists might try to argue that these are not human *persons*, no one can seriously claim that they are not living human *organisms*, living human *beings*.[34]

The longest survivor, whom Shewmon calls T.K., was diagnosed as brain-dead when he was four years old. Although physicians recommended that all life-support systems be discontinued, his mother insisted that he be put on a ventilator and fed. He was eventually transferred home, and is still there (now over 15 years later!) where he remains on the ventilator, assimilates food provided by a stomach tube, spontaneously urinates, and requires little more than nursing care. Although declared brain-dead, he has grown, developed sexual organs, overcome infections, and healed wounds.[35] In a 1999 lecture on brain death at a conference on bioethics sponsored by the Universidad de Navarra in Spain, a conference in which I participated, Shewmon showed slides of T.K., along with a copy of an MRI of his brain, showing that T.K.'s brain was simply a mass of liquefied material: it was clearly irreversibly nonfunctioning and he was surely "brain dead." Nonetheless, despite the claims that the respiratory/circulatory systems of a person known to be brain-dead *cannot* be sustained, *even with mechanical support*, for more than a few days, at the most two weeks (cf. citations above), his major body systems are still functioning.

Granted, they function only because he and other long-term survivors of "brain death" are supported by respiratory machines, and if the support thus provided were to be withdrawn, they would surely die. Moreover, it is apparent that use of ventilators in such instances can surely be judged "extraordinary/disproportionate" and hence discontinued (and Shewmon acknowledges this).[36] But the significant point is this: it is not credible to maintain that T.K. and others like him, human beings who have been declared brain-dead are truly dead, i.e., corpses, cadavers, no longer living human bodies. It is simply not credible to claim that they are really no longer living human beings. In the light of this evidence it is no longer possible, Shewmon concludes, to regard the brain as the central integrating organ of the whole human body and to consider death of the entire brain as equivalent to death of the whole human person. The evidence, Shewmon thinks, falsifies the doctrine that the brain is indeed the integrating factor unifying all the vital organ systems of the body.

B. Criteria for Determining the "Integrative Unity" of the Human Body

Shewmon argues that to "determine whether a given body has integrative unity (hence, is a body as opposed to a collectivity of organs), one must first *define* the term and then examine that body for *properties relevant to the definition*."[37] He then proposes two operational definitions or criteria of "integrative unity."

Criterion 1. "Integrative unity" is possessed by a putative organism...if the latter possesses at least one emergent holistic level property. A property of a composite is defined as "emergent" if it derives from the mutual interaction of the parts, and as "holistic" if it is not predicable of any part or subset of parts but only of the entire composite.[38]

Commenting on this criterion, Shewmon points out that healthy living organisms are characterized by many properties of this kind, but possessing only one suffices for the entity in question to be a *living organism,* "for if the property is truly at the level of the whole, then there must be a whole of which it is predicated." He then goes on to describe the second operational criterion, which is, as it were, a corollary of the first, as follows:

> *Criterion 2.* Any body requiring less technological assistance to maintain its vital functions than some other body that is nevertheless a living whole must possess at least as much robustness of integrative unity and hence also be a living whole.[39]

Shewmon then argues that in light of the first criterion one discovers that "most *brain-mediated* integrative functions are not *somatically integrating*, and conversely, most somatically integrating functions are not brain-mediated." He then gives examples of such bodily (somatically) integrative functions. In light of all this — and other relevant facts that I have not included — Shewmon concludes his critique of the "brain-as-integrating-organ argument" by declaring:

> Far from constituting a "central integrator," without which the body reduces to a mere bag of organs, the brain serves as a modulator, fine-tuner, optimizer, enhancer, and protector of an implicitly *already existing,* intrinsically *mediated* somatic unity. Integrative unity is *not* a top-down imposition from a "central integrator" on an otherwise unintegrated collection of organs.... Rather, it is a *non-localized, holistic property* founded on the mutual interaction among all the parts of the body.[40]

C. New Criteria for Determining That Death Has Occurred
Shewmon in no way wishes to redefine death; he wholeheartedly

agrees that death of a living organism, including a human person, is the irreversible loss of the integrative unity of the body. But, he argues, the *anatomical criterion* "shifts from a single focus (the brain) to the entire body and consists in a critical degree of molecular-level damage (not yet grossly detectable) throughout the body, beyond a thermodynamical 'point of no return.' The body's intrinsic tendency to active, anti-entropic self-development and self-manufacture is irretrievably lost, so that physico-chemical processes now follow the path of increasing entropy characteristic of inanimate things (i.e., decay)." Corresponding to this anatomical criterion, the *clinical tests* to determine that death has occurred shift from ones indicating loss of brain function to those manifesting "thermodynamically supracritical microstructural damage diffusely throughout the body." What kind of test can be used? According to Shewmon, a "*sine qua non* of opposition to entropy is energy, generated by chemical respiration, and a *sine qua non* of somatic integration is the circulation of the blood, by means of which the body parts mutually interact. A clinical test for the 'point of no return' is therefore sustained cessation of circulation of oxygenated blood." Under ordinary circumstances (i.e., normal temperature) Shewmon believes that twenty to thirty minutes of complete cessation of such circulation are enough to show that the "point of no return" has been reached.[41]

Is the "circulatory-respiratory" criterion Shewmon proposes as the clinical test for determining that death has occurred the same as the traditional "cardio-pulmonary" test? Shewmon says no. He points out that neither spontaneous heartbeat nor breathing through the lungs is essential for life — the cardio-pulmonary test. If they were, then persons undergoing cardiopulmonary bypass operations would have to be regarded as dead. But circulation and chemical respiration are essential for life. Shewmon concludes that his proposal of a circulatory-respiratory clinical test to determine that death has occurred represents, "far from a reactionary regression, actually a conceptual advance, bringing our criterion and tests for death more in line with the basic concept [of death]. Because chemical respiration is contingent on the circulation of oxygenated blood, this dual criterion really boils down in practice to the single one of cessation of circulation beyond a thermodynamical 'point of no return.' "[42]

D. A Suggested Protocol for Organ Transplants From the "Brain-Dead"

If, as Shewmon argues — and I find the evidence he marshals compelling—the irreversible cessation of the functioning of the entire brain *cannot* be a criterion for determining that a human person has died, profound questions are then raised about the liceity of removing the vital organs of persons declared "brain dead." Removing such organs would seem to be morally excluded because removing them would be to kill the person or to hasten his death for the benefit of another.

But Shewmon holds that it would be a mistake to conclude that rejection of the "brain death" criterion automatically entails the end of vital organ transplantation from the (still-living) bodies (=persons) of those deemed brain-dead. Shewmon asks, "What if ... in a very particular circumstance it were possible to remove unpaired organs, including even the heart, from a live donor *without causing or even hastening death?*"[43] He then goes on to suggest that this *is* possible and to outline the procedures to be followed.

Here it seems best to cite in full Shewmon's proposal. He writes as follows:

> Consider a patient on morally extraordinary (disproportionate) life support (typically a ventilator), who is about to have that support licitly withdrawn and who, independent of that decision, also wants to donate organs. Suppose also a high probability that the patient will die very quickly upon termination of that support. Instead of the withdrawal taking place in the intensive care unit, however, it is done in the operating room with surgical teams poised. Perhaps, with the patient's consent, arterial catheters have been placed in readiness to perfuse at an appropriate time the organs of interest with a cold ischemia-protective solution. The life support is then discontinued and asystole awaited. After a brief interval (short enough not to damage the transplantable organs but long enough for moral certainty that spontaneous recovery will not occur) the organs of interest are perfused and the surgical teams begin their work.

> In such a scenario, the patient would probably not yet be dead at the moment of organ removal. Cardiopulmonary resuscitation could be successful, but it would constitute an extraordinary means that has been decided ahead of time to be legitimately foregone. In the absence of circulating blood, however, "vital" organs are no longer vital, including even the nonbeating heart; their mere presence in the body con-

tributes nothing to the body's physiological integrity or remaining brief span of life (perhaps on the order of tens of minutes); therefore, their removal would neither cause nor even accelerate death. It is generally accepted that healthy individuals may licitly donate a single kidney or a piece of liver on the dual basis that (1) the functional integrity of their body is not compromised and (2) the gift of life for the recipient sufficiently justifies the risks of surgery and the structural mutilation. The retrieval of unpaired vital organs in the manner described above would seem to be morally equivalent, at least in principle, to these classic examples of licit live donation.[44]

Shewmon believes that this approach to transplant surgery merits further research, and he encourages such study and research "in order to reassure the transplant community that the conceptual demise of 'brain death' would not necessarily entail the demise of organ transplantation, although it would surely require a radical change in the *modus operandi* for obtaining donor organs."[45]

It is surely beyond my competence to judge the merits of Shewmon's proposed protocol from the perspective of medical science and technology, but it seems to be quite reasonable and practicable and, above all, morally acceptable insofar as it does not entail the *willing of evil*. It is surely worthy of intense research. He claims that if this procedure is followed then the pool of prospective organ donors would be increased, not decreased.

It is important to note here that there are other protocols for retrieving vital organs, including non-paired organs, from patients declared dead by traditional cardiopulmonary criteria. One protocol of this kind, analogous in many ways to Shewmon's, has been developed at the Geisinger Medical Center in Pennsylvania. Greg F. Burke, M.D., who was intimately involved in the development of this protocol, has described it in some detail in *Ethics & Medics,* the Bulletin of the National Catholic Bioethics Center.[46] Here I will not describe this protocol in detail since it is many ways similar to Shewmon's, and interested readers can examine Burke's presentation of it. But it is important to note that it was specifically designed to be compatible with core Catholic values. As Burke says, "at its core it must 1) reject euthanasia, 2) respect the longstanding principle of a person's right to refuse disproportionate or excessively burdensome treatment, and 3) afford an opportunity for the donation of unpaired organs to assist in the preservation of life in those suffering from serious life-threatening conditions."[47]

E. Responses to Shewmon's Critique of "Brain Death"

Shewmon notes that at the Second International Symposium on Brain Death, held in Havana, Cuba, February 27 to March 1, 1996, the participants from North America were in general agreement with his thesis that "somatic integrative unity" was "a nonviable rationale for 'brain death.'" For example, neurologist Julius Korein, who had called the brain the "critical organ" for mental and bodily integrity in 1978,[48] in 1996 described the brain's critical function almost entirely in terms of its relationship to consciousness and personhood, regarding as "unimportant" the aspect of bodily integrative unity. Thus Shewmon concluded that this "implicitly acknowledged the validity of my clinical and neurophysiological arguments against the brain as central integrating organ of the body."[49] What disturbed Shewmon about the Second International Symposium on Brain Death was that many participants, while seeming to agree with him that "brain death" is *not* equivalent to the death of the biological human organism, still believed that it is nonetheless "death" of the "person," i.e., the consciously experiencing subject, a view of human death that is, of course, rooted in an unacceptable dualism separating the "person," the experiencing subject, from his or her body.[50]

These were the immediate reactions on the part of the North American scientific community when Shewmon "went public" with his views in 1996. I will now report on the reaction of others to Shewmon's position. Unfortunately, there are not many specific reactions to report. Here I will report on the reactions of (1) Ronald Cranford, M.D., (2) Francis L. Delmonico, M.D., and Joseph E. Murray, M.D., (3) Eugene Diamond, M.D., and (4) Benedict Ashley, O.P.

(1) Ronald Cranford, M. D.

In an editorial appearing in the same issue of the official journal of the American Academy of Neurology, *Neurology,* in which Shewmon's essay "Chronic 'brain death': Meta-analysis and conceptual consequences" appeared, Cranford first says that Shewmon "has accumulated convincing data that, among other things, undermine [the] somatic integration hypothesis.." Continuing, he acknowledges that Shewmon's article "documents and verifies the suspicion that some neurologists have experienced in the diagnosis of brain death: to some extent.... The prediction that patients will inevitably have a cardiac arrest within hours or days is not necessarily accurate." However, after acknowledging, in essence, that Shewmon's research has falsified the presuppositions underlying the equation of brain death with the death of the human bodily person as a whole, Cranford concludes his editorial by declaring: "In the final analysis Shewmon's article will not undermine the medical and legal doctrine of brain death as the death of a human being."[51]

I find Cranford's conclusion astounding. It may be true that Shewmon's work will have no effect in undermining the doctrine of brain death, but if so, it will not do so because those who have accepted it will shift the criterion from the death of the entire brain to death of the neocortex, thus including PVS patients, anancephalic infants, etc., among the dead. And this would indeed be tragic. Cranford gives *no reasons* for setting aside Shewmon's conclusions, which seem to me to have been reached on a reasonable interpretation of relevant medical evidence.

(2) Francis L. Delmonico, M.D., and Joseph E. Murray, M.D.

In a jointly written essay for *Ethics & Medics,* the bulletin of the National Catholic Bioethics Center, Delmonico and Murray refer to Shewmon's *Linacre Quarterly* essay, "Recovery from 'Brain Death: A Neurologist's Apologia" and his claim that brain death is "not really death after all but rather a state of deep and irreversible unconsciousness in a critically lesioned but still live patient." Delmonico and Murray disagree and claim that their support for the brain-death concept is "given from a philosophical and theological perspective." But the perspective from which they give this support seems to me to equate personhood with the functioning of the brain. I say this because they say: "The instrument of consciousness, thought, and free will is the human brain. The loss of these attributes characterizes human death as different from the death of any other form of life.... The central component of human life that distinguishes us from any other living creature is the function of the human brain."[52]

In essence, Delmonico and Murray simply reaffirm, and do not demonstrate, that brain death equals death of the whole person. They in no way seek to rebut the evidence Shewmon has marshaled or to challenge his interpretation of that evidence. I thus consider their response woefully inadequate.

(3) Eugene Diamond, M.D.

Diamond refers several times to Shewmon's *Linacre Quarterly* essay and claims that the protocol he proposes for organ transplantation would "effectively end 90% of all human organ transplantation." He continues by saying that "this would not be an unacceptable price to pay if the result were to be the restoration of a societal respect for the sanctity of human life that had somehow been lost in the acceptance of whole-brain death as tantamount to death of the person" But after saying this, and *without offering* any critique of the argument advanced by Shewmon or of the evidence on which Shewmon's argument is based, Diamond concludes by affirming: "I believe that respect for the sanctity of human life and the declaration of death by whole-brain standards are not mutually exclusive."[53] Frankly, I am puzzled by this statement, unsupported by any argument or evidence. At the conclusion of his essay, Diamond notes that the *Charter for Health Care Workers* accepts the brain-death definition (as did the Pontifical Academy of Sciences, as we have seen). But appealing to these authorities does not answer Shewmon's challenge. I thus regard Diamond's essay as non-responsive.

(4) Benedict Ashley, O.P.

Benedict Ashley, a noted Dominican moral theologian, has offered the most serious response to Shewmon's position that I have seen.[54] His principal argument seems to me to be similar to the "delayed hominization" regarding the beginning of human life which claimed, as we saw in the chapter on abortion, that the spiritual soul cannot be infused into the body formed at conception until it has been prepared to receive that soul by the development of the brain — an argument, incidentally, that Ashley rejects with respect to the beginning of human life. But in considering the criteria for death, or the ending of human life, Ashley seems to me to accept a version of this argument.

I say this because Ashley argues, first, that the intellect, a spiritual faculty, cannot operate without sense data derived from material organs such as the eyes, ears, etc. and that this data must be synthesized and unified by the interior senses of memory, imagination, etc., which require a highly complex and unified organ "differentiated not only from the organs of exterior sensation but from the still simpler organ systems that perform the physiological or vegetative functions of nutrition, growth, reproduction, and locomotion." He then asserts that "modern medicine demonstrates that the brain is this complex organ of interior sensation which acts as the central integrator for animal life. For humans it is only the proximate instrument of the spiritual intelligence by which that intelligence acts as the ultimate central integrator of the whole person."

He then concludes: "Hence, human death occurs when the human brain becomes incapable of performing this synthesis of sense data required for human intellection, even if lower levels of life are sustained in relative integrity in the other organ systems."

Ashley, it seems to me, confuses the vitality of the brain with the vitality of the human person, whose vital principle is the immaterial soul. While the immaterial faculty of the intellect needs sense organs and the brain in order to carry out its operations, the *brain is **not** the mind or intellect,* and trauma to the brain or even the irreversible cessation of its functions does not logically entail loss the mind or intellect, but rather the inability of this spiritual faculty to operate because of its dependence on an organic substrate. Moreover, it seems to me, if Ashley's critique is sound, it then follows that the human person is dead if the neocortex has irreversibly ceased functioning, even if the brain stem is still carrying out all its functions. For, after all, if the neocortex can no longer function, the intellectual cognitive operations of the person can no longer be executed. I thus find Ashley's critique of Shewmon inadequate.

Ashley also says that Shewmon's inference from the data that "'integrative unity' is a nonlocalized emergent property deriving from the mutual interaction of the parts'" is "biologically and philosophically implausible." Ashley claims that in a system of material parts, especially in a system such as the human body/ whose unity is substantial, the single efficient principle needed to unify it "must itself be a differentiated material part, an organ," i.e., the brain. This seems to be another issue central to Ashley's critique. My problem is that Ashley does not offer demonstrative evidence for these claims but rather simply asserts them. I thus do not think that Ashley has shown that Shewmon's critique of brain death is erroneous.

F. Conclusion: Retrieving Organs From Persons Declared Brain-Dead

I find Shewmon's critique of "brain death" compelling. Prior to studying his essays and having the opportunity, at a bioethics conference at the Universidad de Navarra in Spain in October, 1999, to see the remarkable slides depicting the condition of T.K., I had accepted the criterion of brain death.[55] But in my opinion, Shewmon has amply demonstrated, on the basis of irrefutable empirical data, that this criterion can no longer be used. Prior to Shewmon's studies, others had raised important criticisms of the concept of "brain death," although I had not personally found their criticisms completely convincing (some major critiques are referred to in the accompanying endnote).[56] But after reading Shewmon's critique over and over, and after witnessing the visual evidence he marshaled at the meeting in Pamplona, I can no longer in conscience accept "brain death" as equivalent to the death of a human person.

The summary of Pope John Paul II's perceptive observations on death and organ donation early in this chapter make it clear that it is absolutely immoral intentionally to cause a person's death or even to hasten a person's death in order to make that person's vital organs available for another person in need of them. We can never intentionally do evil for the sake of good to come. It is always gravely immoral intentionally to kill an innocent person or to hasten his or her death in order to benefit another.

But, as we saw in reviewing the protocol Shewmon has developed for removing the vital organs of persons said to brain-dead (and other persons in the process of dying for whom any life-preserving measures would be "extraordinary" or "disproportionate"), it is possible to arrange procedures for removing vital organs *without either causing or hastening the death* of the person from whom the organs are, with proper consent, removed. I can find nothing *morally* objectionable to the protocol Shewmon has outlined. It thus, in my opinion, ought to be attempted and the technologies involved in it developed and perfected.

5. ORGAN DONATION FROM THE LIVING (*INTER VIVOS*)[57]

Today the transplanting of vital organs such as a kidney, a portion of the liver, etc., from one living person to another in desperate need of a vital organ is commonplace. We intuitively and instinctively judge that the giving of a part of one's own body to help a gravely or even mortally ill fellow human person is not only morally justifiable but an act of heroic charity. Nonetheless, the proper way to justify organ donations from living persons is a matter of debate among Catholic theologians. In fact, when this kind of surgery became possible around the middle of the twentieth century it stirred controversy among them.[58] Some leading theologians of the time, among them Marcellino Zalba, S.J., wondered how one could justify a procedure in which a healthy human person (the donor) willingly suffers mutilating surgery and the risk of health problems, perhaps serious ones, in the future when his own life and health are not imperiled. The mutilating surgery could hardly be regarded as therapeutic for the donor and hence could not, in their judgment, be justified by the principle of totality, according to which one could justify the mutilation of one's own person (e.g., the amputation of a gangrenous limb or the excision of cancerous testicles) in order to protect one's own life.[59]

Gerald Kelly, S.J., who in many ways led the way for theologians to accept organ transplants *inter vivos* (as we will see shortly), provides the reasons why he and theologians of his day concluded that the principle of totality could not be used to justify such procedures: "This principle [that of totality] can be applied only when there is the subordination of part to whole that exists in the natural body. No such subordination exists between human persons or between the individual and society. Each person is a distinct entity, with a distinct finality. No matter how lowly his condition, he is not subordinated to others in the order of being."[60] Some theologians, nonetheless, sought to justify organ transplants *inter vivos* by "extending" the principle of totality. A radical presentation of this line of thinking, extending the principle to embrace the total good of the person, including the "spiritual" good of the donor, who allegedly benefits spiritually by the self-giving of his vital organs, was presented by Martin Nolan, O.S.A.[61] His attempted justification, rooted in a dualistic understanding of the human person, was soundly criticized by others, in particular by the great Protestant ethicist Paul Ramsey, who characterized it as the "sticky benefits" theory.[62] In addition, Pope Pius XII, who had himself invoked the principle of totality to justify mutilating surgery on one's own person when necessary to protect the person's health and life as a whole, explicitly declared that this principle could not be used to justify organ transplants among the living.[63]

Realizing that organ transplants among the living cannot be justified by the totality principle, other theologians, pre-eminently Gerald Kelly, S.J., followed the lead first suggested by Bert Cunningham, C.M., in his doctoral dissertation, *The Morality of Organic Transplantation* (Washington, D.C.: The Catholic University of America Press, 1944) that the self-giving of one's own vital organs could be justified by the principle of fraternal charity or love when doing so is of great benefit to the recipient, with the proviso that the harm suffered by the donor is limited and morally acceptable. This view, endorsed and developed by Kelly, was soon accepted by many moral theologians. They distinguished between *anatomical* and *functional* integrity, arguing that only the latter was necessary for bodily and personal integrity. Thus Benedict Ashley, O.P., and Kevin O'Rourke, O.P., in their widely used textbook say that "the concept of functional integrity is the key factor in addressing the morality of transplants between living persons." They acknowledge that the donor runs a risk in giving an organ, but such risk is acceptable if it does not impair his own functional integrity (e.g., if he donates one kidney, his functional integrity is not impaired because he still has a functioning kidney). The transplant would be immoral if the organ's removal were to impair the donor's functional integrity (e.g., removing one's cornea to help another person see or removing both kidneys). The risk of giving an organ whose removal does not impair functional integrity may be serious, but it is justifiable because the "donors share in the common good of the community to which they contribute by helping another, that is, by love."[64]

Still other theologians, pre-eminently Germain Grisez, argue that organ transplants from the living can be justified by the principle of double effect. According to this principle an action having two effects, one good, the other bad, is morally good provided that the action is not morally wrong for other reasons, that the evil is not intended, that the evil is not the means to the good, and that there is a "proportionate reason" for tolerating or accepting the bad effect. Grisez argues, correctly in my opinion, that the "principle of totality" is itself, if analyzed properly, an instance of double effect. However, the *physical* "directness" of the causing of harm and the *physical* "indirectness" of the causing of the benefit led many theologians to think that a special principle was needed to justify the "mutilation" involved in necessary surgical interventions on one's own body (the malfunctioning or diseased organ, e.g., the gall bladder, was first removed physically, causing a "mutilation" before the healing would take place).

But if we analyze the matter from a moral perspective, we can see that the "object" morally specifying the chosen act (on this see *Veritatis splendor,* no. 78) is not the harm done to the person but rather the removal of the organ or part of the body, with as its resulting effects the "mutilation" (the evil effect) and the "protection" or "restoration" of health (the good effect). Thus, in analyzing morally the reason why one is justified in submitting to "mutilating" surgery to protect one's own life and health, Grisez writes:

> It can be morally good and even obligatory to remove a part of the body essential to some physiological or psychic function, when doing so of itself also protects or promotes health: the detriment to function may not be intended as a means to the other end, but may only be accepted as a side effect. For example, a person sometimes should consent to the cutting off of an infected or cancerous limb or nonvital

organ when that is necessary to prevent the infection or cancer from doing great harm to the body as a whole. Indeed, this is so even when the part removed is itself healthy, if removing it has natural consequences which are necessary for the health of the body as a whole and which cannot be brought about in another way. For example, a man suffering from breast cancer may consent to the surgical removal of his normal testicles in order to stop the hormones which are aggravating the cancer.[65]

Similarly, Grisez argues, the same norms can be applied to the self-giving of vital organs. The morality of giving them depends on how the freely chosen act relates one to the relevant goods: healthy functioning and life itself. If the harm (including the mutilation) suffered by the donor — but in no way *intended* either by him or those involved in the transplant — does not impair his functional integrity, the evil suffered is an unintended side-effect of an act of self-giving. However, were the donor's own functional integrity and hence his own health and life to be impaired, the choice would be to impede or damage his own health as a means to some good end, but one can never intend or choose evil for the sake of good to come.[66]

I believe that Grisez's analysis of organ donation among the living provides the best moral justification for the self-giving of vital organs.

I will conclude this section on organ donation *inter vivos* by citing relevant magisterial statements.

Pope John Paul II has frequently remarked on the moral liceity of the self-giving of vital organs, and he has likewise clearly indicated the limits of such self-giving. Thus, in his Address to the First International Congress of the Society for Organ Sharing he said, first, that "a transplant, and even a simple blood transfusion, is not like other operations. It must not be separated from the donor's act of self-giving, from the love that gives life. The physician should always be conscious of the particular nobility of his work; he becomes the mediator of something especially significant, the *gift of self* which one person has made ... so that another might live." He then articulated the norm: "A person can only donate that of which he can deprive himself without serious danger or harm to his own life or personal identity, and for a just and proportionate reason."[67]

The *Catechism of the Catholic Church,* in taking up organ transplants *inter vivos,* says: "Organ transplants are in conformity with the moral law if the physical and psychological dangers and risks to the donor are proportionate to the good that is sought for the recipient."[68]

And finally, the Bishops of the United States declare: "The transplantation of organs from living donors is morally permissible when such a donation will not sacrifice or seriously impair any essential bodily function and the anticipated benefit to the recipient is proportionate to the harm done to the donor…. the freedom of the prospective donor must be respected."[69]

ENDNOTES

1. "Uniform Anatomical Gift Act, Section 7 (b)," as printed in Alfred M. Sadler, Jr., M. D., Blair L. Saddler, LL.B., and E. Blythe Stason, J.D., "The Uniform Anatomical Gift Act: A Model for Reform," *Journal of the American Medical Association* 206 (December 9, 1968) 2506.

2. Paul Ramsey, *The Patient as Person* (New Haven: Yale University Press, 1970), p.103.

3. On this, see Ronald E. Cranford, "Death, Definition and Determination of. I. Criteria for Death," *Encyclopedia of Bioethics*, ed. Warren T. Reich (2nd rev. ed. New York: McGraw-Hill, Inc., 1995) 529.

4. See, for example, E. T. Bartlett and S. J. Younger, "Human death and destruction of the neocortex," in *Death: Beyond Whole-Brain Criteria,* ed. R. M. Zaner (Dordrecht/Boston: Kluwer Academic Publishers, 1988), pp. 199-215; Robert M. Veatch, "The Impending Collapse of the Whole-Brain Definition of Death," *Hastings Center Report* 23.4 (July-August 1993) 18-24.

5. Pope John Paul II, "Discourse of John Paul II to the Participants of the Working Group," in *Working Group on the Determination of Brain Death and Its Relationship to Human Death* (December 10-14, 1989) (Pontificiae Academiae Scientiarum Scripta Varia, 83), eds. R. J. White, H. Angstwurm, and I. Carrasco de Paula (Vatican City: Pontifical Academy of Sciences, 1992), no. 2, p. xxiv. This volume will henceforth be referred to as *The Determination of Brain Death...*

6. Ibid., no. 3, p. xxv (emphasis added).

7. Ibid., no. 4, p. xxv (emphasis added).

8. Thus St. Thomas Aquinas says, "my soul is not me" (*anima mea non est ego*): *Super primam epistolam ad Corinthios,* lectura xv, 2.

9. On this theme, see the remarkably perceptive essay of Paul Ramsey, "The Indignity of 'Death With Dignity,' " in *Death, Dying, and Euthanasia,* eds. Dennis J. Horan and David Mall (Frederick, MD:

Aletheia Books: University Publications of America, Inc., 1980), pp.305-330. Ramsey's essay was first published in *Hastings Center Studies* 2 (1974) 47-62.

10. "Discourse of John Paul II to the Participants of the Working Group," *The Determination of Brain Death...*, no. 5, p. xxvi.

11. Ibid., no. 6, p. xxvi.

12. Ibid.

13. Pope Pius XII, "The Prolongation of Life," *AAS* 445 (29257) 1027-1035: "It is in the physician's domain ... to give a clear and precise definition of death and of the 'moment of death' of a patient who dies without regaining consciousness."

14. "Final Considerations Formulated by the Scientific Participants," in *The Determination of Brain Death...*, p. 81.

15. "Conclusion of the meeting of the Working Group held at the Pontifical Academy of Sciences, October 19-21 1985 on 'The Artificial Prolongation of Life and Determination of the Exact Moment of Death,'" in *The Determination of Brain Death...*, p. 208. This document was originally published in *Working Group on the Artificial Prolongation of Life and the Determination of the Exact Moment of Death* (Vatican City: Pontifical Academy of Sciences, 1986), pp. 113-114.

16. See, for example, D. Alan Shewmon, M.D., "Brainstem Death, Brain Death and Death: A Critical Re-Evaluation," *Issues in Law & Medicine* 14.2 (1998) 131.

17. Shewmon cites this text, cited above in our text, in this article on p. 131.

18. James J. Bernat et al., "On the Definition and Criterion of Death," *Annals of Internal Medicine* 94 (1981) 389-390; cited by Shewmon, "Brainstem Death, Brain Death and Death...," 131.

19. "Final Considerations... ," in *The Determination of Brain Death...*, p. 81.

20. Ibid., pp. 81-82.

21. Ibid., p. 82.

22. Cranford, "Death, Definition and Determination of. I. Criteria for Death," 529.

23. U.S. President's Commission for the Study of Ethical Problems in Medicine and Biomedical and Behavioral Research, *Defining Death: Medical, Legal, and Ethical Issues in the Determination of Death* (Washington, D.C.: U.S. Government Printing Office, 1981), p. 41.

24. See, for instance, Alexander Morgan Capron, "Death, Definition

and Determination of. II. Legal Issues in Pronouncing Death," *Encyclopedia of Bioethics,* 536.

25. Among authorities articulating this view are the following: (1) U.S. President's Commission for the Study of Ethical Problems in Medicine and Biomedical and Behavioral Research, *Defining Death....,*; (2) J. L. Bernat, *Ethical Issues in Neurology* (Boston: Butterworth-Heinemann, 1994), pp. 113-143; (3) Pontifical Academy of Sciences, *Determination of Brain Death...,* pp. 81-82.

26. U.S. President's Commission..., *Defining Death...,* p. 35.

27. B. E. Soifer, A. W. Geib, "The Multiple Organ Donor: Identification and Management," *Annals of Internal Medicine* 110 (1989) 814-823.

28. Pallis C. Harley, *ABC of Brainstem Death* (London: BMJ Publishing Group, 1996). I owe references nos. 26, 27, 28 to D. Alan Shewmon, who refers to them in his essay, "Chronic 'brain death': Meta-analysis and conceptual consequences," *Neurology* 51 (December, 1998) 1538.

29. Some of these articles have already been noted. Here I list four major essays in chronological order: (1) "Recovery from 'Brain Death': A Neurologist's Apologia," *The Linacre Quarterly* (February 1997) 30-96; (2) " 'Brainstem Death,' 'Brain Death,' and 'Death: A Critical Re-Evaluation of the Purported Evidence,' " *Issues in Law & Medicine* 14.2 (1998) 125-145; (3) "Chronic 'Brain Death': Meta-analysis and conceptual consequences," *Neurology* 51 (December, 1998)1538-1545; (4) "Determining the Moment of Death: New Evidence, New Controversies"; this essay, delivered at a conference on bioethics at the Universidad de Navarra in October, 1999, has not yet been published. I was one of the participants at this conference. Shewmon accompanied his lecture with slides showing the condition of several individuals recognized as "brain-dead" (in fact, an MRI of the brain of one of the individuals, who had survived "brain death" for more that 15 years, showed that his brain had liquefied!). The second essay noted above was adapted from a lecture Shewmon gave at the Linacre Centre for Health Care Ethics 20th Anniversary International Conference, July 28-31, 1997 at Queen's College, Cambridge University. That lecture has now been published under the title "Is It Reasonable to Use the UK Protocol for the Clinical Diagnosis of 'Brain Stem Death' as a Basis for Diagnosing Death?" in *Issues for a Catholic Bioethic: Proceedings of the International Conference to Celebrate the Twentieth Anniversary of the Foundation of the Linacre Centre 28-31 July 1997,* ed. Luke Gormally (Lon-

don: The Linacre Centre, 1999), pp. 315-333. In the following I will refer to the essay published in *Issues in Law and Medicine.* In addition, Shewmon briefly set forth his position in his essay, "Definitions of Death, the Persistent Vegetative State, and Anencephaly," in the *Bishop and the Future of Catholic Health Care: Proceedings of the Sixteenth Workshop for Bishops,* ed. Daniel P. Maher (Braintree, MA: The Pope John XXIII Medical Moral Research and Education Center, 1997), pp. 136-153.

30. See text above, with accompanying endnotes 26, 27, 28.

31. In the U.K. irreversible cessation of the functioning of the *brain stem* is accepted as a criterion for determining that a human person is dead. The reason for accepting this criterion is that the death of the brain stem is thought to be a necessary and *sufficient* condition for the death of the brain as a whole. The brain, on this view, is the critical system of the living organism and the brainstem is the critical system of the brain. A clear presentation of this position is given by David Lamb in his essay, "What Is Death?" in *Principles of Health Care Ethics,* ed. Raanan Gillon (Chichester/New York: John Wiley & Sons, 1994), pp. 1029-1036.

32. David Lamb, *Death, Brain Death, and Ethics* (Albany, NY: State University of New York Press, 1985), pp. 36-37; cited by Shewmon, "Chronic 'brain death'…," 1539.

33. Shewmon, "Brainstem Death, Brain Death and Death…," 135f; "Chronic 'brain death…,'" 1539-1542; see also "Recovery from 'Brain Death…,' " 62-69.

34. Shewmon, "Brainstem Death, Brain Death and Death…," 136.

35. Ibid., 136.

36. T.K. and most long-term survivors live in cultures quite different from our own (T.K. is Japanese), where much different attitudes toward care of the sick and dying are operative.

37. Ibid., 137.

38. Ibid.

39. Ibid.

40. Ibid., 140.

41. Ibid., 141-142.

42. Ibid., 142.

43. "Recovery from 'Brain Death'…," 81.

44. Shewmon, "Recovery from 'Brain Death'…," 82. In "Brainstem Death, Brain Death and Death," 128-129 Shewmon elaborates on this proposal.

45. "Brainstem Death, Brain Death and Death," 129.
46. Greg F. Burke, M.D., "A Non-Heart-Beating Donor Protocol," *Ethics & Medics* 25.4 (April, 2000) 1-3.
47. Ibid., 1.
48. Shewmon, in "Recovery from 'Brain Death'…, 84, 90, refers to Korein's essay, "The Problem of Brain Death: Development and History," in *Brain Death: Interrelated Medical and Social Issues,* ed. J. Korein, *Annals of the New York Academy of Science* 315 (198) 19-38.
49. "Recovery from 'Brain Death'…, 84.
50. Ibid.
51. Ronald Cranford, M.D., "Editorial: Even the dead are not terminally ill any more," *Neurology* 51 (1998) 1530-1531.
52. Francis L. Delmonico, M.D., and Joseph E. Murray, M.D., "A Medical Defense of Brain Death: Why the Standard Criteria Should Be Preserved," *Ethics & Medics* 24.10 (October, 1999) 2.
53. Eugene F. Diamond, M.D., "Brain-Death Determination of Death Revisited," *The Linacre Quarterly* 65.4 (November, 1998) 71-80, at 77.
54. Ashley's response, so far as I know, has not been published. It was given orally to Shewmon's presentation, "Definitions of Death, the Persistent Vegetative State, and Anencephaly," given at the Sixteenth Workshop for Bishops sponsored by the Pope John XXIII Medical-Moral Research and Education Center February 3-7, 1997 and published in the *Proceedings* of that Workshop. (See above, endnote no. 29.) Ashley's brief response, entitled "A Newly Proposed Definition of Death," was presented orally at the Workshop but was not included in the printed text of the proceedings.
55. See, for example my book *Human Existence, Medicine, and Ethics: Reflections on Human Life* (Chicago: Franciscan Herald Press, 1977), pp. 162-165.
56. Paul A. Byrne, M.D., Seamus O'Reilly, M.D., Paul M. Quay, S.J., "Brain Death: An Opposing Viewpoint," *Journal of the American Medical Association* 242.18 (1979) 1985-1990; Paul M. Byrne, M.D. and R. G. Nilges, "The Brain Stem in Brain Death: A Critical Review," *Issues in Law and Medicine* 9.1 91993) 3-21; Joseph Seifert, "Is 'Brain Death' Actually Death? A Critique of Redefining Man's Death in Terms of 'Brain Death,' " in *Pontifical Academy of Sciences Working Group on the Determination of Brain Death and Its Relationship to Human Death,* pp. 95-143; Joseph Seifert, "Is 'Brain Death' Actually Death?" *The Monist* 76.2 (1993) 175-202.

In some of his writings Dr. Byrne, unfortunately in my opinion, disparages the views of those who disagree with him, referring to them in terms of opprobrium and contempt. For example, in an article co-authored by Rev. George M. Rinkowski, Byrne characterizes the article by Eugene Diamond referred to above as "fraudulent," adding that fraud is legally defined as "an intentional perversion of truth...." (see Paul A. Byrne and Rev. George M. Rinkowski, " 'Brain Death' Is False," *The Linacre Quarterly* 66.1 (1999) 46. This article does little to shed light on the controversy. It is a model example of the way discussion of this topic ought *not* be conducted.

57. Here I adapt and develop material from an earlier essay, "The Ethics of Organ Transplants," *Ethics & Medics* 21.7 (July 1996), 1-3.

58. For a discussion of the debates that took place see a series of articles by Gerald Kelly, S.J., in *Theological Studies* 16 (1955) 391-396; 17 (1956) 341-344, 557-561; 18 (1957) 228-230, 570-572.

59. On the "principle of totality" see John Gallagher, C.S.B., "The Principle of Totality: Man's Stewardship of His Body," in *Moral Theology Today: Certitudes and Doubts*, ed. Donald G. McCarthy (St. Louis, MO: The :Pope John XXIII Center, 1984), pp. 217-242.

60. Gerard Kelly, S.J., *Medico-Moral Problems* (St. Louis, MO: The Catholic Hospital Association, 1957), p. 247.

61. Martin Nolan, O.S.A., "The Principle of Totality in Moral Theology," in *Absolutes in Moral Theology?,* ed. Charles E. Curran (Washington, D.C.: Corpus Books, 1968), pp. 232-248.

62. Paul Ramsey, *The Patient as Person: Explorations in Medical Ethics* (New Haven, CT: Yale University Press, 1970), chapter 4, "The Self-Giving of Vital Organs," pp. 165-197, in particular pp. 178-181.

63. See, for example, Pope Pius XII, "Allocution to a Group of Eye Specialists" (May 14, 1956), as found in *The Human Body: Papal Teaching,* selected and arranged by the Monks of Solemnes (Boston: St. Paul Editions, 1960), nn. 645 ff.

64. Benedict Ashley, O.P., and Kevin O'Rourke, O.P., *Health Care Ethics: A Theological Analysis* (4th ed.: Washington, D.C.: Georgetown University Press, 1997), p. 333.

65. Germain Grisez, *The Way of the Lord Jesus,* Vol. 2, *Living a Christian Life* (Quincy, IL: Franciscan Press, 1993), p. 542.

66. Here I paraphrase and in some ways modify ibid., p. 543.

67. Pope John Paul II, Address to the First International Congress of the Society for Organ Sharing, *L'Osservatore Romano*, English ed. June 24, 1991, 2.

68. *Catechism of the Catholic Church,* no. 2296. **NB.** Here I give the text as required by the "Modifications from the *Editio Typica*" (based on the definitive Latin text promulgated on September 8, 1997). The text found in editions of the *Catechism* prior to that date is somewhat different.

69. National Conference of Catholic Bishops, *Ethical and Religious Directives for Catholic Health Care Services* (Washington, D.C.: United States Catholic Conference, 1995), directive no. 30.

BIBLIOGRAPHY
AND RESOURCES

Note

The endnotes for each chapter provide extensive bibliographical references for the issues specific to each chapter. Here I provide information on (1) a Select Bibliography of Texts, Anthologies, and Reference Works in Bioethics, (2) a list of important Journals and Periodicals, and (3) Bioethical Centers and Web Sites of Particular Value for Catholic Perspectives on Bioethics.

Select Bibliography of Texts, Anthologies, and Reference Works in Bioethics

Ashley, Benedict, O.P., and Kevin O'Rourke, O.P., *Health Care Ethics: A Theological Analysis.* 4th ed. Washington, D.C.: Georgetown University Press, 1997.

_____. *Ethics of Health Care: An Introductory Textbook.* 2nd ed. Washington, D.C, Georgetown University Press, 1994.

Beauchamp, Thomas, and James Childress, *Principles of Biomedical Ethics.* 3rd ed. New York: Oxford University Press, 1994.

Callahan, Daniel, *What Kind of Life: The Limits of Medical Progress.* New York: Simon and Schuster, 1990.

Griese, Orville, *Catholic Identity in Health Care: Principles and Practice.* Braintree, MA: The Pope John XXIII Center, 1987.

Grisez, Germain, *The Way of the Lord Jesus.* Vol. 2, *Living a Christian Life.* Quincy, IL: Franciscan Press, 1993. Chapter Eight of this volume, entitled "Life, Health, and Bodily Inviolability," is a short and excellent treatise on bioethics, pp. 459-552.

_____, *The Way of the Lord Jesus.* Vol. 3, *Difficult Moral Questions.* Quincy, IL: Franciscan Press, 1997. Many of the questions analyzed in detail by Grisez in this volume concern bioethical issues.

McCarthy, Donald, and Edward J. Bayer, *Handbook of Critical Life Issues.* Braintree, MA: Pope John XXIII Center, 1982.

McCormick, Richard A., S.J., *How Brave a New World? Dilemmas in Bioethics.* Garden City, NY: Doubleday, 1978.

_____, *The Critical Calling: Reflections on Moral Dilemmas Since Vatican II.* Washington, D.C.: Georgetown University Press, 1989.

O'Donnell, Thomas, S.J., *Medicine and Christian Morality.* 2nd rev. ed. Staten Island, NY: Alba House, 1991.

Ramsey, Paul, *The Patient as Person.* New Haven: Yale University Press, 1970.

_____, *Ethics at the Edges of Life: Medical and Legal Intersections.* New Haven: Yale University Press, 1978.

Reich, Warren T., ed., *Encyclopedia of Bioethics.* 2nd rev. ed. New York: McGraw-Hill, 1995. Five volumes paginated consecutively. The first edition was published in 1978.

Shannon, Thomas A., ed. *Basic Writings of the Key Ethical Questions That Surround the Major Biological Possibilities and Problems.* 4th ed. New York: Paulist Press, 1993.

Walters, Leroy, ed., *Bibliography of Bioethics.* Detroit: Gale Research Co., 1975-present. An annual bibliography, the most complete of its kind, classified systematically.

Important Journals and Periodicals

Catholic Medical Quarterly: Journal of the Guild of Catholic Doctors. A quarterly journal published by the Guild of Catholic Doctors in England.

Ethics and Medics: The Bulletin of the National Catholic Bioethics Center on Moral Issues in the Health Care Sciences. Inaugurated in 1975, this is a very useful monthly periodical, ordinarily four pages in length and containing two brief but significant essays on an issue in bioethics. It is published by the National Catholic Bioethics Center (formerly called The Pope John XXIII Medical Moral Research and Education Center).

Hastings Center Report. This is published bimonthly by the Hastings Center, a nonpartisan organization that carries out educational and research programs on ethical issues in medicine. In addition to the bimonthly *Report,* the Center issues occasional Studies on selected topics.

Health Progress. This journal, formerly called *Hospital Progress,* is published ten times a year by the Catholic Health Association of the United States.

Issues in Law and Medicine. This is a quarterly publication of the National Legal Center for the Medically Dependent and Disabled, Inc., the Horatio P. Storer Foundation, Inc., and the American Academy of Medical Ethics, Inc. Essays in this journal are uniformly of high scholarly quality and pro-life in orientation.

Journal of the American Medical Assocation (JAMA). A weekly, professional journal for physicians; many articles are quite technical; others deal with ethical issues from various perspectiives.

Linacre Quarterly. This is the official publication of the Catholic Medical Association, formerly called the National Federation of Catholic Physicians' Guilds.

The NaProEthics Forum. Bimonthly publication of Pope Paul VI Institute, Omaha, NE.

New England Journal of Medicine. A weekly professional journal for physicians usually featuring several essays of ethical significance.

Centers and Web Sites of Particular Value for Catholic Perspectives on BioethicS

The most important center for Catholic perspectives on bioethics in the United States is the **National Catholic Bioethics Center**, formerly called The Pope John XXIII Medical Moral Research and Education Center. It is located at 159 Washington Street, Boston, MA 02135-4325. It publishes its bulletin, *Ethics and Medics,* and numerous monographs on bioethical issues. For many years it sponsored, with the help of the Knights of Columbus, annual workshops on specific topics in bioethics for the bishops of the United States, Canada, and Latin America, publishing papers given at these workshops in annual proceedings. The web site for the **NCBC** is http://www.ncbcenter.org.

Another very important center for Catholic perspectives on bioethics is the **Linacre Centre**, 60 Grove End Road, London NW8 9NH, England. Now a little over a quarter of a century old, the Centre has sponsored excellent research in bioethics. Among its publlications is its Workking Party Report on Euthanasia, *Euthanasia, Clinical Pracice and the Law,* edited by Luke Gormally, and cited frequently in the Endnotes. The web site for the London **Linacre Centre** is http://www.linacre.org.

The **Center for Health Care Ethics,** St. Louis University Health Sciences Center, 1402 S. Grand Blvd., St. Louis, MO 63104. While representing the Catholic tradition, this Center seeks dialogue with the many other ethical traditions represented in the U.S.

The **Joseph and Rose Kennedy Institute of Ethics,** Georgetown University, Washington, D.C., 20057. Although located on the campus of a major Catholic university, this Institute does not support magisterial teaching and presents a wide variety of views on bioethical matters.

Additional Web Sites

In addition to the Web Sites noted above, the following organizations, with their web sites, are valuable resources for those interested in Catholic perspectives on bioethics:

The **Culture of Life Foundation,** http://www.culture-of-life.org. This is an excellent source for relevant essays and other information on contraception, abortion, the generation of human life, euthanasia, etc.

The **International Anti-Euthanasia Task Force,** http://www.iaetf.org. An excellent source for material on euthanasia and allied subjects.

Index

abortion, arguments defending presented and criticized, 156-170; *Catechism of Catholic Church*, 152; *Declaration on Procured Abortion*, 39ff; defined, 153; "direct" vs. "indirect," 154ff; *Gaudium et spes*, 152; intentional (direct), always gravely immoral, 27; "removal" vs. "killing," 176ff; resumé of Church teaching, 152f; special moral gravity of, 170ff

adultery, and generation of human life, 66

advance directives, 270ff

agametic reproduction (cloning), 78

agathanasia, *see* benemortasia

Alexander, Leo, medical science under dictators, 277

American Academy of Neurology, PVS patients, 265, 280

American Medical Association, free and informed consent, 202, 229; PVS patients, 279f

amniocentesis, 220ff

Anderson, Barbara Hilkert, marriage and other domestic partnerships, 111

Anderson, W. French, gene therapy, 217f, 232

Annas, George, sperm vending, 74, 111

Anscombe, Elizabeth, member of Linacre Centre (London) Working Party on euthanasia, 190, 276

Anti-Euthanasia Task Force, Protective Medical Decisions Document, 272, 282

artificial fertilization and insemination, kinds of, 73-78; moral evaluation of, 79ff; *see also in vitro* fertilization, reproductive technologies.

Ashley, Benedict, O.P., critique of delayed hominization theory, 163, 191; critique of Ford, et al., on twinning, 168, 193; critique of McCormick's views on homologous IVF, 84, 113; kinds of experimentation, 228; opposes GIFT, 92f, 114; organ transplants *inter vivos*, 307, 315; proxy consent in nontherapeutic situation, 231; response to Shewmon, 304, 314

Our Sunday Visitor

Your Source for Discovering
the Riches of the Catholic Faith

Our Sunday Visitor has an extensive line of materials for young children, teens, and adults. Our books, Bibles, booklets, CD-ROMs, audiocassettes, and videos are available in bookstores worldwide.

To receive a FREE full-line catalog, or for more information, call **Our Sunday Visitor** at **1-800-348-2440**. Or write: **Our Sunday Visitor**, 200 Noll Plaza, Huntington, IN 46750.

- -

❑ Please send me a catalog.

Please send me material on:

❑ Apologetics/Catechetics   ❑ Reference works
❑ Prayer books   ❑ Heritage and the saints
❑ The family   ❑ The parish

Name _____
Address _____
City _____ ST _____ Zip_____
Telephone (_____) _____

                                           AO3BBABP

- -

❑ Please send a friend a catalog.

Please send a friend material on:

❑ Apologetics/Catechetics   ❑ Reference works
❑ Prayer books   ❑ Heritage and the saints
❑ The family   ❑ The parish

Name _____
Address _____
City _____ ST _____ Zip_____
Telephone (_____) _____

                                           AO3BBABP

- -

OUR SUNDAY VISITOR BOOKS

Our Sunday Visitor
200 Noll Plaza
Huntington, IN 46750
1-800-348-2440
E-mail us at: osvbooks@osv.com
Visit us on the Web: http://www.osv.com

Your source for discovering the riches of the Catholic Faith